THE POWER OF CREATIVE DESTRUCTION

THE

POWER

OF

CREATIVE

DESTRUCTION

▲

Economic Upheaval and the Wealth of Nations

PHILIPPE AGHION   CÉLINE ANTONIN   SIMON BUNEL

Translated by Jodie Cohen-Tanugi

The Belknap Press of Harvard University Press

CAMBRIDGE, MASSACHUSETTS ▲ LONDON, ENGLAND

First Harvard University Press paperback edition, 2023
First printing

First published as *Le Pouvoir de la destruction créatrice,* copyright © 2020 Odile Jacob

Library of Congress Cataloging-in-Publication Data

Names: Aghion, Philippe, author. | Antonin, Céline, author. | Bunel, Simon, author.
Title: The power of creative destruction : economic upheaval and the wealth of nations / Philippe Aghion, Céline Antonin, Simon Bunel; translated by Jodie Cohen-Tanugi.
Description: Cambridge, Massachusetts : The Belknap Press of Harvard University Press, 2021. | "First published as Le Pouvoir de la destruction créatrice, copyright 2020 Odile Jacob"—Title page verso. | Includes bibliographical references and index.
Identifiers: LCCN 2020048914 | ISBN 9780674971165 (cloth) | ISBN 9780674292093 (pbk.)
Subjects: LCSH: Capitalism. | Disruptive technologies. | Business cycles. | Income distribution.
Classification: LCC HB501 .A459 2021 | DDC 330.12/2—dc23
LC record available at https://lccn.loc.gov/2020048914

Contents

CONTENTS

Preface

We began writing this book in November of 2019. Four months later an unprecedented, worldwide pandemic crisis struck. This crisis stimulated existential debate on how our society will look—and how we want to reshape it—when we emerge from the crisis. At the heart of the debate we find creative destruction. Indeed, COVID-19 has destroyed jobs and pushed huge numbers of firms into bankruptcy. Yet at the same time, the crisis has created room for new, innovative activities.

As Barry Eichengreen explained in a recent article in *Prospect* (May 26, 2020) with the evocative title, "Schumpeter's Virus: How 'Creative Destruction' Could Save the Coronavirus Economy," the retail sector will utilize artificial intelligence and automation more than ever, because consumers will not give up the habit of ordering online that they acquired during social confinement. Similarly, confinement revealed the virtues of remote working and of videoconferences. We also became acquainted with medical consultations by telephone or video.

However, the realization that creative destruction can serve as a lever of growth after COVID presents a challenge to policy makers. On the one hand, they must "protect": support viable firms in order to save jobs and preserve the human capital accumulated in those firms. On the other hand, they must "reallocate": encourage the entry of new firms and new activities that are more efficient or more responsive to the new needs of consumers. In other words, they must accompany the process of creative destruction, without obstructing it.

More importantly, the COVID-19 crisis acted as a wake-up call by revealing deeper problems that plague capitalism in the different forms it takes throughout the world: dysfunctional social welfare and health-care systems in the United States; inadequate innovation systems in Europe; and the lack of transparency or the excessive centralization of power in yet other countries.

More generally, in light of the rise of inequality, the concentration of rents, increasing job insecurity, and the deterioration of health and the environment that we have observed for decades, we hear more and more calls for radical change, even the overthrow of capitalism. However, in this book we argue that the answer to our problems is not to abolish capitalism. It is to invent a better capitalism by harnessing the power of creative destruction—innovation that disrupts, but that over the past two hundred years has also lifted societies to previously unimagined prosperity.

The challenge we face is therefore to understand the underpinnings of creative destruction in order to steer its power in the direction we choose. How can we direct creative destruction toward greener and more equitable growth? How can we prevent yesterday's innovators from using their rents to block new innovation? How can we minimize the potentially negative effects of creative destruction on employment, health, and happiness? What are the forces—firms, governments, constitutions, civil society—that enable us to steer creative destruction in the direction we desire? These are the questions we will attempt to answer in the following chapters.

The raw material of this book comes from five years of lectures at the Collège de France, which themselves encompass more than thirty years of research on the economics of innovation and growth. This material was enriched and reorganized around a central theme: the power of creative destruction and how the transformation of capitalism can direct this power toward achieving more sustainable and inclusive prosperity.

THE POWER OF CREATIVE DESTRUCTION

▼

1

A NEW PARADIGM

This book is an invitation to a journey: a journey through economic history, more specifically a journey to explore the enigmas of economic growth through the lens of creative destruction.

Creative destruction is the process by which new innovations continually emerge and render existing technologies obsolete, new firms continually arrive to compete with existing firms, and new jobs and activities arise and replace existing jobs and activities. Creative destruction is the driving force of capitalism, ensuring its perpetual renewal and reproduction, but at the same time generating risks and upheaval that must be managed and regulated.

Our purpose in this book is to:

1. *Penetrate some of the great historical enigmas associated with the process of world growth,* such as industrial takeoff, major technological waves, secular stagnation, the evolution of inequality, convergence and divergence across countries, the middle-income trap, and structural change.

2. *Revisit the great debates over innovation and growth in developed nations:* Can we foster innovation and creative destruction while at the same time protecting the environment and reducing inequality? Can we avoid creative destruction's potentially detrimental effects on employment, health, and well-being? Must we fear the digital and artificial intelligence revolutions?

3. *Rethink the role of the state and civil society:* What role can each of them play to stimulate innovation and creative destruction and thereby increase the wealth of nations? How can we protect citizens and the economy from the excesses of capitalism?

Even as he extolled the merits of creative destruction as the driving force of growth, Joseph Schumpeter was pessimistic about the future of capitalism. In particular, he anticipated that large conglomerates would push out small and medium-sized firms, leading inexorably to the disappearance of entrepreneurs and the triumph of bureaucracy and vested interests.[1] The final chapters of this book (Chapters 14, 15, and the Conclusion), which deal with the state and regulating capitalism, conclude our journey on an optimistic note, but a fighting optimism, adopting Karl Marx's famous words: "The philosophers have hitherto only *interpreted* the world in various ways. The point, however, is to *change* it."[2]

1. Measuring the Wealth of Nations

The preferred measure of the wealth of nations is per capita gross domestic product (per capita GDP). Why should we focus on this dry statistic rather than on more literal measures, such as indexes of well-being, consumption, or happiness? One argument is that the material well-being of billions of human beings is closely linked to per capita GDP of the country where they live. For example, the industrial takeoff at the beginning of the nineteenth century corresponded to a takeoff of per capita GDP after a long period of stagnation (see Chapter 2).

The growth of per capita GDP enabled a large part of the populations of developed nations to attain a standard of living that only a few privileged people enjoyed at the beginning of the nineteenth century. By contrast, inadequate growth of per capita GDP in poor nations means that hundreds of millions of people still live in extremely difficult and precarious conditions. Consequently, it is important to understand what governs the growth of per capita GDP in order to understand why some countries have prospered and others languished, and why wealth is so inequitably distributed across countries. In addition, per capita GDP has the advantage of enabling comparisons between nations not only at a given point in time but also over time.

This book focuses on the growth of "utils," a measure of what is useful or procures well-being within a nation. Many of these "utils" are traded on the market for goods and services and are therefore included in the calculation of GDP, but others are not. For example, GDP does not take into account the time saved by reserving train tickets over the internet rather than queuing at the train station or a travel agency. Similarly, the photos we take with our smartphones cost us nothing and accordingly are not included in GDP. In the past, before digital cameras, we had to buy film, then pay to have our pictures developed, and all these expenditures entered into the calculation of GDP. Or consider the technological improvements that have made a visit to the dentist much less unpleasant than it was forty years ago. Those improvements do not show up in GDP. How can we measure them?

One approach is to utilize surveys to evaluate individuals' life satisfaction. As Daniel Kahneman and Angus Deaton have emphasized, international comparisons show a positive correlation between per capita GDP and life satisfaction.[3] Chapter 11 looks in detail at the relationship between creative destruction and life satisfaction. A second approach is to measure economic development directly by innovation, either by the number of new products and new activities or by the type of innovation. In particular, in Chapter 9 we will focus on green innovation and explore ways to measure and foster it. Finally, there are indexes that measure the inclusiveness and equality of a nation's economic growth. The most commonly used indicator is the Gini coefficient, which measures how much a nation's income distribution differs from perfect equality. We can also measure inequality more dynamically by using indicators of social mobility. We return to these questions of inequality and social mobility in Chapters 5 and 10.[4]

2. Why Do We Need a New Paradigm to Explain the Wealth of Nations?

The answer is simple: existing paradigms have proved inadequate to explain major trends and to solve the enigmas of growth and the wealth of nations. For both theoretical and empirical reasons, it has become urgent to introduce a new paradigm.

The theoretical reason. Up to the late 1980s, the dominant theory of economic growth, known as the neoclassical model, was one of a growth process based on capital accumulation. The most elegant version of the neoclassical model was developed in 1956 by Robert Solow, whose work was awarded the Nobel Prize in 1987.[5]

The simplicity and elegance of Solow's model make it the necessary starting point for any course on economic growth. In a nutshell, it describes an economy in which production requires capital, and where growth of GDP comes from increasing the stock of capital. What causes the stock of capital to grow? The answer is households' savings, which are presumed to be equal to a constant fraction of production (that is, of GDP).

It would seem that all is well in this economy: more capital, financed by savings, increases GDP, which leads to more savings and therefore more capital, further increasing GDP, and so forth. In other words, this economy seems to generate durable growth even in the absence of technical progress, merely as a result of capital accumulation.

The problem with this model lies in the fact that there are decreasing returns on producing solely with capital. The greater the number of machines, the less GDP increases by adding one more machine. At some point, the economy runs out of steam and stops growing. As Robert Solow explained very clearly, generating sustained growth necessitates technical progress that makes it possible to improve the quality of machines—in other words, their productivity. But Solow did not describe the factors that determine technical progress and in particular the factors that stimulate or inhibit innovation.

The empirical reason. Neoclassical theory does not explain the determinants of long-term growth, as we have just seen. Even less does it enable us to understand a whole set of enigmas related to growth, for example, why some nations grow more quickly than others, and why some nations converge to the levels of GDP per capita of the developed world and others remain far behind or stall along the way.

Thus, both theoretical and empirical considerations motivated the introduction of a radically new framework.

3. The Paradigm of Creative Destruction[6]

The model of growth through creative destruction is also known as the Schumpeterian paradigm because it was inspired by three ideas put forward by the Austrian economist Joseph Schumpeter but that had never before been formalized or tested.[7]

The first idea is that *innovation and the diffusion of knowledge are at the heart of the growth process.* Long-term growth results from cumulative innovation, in that each new innovator "stands on the shoulders of giants" who preceded him. This idea echoes Solow's conclusion that technical progress is a prerequisite of long-term sustained growth. Only with the diffusion and codification of knowledge can innovation be cumulative, without which we would have to continually reinvent the wheel and, like Sisyphus, climb the same mountain over and over.

The second idea is that *innovation relies on incentives and protection of property rights.* Innovation comes from the decision to invest, especially in research and development (R&D), by entrepreneurs motivated by potential returns—innovation rents. Anything that secures those rents, in particular protecting intellectual property rights, will incentivize entrepreneurs to invest more in innovation. And on the contrary, anything that jeopardizes rents, such as the absence of protection against imitation or confiscatory taxes on revenues from innovation, will discourage investment in innovation. More generally, innovation responds to positive or negative incentives from institutions and public policy: innovation is a social process.

The third idea is *creative destruction:* new innovations render former innovations obsolete. In other words, growth by creative destruction sets the stage for a permanent conflict between the old and the new: it is the story of all incumbent firms, all the conglomerates, that perpetually attempt to block or delay the entry of new competitors in their sectors.

Creative destruction thus creates a dilemma or a contradiction at the very heart of the growth process. On the one hand, rents are necessary to reward innovation and thereby motivate innovators; on the other hand, yesterday's innovators must not use their rents to impede new innovations. As we mentioned above, Schumpeter's answer to this dilemma was that capitalism was condemned to fail precisely because it was impossible to prevent incumbent firms from obstructing new innovations. Our response is that it is indeed possible to overcome this contradiction, in other words to regulate capitalism or, to take the title of Raghuram Rajan's and Luigi Zingales' 2004 book, to "save capitalism from the capitalists."[8]

4. Creative Destruction: A Reality

Creative destruction is not merely a concept; it is a tangible and measurable reality. We can perceive it through the arrival of new products and new technologies, measured by the number of patents filed each year in a country or region.[9] Figure 1.1 shows how the average annual growth rate of per capita GDP in American states varied with the average annual number of patents registered in those states from 1900 to 2000.[10] We observe a very clear positive correlation between the intensity of innovation and the growth of per capita GDP: states that innovate more grow more quickly.[11]

Another way to measure creative destruction is to examine more closely the life cycle of new firms: their entry, their growth, and their exit from the market. The comprehensive data collected by the US Census Bureau in the Longitudinal Business Database provide a good starting point, as the database enables us to find the number of jobs created annually by firms broken down by their age and size. We can see from Table 1.1 that in 2005 startups—defined as firms that have existed less than one year—generated 142 percent of net new jobs in the United States.[12]

Figure 1.2a illustrates the rate of growth of employment as a function of firm age: the youngest firms exhibit stronger net job growth than long-established firms. Figure 1.2b shows the exit rate for firms at different ages. Younger firms have a much higher exit rate than long-established firms. This is what we call "up or out": each new generation of startups creates a large number of new jobs. Since many of these startups disappear in the early years of their existence, many of

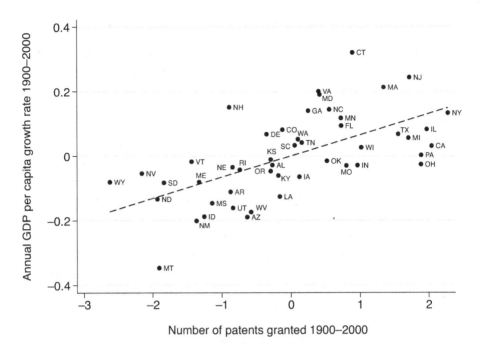

FIGURE 1.1. Positive correlation between growth of per capita GDP and patents. *Note:* The horizontal and vertical axes plot the variables residualized against 1900 log GDP.

Reformatted from U. Akcigit, J. Grigsby, and T. Nicholas, "The Rise of American Ingenuity: Innovation and Inventors of the Golden Age" (NBER Working Paper No. 23047, National Bureau of Economic Research, Cambridge, MA, January 2017), figure 6.

Table 1.1. Net Job Creation by Firm Age, US Private Sector, 2005

Firm Age (in years)	Net Job Creation (in thousands)	Percentage of Net Job Creation
0	3,518	142%
1	−189	−8%
2	−178	−7%
3	−151	−6%
4	−74	−3%
5	−103	−4%
6–10	−339	−14%
11–15	−161	−6%
16–20	−154	−6%
21–25	−141	−6%
26+	417	17%
All	2,481	100%

Source: J. Haltiwanger, R. S. Jarmin, and J. Miranda, "Who Creates Jobs? Small versus Large versus Young," *Review of Economics and Statistics* 95, no. 2 (2013): 347–361.

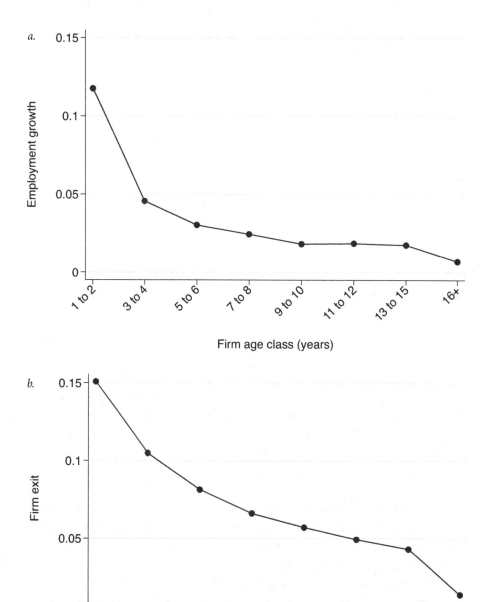

FIGURE 1.2. Net employment growth and exit rate by firm age. *a.* Net employment growth. *b.* Exit rate.

Extracted and reformatted from J. Haltiwanger, R. S. Jarmin, and J. Miranda, "Who Creates Jobs? Small versus Large versus Young," Review of Economics and Statistics *95, no. 2 (2013): 347–361, figures 4B, 5.*

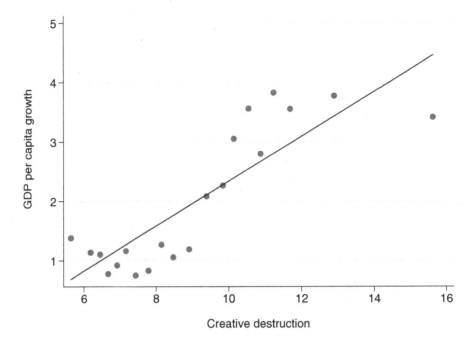

FIGURE 1.3. Positive correlation between growth of per capita GDP and rate of creative destruction. *Note:* The countries included in the data are Austria, Bulgaria, the Czech Republic, Croatia, Denmark, Estonia, Finland, France, Hungary, Italy, Latvia, Lithuania, Poland, Portugal, Romania, Slovakia, and Spain.

Data source: Eurostat.

these jobs will be destroyed. But those that survive this Darwinian process continue to create jobs and therefore to grow in size. We recognize the image of the Schumpeterian entrepreneur, who has a strong probability of failing but encounters spectacular growth if he manages to survive.

Lastly, we can measure creative destruction by the average between the rate of firm creation and the rate of firm destruction. This is the most commonly used measure in the literature on firm and employment dynamics.[13] How is this measure of creative destruction related to the growth of GDP per capita? Figure 1.3, constructed from data covering 587 regions in seventeen European countries between 2012 and 2016, shows that the average annual growth of per capita GDP during this period was greater in regions where average creative destruction was higher.

What is the relationship between creative destruction as measured by the creation and destruction of jobs or firms and creative destruction as measured by the number of new patents? We find a positive correlation between the two measures: on average, the American counties with the highest rates of job creation and destruction were also the counties that produced the most new patents between 1985 and 2010. This data covers more than 1,100 counties, and the correlation is 0.456. This correlation is largely due to the fact that the most innovative firms are the small, young firms that also create and destroy the most jobs. In fact, Figure 1.4 shows clearly how the intensity of innovation, measured by the number of patents per employee, decreases with the size of the firm measured by the number of employees. The larger the firm grows, the less likely it is to innovate. In addition, innovations generated by smaller firms are more radical and more significant than those generated by larger firms.[14]

In closing this introduction to the reality of creative destruction, there are two additional "seeds" that we would like to share with the reader. Figure 1.5 shows the evolution of plant size—measured by the number of employees—as a function of the plant's age in the United States, Mexico, and India.[15] We can see that plant size increases more sharply with age in the United States than in Mexico or India. This reflects two closely intertwined realities. The first is that it is easier for an American firm to find the financing necessary for growth. The second is that the American financial system selects the highest performing firms, in other words those with the greatest potential to grow.

A similar contrast between the United States and France appears in Figure 1.6, which shows employment share according to the age of establishments: this reflects the fact that long-existing establishments in the United States perform better and have had easier access to financing in order to grow, compared to their counterparts in France.[16] It is thus not surprising that the oldest establishments account for a much greater fraction of total employment in the United States than in France.

5. A Few Growth Enigmas

We judge economic models and paradigms by their ability to elucidate certain phenomena in order to help us understand them. The paradigm of creative destruction penetrates a number of enigmas pertaining to growth. We will confine ourselves to mentioning five of them here.

The Transition from Stagnation to Growth

As we will see in detail in Chapter 2, growth is a recent phenomenon. According to the economist Angus Maddison's 2001 estimates, world per capita GDP was the same in the year 1000 as in the year 1 CE.[17] This world per capita GDP was only 53 percent higher in 1820 than it had been in the year 1000, which corresponds to an

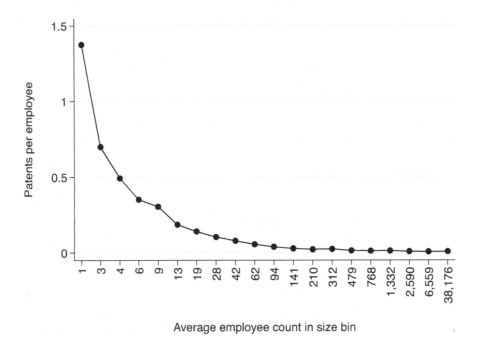

FIGURE 1.4. Innovation intensity by firm size in the United States.

Reformatted from U. Akcigit and W. R. Kerr, "Growth through Heterogeneous Innovations," Journal of Political Economy *126, no. 4 (2018), figure 2.*

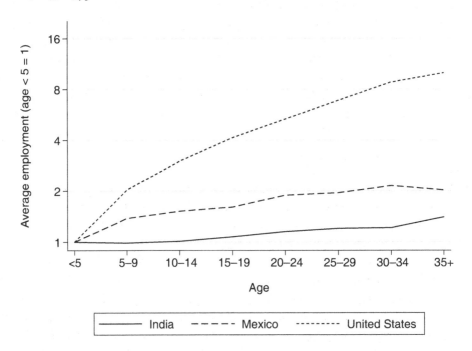

FIGURE 1.5. Plant size as a function of age.

Reformatted from C. T. Hsieh and P. J. Klenow, "The Life Cycle of Plants in India and Mexico," Quarterly Journal of Economics *129, no. 3 (2014): 1035–1084, figure IV.*

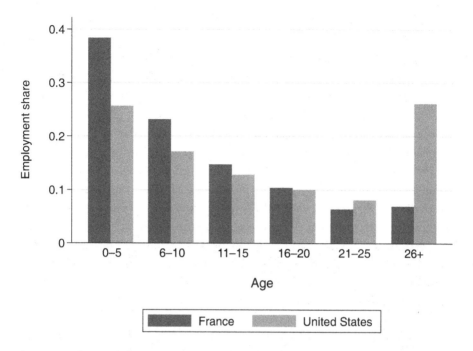

FIGURE 1.6. Employment share of establishments by age.

Reformatted from P. Aghion, A. Bergeaud, T. Boppart, and S. Bunel, "Firm Dynamics and Growth Measurement in France," Journal of the European Economic Association *16, no. 4 (2018): 933–956, figure 6.*

average rate of growth of barely 0.05 per year for 820 years. The takeoff started in 1820, first in the United Kingdom, then in France. The takeoff in these two countries was of such magnitude that the average annual rate of growth jumped from 0.05 before 1820 to 0.5 percent from 1820 to 1870. And after that, global growth continued to accelerate, reaching approximately 3 percent between 1950 and 1973.

How can we explain such a recent and sudden takeoff of growth? Why did it take place in Europe and not in China, where so many important discoveries had been made since the Middle Ages? More generally, what explains other transitions, such as from manufacturing to services, or from catch-up economies to innovation economies?

The neoclassical model is silent on these questions. In particular, it does not explain the increase in growth over time; on the contrary, in the neoclassical paradigm, a nation's growth tends to decline over time as the nation accumulates more capital increases, given that the returns to capital are decreasing. We will see in Chapters 2, 7, and 8 that the Schumpeterian paradigm sheds light on these issues.

Competition and Growth

One might think that everything that reduces profits, such as heightened competition on product markets, would automatically decrease the incentive to innovate, and that more competition implies less innovation and therefore less growth. Yet empirical studies carried out by British economists on firm data demonstrated a positive correlation between competition and innovation in a sector as well as between competition and productivity growth in that sector.[18] What explains this paradoxical result?

The neoclassical theory has little to say on this enigma, as it assumes perfect competition. Can the Schumpeterian paradigm tell us more despite the apparent contradiction we just revealed? How can we reconcile theory and empirical evidence on growth and competition? Must we discard all of our models, including the Schumpeterian model, and return to the drawing board? Or, at the opposite extreme, should we ignore empirical challenges and continue to work on our model as if the problem didn't exist? We will see in Chapter 4 how the paradigm of creative destruction solves this enigma.

The Middle-Income Trap

In 1890, Argentina's per capita GDP had reached 40 percent of that of the United States, making it a middle-income country. Argentina maintained this status until the 1930s, without reducing the gap. But starting in the 1930s, Argentina's productivity began to drop relative to that of the United States. Why did the convergence of Argentina's standard of living toward that of the United States stall and instead begin to retreat? Growth interruptions also occur in more advanced countries. Japan provides a particularly useful example. Between the end of World War II and 1985, Japan experienced spectacular growth in per capita GDP and in its technology level before entering a long period of stagnation.

Neoclassical theory cannot explain such breaks in economic trends. In the neoclassical model, the growth rate declines progressively as capital accumulates, but without trend breaks. The explanation offered by the Schumpeterian theory of growth is that countries like Argentina had institutions or adopted policies favoring growth by accumulation of capital and economic catch-up—in particular a policy of import substitution. But they failed to adapt their institutions in order to transition to innovation economies. We explore this topic in detail in Chapter 7.

Secular Stagnation

In his presidential address to the American Economic Association in 1938, the economist Alvin Hansen explained that he believed the United States was doomed to long-term weak growth, a condition he dubbed "secular stagnation."[19] The country had just emerged from the Great Depression. More recently, the 2008 financial crisis led Lawrence (Larry) Summers and other economists to revive the term *secular stagnation* to describe a situation they saw as similar to that portrayed by Hansen in 1938.[20]

Why has American growth fallen off since 2005 despite the information technology (IT) and artificial intelligence revolutions? The neoclassical model fails to explain the mystery of secular stagnation, as it predicts a continuous decline in growth due to diminishing returns from the accumulation of capital. Can the paradigm of creative destruction do better?

The paradigm of creative destruction suggests, for at least two reasons, a more optimistic vision of the future than that of Larry Summers or Robert Gordon.[21] First, the IT revolution fundamentally and permanently improved the technology of producing new ideas.[22] Second, the process of globalization, contemporaneous with the IT wave, substantially increased the potential rewards of innovation (scale effect) and at the same time the potential cost of not innovating (competition effect). Accordingly, innovation has been accelerating both in quantity and in quality over recent decades. Why doesn't this acceleration show up in the observed evolution of productivity growth? This is the question we will answer in Chapter 6.

Inequality and Innovation

Over recent decades, income inequality has increased rapidly in developed countries, especially at the very top of the income scale. The share of the "top 1 percent" in total income has risen sharply.[23] How can we explain this evolution?

One approach, based on the neoclassical model, is to view the accumulation of capital as the sole source of enrichment. An alternative approach, based on the paradigm of creative destruction and developed in Chapters 5 and 10, sees innovation and the rents it generates as another source of enrichment and of inequality at the top of the income distribution.[24]

What are the different ways to measure inequality? How does innovation affect these different measures? Why is it important to know that the increase in the share of income going to the top 1 percent results partly from innovation and not solely from income from real property rents and speculation?

Without getting ahead of ourselves here, we shall argue in Chapter 5 that innovation has virtues that other sources of top income inequality do not share. Innovation is an engine of growth in developed economies. And if it is true that in the short term innovation benefits those who generated or enabled it, in the long term innovation rents dissipate due to imitation and creative destruction. In other words, the inequality generated by innovation is temporary. Finally, innovation creates social mobility; it allows new talents to enter the market and displaces, fully or partly, incumbent firms.

The contrast between innovation and other sources of inequality at the top of the income ladder will lead us to investigate the contours of a tax policy that is redistributive and at the same time fosters innovation and growth, and that distinguishes between innovation and other sources of inequality. By contrast, a tax policy that discourages innovation would not only hinder growth, but might also impede social mobility by failing to encourage creative destruction.

6. Public Policy, the State, and Civil Society

We also judge economic paradigms by their ability to guide economic policy decisions.

Growth Policies with No Paradigm

The quintessential example of a growth policy not based on any paradigm is what our colleague John Williamson labeled the Washington Consensus.[25] The word *consensus* referred to the fact that the World Bank, the International Monetary Fund, and the US Treasury all supported the same growth policy for Latin American, Asian, and former Soviet bloc countries that were undertaking reforms. The consensus consisted of three key precepts: stabilize the economy, liberalize markets, and privatize firms. These policies were not devoid of any basis, but they did not come from systematic reasoning within a defined theoretical framework.

The Washington Consensus had some critics. In particular, our colleagues Ricardo Hausmann, Dani Rodrik, and Andres Velasco rightly observed in 2008 that countries like China and South Korea experienced high growth rates without rigorously following these recommendations: China never privatized its large state-owned firms, and South Korea did not entirely liberalize trade.[26] By contrast, compliance with the Washington Consensus by some of the Latin American countries did not noticeably stimulate their growth. These three economists proposed a different approach, also pragmatic, based on the idea of growth diagnostics. Their idea was to identify for each country the main barriers to growth, for example, inefficiencies in the education system, credit constraints, or lack of infrastructure.

Growth Policies and the Neoclassical Paradigm

A second approach is to use the neoclassical paradigm to design growth policies. This model suggests that investing in the accumulation of physical capital equipment stimulates growth of per capita GDP, but only up to a certain point, because of diminishing returns on capital. This model also suggests that investing in human capital, in particular in education and knowledge, generates growth. But the theory stops there; it does not deal with the role of policies protecting intellectual property rights, the role of competition policy, the role of structural reforms of the labor market, or how to combine education policy and investment in research and innovation.

Growth Policies and the Paradigm of Creative Destruction

As the reader will recall, the first key idea of the paradigm of creative destruction is that cumulative innovation is the first source of growth: it follows that all individuals will underinvest in innovation because they do not internalize the improvement in collective knowledge that their innovations bring to society or the fact that future innovators will be able to build on this knowledge. As a result, the state has a role to play as an *investor* in innovation. We discuss this topic in Chapter 10, which is devoted to the role of education and science in the innovation process, then in Chapter 12, devoted to the financing of innovation, and again in Chapter 14 on the emergence of the state as an investor.

The second key idea of the paradigm is that innovation is motivated by the prospect of monopoly rents as a reward for innovating. This principle suggests a second role for the state as protector of property rights in innovations. We explore this role in Chapter 4 in connection with the complementary character of intellectual property rights and competition, and again in Chapter 5 in connection with the relationship between tax policy and innovation.

The third key idea of the paradigm is creative destruction: every new innovation destroys the rents generated by prior innovations. Creative destruction implies that any new innovation will be resisted by incumbent firms, as they wish to protect their rents at all costs. As Raghuram Rajan and Luigi Zingales explain very clearly, these firms can in addition benefit from the support of employees who fear they will find themselves unemployed as a result of the destruction of existing activities.[27]

The state has a double role to play in response to this objective alliance against innovation. First, it should preserve competition and the free entry of new innovators in the market for goods and services. This is the whole point of competition policy and of policies aimed at regulating lobbying and combating corruption, which we discuss in detail in Chapters 4, 6, and 15. Second, the state must insure employees against the potentially adverse consequences of job loss. We discuss this topic in Chapter 11 on the connection between creative destruction, health, and happiness as well as in Chapter 14 on the emergence of the insurer-state.

Two Further Implications of the Paradigm of Creative Destruction

The lens provided by the paradigm of creative destruction enables us to explore two additional fundamental aspects of the process by which nations increase their wealth.

Imitation vs. Frontier Innovation.[28] There are two ways to generate productivity growth and technical progress. First, technological imitation makes it possible to adapt best practices in each sector of activity, in other words, to imitate what is happening at the technological frontier. Second, innovating at the frontier enables a firm that is already at the technological frontier to innovate relative to itself, since it has no one else to imitate.

As we will discuss in detail in Chapter 7, some countries experienced an initial period of strong growth thanks to institutions and policies favoring growth by accumulation of capital and economic catch-up. But they were unable to adapt their institutions and policies to become innovating economies. Yet the more developed a country becomes, meaning the closer it gets to the technological frontier, the more frontier innovation takes over from technological catch-up and becomes the engine of growth.[29] Consequently, some countries were unable to maintain strong growth or to converge completely to the levels of per capita GDP of the most developed countries.

The Environment and Directed Innovation. The problem with established firms is not solely that they try to prevent the entry of new, innovative firms. There is another problem relating to their conservatism regarding innovation and technical progress. As we will see in detail in Chapter 9, a car manufacturer that has innovated in combustion engines in the past will tend to innovate in combustion engines in the future because that is where it excels. It will not spontaneously choose to innovate in electric vehicles. This phenomenon is called path dependence. State intervention, through a variety of instruments, is necessary to redirect firms to innovate in green technologies.

Why Would the State Do What We Expect It to Do?

Why would the government play the role that we expect from it by stimulating innovation and creative destruction? Why would state actors encourage the entry of new innovators and resist corruption by incumbent firms? Why would they set up safeguards and checks and balances to thwart abuses of power?

We attempt to answer these questions in Chapters 14 and 15. In these two chapters that deal with the state, we identify international competition and civil society—what Marx called productive forces—as the two levers that obligate governments to pursue the common good. When we take these forces into account, we are less pessimistic about the future of capitalism than Schumpeter was. These forces compel the market economy to continually improve itself and its regulation; they give us hope for prosperity that will be both greener and more inclusive.

7. Outline and User Manual for This Book

Chapter 2 explores the enigma of the takeoff of growth. What explains the long stagnation of world GDP until the beginning of the nineteenth century, followed by the industrial takeoff in the United Kingdom and then in France? This chapter shows how the paradigm of creative destruction provides a useful lens to understand this takeoff.

Chapter 3 deals with the major technological waves: Why does technical progress take the shape of waves, and why did past technological revolutions and automation create more jobs than they destroyed?

Chapter 4 analyzes the relationship between innovation and competition on the market for goods and services: Why and when does competition foster innovation and growth; how can we reconcile competition with the protection of intellectual property rights; and why are competition and industrial policy not contradictory?

Chapter 5 looks at the relationship between innovation and inequality: How do we measure inequality; why is innovation a source of "inequality at the top" that is different from other sources of inequality; how and why does innovation generate social mobility; and how does lobbying affect growth and inequality? And why is taxing capital not the only instrument to make growth more equitable?

Chapter 6 examines the enigma of secular stagnation and seeks in particular to explain the decline in productivity growth in the United States since 2005. Why is productivity growth mismeasured; why has the decline in business dynamism gone hand in hand with rising rents and the emergence of superstar firms? And why is secular stagnation not inevitable?

Chapter 7 sheds light on the enigma of the middle-income trap, also known as the "Argentine Paradox": Why do some countries begin to grow rapidly, then stop midstream? Why are the institutions that foster growth by innovation at the technological frontier not the same as those that encourage catch-up growth; why is freedom especially favorable to innovation and growth at the technological frontier; and how have crises helped some countries escape from the middle-income trap?

Chapter 8 examines the causes of deindustrialization and the transition to a service economy: What causes this transition? Is industrialization a necessary step in the development process, or can an economy transition directly from agriculture to services without large-scale industrialization?

Chapter 9 looks at green innovation: Why doesn't a laissez-faire economy move spontaneously toward green innovation? Why and how should the state intervene to redirect innovation toward green technologies, and why is a carbon tax not the unique instrument to achieve greener growth?

Chapter 10 goes behind the scenes of innovation. Who are the innovators? What do we know about their social origins? Why are education policy and R&D policy complementary to stimulate innovation-led growth? Why can't innovation happen without basic research, and why does basic research rely on academic freedom and openness?

Chapter 11 analyzes the relationship between creative destruction, on one hand, and unemployment, health, and happiness on the other: Why does creative destruction generate unemployment? What is the emotional impact of job loss on individuals, and what are its consequences on their health? Why, accompanied by appropriate public policies, is creative destruction not detrimental to health and happiness?

Chapter 12 focuses on funding innovation: Why are equity and venture capital financing so well adapted to finance frontier innovation; why do institutional investors and philanthropists also play an indispensable role in encouraging risk-taking; why might the state end up focusing research subsidies on large firms to the detriment of more innovative small- and medium-sized enterprises (SMEs)?

Chapter 13 focuses on the relationship between innovation and globalization—globalization of goods but also of individuals. How does the increase in imports from China affect employment and innovation in developed nations? Why does the expansion of export markets stimulate innovation, and why are investment and innovation more effective ways to gain control of our value chains than protectionism? Also, why does skilled immigration make such a strong contribution to innovation in the destination country?

Chapter 14 analyzes how, historically, states were built that were capable of simultaneously investing in innovation and managing the risks associated with it: How did the risks of war and international competition lead progressively to the emergence of states that invest in education, research, and industrial policy? How did wars and major economic crises push states to adopt policies that protect individuals from the risks inherent in creative destruction or to protect firms from the risks of economic cycles?

In Chapter 15 we analyze how checks and balances on the executive can prevent abuses of power and corruption that impede the entry of new, innovative activities. We identify several constitutional tools that make it possible to oversee the exercise of executive power. In many cases, however, these tools are not put into practice without the intervention of civil society. How and why does civil society act as the ultimate guarantor of the separation of powers and of oversight of executive power? Why is the "markets-state-civil society" triangle indispensable to a properly functioning innovation economy?

Finally, on the basis of the analyses and discussions in the earlier chapters, the Conclusion invites the reader to consider the future of capitalism. It posits why, rather than seeking to leave capitalism behind, we should instead reform it in order to attain the objective of sustainable and equitable prosperity.

In closing this introductory chapter, we make three additional remarks. The first is that we are offering a particular paradigm, the Schumpeterian paradigm—or paradigm of creative destruction—to analyze the enigmas and questions associated with the growth process. As we mentioned above, other approaches have been proposed to shed light on the growth process. But at the end of the day, it is the process of creative destruction—applied this time to economic thought—that selects the models and paradigms that best withstand the test of time. The second remark is that in conveying our analyses and reasoning, we have relied first on *suggestive* empirical evidence, meaning simple correlations between explanatory variables and explained variables, and second on empirical evidence progressively approaching a *causal* interpretation, by including control variables, by using instrumental variables, or by relying on natural or random experiments. In every instance, we have tried to be as explicit as possible as to the suggestive or more directly causal nature of the empirical facts we submit to the reader. Third, we have chosen to illustrate our reasoning with numerous graphs and figures. Our purpose is to make notions that are sometimes not obvious clearer, more reader-friendly, and more entertaining.

▼

2

THE ENIGMA OF TAKEOFFS

The onset of sustained and uninterrupted growth at the end of the eighteenth century was without a doubt the first momentous event in the history of economic growth. Out of a world dominated by small cyclical movements around a trajectory of stagnation, an unprecedented process of cumulative expansion suddenly emerged, bringing exponential progress in the average per capita standard of living. Living conditions in the eighteenth century, especially with respect to housing, nutrition, and public health, are unrecognizable to us today. In developed countries, deaths from famine or hypothermia have almost entirely disappeared, whereas they were rampant until the end of the nineteenth century. In the seventeenth century, 25 to 30 percent of newborns died before the age of one; 50 percent before they reached age twenty. Today, infant mortality in the European Union is four per thousand.

What explains the stagnation of both global GDP and population prior to 1820? Why did a sustained growth takeoff occur only in 1820 even though Europe had been the scene of important discoveries since the Middle Ages? Why did the first Industrial Revolution happen in Europe and not elsewhere, in particular in China, where the wheel and the compass had been invented? What was the engine of takeoff: technological development or institutional development? In this chapter we will attempt to answer these questions by confronting the various growth theories with historical facts and data.

1. What Long Series Teach Us: Angus Maddison[1]

Sustained Growth of Income and Population Is a Recent Phenomenon

Between 1000 and 2000 CE, global GDP grew by a factor of 300, while the population grew by a factor of twenty-three. Consequently, per capita income

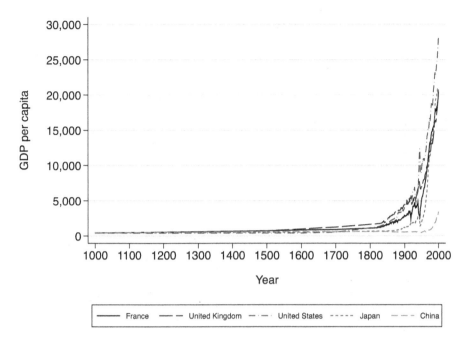

FIGURE 2.1. Per capita GDP, 1000–2008. *Note:* In 1990 dollars.

Data source: Maddison Historical Studies Project (2010), Groningen Growth and Development Centre, University of Groningen.

was multiplied by thirteen during this period, in sharp contrast to the preceding millennium, when the population increased by one-sixth and per capita income remained unchanged. The true breakthrough in the history of growth occurred in 1820, barely 200 years ago. The growth of per capita GDP, which seems self-evident today, is thus an extremely recent phenomenon on the scale of human history (Figure 2.1). Between 1000 and 1820, the average growth rate of global per capita GDP was extremely low, less than 0.05 percent per year. Between 1820 and 1870, it reached 0.5 percent and exceeded 3 to 4 percent from 1950 to 1973.

Growth increased hand in hand with an increase in life expectancy. In 1000, newborns could hope to live to the age of twenty-four; one-third of them died during their first year. Here, too, 1820 marked a turning point. The rise in life expectancy was extremely limited until that date: the average worldwide life expectancy at birth, which was twenty-six years in 1820, grew exponentially thereafter, reaching sixty-six in 1999.

Demography followed a trajectory very similar to that of GDP. Over the very long term, the mortality rate was quite high (approximately thirty-eight per thousand),

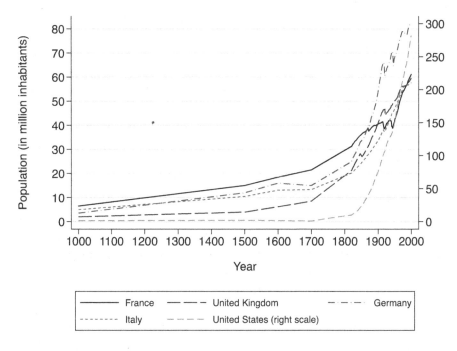

FIGURE 2.2. Evolution of the population in the major European countries and the United States.

Data source: Maddison Historical Studies Project (2010), Groningen Growth and Development Centre, University of Groningen.

as was the birth rate (approximately forty per thousand), hence population growth remained small. World population grew only 18 percent between the year zero and the year 1000 but increased by a factor of twenty-three between 1000 and 2000. Just as they had been the first to experience a takeoff, the European countries were the first to witness substantial demographic growth. In fact, France's population began to grow markedly in 1750 (Figure 2.2). With only a few exceptions, including France, the decline in fertility didn't begin until after 1880. Some nations, such as France, Germany, and the Netherlands, experienced a simultaneous decrease in infant mortality and fertility, while for others (Sweden, Belgium, and Denmark), the decline in infant mortality substantially preceded the drop in fertility. This concomitant explosion of economic and demography growth is intriguing: Were the two phenomena self-sustaining? Or did the growth of GDP bring about the population explosion? What was the spark that ignited the powder keg?

In addition to demographic evolution, the geographic distribution of the population underwent a metamorphosis over the course of the nineteenth and

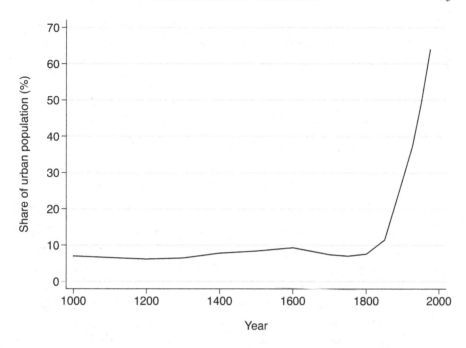

FIGURE 2.3. Urban population as a percentage of total population in Europe, 1000–1975.
Note: Urban population is defined as the population living in cities of more than 5,000 inhabitants.

Data source: J. V. Grauman, "Orders of Magnitude of the World's Urban Population in History," Population Bulletin of the United Nations 8 *(1976): 16–33.*

twentieth centuries. A rural exodus began early in the nineteenth century. In pre-industrial Europe, the population was mostly rural and the rate of urbanization was low, with the highest levels of urbanization occurring in northern Italy and the Netherlands. Thus, the Netherlands had the highest urbanization rate in Europe, at 37 percent, followed by the United Kingdom and Belgium, both of which had urbanization rates of 20 percent. Other European countries (Italy, Spain, Denmark, and Portugal) had urbanization rates exceeding 15 percent as a result of commercial development in the preceding centuries.[2] Yet until the beginning of the nineteenth century, the rural population made up approximately 90 percent of the total population in Europe (Figure 2.3).[3] This share began to decrease in 1800, reaching 36 percent in 1975.[4] The number of cities with more than 100,000 inhabitants increased by a factor of forty-two between 1800 and 1980!

For many years, quantitative research in the history of economics focused nearly exclusively on periods contemporary with or after the takeoff, namely the nineteenth and twentieth centuries. Only with the work of Angus Maddison did quantitative research on growth long before the takeoff begin to develop. Maddison was a pioneer in the reconstruction of national accounts over the long run. His work *The World Economy: A Millennial Perspective* offered a remarkably detailed analysis of income and world population since the year zero. Going that far back in time, to an era when data was fragmentary and national accounting nonexistent, necessitated relying on clues and conjecture (see Box 2.1).

BOX 2.1. THE INVENTION OF NATIONAL ACCOUNTING

Maintaining national accounts only dates to the mid-twentieth century, even though censuses, as a means for rulers to know their resources in human beings and in goods, go back much further. Indeed, political authorities have always attempted to measure the creation of wealth in the territories they controlled. In the feudal age, the national economy was almost entirely limited to agriculture, which served as the basis for calculating taxes. In England in 1690, William Petty (1623–1687) invented the concept of political arithmetic, ancestor of national accounting. The desire to increase revenues led William Petty and later Gregory King to attempt to estimate national income either as the sum of income generated by the various production factors or as aggregate expenditures.[1] In France, Pierre de Boisguillebert and Marechal Vauban used similar approaches to estimate national income. François Quesnay (1694–1774), founder and leader of the Physiocrats, invented the first dynamic model encompassing the totality of national accounting from a macroeconomic perspective, even though the Physiocrats' model was one of an economy based entirely on agriculture.[2]

Only with the appearance of classical economic theory did production become a central concept as a flow of newly created value, rather than a stock of accumulated wealth. In addition, the idea that not only goods but also services must enter the calculation of value added did not emerge until the end of the nineteenth century. The Great Depression of 1929 played a key role in the recognition of the importance of national accounts. Authorities had only incomplete information available with which to develop policies to combat the crisis: market indexes, quantities of shipped merchandise, and incomplete indexes of manufacturing production.

In the United States, the Department of Commerce tasked Simon Kuznets at the National Bureau of Economic Research to develop a set of national accounts. To do so, Kuznets invented the idea of gross domestic product, for which he presented estimates in a 1934 report to the Senate.[3] World War II stimulated the creation of input / output tables, which, following Wassily Leon-tief's work, were integrated into the national accounts.[4] In parallel, at the re-quest of the British government, Richard Stone and James Meade, encouraged and advised by John Maynard Keynes, prepared a set of national revenue and expenditure estimates.[5]

In France, the pioneer was François Perroux, who initiated quantitative work at the Institut de Science économique appliquée in 1955.[6] But the key reference on French growth during the three decades after World War II is the work of Jean-Jacques Carré, Paul Dubois, and Edmond Malinvaud.[7] These authors' goal was to identify and evaluate the determinants of the growth of GDP by looking at the progress that had been made in national accounting. This work, carried out in parallel in several different countries, led to the creation of sys-tems of national accounts (SNA) after World War II. Over time these SNAs were improved and harmonized under the auspices of international working groups of experts from the United Nations, the Organisation for Economic Co-operation and Development (OECD), Eurostat, the International Monetary Fund (IMF), and the World Bank.

1. William Petty, "Political Arithmetick" (1676; pub. London, 1690), in *The Economic Writings of Sir William Petty*, 2 vols., ed. Charles H. Hull (Cambridge: The University Press, 1899), vol. 1, 233–313; Gregory King, "Natural and Political Observations and Conclusions upon the State and Condition of England" (1696), in *Two Tracts by Gregory King*, ed. George E. Barnett (Baltimore: Johns Hopkins Press, 1936).

2. The reader can consult the *Tableau économique* in François Quesnay, *Œuvres économiques complètes et autres textes*, ed. C. Théré, L. Charles, and J.-C. Perrot, 2 vols. (Paris: Institut national d'études démographiques, 2005). For a more exhaustive picture of the history of national accounting, see Alfred Sauvy, "Historique de la comptabilité nationale," *Economie et statistique* 14, no. 1 (1970): 19–32.

3. Simon Kuznets, "National Income, 1929–1932" (Bulletin 49, National Bureau of Economic Research, New York, 1934).

4. Wassily Leontief, *The Structure of the American Economy, 1919–1939: An Empirical Application of Equilibrium Analysis*, 2nd enl. ed. (Oxford: Oxford University Press, 1951).

5. J. Meade and R. Stone, *National Income and Expenditure*, 4th ed. (London: Bowes and Bowes, 1957).

6. François Perroux, "Prise de vues sur la croissance de l'économie française, 1780–1950," *Review of Income and Wealth* 5, no. 1 (1955): 41–78.

7. J. J. Carré, P. Dubois, and E. Malinvaud, *La Croissance française: un essai d'analyse économique causale de l'après-guerre* (Paris: Seuil, 1972).

Maddison and the Reconstruction of Historical Data

Maddison had national accounting data for most countries starting in 1950. How-ever, reconstructing earlier GDP and population data required techniques spe-cific to each period.

For the years from 1820 to 1950, Maddison used historic income and popula-tion data collected from registries and administrative sources. He relied on the work of historians and economists in different countries to carry out this task of collecting data; he then marginally corrected the estimates as a function of differences in the techniques that had been utilized, in order to obtain uniform estimates across countries. For example, in the case of France, Maddison relied particularly on Jean-Claude Toutain's 1987 work.[5] To evaluate GDP, he looked mainly at production in the major economic sectors. Maddison evaluated agricultural production from archives of French agricultural production (such as grains, wine, wood, and meat) and production prices. For the manufacturing sector, 113 series were assembled in twenty-three branches covering the entire industrial structure between 1789 and 1938 (such as extraction industries, metallurgy, food, textiles, chemicals, and construction). Maddison then cross-checked the results with those obtained by Maurice Lévy-Leboyer and François Bourguignon in 1985.[6] Adjusting for changes in the national boundaries during the nineteenth century, he arrived at the evolution of per capita GDP since 1820 (Table 2.1).

For the period 1500 to 1820, Maddison used approximations to estimate GDP. He utilized population data from registries, which were reasonably reliable in particular for European countries. He corrected these data by considering historical events (such as wars and epidemics). To estimate GDP, there were three possible scenarios: Sectoral production data was available in some countries, notably Belgium. Other countries had no such data but their economies were very similar to those of neighboring countries; thus Maddison assumed that the growth of per capita GDP in France was the same as that in Belgium. In the last scenario, in the absence of data for the country or for neighboring countries, Maddison was forced to make educated guesses; for example, he assumed that per capita GDP grew by 0.1 percent per year in Russia. Although these guesses were to some extent arbitrary, per capita GDP and its growth before the Industrial Revolution were so low that possible variations between countries are flattened over a long time scale.

Between the year zero and 1500, the estimates of the evolution of per capita income are much rougher, as Maddison's only source is demographic data. He knew the rate of urbanization in Europe and Asia in the year 1000 (the percentage

Table 2.1. Estimates of Per Capita GDP in France, 1820–1913 (in thousands of 1990 international dollars)

	1820	1870	1913
Maddison	1.218	1.858	3.452
Toutain (1987)	0.983	1.858	3.452
Lévy-Leboyer (1985)	1.123	1.836	3.452

Source: A. Maddison, The World Economy, Development Centre Studies (Paris: OECD, 2001).

of the population living in cities with more than 10,000 inhabitants), which was available. He then hypothesized that an increase in the rate of urbanization within a country implied that there was excess agricultural production and that the share of nonagricultural activity in the economy increased. The urbanization rate in Europe was close to zero between the year zero and 1000; Maddison thus posited that per capita GDP was close to subsistence level, evaluated at 400 dollars per year per person. In China, where the urbanization rate was slightly higher, on the order of 3 percent, Maddison inferred that per capita GDP reached 450 dollars.

One of Maddison's most important contributions was to enable us to revise our understanding of long-term economic growth in Western Europe. To continue the work of Maddison, who died in 2010, the University of Gröningen initiated the Maddison Project with the goal of continuing to collect historical data on GDP, per capita GDP, and labor productivity. For the period after 1820, corrections to Maddison's estimates were marginal. However, significant cliometric work was carried out for the period from 1300 to 1820.[7] Over the long term, growth appears negligible compared with growth after the takeoff of 1820.

The Preindustrial Period in Europe: "eppur si muove"

Although growth over the long term was vastly overshadowed by the post-1820 takeoff, the economy prior to that time was not in a situation of permanent stagnation devoid of any growth.[8] Keynes himself, in his essay "Economic Possibilities for Our Grandchildren," took a nuanced position, affirming that although there had not been an abrupt change in the standard of living, there had been ups and downs, with fluctuations that could even double wealth per capita over a period of several decades.[9] More recently, Roger Fouquet and Stephen Broadberry showed that when we focus on the period from 1300 to 1820, we find noticeable movement of per capita GDP, both rising and falling (Figure 2.4).

Two countries stand out for their long and sustained periods of growth.[10] Between 1350 and 1420, at the beginning of the Renaissance, Italy experienced a 40 percent increase in per capita GDP, which represented an average yearly increase of 0.8 percent for seventy years. The causes of this phenomenon were the sharp decline in population due to the Great Plague, which increased the quantity of land and capital per individual, along with Italian cities' pivotal role in maritime trade.

The Republic of Venice, in particular, played a key role in the development of trade within Europe (Flanders, France, Germany, and the Balkans), between the West and the eastern Mediterranean, and between the West and the Far East. Venice was not only responsible for the flourishing of trade in goods (such as spices and silk), but also fostered the transfer of technologies from Asia, Egypt,

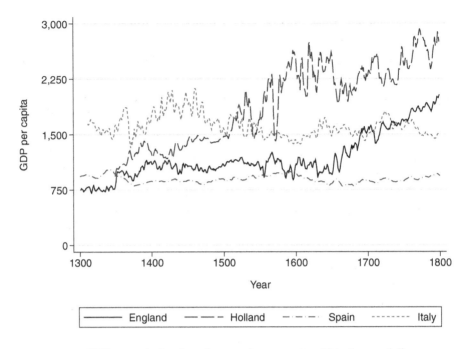

FIGURE 2.4. GDP per capita in selected economies, 1300–1800. *Note:* In 1990 dollars.

Extracted from R. Fouquet and S. Broadberry, "Seven Centuries of European Economic Growth and Decline," Journal of Economic Perspectives 29, no. 4 (2015): 227–244, figure 1.

and Byzantium (such as textile production, glass-blowing, rice cultivation, and sugar cane cultivation). Venice was also at the forefront of institutional innovation, notably by introducing new types of contracts to organize twelfth-century trade and investment. More specifically, trade with Constantinople necessitated significant investments and carried great risk (such as piracy, shipwrecks, and delays), with an exceedingly low probability of substantial financial reward. In order to achieve tolerable risk-sharing, Venetians invented a contract called the *colleganza,* one of the first joint-stock companies. In its most elementary form, the *colleganza* was an agreement between two parties, the investor and the merchant. The investor provided the merchant with merchandise and the merchant shipped it in order to sell it. The contract fixed in advance the division of potential profits. This type of contract allowed a large part of the population to participate in international trade, and it was during this period that Venice reached the height of its prosperity and power.

In the seventeenth century, it was England's turn to experience rapid growth, with the doubling of per capita GDP over the course of the century. The Civil War (1642–1660) marked a crucial step in the transformation of royal power, which, following an ephemeral republic, moved definitively in the direction of a consti-tutional monarchy, proclaimed at the end of the Glorious Revolution of 1688. With a constitutional monarchy, Parliament had supremacy over the king, which al-lowed for better protection of intellectual property rights.[11] This hitherto unknown political configuration created a propitious setting for innovations and thus set the stage for the Industrial Revolution.

The period from 1300 to 1800 also witnessed periods of decline. For instance, Italy experienced three periods of a drop in the growth of per capita GDP: 1450–1600, 1650–1700, and 1750–1800. These downturns were in part due to the return of demographic growth, the fragmentation of markets among several rival city-states (such as Florence and Venice), and the shift of European trade from the Mediterranean to the Atlantic after Europeans reached America at the end of the fifteenth century.

Far from being stagnant, European economies prior to 1820 experienced a se-ries of phases of growth and decline. This raises a question: How did the pre-1820 period differ from the takeoff that started with the first Industrial Revolu-tion? In order to answer this question, Fouquet and Broadberry in 2015 analyzed, for each century, a country's probability of experiencing a prolonged phase of con-tinuous growth, defined as greater than 1.5 percent for at least four consecutive years (Table 2.2), their assumption being that four consecutive years of growth

Table 2.2. Periods of Sustained Economic Growth and Decline in Six Countries, 1300–2000 (in percent)

	Percentage of Years in Four-Year Consecutive ≥1.5% Annual Growth Rate	Percentage of Years in Three-Year Consecutive ≤−1.5% Annual Growth Rate
Fourteenth century	1.1	1.6
Fifteenth century	1.0	8.0
Sixteenth century	2.3	8.7
Seventeenth century	1.3	4.3
Eighteenth century	1.3	5.8
Nineteenth century	5.3	2.0
Twentieth century	40.0	3.2

Note: The countries included in the data are England / United Kingdom, Italy, Holland / Netherlands, Sweden, Spain, and Portugal.

Source: R. Fouquet and S. Broadberry, "Seven Centuries of European Economic Growth and Decline," Journal of Economic Perspectives 29, no. 4 (2015): 227–244.

greater than 1.5 percent corresponds to the beginning of a takeoff.[12] Over the five centuries between 1300 and 1799, the six countries they examined—England / Great Britain, Italy, Holland, Sweden, Spain, and Portugal—had only a very weak probability (between 1 and 2 percent) of experiencing a prolonged phase of growth. This probability increased to 5 percent in the nineteenth century and to 40 percent in the twentieth century. Fouquet and Broadberry thus confirmed the hypothesis that sustained economic growth is a recent phenomenon.

2. The Technological Explanation for the Takeoff

Why didn't growth take off until the beginning of the nineteenth century? Why didn't inventions prior to the Industrial Revolution, such as the wheel, the printing press, or the compass, generate cumulative growth? Why did everything start in the United Kingdom, a small European nation, rather than in a large country such as China?

Before the Takeoff: The Malthusian Trap

Thomas Robert Malthus (1766–1834) offered a particularly convincing explanation for the failure of the global economy to take off before 1820. Malthusian theory explains the coexistence of two phenomena: the stagnation of per capita GDP and the stagnation of the population until the nineteenth century. In his work *An Essay on the Principle of Population,* Malthus started with the premise that agricultural production results from a combination of labor and land.[13] Since land is a fixed production factor, any increase in the population automatically lowers per capita GDP, as more people are working on the same fixed amount of land. But at the same time any increase in per capita GDP—that is to say, the average standard of living—due, for example, to new inventions or to greater openness to trade, leads to an increase in the population, either because it encourages families to have more children (which gives us the story of Hansel and Gretel or Tom Thumb) or because the improvement in the standard of living temporarily reduces mortality. The combination of the two forces produces what we call a Malthusian trap: Technological progress can never bring about a durable increase in an economy's per capita GDP, because any increase in per capita GDP will cause the population to rise, which in turn brings per capita GDP back down to subsistence level.

In Malthus's world, only demographic decline, brought about by abstinence from or restriction of childbearing, can increase per capita GDP. The Malthusian idea that every increase in productivity gives rise to an increase in population may seem to provide a convincing explanation of the preindustrial era. But the conjunction of economic growth and tremendous demographic growth after 1820 showed the limits of the Malthusian approach. How and why did we ultimately escape from the Malthusian trap?

The Technological Approach

Can purely technological arguments explain the escape from the Malthusian trap? A frequently invoked explanation is that the transition from agriculture to manufacturing made it possible to escape the fixed factor—land—by replacing it with capital. Unlike land, capital accumulates over time. Thus replacing land with capital eliminates the negative effect of population growth on per capita GDP in the Malthusian paradigm. But if this were the case, why continue agricultural production rather than immediately replacing land with capital? Once again, we refer to a purely technological argument, that the introduction of manufacturing technology is costly and is not worth the investment until the population has sufficiently increased, and as a result per capita agricultural production has sufficiently decreased. A variant of this explanation of the shift from agricultural production to manufacturing is that when population reaches a critical threshold, there is a rural exodus, freeing up labor for manufacturing. Other authors have underscored the importance of demand effects: only when demand surpasses a certain threshold does it become profitable for various sectors to simultaneously adopt new production technologies.[14] In summary, the shift from agriculture to manufacturing relies on a threshold effect: population threshold, demand threshold, investment threshold. But why, then, did the takeoff happen in 1820, and why did it not happen in a country like China, which was both innovative and densely populated?

Scale Effect and Demographic Transition

A second explanation, modeled by Michael Kremer in 1993 and developed by Oded Galor and David Weil in 2020, relies on the combination of two effects: a scale effect of population on innovation and a demographic transition effect.[15]

We can summarize the scale effect as follows. An increase in population density or size increases innovation rents by increasing the size of the market for all new products, hence a positive effect of population on innovation and growth.[16] In addition, higher population density facilitates the exchange of ideas among individuals, thereby accelerating the production of innovations and consequently growth.[17] Does the acceleration of technical progress caused by the scale effect suffice on its own to extricate an economy from the Malthusian trap? The answer is negative: in the Malthusian world, every acceleration of technical progress translates into accelerated population growth. In other words, it generates a demographic explosion, which ultimately prevents a takeoff of per capita GDP.

Another lever is thus necessary to enable us to escape from the Malthusian trap, and that lever is demographic transition. Simply put, with the acceleration of technological progress, individuals have to study more in order to master the latest technologies. As a consequence, the more advanced a nation's technology, the more parents must invest in their children's education to enable them to adapt to the new technologies.[18] The necessity of investing in education will in turn affect parents' choice between the number of children and the education level of their children, leading them to prefer having fewer but more highly educated children.[19]

This demographic transition lever will mitigate the Malthusian effect of per capita GDP growth on demography. It thus prevents the productivity boom induced by the scale effect from leading automatically to accelerated population growth. Instead, beyond a certain level of per capita GDP, parents will choose to have smaller families in order to invest more in their children's education and benefit more from technical progress.[20] Hence, demographic transition combined with the scale effect enables an economy to escape from the Malthusian trap.

At first glance, historical data seems to confirm this approach based on demographic transition: until 1870, the acceleration of the growth of per capita GDP was accompanied by an acceleration of population growth. After 1870, however, the growth of per capita GDP coincided with a decrease in the rate of population growth. Indeed, the most advanced countries are those with the lowest rates of population growth.

Toward an Institutional Explanation

The idea that takeoff resulted from the conjunction of the scale effect and demographic transition has encountered a number of empirical challenges from economic historians such as Joel Mokyr and Hans-Joachim Voth.[21] In the first place, as these authors point out, the population of England was stagnant from 1700 to 1750, prior to the Industrial Revolution; there was thus not a demographic explosion leading to a scale effect. In addition, China, whose population grew by a multiple of 3.2 between 1650 and 1750, and which innovated at least as much as Europe, did not experience a takeoff. Finally, the largest countries did not experience stronger growth than other countries. These considerations prompt us to seek an explanation for takeoff that is not purely technological but that integrates technological factors with an institutional dimension.

3. The Articulation between Technology and Institutions: Joel Mokyr[22]

The institutional approach developed in this section will constantly bring us back to the paradigm of creative destruction described in Chapter 1, with its three basic ideas: (1) growth comes from the progressive accumulation of knowledge: every innovation uses the knowledge contained in preceding innovations, and every innovator stands "on the shoulders of giants" that preceded him; (2) innovation needs a favorable institutional environment, starting with strong protection of property rights; and (3) innovation destroys existing rents and consequently requires a competitive environment so that innovative new firms can continuously enter.

Joint Evolution of Science and Technique

Well before the Industrial Revolution, the history of humanity was punctuated by technological innovations. But unlike during the industrial era, these innovations were isolated and idiosyncratic and did not engender a sustained period of innovation and growth. In *The Gifts of Athena,* Joel Mokyr highlights the dialogue between theoretical knowledge and practical knowledge to explain the takeoff. He first distinguishes between what he labels propositional (theoretical) knowledge and prescriptive (practical) knowledge. Propositional knowledge refers to scientific knowledge, which seeks to understand natural phenomena. Prescriptive knowledge designates knowledge of technique; its objective is production. Progress in propositional knowledge is a discovery, whereas progress in prescriptive knowledge is an innovation. Preindustrial growth was grounded in progress in prescriptive knowledge, meaning an accumulation of techniques that worked without the user having to understand the scientific knowledge underlying them. By contrast, beginning in the nineteenth century, industrial societies sought to understand the underlying principles that made the techniques effective, adopting a scientific approach. They moved from "How does it work?" to "Why does it work?" This emergence of scientific thinking constituted a breakthrough that paved the way for the generalization of propositional knowledge and its application to new fields.

As our colleague David Encaoua wrote in 2011, "This period gave rise to the passage from a state of knowledge governed by technique to a state of knowledge governed by technology, that is to say a combination of science and technique."[23] Thus, in the field of chemistry, the formulas for various compounds had been known for centuries, but only once we had conceptualized chemical compounds could we produce new chemical compounds. Likewise, the invention of the microscope made possible the development of microbiology.

Mathematics in particular paved the way for this dialogue between science and technique. For example, mathematics provided the means to formulate Newton's laws, which made it possible to explain the movement of projectiles, promoting progress in ballistics and leading to new scientific discoveries. This coevolution of science and technology is the defining characteristic of the Industrial Revolution.

But what made this coevolution possible? Mokyr points to three factors, which coincide precisely with the three tenets of the paradigm of creative destruction: the diffusion of knowledge and information that enable cumulative innovation, competition among nations that makes creative destruction possible, and the emergence of institutions that protected innovators' property rights.

Diffusion of Knowledge and Information

The diffusion of knowledge and information played a crucial role in the eighteenth century, thanks to the emergence of affordable postal service and the decreasing cost of printing. The number of newspapers exploded (Table 2.3) and numerous encyclopedias appeared.[24] For example, in London in 1704, John Harris published his *Lexicon Technicum,* considered the first modern English-language encyclopedia, which served as the basis of Ephraim Chambers's *Cyclopaedia or an Universal Dictionary of Arts and Sciences,* published in 1728. In fact, before embarking on their more ambitious project, Denis Diderot's and Jean le Rond d'Alembert's initial project was to translate the *Cyclopaedia.* The objective of their *Encyclopédie ou Dictionnaire raisonné des sciences, des arts et des métiers,* the first volumes of which appeared in 1751, was to codify all knowledge and know-how available at the time, calling for contributions from specialists in the various disciplines.[25] The diffusion of these works made technical and scientific knowledge accessible and greatly facilitated the process of knowledge accumulation.

In return, these developments favored the exchange of ideas through the emergence of societies and clubs that encouraged the sharing and advancement of knowledge. This situation contrasts sharply with that of the fifteenth century, when knowledge was jealously guarded by guilds and trade organizations. In the eighteenth and nineteenth centuries, on the contrary, a true culture of sharing information arose. As a result, inventors did not begin from scratch for each invention; they inherited the wealth of all the preceding inventions and were able to "stand on the shoulders of giants."

Openness, that is, the free circulation of ideas between inventors and between countries, also played a major role in the cumulative process of innovation and consequently in takeoff. Mokyr insists on the preeminent role of the transnational Republic of Letters uniting all European humanists, scholars, and literati around Latin as a common language. From the time of the Renaissance, this Republic of Letters put the innovator in a European and supranational environment, and provided him with an audience larger than just his compatriots. In Chapter 10, we will return to the importance of openness for the process of innovation, particularly for basic research.

Table 2.3. Letters and Newspapers Transmitted by the US Postal Service, 1790–1840

Year	Letters (millions)	Letters per capita	Newspapers (millions)	Newspapers per capita
1790	0.3	0.1	0.5	0.2
1800	2.0	0.5	1.9	0.4
1810	3.9	0.7	–	–
1820	8.9	1.1	6.0	0.7
1830	13.8	1.3	16.0	1.5
1840	40.9	2.9	39.0	2.7

Source: R. R. John, *Spreading the News: The American Postal System from Franklin to Morse* (Cambridge, MA: Harvard University Press, 1995).

The Importance of Competition

The second institutional impetus of takeoff occurred in Europe: competition among nations. This competition enabled innovation and creative destruction to take place notwithstanding the resistance or opposition of vested interests in the different nations. In a politically fragmented Europe, nations competed for the most brilliant minds. Thus, despite the presence in each country of forces resisting innovation, the fear of being surpassed by other countries won out over all other considerations.

By contrast, the absence of competitive pressures in China enabled incumbent economic and political powers to have the last word. Thus, in 1661, Emperor Kangxi ordered everyone living along the southern coast to move thirty kilometers inland. Until 1663, navigation along the entire coast was forbidden. This prohibition was periodically reinstated in the eighteenth century, delaying the emergence of overseas trade. Chinese rulers acted in response to a fear of creative destruction because they believed it threatened their political stability. The only innovations that were allowed to emerge in China were those handpicked by the emperor. Unlike in Europe, there were few opportunities of emigration for Chinese innovators whose inventions had not been selected. The consequence of this absolute control was stagnation of the Chinese economy throughout the nineteenth century and into the early twentieth century, while other economies were industrializing.

The absence of competition also engendered the decline of Venice.[26] In 1297, fearing an erosion of their status, the richest and most powerful families passed the first of a series of laws known as the *Serrata* that made participation in the Maggior Consiglio a hereditary right limited to members of a few noble families. From that moment, access to political power was limited, wealth became concentrated in a small number of families, and the city-state began its decline as a maritime and economic power. In Chapter 15, we will return in detail to the example of Venice.

Property Rights

The establishment of institutions protecting intellectual property rights was a key factor in the takeoff of growth, explaining in part why the takeoff happened first in England, and only afterward in France. Technology cannot be the entire explanation, because at the end of the eighteenth century, both nations had achieved comparable scientific and technological levels—remember that France was the birthplace of Diderot's groundbreaking codification of knowledge with the *Encyclopédie*. However, England was far more advanced than France in protecting property rights. The English Parliament's supremacy over the king, achieved in the Glorious Revolution (1688–1689), secured property rights from political interference for the first time, thereby encouraging innovation.[27] The Glorious Revolution took place a century before the French Revolution, which itself only progressively paved the way to the creation of new institutions that were more favorable to entrepreneurship and innovation, starting with the Napoleonic Code, through Jules Ferry's revolutionary education reform during the Third Republic.

It was thus England that led the way in recognizing inventors' property rights and that inspired the rest of Europe in this direction. As early as 1624, the Statute of Monopolies prohibited the monarchy from granting exclusive privileges in commercial matters, except for the "true and first inventor[s]", who could obtain a fourteen-year monopoly on the exploitation of their inventions. This step marked the institutionalization of a system of letters patent, which subsequently inspired America's Founders and the French revolutionaries: the first laws concerning patents date to 1790 in the United States and 1791 in France.

Before this time, trades had been protected by guilds that maintained strict secrecy over their accumulated technical knowledge. These guilds strove to establish monopolies in their respective cities and attempted to exclude neighboring cities from their markets, as witnessed by the intense rivalry between Bruges and Ghent or between Genoa and Venice. Only apprentices deemed worthy were given access to a full understanding of the techniques used in the trade. And woe betide anyone who betrayed the guild's secrets! Georges Renard described the following Venetian law from 1454: "If a worker takes an art or craft to another country, to the detriment of the Republic, he will be ordered to return; if he disobeys, his closest relatives will be imprisoned so that family solidarity will persuade him to return; if he persists in disobeying, secret measures will be taken to put him to death wherever he is."[28] Hal Varian reported the example of fifteenth-century

Venice, city-state at the cutting edge of two technical fields: Murano glass and shipbuilding. The secrets of Murano glass-making were so strictly guarded that anyone born on the island of Murano could never leave, to avoid the risk that he might reveal them. Similarly, foreigners were prohibited from observing the building of ships in the Arsenal of Venice.[29]

The emergence of the patent system had a twofold effect on innovation and technological progress. First, patents created an incentive for inventors to innovate by granting them at least a temporary monopoly on the use of their innovations, thereby guaranteeing an innovation rent. Second, patents obliged inventors to diffuse the knowledge underlying their inventions, which enabled others to subsequently innovate upon them by exploiting the knowledge contained in the patent.[30]

Financial Development

Financial development played a central role in stimulating innovation and enabling industrial takeoff in Europe in the nineteenth century: the creation of commercial banks and development banks, the emergence of equity financing and stock exchanges, the appearance of limited liability companies—these financial innovations dynamized real innovation and risk-taking, thereby enabling sustained and robust growth such as the world had never seen before 1820. As Raghuram Rajan and Luigi Zingales explain so well in the introduction to their book *Saving Capitalism from the Capitalists,* financial markets make it possible to mobilize resources and capital to finance daring ideas; in so doing they sustain the process of creative destruction, which generates prosperity.[31] In particular, the authors show how the growth of per capita GDP in developed countries has historically gone hand in hand with the growth of indicators such as the ratio between bank deposits and GDP, the ratio between market capitalization and GDP, or the ratio between equity financing and fixed investments. Yet, Rajan and Zingales are not naive about the dark side of finance, namely the excesses and dangers of unregulated finance. A major focus of their work is the identification of these dangers and the means of preventing or at the very least curbing them. In Chapter 12, we will look in detail at the financing of innovation.

David Séchard or the Ordeals of the Inventor

Few novelists have described the misery suffered by a nineteenth-century inventor in the face of imperfect protection of intellectual property rights, combined with lack of access to financing, as well as Honoré de Balzac in *Lost Illusions.* Entitled "Les Souffrances de l'Inventeur" (The Ordeals of the Inventor), the third part of this book describes the tribulations of David Séchard.

Séchard, son of a printer, invents a process for producing paper using plant fibers. This process enables him to produce at a lower cost than rivals. However, his closest competitors, the Cointet Brothers, manage to claim ownership of the process by means that are unethical but nonetheless legal. They force Séchard and his printshop into bankruptcy by demanding payment of a debt incurred by David's friend—and the hero of the novel, Lucien de Rubempré—by forging his signature. The Cointet Brothers then have the upper hand and can pressure David, in exchange for forgiving his debt, to grant them the right to use his invention freely and indefinitely. Although the discounted value of the income generated by the invention far surpasses the amount of the debt, David has no choice but to accept a deeply unfavorable agreement.

Such misfortune would be less likely to occur in France today than in Séchard's time, the first half of the nineteenth century, for at least two reasons. One reason has to do with the cost of filing a patent: today the cost is €600, whereas at the time Balzac's novel took place, it corresponded to 10 percent of the market value of Séchard's print shop. The second reason is that it is much easier today for an inventor like Séchard to find financing (from banks, venture capitalists, institutional investors, or elsewhere), given that there is an actual market for intellectual property, in which patents have a value and accordingly can serve as collateral for fundraising and borrowing.

If David Séchard were to return today, he could thus patent his invention and then obtain financing from a bank or venture capitalist to implement it. The bank or venture capitalist would then repay the debt owed to the Cointet Brothers. Or Séchard could choose to sell his patent and use the proceeds to repay his debt, but he would retain the difference between the value of the patent and the amount of the debt.

Thus, Balzac's novel illustrates the benefits of a more advanced capitalist system, in which intellectual property rights in inventions are guaranteed by a patent system more easily accessible than that of the nineteenth century, together with a more developed financial system that protects the inventor from being held up by a single creditor, *a fortiori* a creditor who is also a competitor.

Eli Whitney and His Cotton Gin

In 1793, the American Eli Whitney invented the cotton gin, a machine that separated cotton seeds from stems. This invention was patented in March 1794. However, with the institutions in place at the time, it was not possible in practice to enforce the intellectual property rights in the patent. The expenses Whitney incurred to protect his invention from counterfeits used up all of the profits from his invention, leading his firm to declare bankruptcy in 1797. The inventor decided never again to file for a patent, famously declaring, "An invention can be so valuable as to be worthless to its inventor." Today, Eli Whitney would undoubtedly have succeeded in protecting his invention and in obtaining the financing to keep his firm afloat.[32]

4. Conclusion

The miracle of takeoff was linked to multiple factors, the conjunction of which gave rise to an unprecedented accumulation of wealth starting in the nineteenth century. But the articulation between technology and institutional factors offers the best understanding of why takeoff occurred at the beginning of the nineteenth century and not earlier, and why it started in Europe—first in England and then in France—and not elsewhere. The impact of technologies such as printing and postal services enormously facilitated the production and diffusion of knowledge, while the emergence of new institutions protected innovators and thereby encouraged investment in innovation.

In sum, the Industrial Revolution serves as an illustration of three fundamental principles of the paradigm of creative destruction, namely: cumulative innovation is a driving force of growth; institutions are critical, starting with property rights to protect innovation rents and more generally to foster innovation; and competition is necessary to combat the barriers to entry that existing firms and governments create to thwart the process of creative destruction in order to prevent new entrants from challenging their rents or their power. This paradigm will guide our analysis throughout this book, but at the same time we will continuously test it against empirical data in the chapters to come.

▼

3

SHOULD WE FEAR

TECHNOLOGICAL REVOLUTIONS?

Should we fear or wish for technological revolutions? On the one hand, we may fear them because they seem to accelerate the automation of tasks and thus the replacement of human workers by machines to perform these tasks. On the other hand, we welcome them, as they induce a series of secondary innovations that affect all sectors of the economy, thereby fostering growth.

The most well-known example is undoubtedly the invention of the steam engine by James Watt in the 1770s, which triggered the first Industrial Revolution—the first major technological wave—discussed in the preceding chapter. This revolution started in England and France before spreading to other western countries, in particular the United States. The invention of electricity set off the second Industrial Revolution, whose golden age was in the first half of the twentieth century. This second revolution originated with the invention of the light bulb by Thomas Edison in 1879 and of the dynamo by Werner von Siemens in 1866. This second technological wave, which Robert Gordon baptized the "one big wave," crossed the Atlantic in the opposite direction: it began in the United States in the 1930s before diffusing to the other industrialized nations after World War II, as we see in Figure 3.1.[1] This wave was of greater magnitude in Europe and Japan than in the United States, because of both postwar reconstruction and the need to catch up with the United States technologically. Finally, the third Industrial Revolution, the revolution in information technologies (IT), grew out of the invention of the microprocessor by Federico Faggin, Marcian (Ted) Hoff, and Stan Mazor at Intel in 1969.

Yet there is a significant delay between the invention of the technology that initiates the wave and the growth takeoff that materializes the wave. The first steam engine was on the market in 1712, but not until 1830 do we observe an acceleration

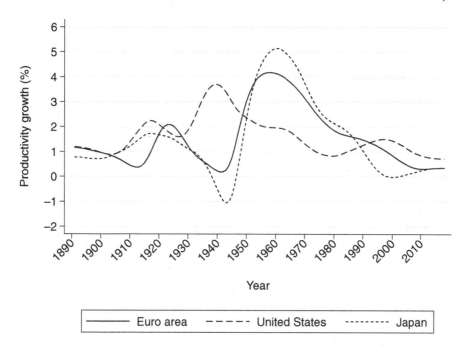

FIGURE 3.1. Annual growth of total factor productivity.

Data source: A. Bergeaud, G. Cette, and R. Lecat, "Productivity Trends in Advanced Countries between 1890 and 2012," Review of Income and Wealth 62, no. 3 (2016): 420–444.

in the growth of per capita GDP in the United Kingdom.[2] Similarly, although the lightbulb was invented in 1879, more than fifty years passed before we observed an acceleration of productivity growth in the United States. In addition, we observe a decline in productivity growth in the United States and the eurozone since the beginning of the 2000s.[3]

What explains this time lag between a general-purpose invention and the ensuing acceleration of growth? Why have technological revolutions so far not brought about the mass unemployment feared by the Luddites in nineteenth-century England and by Keynes in 1930?[4] What can we expect from the artificial intelligence revolution: will it create jobs or destroy them? These are the enigmas we will explore in this chapter.

1. Why Is There a Delay in the Diffusion of Waves?

In 1987, Robert Solow wrote, "You can see the computer age everywhere except in the productivity statistics."[5] He first formulated what is now known as the *Solow paradox* eighteen years after the invention of the microprocessor, and yet growth of American productivity remained sluggish. The growth wave associated with IT did not begin until several years later, in the mid-1990s, and continued through the middle of the 2000s in the United States.

In order to understand this delay in the diffusion of IT, it is helpful to look more closely at the characteristics of a technological revolution. To start with, technological revolutions originate in a fundamental innovation that produces a general purpose technology or GPT, one that will alter the entire economy.[6] Three fundamental properties characterize GPTs. First, they spawn successive waves of secondary innovations, each of which corresponds to the adaptation of the GPT to a specific sector of the economy. Second, these technologies improve, allowing their cost to users to decrease over time. Third, they are pervasive: these technologies spread to all sectors of the economy.[7]

Let us now explore how these characteristics enable us to explain the delay between the innovation behind the GPT and the time we observe a significant increase in economic growth.

The Importance of Secondary Innovations

A GPT is not "ready-to-wear." Its implementation in the various sectors of the economy necessitates secondary "process" innovations. Each secondary innovation adapts the GPT to the needs of a particular sector. For example, the assembly line was a secondary innovation that emerged from the application of the electricity revolution to the automobile manufacturing sector. Online shopping is an innovation derived from the IT revolution and applied to the commercial services sector. Secondary innovations like these improve firms' production processes, thereby increasing their productivity, which is why they are sources of long-term growth.

Nevertheless, these secondary innovations take time. This is one factor that explains the delay in growth. Furthermore, generating secondary innovations takes resources away from production. This in turn causes GDP growth to slow down in the short term, or at the very least delays the surge in growth that the GPT is supposed to spark.[8]

Every wave of secondary innovations coming from a new GPT corresponds to a surge in innovation, reflected in a sharp increase in the number of patents per capita over the time period in question (Figure 3.2).

Each sector requires a unique secondary innovation, and the invention of these secondary innovations takes different amounts of time from one sector to another. This explains why, for the economy as a whole, the replacement of the old GPT by the new GPT takes place only gradually.

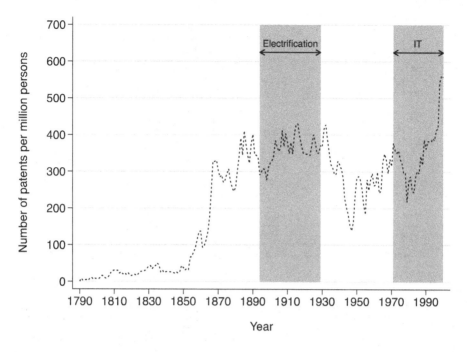

FIGURE 3.2. Patents issued on inventions in the United States per million persons, 1790–2002.

Extracted and reformatted from B. Jovanovic and P. L. Rousseau, "General Purpose Technologies," in Handbook of Economic Growth, *ed. P. Aghion and S. Durlauf (Amsterdam: Elsevier, 2005), vol. 1, 1181–1224, figure 12.*

Thus, between 1869 and 1900, the use of waterwheels and hydraulic turbines in the manufacturing sector dropped gradually, in parallel to the gradual increase in the use of steam—steam engines and turbines (Figure 3.3). Then, starting in the twentieth century, steam-powered machines gave way to electricity-powered machines, slowly at first, then at an accelerated pace. Ultimately, the diffusion of a new GPT follows an S-shaped curve, similar to the one describing the evolution of an epidemic like COVID-19—slow and progressive at first, then rising rapidly, and finally reaching a plateau.

The Delay in Technological Diffusion within Firms: The Dynamo and the Computer

The economist Paul David provides a particularly good illustration of the process of diffusion of new GPTs by comparing the adoption of electricity to the adoption of computer technology within firms.[9] Despite the enormous transformative potential that engineers foresaw, electricity was barely in use in US firms

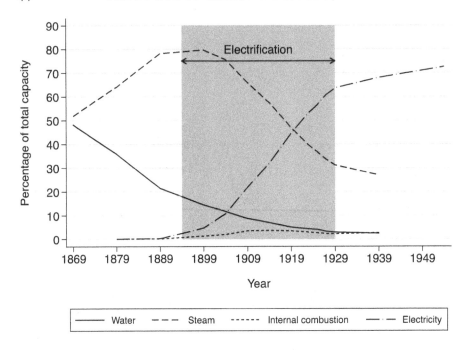

FIGURE 3.3. Shares of total power generated by the main sources of energy in US manufacturing, 1869–1954.

Reformatted from B. Jovanovic and P. L. Rousseau, "General Purpose Technologies," in Handbook of Economic Growth, *ed. P. Aghion and S. Durlauf (Amsterdam: Elsevier, 2005), vol. 1, 1181–1224, figure 2.*

in 1899. In fact, the internal organization of factories had not changed since the era when they were powered by waterwheels: they were still structured around a line shaft. The force of the water turned a line shaft attached to the factory ceiling, and each machine was directly connected to this shaft by a system of belts.

With the advent of the first Industrial Revolution, steam started to progressively replace water as the energy source in factories, yet the production system remained unchanged. Then came the second Industrial Revolution. Some plants chose to retain steam power while others converted to electrical power, but they did so initially with an unchanged organizational structure, that is to say, without questioning the line shaft system.

However, the line shaft system entailed major disadvantages that limited its effectiveness. For example, similar machines had to be placed alongside each other in order to facilitate the transmission of power from the shaft. This suboptimal layout necessitates a long physical distance in the plant between the first and last steps in manufacturing a product.

This is where secondary innovations play a role. In the early 1910s, Henry Ford realized that electricity made possible two things that were not possible with steam power: using wires to transmit energy and miniaturizing motors. These two secondary innovations changed everything. As a result of these innovations, machines could be totally independent of each other, powered directly by electrical wires. Ford could thus eliminate the line shaft and arrange machines according to the sequence of tasks they performed in the production process: the assembly line was born, and it would vastly boost productivity.

Paul David draws a parallel between the inefficient use of electricity at the end of the nineteenth century and the inefficient use of computer technology at the end of the twentieth century. Although computers could and should have led to the digitization of numerous data processing tasks as soon as they emerged, in fact traditional paper procedures continued, with a duplication of tasks and little gain in productivity by the end of the 1980s. Without the discovery and general acceptance of secondary innovations, there are even cases where we never converge to optimal utilization of a new technology. The overwhelming dominance of the QWERTY keyboard presents a glaring example of how we deprive ourselves of a source of productivity growth by ignoring secondary innovations (see Box 3.1).

BOX 3.1. THE QWERTY KEYBOARD: AN EXAMPLE
OF PATH DEPENDENCE

The QWERTY keyboard has been adopted in virtually all Anglo-Saxon countries. Yet this keyboard arrangement is far from optimal, and other keyboards permit much faster typing. Why, then, do we continue to use the QWERTY keyboard? The history of this keyboard helps us understand. The story begins in 1873, when Remington developed the first commercially successful typewriter. It utilized the QWERTY keyboard, designed to keep the metal arms of the keys from jamming.

In 1936, August Dvorak filed a patent for a new layout of the keys on the keyboard, the Dvorak Simplified Keyboard. This layout allowed record-breaking typing speeds in English with ergonomics superior to QWERTY. In 1940, the US Navy conducted tests that showed that in ten days the increase in efficiency with the Dvorak keyboard would absorb the cost of retraining a group of typists. Nonetheless, the Dvorak standard did not replace the suboptimal QWERTY standard. Why?

Paul David suggests two reasons.[1] The first comes from a problem of coordination: an employer was better off buying QWERTY typewriters, because he assumed typists had been trained on this keyboard. And typists were well advised to learn the QWERTY keyboard on the assumption that most firms were equipped with them. This technical interdependence favors the earlier technology, in our example the QWERTY keyboard. The second factor has to do with the economies of scale in the adoption of a new standard: As an industry converges to a single standard, the average costs of using this standard decrease, and it becomes more costly for a firm to move toward an alternative keyboard.

The secondary innovation inherent in the Dvorak keyboard arrived too late, or to put it another way, no one seized on it quickly enough to make possible a radical change in typing. As a result, firms and users are stuck with the suboptimal QWERTY standard.

---

1. Paul David, "The Dynamo and the Computer: An Historical Perspective on the Modern Productivity Paradox," *American Economic Review* 80, no. 2 (1990): 355–361.

Finally, we note that the transition from an old to a new GPT fosters the process of creative destruction. This is because new firms have an advantage insofar as they, unlike existing firms, are not subject to the costs of switching from old to new GPTs. Accordingly, the arrival of a GPT should lead to entry and exit of firms. If we measure entry based on the stock market valuation of newly listed firms on the New York Stock Exchange, the American Stock Exchange, or NASDAQ as a percentage of the total valuation of these stock markets, we indeed observe, during both the diffusion of electricity and the diffusion of IT, an increase in the flow of entry and exit of firms—in other words, an acceleration of creative destruction.

Improvements in the Use of GPTs

A new GPT is not immediately efficient. It takes time to learn how to use it effectively. The process of learning by doing shows up in the evolution over time of the price of capital incorporating the new GPT: as new machines integrate the GPT more efficiently, prices will drop for existing machines that use an earlier version of the same technology. For example, in France, the arrival of the second generation of high-speed trains with a cruising speed of 320 kilometers per hour caused prices to fall for the first generation of high-speed trains, whose maximum speed was 260 kilometers per hour. Between the beginning of the twentieth century and the 1960s, the price of electricity was divided by 100. Over a twenty-five-year period, the price of a computer of a given quality has fallen by a factor of 10,000.

Adoption of New GPTs by Households

Mirroring the delay followed by an acceleration in the adoption of new GPTs by firms, there is a similar delay and acceleration for households, stemming largely

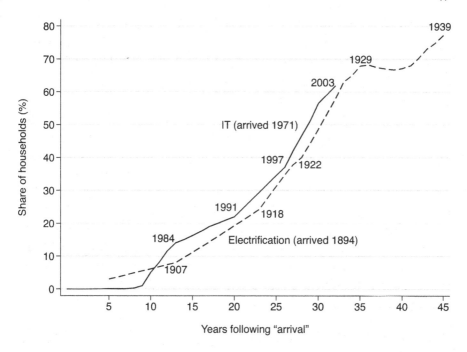

FIGURE 3.4. Percentage of households with electric service and personal computers during the two GPT eras.

Reformatted from B. Jovanovic and P. L. Rousseau, "General Purpose Technologies," in Handbook of Economic Growth, *ed. P. Aghion and S. Durlauf (Amsterdam: Elsevier, 2005), vol. 1, 1181–1224, figure 8.*

from the fall in prices. For example, the rapid fall in the price of portable computers in the 1990s resulted in accelerated adoption of IT by households (Figure 3.4). It is interesting to note that the share of households with electricity followed a similar evolution to that of household adoption of IT. In both cases, improvements in the quality of the GPT that persuaded households to adopt it depended on a network effect: The adoption of electricity expanded as the geographic extension and the quality of the electrical network grew. In the same way, the adoption of IT depends on the establishment of sufficiently fast internet access.

Inadequate Local Infrastructure and Institutions

As Figure 3.1 shows, the technology wave associated with the electricity revolution took nearly twenty years to spread from the United States to other developed nations, in particular Western Europe and Japan. Antonin Bergeaud, Gilbert Cette, and Rémy Lecat account for this delay by several factors: the dilapidated state of manufacturing facilities, the disorganization of production, and the loss of human capital in those nations as a result of World War II.[10] After the war, it was necessary both to build new factories adapted to the use of electricity and to change managerial methods. None of that could be accomplished until the war had ended and international trade had resumed. It was thus due to structural changes that the electricity wave was able to spread in Europe.

Figure 3.1 shows that the IT revolution has followed a path similar to the electricity revolution. The IT revolution, also initiated in the United States, produced a technological wave that crested there in 2000, but it has not yet produced similar waves in Japan and the eurozone. In this case, the authors account for the delays in the diffusion of IT by the difficulty of setting up adequate economic policies and institutions. In particular, they identify the failure to open up labor markets and the markets for goods and services, and the failure to invest adequately in higher education and research as key reasons for the delay in IT diffusion. Once again, we see that structural modifications were a prerequisite for the propagation of the technological wave. We will return to the notion of appropriate growth policies in Chapter 7.

The Difficulty of Measuring Productivity: The Case of the IT Revolution

The gains in productivity from a new GPT are sometimes difficult to measure, especially during the period immediately following introduction of the GPT. This brings us back to the Solow paradox, mentioned at the beginning of this chapter. It is undeniable that the IT revolution generated gains in productivity, not only in the production of goods and services but also in the production of ideas. For example, thanks to Skype and Zoom, researchers in different universities and different countries can communicate with far greater ease and thus collaborate more easily on research projects. The productivity gains brought about by IT in the production of ideas are even harder to measure than the productivity gains brought about by IT in the production of goods and services.[11]

Moreover, the output generated by IT is concentrated in the services sector, and productivity is harder to measure in the services sector than in the manufacturing sector. As Eric Brynjolfsson and Shinkyu Yang write, "Increased variety, improved timeliness of delivery and personalized customer service are other services that are poorly represented in productivity statistics."[12] In Chapter 6, we will look more closely at these measurement problems.

Artificial Intelligence: A New Growth Wave Ahead?

Are we on the threshold of a new growth wave driven by artificial intelligence (AI)? AI allows us to anticipate the automation of tasks we believed could not be automated, such as driving cars or reading electrocardiograms. This large-scale automation can in turn fuel growth by replacing labor, which is in limited supply, with capital, which can accumulate without bound, for the production not only of goods and services but also of new ideas and innovations.[13]

Why, then, haven't we observed a burst of growth in developed countries, even though automation and AI are affecting a growing share of activities? One possible explanation is that some essential inputs to production or research cannot be automated.[14] Accordingly, labor remains indispensable in the production process, even if many other tasks are automated. Labor then becomes a scarce factor, which leads its price—that is, wages—to increase over time. At the same time, being indispensable and in limited supply, labor inhibits the potential for AI to generate accelerated growth. We will return to this point in greater detail in Chapter 8.

A second explanation, developed in Chapter 6, is that in the absence of the appropriate institutions, a technological revolution can itself become an obstacle to growth rather than a catalyst of growth. More specifically, we will see why, without an effective competition policy, the IT revolution can actually end up discouraging innovation.

2. Industrial Revolutions and Employment: Irreconcilable Antagonists?

A Historical Perspective

The fear that machines will destroy human jobs began long ago. As early as 1589, when William Lee invented a machine to knit stockings, the working class was so fearful of the consequences that he was rejected everywhere and even threatened. When he presented his invention to Queen Elizabeth I, in the hopes of obtaining a patent, she refused, declaring, "Consider what thy invention could do to my poor subjects. It would assuredly bring them ruin by depriving them of employment, thus making them beggars."[15] Gradually, professional guilds, which jealously defended their trades from encroachment by technology, lost their influence. Despite a 1769 law protecting machines from being destroyed, destruction intensified as the weaving loom became widespread, culminating with the Luddite rebellion in 1811–1812. This rebellion pitted textile craftsmen under the leadership of the apocryphal Ned Ludd against manufacturers who favored the use of machines for producing cotton and wool textiles. In 1812, Parliament passed a law making machine breaking a capital crime. What accounts for this turnaround in the official attitude toward technical progress? Above all, the owners of capital, who profited from exporting manufactured goods, pleaded the positive effects of technical progress for production, exports, and employment. These "capitalists" gained increasing representation in the British Parliament, which over time obtained supremacy over the Crown.[16]

Starting in the 1930s, economists began to express concern about *technological unemployment,* a term that had been introduced by John Maynard Keynes. In 1930, Keynes wrote, "We are being afflicted with a new disease of which some readers may not yet have heard the name, but of which they will hear a great deal in the years to come—namely, technological unemployment."[17] Two decades later, in 1952, Wassily Leontief wrote, "Labour will become less and less important . . . More and more workers will be replaced by machines. I do not see that new industries can employ everybody who wants a job."[18]

Which jobs are the most vulnerable? In the nineteenth century, as capital replaced skilled labor, craftspeople were most at risk of losing their jobs to machines. But in the twentieth century, this paradigm changed, as capital and education became complementary inputs. This time around, unskilled workers were the victims of automation. The IT revolution reinforced this phenomenon. This led to the development of a significant body of literature in the 1990s based on the notion of "skill-biased technological change," according to which technological progress increases the demand for skilled labor as opposed to unskilled labor. Consequently, unemployment among lower-skilled workers grows, as does the wage gap between skilled and unskilled workers.[19]

Automation and Employment at the Aggregate Level

How can we measure the effect of automation on employment? Finding a measure of automation with which to study its correlation with employment is a difficult challenge. We quickly encounter the problem of trade secrets, but the most important difficulty is measuring automation itself: Is it enough to count machines, and if so, which machines? How should we "add up" machines? Should we take into account their efficiency?

The International Federation of Robotics (IFR) provided a first possible measure of automation in some countries by tracking the number of industrial robots by sector since the early 1990s.[20] A pioneering study by Daron Acemoglu and Pascual Restrepo in 2020 uses the IFR data on the total number of robots per sector to estimate the impact of robots on US employment between 1993 and 2007.[21] To do so, they compare employment in 722 commuting zones as a function of these zones' exposure to automation. The problem was that existing data on robots were national and were not broken down by commuting zone. The authors thus constructed an index of automation at the commuting zone level by weighting the evolution of the number of robots per sector at the national level according to the relative weights of the sectors in total employment in the zone.

Using this measure of local exposure to automation, the authors find that automation has a negative effect on employment and wage growth: every additional robot in a zone leads to a loss of six jobs and to a decrease in hourly wages. When we reproduce this analysis using French data, the results are of similar magnitude but even more pronounced: each additional robot in a commuting zone leads to the loss of eleven jobs. Furthermore, it appears that robotization poses a greater threat to the jobs of less-educated workers.

This analysis nonetheless has some limitations. First of all, why should we look only at robots? Are robots truly different from other machines? It is true that they are more autonomous, but they do not necessarily differ from other types of machines in the tasks they accomplish. The IFR's definition of robots is actually very restrictive in that it corresponds essentially to robots used in automobile manufacturing. Another problem with this measure concerns the lack of data on a local level, necessitating the reconstruction of local data under the assumption that in a given industry all factories have the same number of robots and thus the same level of technology. However, we can legitimately presume that it is precisely the difference in the level of technology between two plants that explains the creation and destruction of jobs.

Automation and Employment at the Firm Level

Measuring automation at firm level or at plant level presents several difficulties, which we have already mentioned. In a recent study with Xavier Jaravel, we attempted to overcome these difficulties by introducing a new measure of automation at the microeconomic level of individual plants.[22] We defined automation technology as a "class of electromechanical equipment that is relatively autonomous once it is set in motion on the basis of predetermined instructions or procedures."[23] On the basis of this definition, we examined annual electricity consumption for motors directly utilized in the production process as a measure of plant-level automation.

We then sought to measure, at individual plant level, the impact of an increase in automation at a given moment in time on employment at that moment, and two, four, and ten years later.

Our results show that the impact of automation on employment is positive, and in fact increases over time. Thus, a 1 percent increase in automation in a plant today increases employment by 0.25 percent after two years and by 0.4 percent after ten years (Figure 3.5). It is especially noteworthy that this effect was positive even for unskilled manufacturing workers. In other words, automation creates more jobs in the plant than it destroys, contrary to preconceived notions.

It is worth noting that the positive effects of automation go beyond employment. We also observe that it brings about increased sales and lower consumer

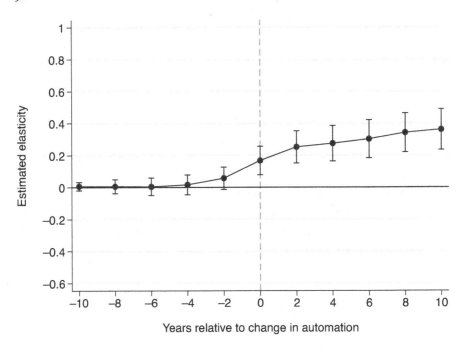

FIGURE 3.5. Effect of variation in automation on variation in employment at plant level.

Reformatted from P. Aghion, C. Antonin, S. Bunel, and X. Jaravel, "What Are the Labor and Product Market Effects of Automation? New Evidence from France," CEPR Discussion Paper no. DP14443, Centre for Economic Policy Research, March 2020, figure 3 panel B.

prices. Automation thus generates productivity gains that are shared by employees, consumers, and firms.

What explains this positive relationship between automation and employment at the level of each individual plant? One explanation that comes immediately to mind is that firms that automate more become more productive. This enables them to obtain larger market shares, because their products offer consumers better value for money than their competitors. The resulting gain in market share prompts those firms that automate to produce on a larger scale, and therefore to hire more employees.

What happens at the aggregate level, that is, when we go from the level of individual firms to the level of a sector or the entire economy? Does employment grow in more automated sectors, or does it in fact decline? Once again, we find a positive relationship between automation and employment: the industries that automate the most are the ones where employment increases the most. Overall, more automation goes hand in hand with employment growth. And for this

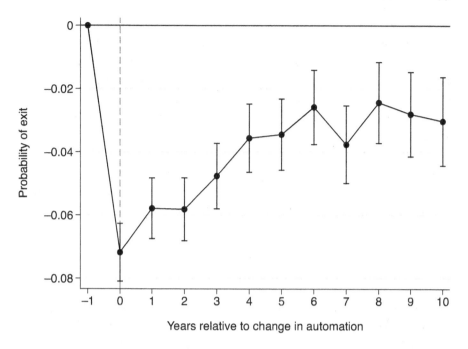

FIGURE 3.6. Effect of a substantial investment in industrial equipment on probability of firm exit. *Note:* A firm that invests more than the median in industrial equipment reduces its probability of exit in the following years, compared with a firm that invests less than the median.

Data source: P. Aghion, C. Antonin, S. Bunel, and X. Jaravel, "What Are the Labor and Product Market Effects of Automation? New Evidence from France," CEPR Discussion Paper no. DP14443, Centre for Economic Policy Research, March 2020.

reason, any attempt to slow down automation by domestic firms—for example, by taxing robots—may turn out to be counterproductive.

Automation is thus not in and of itself an enemy of employment. By modernizing the production process, automation makes firms more competitive, which enables them to win new markets and therefore to hire more employees. This is what we call a *productivity effect*. This same productivity effect was at work in prior industrial revolutions—those induced by the steam engine and then by electricity—and explains why neither of these revolutions produced the mass unemployment that some had predicted.

How can we reconcile this optimistic conclusion with the more pessimistic finding, mentioned earlier, that automation has a negative effect on employment at the level of commuting zones? One response is to invoke the difficulty of measuring automation or robotization at the commuting zone level, as we discussed

earlier. A second possible explanation is that firms that do not automate sufficiently end up downsizing their employment, outsourcing their production, or
simply going under. This would reflect an *eviction effect* of automation on employment. Figure 3.6 illustrates this eviction effect: firms that invest significantly
in new industrial equipment substantially lower their likelihood of going out of
business over the following ten years compared to firms that do not make such
an investment.

It is thus not automation of manufacturing processes that causes firms to
eliminate jobs but rather missing the critical juncture of automation and consequently finding themselves forced to reduce the scope of their activities or even
to exit the market. In other words, it is through the process of creative destruction that automation can lead to job losses.

3. Conclusion

In this chapter we have challenged two common preconceptions about technological revolutions. The first was that these revolutions necessarily lead to an acceleration of growth. The second is that technological revolutions are necessarily
detrimental to employment. The reality is in fact quite different. Although it
is true that growth accelerates, in most cases this occurs only after a delay. In
particular, inappropriate institutions can inhibit the growth potential generated
by the appearance of a new technological revolution. In addition, the history of
past technological revolutions shows that none of them gave rise to the mass
unemployment that many anticipated. In fact, as we have seen, firms or plants that
automate their production activities end up being net job creators; it is rather
those firms that do not sufficiently automate that destroy jobs, because their failure
to automate leads them to decline and possibly exit the market. An interesting
implication of our analyses in this chapter is that taxing robots can be counterproductive: discouraging automation will inhibit firms' potential to innovate, expand their markets, and thereby create new jobs.

IS COMPETITION A
GOOD THING?

Competition seems to have two very different faces. Some see it as a process of copying or imitation or more broadly as a force that erodes innovation rents and therefore discourages innovation. Others see it as an unceasing impulse to improve, to innovate more in order to remain in the lead. As a practical matter, which of these two contrary forces predominates? More generally, how can we rethink the relationship between competition and innovation and between competition and growth? Has competition declined in the United States, and is that the cause of the downturn in American growth? How can we coordinate competition policy and intellectual property rights? Are these two policies contradictory, or do they play complementary roles? Can we reconcile competition policy and industrial policy, and in particular can we design an industrial policy that stimulates competition and the entry of new firms rather than hindering them?

But a prerequisite to exploring these questions is knowing how to measure competition.

1. Measuring Competition

One of the first things a student of economics learns is that a firm is in a monopoly situation if it is the only firm in the market for a given product, and that it is in an environment of perfect competition if other firms operate (or can operate) in this market to produce the same product or a perfect substitute.

Most of the time, however, firms exist in an environment somewhere between monopoly and perfect competition. To evaluate this "in-between" state, empiricists' preferred measure of competition is the Lerner index. At firm level, the Lerner index is defined to be one minus the ratio between the firm's net profits and its value added. The closer the index is to one, the lower the firm's monopolistic rents, indicating the existence of real or potential competitors in the firm's market. Competition in a sector is equal to the weighted sum of the Lerner indexes of firms in the sector. This is the index used to measure competition in the pioneering studies of Richard Blundell, Rachel Griffith, Steve Nickell, and John Van Reenen.[1]

A second measure of competition is the rate of entry of new firms or the rate of creative destruction, defined as the average of the entry rate and the exit rate of firms or jobs. It allows us to test the Schumpeterian paradigm, which predicts a positive relationship between growth and the rate of creative destruction. We have already seen (Figure 1.3) that the average annual rate of growth of per capita GDP is higher in European regions where the average annual rate of creative destruction is higher.

Thus, when we measure competition by the rate of creative destruction, the empirical analysis of the correlation between competition and growth is consistent with Schumpeterian theory. However, as we shall see below, when competition is measured by rents and the Lerner index, theory seems to be at odds with empirical analyses: theory seems to predict a negative relationship between competition and growth, whereas the empirical analysis points to a positive relationship between competition and growth. How do we solve this enigma?

A third measure of competition in a sector is the concentration of production in that sector. Concentration, in turn, is measured by the share of total sales or total employment attributable to the largest firms in the sector, ranked by sales (or employment). The degree of concentration increases when this share increases, and the maximum degree of concentration is achieved when one firm monopolizes the entire production of the sector. Figure 4.1 shows an increase in the concentration of production in the US service sector over the past two decades.[2] The curve with black circle markers shows a sharp increase in the share of total sales attributable to the four largest (twenty largest for the curve with grey circle markers) firms ranked by sales in the service sector between 1982 and 2012. The curve with black triangle markers shows an increase in the share of employment attributable to the four largest firms ranked by employment in the service sector for the same period. The curve with grey triangle markers shows a similar pattern for the share attributable to the twenty largest firms ranked by employment.

The use of concentration indexes to measure competition warrants precaution, as it can be misleading in some instances. There are sectors in which a single firm operates but that are nonetheless highly competitive according to the Lerner index. These sectors are known as "contestable markets," meaning that a new firm could enter freely and exit at no cost, so that any price increase by the incumbent

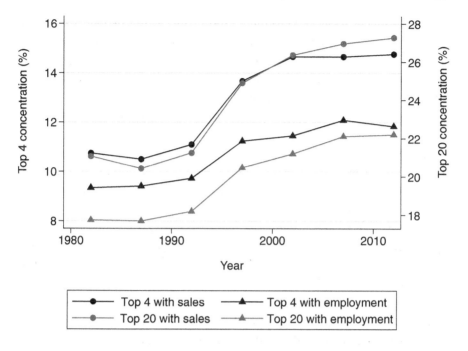

FIGURE 4.1. Concentration index in the service sector. *Note:* Top X concentration represents the share of employment (resp. sales) of the X largest firms in terms of employment (resp. sales).

Reformatted from D. Autor, D. Dorn, L. F. Katz, C. Patterson, and J. Van Reenen, "The Fall of the Labor Share and the Rise of Superstar Firms," Quarterly Journal of Economics 135, no. 2 (2020): 645–709, figure IV, panel D.

firm would promptly lead to the entry of another firm making the same product. This notion of contestable markets was introduced by the economist William Baumol.[3] This leads us to mention a fourth measure of competition, namely the degree to which a market is "contestable." Contestability, in turn, is measured by the probability of entry of a new firm into a market if incumbent firms in that market raise their prices above a "limit price."[4]

2. The Enigma of the Relationship between Competition and Growth

We recall that one of the three central tenets of the paradigm of creative destruction is that innovation comes from investment by entrepreneurs, in particular research and development; and that these investments are in turn motivated by the prospect of the monopoly rents that reward innovation. It would thus seem logical that anything that might diminish innovation rents, and in particular increased competition on the product market, would reduce the incentive to innovate. Thus, increased competition would curtail innovation and consequently growth. The earliest Schumpeterian models of growth did indeed predict that competition would have a negative impact on innovation and growth.[5]

However, empirical studies carried out in the 1990s using firm-level data by Richard Blundell, Rachel Griffith, and John Van Reenen, and also by Steve Nickell, show a positive correlation between the intensity of competition in a sector, measured by the Lerner index, and the rate of productivity growth in that sector.[6] In other words, more competition seems to be associated with more intense innovation and higher productivity growth.

How can we resolve this enigma and reconcile theory with empirical analysis? Should we discard the Schumpeterian model altogether and go back to the drawing board, even though it generates other predictions that empirical studies have validated? Or should we simply ignore these empirical challenges?

The path we chose was to reexamine the basic Schumpeterian model in order to identify the restrictive assumptions that led to the prediction of a negative relationship between competition and growth.[7] We were ultimately able to identify the source of the problem: the initial Schumpeterian model assumed that only newly entering firms innovated, and not firms that were already operating in the market. Firms that innovate thus go from zero profits before innovation to positive profits postinnovation. Increased competition reduces postinnovation profits, thus also reducing the incentive to innovate.

In reality, however, there are two types of firms present in the economy, and they react differently to competition. On the one hand there are firms that are close to the technological frontier in their sectors, meaning their productivity is close to the maximum level of productivity in the sector.[8] And on the other hand there are firms far from the technological frontier, meaning their productivity is far below the maximum productivity in the sector. The firms close to the frontier—which Richard Nelson and Edmund Phelps call "best practice"[9]—are active and earn substantial profits even before innovating. The others, far from the frontier and inactive, have low or zero profits and seek to innovate in order to catch up to the technological frontier.

To understand why these two types of firms react differently to competition, imagine that we are considering not firms but a class of students. Some students are at the top of the class and have good grades (the students' grades are equivalent to profits for firms), and others are at the bottom of the class with low grades. Imagine that one day a brilliant new student arrives in this class. How will the students in the class react to this intensified competition? The arrival of the brilliant new student will incite the best students, those who already have very high grades, to work even harder in order to remain at the top, but it will discourage the weaker students, for whom it becomes even more difficult to catch up.

Strikingly, empirical studies confirm that firms behave the same way as students. Firms close to the technological frontier innovate more in order to escape competition, whereas firms that are far from the technological frontier will be discouraged by competition, just as in the basic Schumpeterian model, where only outsiders innovate. The first study to test this prediction looked at data from UK firms.[10] In this study, competition in a given sector was measured by the rate of entry of foreign firms (calculated as the percentage of jobs in the sector that is accounted for by foreign firms). Innovation was measured by the number of patents at firm level (see Figure 4.2). The upper curve represents firms close to the technological frontier, and the lower curve represents firms that are far from the technological frontier. The result confirms that innovation by firms close to

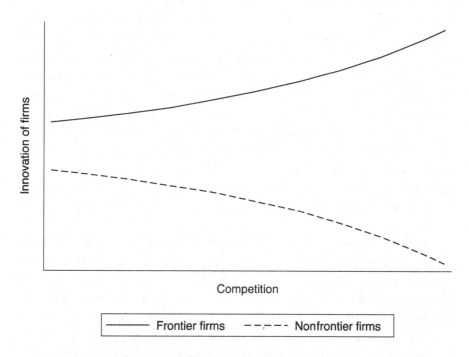

Competition

———— Frontier firms   — — · — — Nonfrontier firms

FIGURE 4.2. Intensity of competition and innovation, as a function of distance to the technological frontier. *Note:* The upper curve corresponds to the average of firms closer to the technological frontier than the median firm. The lower curve corresponds to the average of firms that are farther from the technological frontier than the median firm.

Reformatted from P. Aghion, Repenser la croissance économique *(Paris: Fayard, 2016), figure 3.*

the frontier increases with competition while innovation by firms far from the frontier falls with increased competition.

3. Three Predictions

Extending the Schumpeterian model in this way—by allowing for innovation by incumbent firms and by distinguishing between frontier firms and nonfrontier firms—enabled us not only to understand the positive relationship between competition and growth, but also to generate new predictions that can also be tested empirically using microeconomic data.

Distance to the Frontier and the Effect of Competition on Innovation

As we have just seen, the first such prediction is that competition has a positive effect on innovation for firms that are close to the technological frontier and a negative effect for firms far from the technological frontier.

One consequence of this result involves the effect of international trade on innovation and growth. The expansion of export markets has led to demonstrably more innovation by French firms initially close to the technological frontier than by firms initially far from the frontier.[11] The explanation is that the appearance of new outlets encourages the entry of new firms from other countries who export to these same markets, and the resulting increase in competition stimulates innovation by the most productive French firms, despite the increase in the size of the market resulting from its expansion. Similarly, opening domestic markets to imports has a stronger negative effect on innovation by French firms far from the technological frontier than by French firms close to the technological frontier. We will return to these predictions in Chapter 13.

Another consequence involves the relationship between growth and development; it is relevant for growth policy design. The closer a country is to the technological frontier—in other words the closer its aggregate productivity is to the productivity of the most productive country in the world (currently the United States)—the more competition will boost innovation and growth in the country. Indeed, the closer a nation is to the world technological frontier, the higher the proportion of firms in that country that are close to the frontier relative to firms in the country that are far from the frontier. And the higher the proportion of firms close to the technological frontier, the more the "escape-competition" effect will predominate over the discouragement effect on average in that country.

Thus the closer a country is to the technological frontier, the more its growth benefits from increased competition. In other words, countries should adopt more procompetition policies as they become more developed. However, in practice, things do not happen that way. In Chapter 7, we will show how the inability of certain developing countries to converge toward the income levels of developed nations is in part due to the anticompetitive attitude of large incumbent firms in those countries. Not only do the incumbents block the entry of new competitors; they also resist the adoption of public policies aimed at increasing competition. Yet these are the policies that would maximize innovation and growth as the country becomes more technologically developed.

The Inverted U Relationship between Competition and Growth

The overall effect of competition on innovation and growth takes the shape of an inverted U curve (see Figure 4.3). This curve results from a *composition effect* that encompasses both the positive effect of competition on innovation in "frontier" firms—those close to the frontier—and the negative effect of innovation on "laggard" firms—those far from the frontier.[12] This inverted U relationship has been confirmed in nearly all countries for which data on competition and innovation are available. Intuitively, this phenomenon can be understood as follows.

When competition is initially weak, we are on the left side of the graph in Figure 4.3; in this case, firms initially below the frontier have a strong incentive to catch up to the frontier because their profits will increase significantly if they catch up. Thus most firms that are initially far from the frontier will quickly become frontier firms. Consequently, if we take a picture of the overall economy at a given point in time, we will see that most firms are frontier firms. However, as we have seen before, innovation by frontier firms reacts positively to an increase in competition. It follows that when we start from a low level of competition, intensifying it will have a positive effect on innovation economy-wide, as the escape-competition effect will dominate on average.

But when competition is initially strong, we are on the right side of the graph. The high degree of competition spurs frontier firms to innovate in order to surpass their rivals (to escape competition). The technological frontier will then quickly move forward, leaving most firms behind the new frontier. Consequently, if we take a picture of the overall economy, we will see that most firms are far below the frontier. However, we know that innovation by firms far below the frontier reacts negatively to an increase in competition due to the discouragement effect. Therefore, when competition is initially strong, intensifying it will have a negative effect on innovation economy-wide, as the discouragement effect will dominate on average.

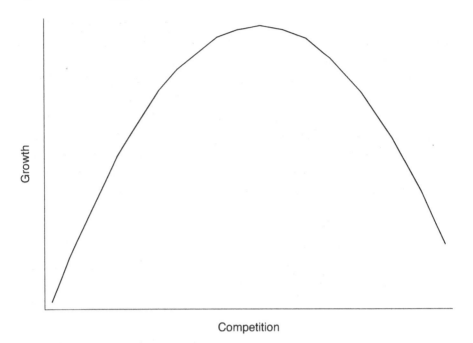

FIGURE 4.3. Effect of competition on innovation and growth.

Data source: P. Aghion, N. Bloom, R. Blundell, R. Griffith, and P. Howitt, "Competition and Innovation: An Inverted-U Relationship," Quarterly Journal of Economics 120, no. 2 (2005): 701–728.

Complementarity between Competition and Protection of Intellectual Property Rights

According to a somewhat superficial but nonetheless widespread view, there is a conflict between antitrust policy, on the one hand, and patents, or more generally the protection of intellectual property (IP) rights, on the other.

On one side are the most ardent advocates of IP protection. This faction maintains that IP rights are crucial because they protect innovation rents, shielding the innovator from imitation by potential competitors. As a corollary, they call for limiting competition in order to preserve innovation rents and thereby encourage firms to innovate. This extreme position results from a view of the world in which only new market entrants innovate, never existing firms: in such a world, innovation takes a firm's profits from zero to a positive number, thus stronger protection of IP rights increases profits, and greater competition decreases profits.[13]

On the opposing side are the procompetition, antipatent advocates, in particular Michele Boldrin and David Levine.[14] These authors see competition and new market entrants as the primary source of innovation-led growth. In their vision of the world, anything that constrains competition and market entry, especially patents, is detrimental to innovation-led growth.

Beyond their disagreement as to the pros and cons of patents, both of these factions share the view that competition and IP protection are contrary forces: if one fosters innovation, the other necessarily hinders it.

The more sophisticated model we have described above—which allows for innovation by incumbent firms and distinguishes frontier firms, close to the frontier, from laggard firms, far from the frontier—opens a totally new perspective. It suggests that competition is in fact complementary to IP protection. Consider a frontier firm competing neck and neck with other frontier firms—at the "top of the class," but tied with other firms for first place. Increased competition will decrease this firm's rents P_0 if it does not innovate. Stronger IP protection will increase the firm's rents P_1 if it innovates. Both policies thus contribute to increasing the net gain from innovation, measured by $P_1 - P_0$. This is the story of the carrot and the stick. Protecting IP rights makes the carrot bigger, whereas increased competition makes the stick harder. Accordingly, it is important to pursue both types of policies simultaneously: protecting IP rights on innovation on the one hand and safeguarding competition on the other. This touches on one of the key ideas of this book: namely that capitalism must be regulated. Capitalism must reward innovation, but it must be regulated to prevent innovation rents from stifling competition and thus jeopardizing future innovation.

This complementarity between competition and patents has been tested, with results demonstrating that the implementation of the European Single Market, which favored competition, stimulated innovation more in those European member states with stronger protection of IP rights.[15]

A Fruitful Dialogue between Theoreticians and Empiricists

Overall, this dialogue between theory and empirical analysis has been mutually enriching. Growth theorists learned why and how they could refine their models. They were able to bring to light not one but two fundamental effects of competition on growth and to identify the conditions in which each of these effects dominates the other, which is what gives rise to the inverted U curve. Empiricists understood that the relationship between competition and growth is more nuanced than what they had foreseen on the basis of their earlier studies.

4. Competition and Growth in the United States

In his book entitled *The Great Reversal: How America Gave Up on Free Markets*, Thomas Philippon points to a decline in competition and antitrust policy in the

United States and ties this decline to the downturn in productivity growth since the early 2000s.[16]

A Decline in Competition?

Various indicators suggest that American antitrust policy has slackened over the past several decades. Thomas Philippon has developed a number of highly relevant case studies in his book. He starts from a personal observation. When he first arrived in the United States in the late 1990s, subscriptions to internet and telephone service, as well as fares for domestic flights, were far less expensive in the United States than in Europe, for the same quality. Twenty years later, the situation is totally reversed: the European consumer now has far better value for money on these products. Thomas Philippon attributes this change to the difference in competition policy in the United States and in Europe. To further illustrate his point, he relies on a number of case studies. First, he cites the financial sector, where technological progress has not led to lower costs for consumers. Philippon attributes this to the lack of competition in this sector: there are very few new entrants and a particularly weak rate of creative destruction, due in particular to intense lobbying by incumbent firms to limit the granting of new licenses.

The second example is the health-care system. Thomas Philippon notes that Americans' life expectancy declined between 2014 and 2016, after increasing continuously since the early 2000s, even though health-care expenditures remained extremely high for American households. The author explains this fact by the increase in concentration in the health-care sector in the United States since 2000, with hospitals' market power constantly growing. By way of example, since 2010 there have been more than seventy mergers of hospitals each year. This growing concentration of hospitals is tied to a phenomenon of increasing concentration in the insurance sector. In order to maintain their negotiating power against insurers, which have become a quasi-monopoly, hospitals are compelled to merge.

The third example is the GAFAM (Google, Amazon, Facebook, Apple, and Microsoft) and "superstar" firms more generally, although Thomas Philippon minimizes their significance in explaining the decline of growth in the United States.

In addition to the work of Thomas Philippon, there are other signs suggesting that competition in the United States has stalled in recent decades. Of particular interest is the work of Matilde Bombardini and Francesco Trebbi on the escalation of lobbying in the United States, which we will describe in greater detail in Chapter 5.[17]

Other indicators also suggest a decrease in competition in the United States over the past two decades. In particular, concentration, as measured by the share of sales or employment of the largest firms, has substantially increased over the

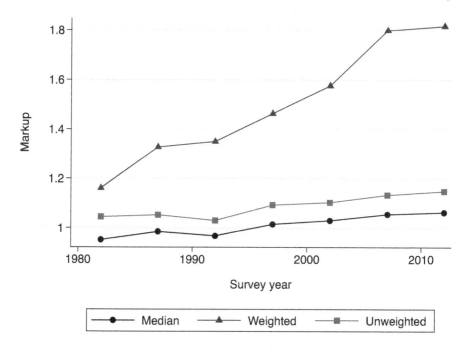

FIGURE 4.4. Evolution of markups.

Reformatted from D. Autor, D. Dorn, L. F. Katz, C. Patterson, and J. Van Reenen, "The Fall of the Labor Share and the Rise of Superstar Firms," Quarterly Journal of Economics 135, no. 2 (2020): 645–709, figure X panel B.

past twenty years in all sectors of the American economy.[18] In addition to the service sector (Figure 4.1), the same trend affected retail trade, financial services, transportation, and, to a lesser extent, wholesale and manufacturing. In addition, American companies increased their markups over the past two decades, as illustrated by Figure 4.4. Finally, the labor share in total income has declined markedly over the same period (Figure 4.5).

Two remarks are warranted at this point. First, an increase in concentration does not automatically mean competition has deteriorated. We have already seen that some markets appear monopolistic but are in reality contestable, meaning that the threat of a new entrant forces the incumbent firm to keep its prices low. More importantly, an increase in concentration can result when a firm's innovations enable it to acquire a larger market share. The innovation allows it to either produce the same product as its competitors at a much lower unit cost or produce a better-quality product.

The second remark is directly related to the first: an increase in average markups for the overall economy may reflect either an increase in markups within firms

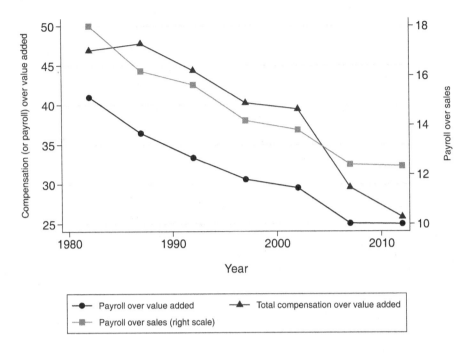

FIGURE 4.5. Labor share in manufacturing.

Reformatted from D. Autor, D. Dorn, L. F. Katz, C. Patterson, and J. Van Reenen, "The Fall of the Labor Share and the Rise of Superstar Firms," Quarterly Journal of Economics 135, no. 2 (2020): 645–709, figure II.

or a composition effect. The latter means that over time high-markup firms account for an increasingly large share of the economy.

Overall, one cannot be certain that the observed increase in average markups or concentration reflects a deterioration of competition in the United States over the past two decades.

Decline in American Growth

While it is difficult to establish clearly that competition in the United States has decreased over the past twenty years, there is no doubt that productivity growth since 2005 has fallen. Three facts call for more detailed examination.[19] First, the decline in growth since 2005 follows a decade (1996–2005) during which productivity growth was particularly high, approaching 3 percent per year (Figure 4.6). Second, the increase and the subsequent decline in growth were especially significant in sectors that produce or utilize information technologies. Third, the period of strong growth partially coincided with the period of fastest increase in concentration, namely 1995 to 2000. In other words, during this period, the rapid

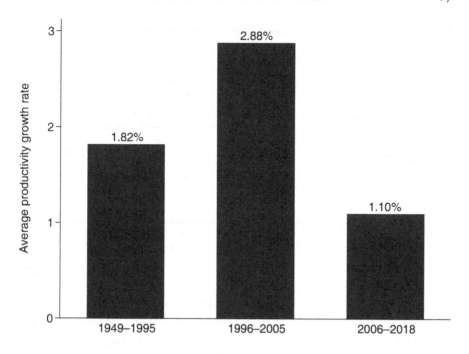

FIGURE 4.6. US productivity growth rate, 1949–2018.

Reformatted from P. Aghion, A. Bergeaud, T. Boppart, P. J. Klenow, and H. Li, "A Theory of Falling Growth and Rising Rents" (NBER Working Paper No. 26448, National Bureau of Economic Research, Cambridge, MA, November 2019), figure 1.

increase in concentration was not accompanied by a decrease in innovation and growth.

These three facts cast doubt upon the theory that competition declined after 1990 and that this decline was the main cause of the slowdown in growth that we observe since 2005. We will return to the sources of declining American growth in Chapter 6.

5. Competition and Industrial Policy

In the years following World War II, national industrial champions were at the forefront of industrial policy in many developed countries. In France, this pro-champion policy was a pillar of the reconstruction of the economy and of the thirty years of postwar growth. In the United States, it played a decisive role in particular for the defense, aeronautics, and aerospace industries in pursuit of supremacy over the Soviet Union. At the same time, the World Bank, under the direction of Robert McNamara, supported trade protection and import substitution in developing countries to allow them to nurture their infant industries.

Initially formulated by Alexander Hamilton and then Friedrich List, the infant industry doctrine can be summarized as follows.[20] Consider a developing country with two sectors of activity, a large agricultural sector and a nascent domestic manufacturing sector. This country wishes to develop its manufacturing sector because of the resulting positive technological externalities on the economy as a whole. Manufacturing, however, entails high initial fixed costs that will decrease over time thanks to experience and "learning by doing." Total and immediate liberalization of international trade would lead this country to import manufactured products from developed countries, where they are initially cheaper to produce. This in turn would lead to less local manufacturing activity, less "learning by doing," and thus less technological progress and domestic growth. To avoid this repercussion, proponents of the infant industry argument endorse temporary protectionist policies, such as provisional tariff barriers, so that infant industries can grow and catch up to the technological frontier.

Over time, industrial policy fell out of favor. Little by little, economists became aware of the problems it creates in practice. First, it favors existing large domestic firms—the national champions—thus limiting or distorting competition. But product market competition stimulates innovation and productivity growth by pushing firms to innovate in order to surpass their rivals. Second, governments are not great at picking winners, that is, choosing which firms they should support with subsidies or tariffs, as they do not have access to all of the relevant information. Furthermore, they may be receptive to lobbying by large incumbent firms. The greater these firms' resources, the more they are in a position to influence public policy. Anne Krueger was one of the economists who challenged the soundness of industrial policy.[21]

This challenge led to a preference for what are known as "horizontal" policies for stimulating innovation and growth, meaning policies that apply to all sectors of the economy.[22] Among the main vectors of horizontal policy are (1) investing in the knowledge economy (especially higher education and research), (2) reforming labor and product markets to make them more dynamic, through appropriate policies for competition, unemployment insurance, and professional training, and (3) developing venture capital and private equity to provide funding for innovation.

Do these horizontal actions suffice? Or does the state still have a role to play in industry, and if so, what is that role? Objections to industrial policy from the 1950s through the 1980s are difficult to counter, all the more because later work, such as that of Jean-Jacques Laffont and Jean Tirole, pointed to several sources of inefficiency in state intervention, due to asymmetric information or the potential for collusion between some private actors and the state.[23] Still, this alone does not suffice to disqualify state intervention, which remains legitimate for several reasons. One reason is the existence of positive knowledge externalities, such as patents, that individuals do not take into account. An individual deciding whether to invest in education or in R&D does not take into account the positive externalities on his or her coworkers or on the economy as a whole. As a consequence, individuals tend to underinvest in education and in R&D. Moreover, credit constraints exacerbate this tendency. Still, this does not justify state intervention that is not purely horizontal.

A first argument in support of a nonhorizontal industrial policy is the phenomenon known as path dependence. The notion of path dependence, which we developed in Chapter 3 with the example of the QWERTY keyboard, shows how the weight of habit and the high cost of change hamper the adoption of a new technology, even if it performs better. The quintessential example is green innovation. A recent study by Philippe Aghion, Antoine Dechezleprêtre, David Hémous, Ralf Martin, and John Van Reenen shows that car manufacturers that had innovated in combustion engine technology in the past will tend to innovate in combustion engine technology in the future because of path dependence.[24] Imposing a carbon tax or subsidizing green innovation makes it less costly to adopt a new technology and redirects car manufacturers' innovation toward electric engines. This example shows that governments have a role to play, not only in stimulating innovation in general, but also by directing innovation through targeted interventions. We return to this in Chapter 9.

Another argument has to do with problems of coordination. Patrick Bolton and Joseph Farrell, and separately Rafael Rob, have suggested that government action can help resolve coordination problems, thereby enabling or accelerating entry into strategic sectors where the initial fixed costs of entry are high.[25] Consider a new potential market where entry is costly and where future profits are uncertain and depend on information (such as the level of consumer demand) that cannot be known until the market is active. No single firm wants to be the first to pay the fixed costs of entry. Every firm prefers to let other firms bear the fixed costs first and then to benefit from the information they generate, without bearing the risk and cost of acquiring this information. In other words, the absence of state intervention leads to the "free rider" phenomenon, which results in delay or even an impasse in creating the market. To solve this problem, the state can subsidize the first entrant, which encourages other firms to follow its example.

This argument explains the success of state intervention in the aeronautics industry (Boeing, Airbus), where fixed costs are high and demand is uncertain. It also explains the success of the Defense Advanced Research Projects Agency (DARPA) program, established in the United States in 1958 to facilitate the transition from basic research to applied research and marketing for breakthrough innovations ("tough technologies") where this transition entails substantial fixed costs and requires coordinated efforts by various economic actors.[26] DARPA enabled America to send men into space and then to the moon, and it ultimately led to important innovations such as the internet and global positioning system (GPS).

Once we recognize that industrial policy can be useful, how can we determine in which sectors the state should intervene? Policymakers should first address economic and social priorities such as fighting climate change and developing renewable energies, health, and defense. After that, they should focus on sectors using highly skilled labor or having a high degree of competition. Thus a study by Nathan Nunn and Daniel Trefler analyzing international microeconomic data showed that public investments targeting skill-intensive sectors are more effective in stimulating productivity growth.[27] Similarly, a study based on Chinese data showed that targeting more competitive sectors helps stimulate productivity growth.[28]

The question then arises of the governance of sectoral state aids. Sectoral aids stimulate productivity growth more when they are not concentrated on a single firm or a small number of firms, in other words if the aid operates to maintain or increase competition in the sector. Furthermore, sectoral state aids should be regularly reassessed in order to avoid the perpetuation of programs that prove to be ineffective. Cofinancing by state and private investors, such as development banks, can facilitate the establishment of adequate exit mechanisms. Finally, as we will explain in greater detail below, subsidizing established firms can hinder the entrance of new, more innovative firms as a result of a reallocation effect: incumbent firms increase the cost of skilled labor and other factors of production. The state should thus implement sectoral aid that does not impede potential new entrants and that reconciles, as much as possible, industrial policy and competition policy.

In a word, industrial policy is not a "yes or no" issue; the question is rather to redesign the governance of industrial policy to make it more compatible with competition and more generally with innovation-led growth.

6. Firm Dynamics and the Cost of Subsidizing Incumbent Firms

How does the life cycle of firms—market entry, growth, and exit from the market— interact with the process of growth, and how does subsidizing incumbent firms affect the entry and growth of new, innovative firms? The COVID-19 crisis has demonstrated how important this question is: on the one hand, governments are faced with the necessity of helping existing firms in order to minimize the number of bankruptcies and to sustain employment and accumulated human capital; on the other hand, they must not hinder new potential entrants on the market. In other words, we must find a way to provide the necessary governmental support of existing firms without blocking the process of creative destruction and the entry and growth of new, innovative activities.

We saw in Chapter 1 the positive correlation, predicted by the Schumpeterian model, between creative destruction and productivity growth. There is, however, more to be said about the relationship between firm dynamics and growth.[29] When we compare the distribution of jobs by the age of establishments in the United States and in France, we find that the oldest establishments (establishments that have existed more than twenty-six years) account for a larger employment share in the United States than in France (Figure 4.7). This finding bears witness to the greater ability of American companies, relative to French companies, to grow and remain in the market. Furthermore, the phenomenon of creative

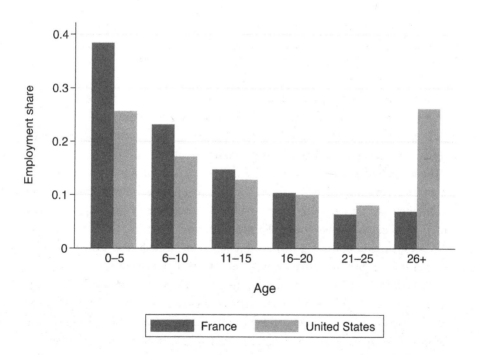

FIGURE 4.7. Employment share of establishments by age.

Reformatted from P. Aghion, A. Bergeaud, T. Boppart, and S. Bunel, "Firm Dynamics and Growth Measurement in France," Journal of the European Economic Association *16, no. 4 (2018): 933–956, figure 6.*

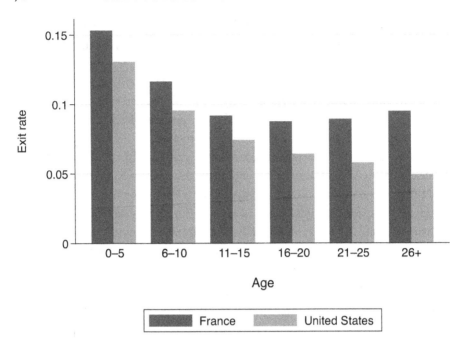

FIGURE 4.8. Exit rate of establishments by age.

Reformatted from P. Aghion, A. Bergeaud, T. Boppart, and S. Bunel, "Firm Dynamics and Growth Measurement in France," Journal of the European Economic Association 16, no. 4 (2018): 933–956, figure 8.

destruction is more pronounced in France than in the United States. Figure 4.8 compares the exit rates of establishments in France and in the United States respectively. Whatever the age of the establishment, the exit rate is consistently higher in France, especially for young establishments.

These two figures tell two sides of the same story. The inability of even the most productive and innovative firms in France to grow beyond a certain size enables less productive firms to hold onto market outlets and thus to survive. In the long run, this affects the growth of the French economy as a whole.

What factors inhibit the growth of French firms? One factor is the lack of access to funding for innovative firms.[30] Venture capital, private equity, and institutional investors, all of which play an important role in financing innovation, are far more developed in the United States than in France. We will come back to this in Chapter 12. A second factor is the body of regulations, especially labor regulations, that apply once total employment in a company reaches a certain threshold. These regulations discourage innovation in firms that are close to that threshold.[31] Should the state mitigate these constraints by subsidizing R&D in existing firms?

A recent study warns us of the negative effect of this type of subsidy, namely the risk of discouraging entry of new, higher-performing firms.[32] Subsidizing existing firms increases the demand for skilled workers, thereby increasing its cost. This extra cost in turn reduces the profits that potential new entrants can expect, thereby discouraging them from entering the market.

This reallocation effect is illustrated by a more recent study that analyzes how the Eurosystem's Additional Credit Claims (ACC) program implemented in February 2012 by the European Central Bank (ECB) affected firm dynamics in France.[33] Mario Draghi, then president of the ECB, created this program to prevent a recession in the eurozone following the 2008–2009 financial crisis. The idea was as follows: In the eurozone, banks can pledge high-quality corporate loans as collateral for refinancing from the ECB. These loans thus enable banks to obtain additional liquidity. Firms that are most likely to repay their debt have a rating of 1. They are followed by the firms rated 2, then 3, then 4, then 5, with decreasing probabilities of repaying their debt. A rating of P means the firm is close to bankruptcy. Before February 2012, commercial banks could use only loans to firms rated better than 4 as collateral for refinancing from the ECB. The ACC program extended eligibility to firms rated 4.

What happened after implementation of the ACC program? The first consequence was that loans to firms rated 4 increased relative to loans to firms with a rating worse than 4, in particular those one step below, at 5+. The second consequence was that productivity growth of firms rated 4 increased; in other words relaxing credit constraints on these firms allowed them to invest, in particular in innovation. But this positive effect was offset by a reallocation effect: the implementation of the ACC program reduced the fraction of firms rated 4 exiting the market, and the biggest impact was on the lowest-performing firms in terms of initial productivity. In other words, the ACC program impeded the replacement of the lowest-performing firms rated 4 by new, potentially higher-performing firms.

The existence of a reallocation effect pointed out by the above-mentioned studies suggests that any public policy subsidizing firms should take into account the impact of the policy not only on existing firms but also on potential new entrants in the sector.

7. Conclusion

In this chapter we examined the relationship between competition and innovation. We saw that on average, competition stimulates innovation and growth, and the effect of competition on innovation and growth is positive for firms close to

the technological frontier, whereas it is negative for firms far from the technological frontier. We explored the decline of competition in the United States as
an explanation of the decline of US growth. We then showed that competition
and protection of IP rights are complementary, and we defended the idea that
competition is not inconsistent with a well-designed industrial policy.[34] In the
coming chapters we will return to several of these topics, in particular the slowdown in American growth in Chapter 6, the middle-income trap in Chapter 7,
and globalization in Chapter 13.

▼

5

_____

INNOVATION, INEQUALITY, AND TAXATION

The question of income inequality, recurring in public debate, has found particular resonance since the publication of work by Tony Atkinson, Thomas Piketty, and Emmanuel Saez.[1] These authors have endeavored to draw attention to the explosion of the share of income going to the very top levels of the income distribution ("top income inequality" or "inequality at the top") since the 1980s. Figure 5.1 shows, in the case of the United States, the evolution of the share of income going to the top 1 percent, that is, households in the highest percentile of the income distribution.[2]

This graph raises a series of questions. First, should we focus on the income of the top 1 percent as the measure of inequality, or are there other equally pertinent measures? Another question that comes immediately to mind relates to the source of inequality: in particular, how do the rich become rich? Does innovation-led growth generate inequality, and if so, what types of inequality? How is innovation different from other sources of inequality? Should we focus mainly on taxation to increase social mobility? How can we make growth more inclusive without destroying it?

These are the questions we will examine in this chapter.

1. How Can We Measure Inequality?

When thinking about inequality, the first question we should ask is, "What type of inequality are we talking about?" There are several ways to measure income inequality, and they are by no means equivalent. First, there are broad measures

FIGURE 5.1. Income share of the top 1 percent in the United States.

Extracted and reformatted from T. Piketty, Capital in the Twenty-First Century *(Cambridge, MA: Harvard University Press, 2014), figure 8.6. Copyright © 2014 by the President and Fellows of Harvard College.*

of inequality, which reflect how far a country is as a whole from a situation of "perfect equality," where all individuals have the same income. The most widely used of these measures of overall income inequality is the Gini coefficient (see Box 5.1). The closer a nation gets to perfect equality, the closer the Gini coefficient is to zero; conversely, the greater the concentration of income among a small number of individuals, the closer the Gini coefficient is to one.

BOX 5.1. THE GINI COEFFICIENT AND THE LORENZ CURVE

The dotted black curve in Figure 5.A is called the Lorenz curve. It matches each share of the population, ranked by increasing income, with the share its income represents in total income. It is constructed as follows. Point A plots the share of total income that goes to the 20 percent of the population with the lowest income, that is, the first two deciles. In the graph below, the first two deciles receive 3.4 percent of total income. Point B plots the share of total in-

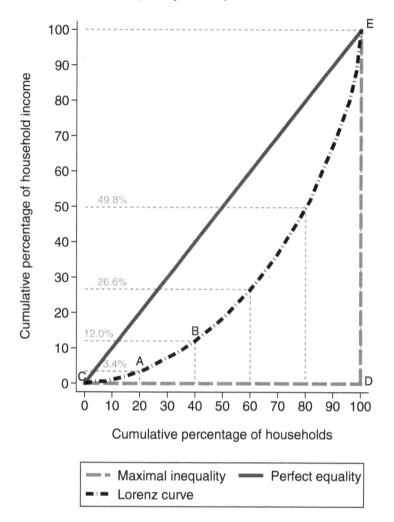

FIGURE 5.A. Lorenz curve for the United States in 2009.

Data source: C. DeNavas-Walt, B. D. Proctor, and J. Smith, "Income, Poverty, and Health Insurance Coverage in the United States: 2009," Current Population Reports P60-238, U.S. Census Bureau, September 2010.

come that goes to the first four deciles (here, 12 percent) and so forth, through the last decile of income.

If income distribution were perfectly equal, the dotted curve would be identical to the solid curve (which we call the 45° line): the first decile would have 10 percent of total income, the first two deciles would have 20 percent, and so forth. By contrast, if all income were in the hands of a single person and everyone else had an income of zero, then the Lorenz curve would be very convex: it would co-incide with the horizontal axis as long as we are below 100 percent and jump abruptly to one when we reach 100 percent on this axis. The income of 99.9999 percent of the population would be zero, and the income of 0.0001 percent would be 100 percent. This situation corresponds to the gray dashed curve.

The Gini coefficient, which measures overall inequality, is equal to the surface S between the straight solid line and the dotted curve, divided by the surface T of the triangle CDE. Perfect equality is the case where $S = 0$ (the dotted curve is perfectly aligned with the solid line) and the Gini coefficient is thus zero, and maximum inequality is the case where $S = T$ and consequently the Gini coefficient is equal to one.

A second way to measure inequality is to focus on inequality at the top of the income distribution. The most commonly used measure of inequality at the top looks at the share of total income that goes to the highest earning 1 percent; Figure 5.1 shows how the top 1 percent income share has evolved in the United States over recent decades. This measure is calculated in a simple manner: we first make a group beginning with the person with the highest income in the country, then we add the person with the second highest income, then the third, and so on until we have accounted for the richest 1 percent of the population. We then add up the income of the individuals in this group and calculate the ratio between this sum and the income of the entire active population of the country. This ratio represents the share of total income that goes to the top 1 percent. Figure 5.1 shows that the evolution of this top 1 percent in the United States follows a U-shaped curve: it decreased until 1980 and has traced a steep increase since 1980.

The third way to measure income inequality is of a dynamic nature. It reflects the lack of social mobility, in other words the probability that children will have incomes similar to that of their parents. The greater the correlation between the children's and the parents' incomes, the less social mobility there is in the country. Figure 5.2 shows how different OECD countries line up, both with respect to overall income inequality, measured by the Gini coefficient (horizontal axis) and with respect to dynamic inequality as measured by the correlation between parents' income and their children's income (vertical axis). Unsurprisingly, the Scandinavian countries (Denmark, Norway, Sweden, and Finland) have both the lowest overall inequality and the lowest dynamic inequality; in other words, their overall income inequality is the lowest, and their social mobility is the highest. By contrast, the Anglo-Saxon countries (Great Britain and the United States) have the highest overall inequality and dynamic inequality and thus the highest overall income inequality and the lowest social mobility. Most importantly, there is a pos-

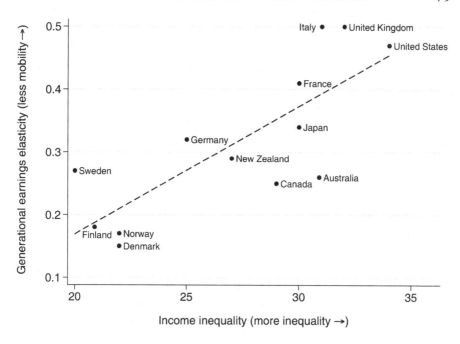

FIGURE 5.2. The Great Gatsby curve: comparison between nations.

Reformatted from Miles Corak, "Income Inequality, Equality of Opportunity, and Intergenerational Mobility," Journal of Economic Perspectives 27, no. 3 (2013): 79–102, figure 1.

itive correlation between overall inequality as measured by the Gini coefficient and dynamic inequality: the *least squares line,* which minimizes the sum of the squares of the distance between the line and the data points, is clearly upward-sloping. This line shows us that the greater a country's social mobility, the less income inequality there is in that country.[3] Economists call this line the Great Gatsby curve, in homage to F. Scott Fitzgerald's iconic protagonist, a millionaire symbolizing the American Dream but also the disillusionment that accompanied it in the United States of the 1920s.

More recently, economists Raj Chetty, Nathaniel Hendren, Patrick Kline, and Emmanuel Saez computed the degree of social mobility on a very detailed geographic level, namely by commuting zone.[4] Figure 5.3 shows that the Great Gatsby curve applies when comparing commuting zones: the areas with greater social mobility have less income inequality.

Do we find a similar relationship between dynamic inequality (that is, social mobility) and the share of income going to the top 1 percent? The answer is yes, according to Figure 5.4. In American commuting zones, we find that the greater

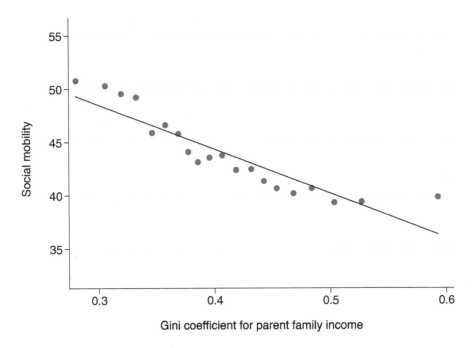

FIGURE 5.3. The Great Gatsby curve in the United States.

Data source: R. Chetty, N. Hendren, P. Kline, and E. Saez, "Where Is the Land of Opportunity? The Geography of Intergenerational Mobility in the United States," Quarterly Journal of Economics *129, no. 4 (2014): 1553–1623.*

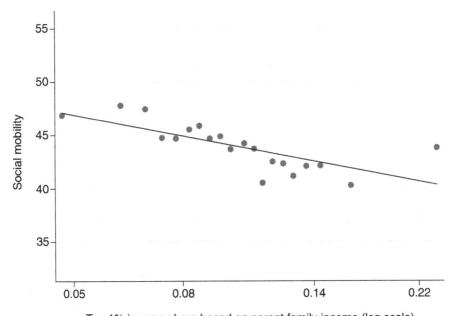

FIGURE 5.4. Social mobility and the top 1 percent income share.

Data source: R. Chetty, N. Hendren, P. Kline, and E. Saez, "Where Is the Land of Opportunity? The Geography of Intergenerational Mobility in the United States," Quarterly Journal of Economics *129, no. 4 (2014): 1553–1623.*

the social mobility, the lower the percentage of income captured by the top 1 percent. However, the connection between these two variables is not conclusive: the correlation coefficient is only −0.190, far lower than in Figure 5.3, where it was −0.578 between social mobility and overall inequality. The commuting zones where the top 1 percent's share of income is the highest are typically in states such as California, Connecticut, and Massachusetts, which are particularly innovative states. This observation naturally leads us to introduce innovation as a possible determinant of inequality and social mobility.

2. Innovation and the Different Types of Inequality

Each of the two main ideas underlying the theory of innovation-led growth under the paradigm of creative destruction has implications on the relationship between growth and inequality.

The first idea holds that innovation comes from entrepreneurial activity that is motivated by the prospect of innovation rents. These rents depend on the institutional environment, and in particular the degree of protection of intellectual property rights. As Abraham Lincoln (quoted by Joel Mokyr) said, the patent system "added the fuel of interest to the fire of genius."[5] Innovation rents increase the chances that an innovator will climb the income ladder and join the top 1 percent. Niklas Zennström, one of the founders of Skype, became one of the wealthiest people in Sweden thanks to his invention, joining the ranks of such innovators as Steve Jobs (Apple) and Bill Gates (Microsoft).

More generally, every innovation enables the innovating firm to increase the quality of its production compared to its existing or potential competitors. This in turn allows the innovator to expand its market and therefore its profits. Innovation also enables the innovator to reduce costs, in particular unit labor costs. This further increases the innovator's profits—and thus her income—relative to wages.[6] Accordingly, the paradigm of creative destruction predicts that innovation leads to increased inequality at the top of the income scale. The more innovative a country or region is, the greater the top 1 percent's share of income should be in that country or region.

The second idea underlying Schumpeterian growth theory is the idea of creative destruction: new innovations replace older technologies and, consequently, destroy the rents that rewarded yesterday's innovators. These new innovations are closely related to new market entrants. New innovators' rents increase, while those of incumbent firms decline. Thus the inventor of Skype was not in the top 1 percent twenty years ago, nor was Steve Jobs before the creation of Apple in 1976. Hence, a second prediction of the Schumpeterian paradigm is that innovation, especially when it comes from new entrants, is a source of social mobility.

It may seem paradoxical that innovation should increase both the share of income of the richest 1 percent (top income inequality) and social mobility. Yet the comparison among different American states suggests that this is indeed the case. For example, if we compare California, currently among the most innovative states in the United States, with Alabama, which is among the least innovative, we find that the share of the state's total income that goes to the top 1 percent is significantly higher in California than in Alabama. At the same time, social mobility is substantially higher in California than in Alabama.

The fact that innovation increases inequality at the top as well as social mobility implies that it is difficult *a priori* to predict how innovation will affect broader measures of inequality such as the Gini coefficient. Consequently, a third prediction of the Schumpeterian paradigm is that the relationship between innovation and broad measures of inequality is ambiguous.

But what do the data tell us about the relationship between innovation and the different measures of income inequality? By looking at production data, the quality of patents, and income distribution in the various American states between 1975 and 2010, Philippe Aghion, Ufuk Akcigit, Antonin Bergeaud, Richard Blundell, and David Hémous show in a 2019 study that innovation is a key factor explaining income inequality at the top.[7]

Figure 5.5 and Figure 5.6 illustrate this point particularly well. Figure 5.5 shows a significant positive causal effect of innovation on the share of income going to the top 1 percent (the solid curve). It also shows that innovation is not correlated with the Gini coefficient measuring overall inequality (the dotted curve). Figure 5.6 describes the relationship between innovation and social mobility derived from the analysis of commuting zones. Social mobility is defined as the probability for an individual from a modest background, that is, one whose parents belonged to the bottom 20 percent of the income distribution in 1996 to 2000, to reach the top of the scale—the highest 20 percent—when he or she reached adulthood in 2010. The intensity of innovation is measured by the number of patents filed with the US Patent and Trademark Office per resident in the commuting zone. The graph shows a positive relationship between innovation and social mobility.

This 2019 article also showed that innovation by new entrants is positively correlated with social mobility. This finding is consistent with the idea that creative destruction is a mechanism by which innovation generates social mobility.

In sum, innovation does increase top income inequality, but it comes with a trio of virtues: it does not increase overall inequality, it fosters social mobility, especially

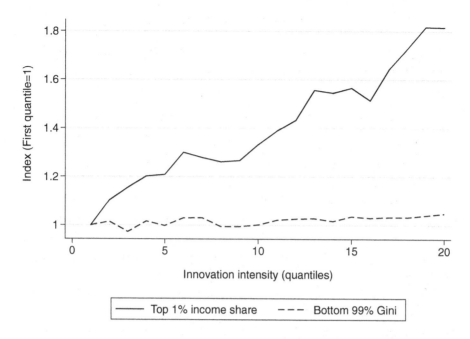

FIGURE 5.5. Innovation, top 1 percent income share and Gini coefficient. *Note:* The Gini coefficient is the Gini coefficient of the 99 first centiles; it is the Gini coefficient when the top 1 percent of the income distribution is excluded.

Reformatted from P. Aghion, U. Akcigit, A. Bergeaud, R. Blundell, and D. Hémous, "Innovation and Top Income Inequality," Review of Economic Studies 86, no. 1 (2019): 1–45, figure 2.

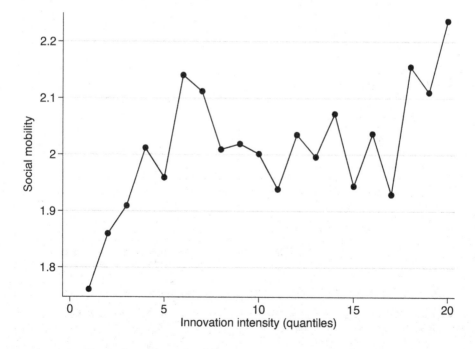

FIGURE 5.6. Innovation and social mobility.

Reformatted from P. Aghion, U. Akcigit, A. Bergeaud, R. Blundell, and D. Hémous, "Innovation and Top Income Inequality," Review of Economic Studies 86, no. 1 (2019): 1–45, figure 3.

when it involves new innovators entering the market, and it stimulates productivity growth.[8]

3. Innovative Firms as a Lever of Social Mobility

The positive relationship between innovation and social mobility does not come solely from the fact that new innovators replace yesterday's innovators. The innovative firm is itself a potential lever of social mobility insofar as it trains and promotes its employees, especially the least skilled among them. A recent study based on British data for the period 2004 to 2015 shows that innovative firms act as a social ladder above all for workers, including such low and middle-skilled employees as warehouse workers, secretaries, security guards, specialized blue-collar workers, transport operators, and salespeople.[9]

Figure 5.7 depicts the evolution of the hourly wage for a low-skilled worker according to age, respectively if the worker is employed by an innovative firm (solid curve) or by a noninnovative firm (dotted curve). A firm is defined as

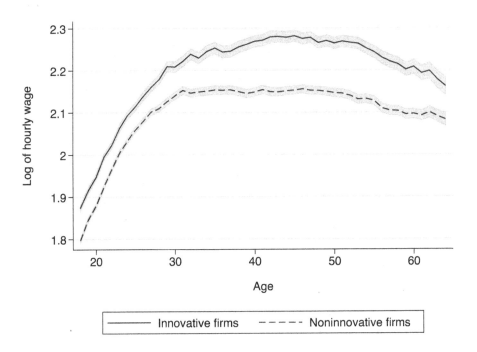

FIGURE 5.7. Average wage of workers in low-skilled occupations.

Reformatted from P. Aghion, A. Bergeaud, R. Blundell, and R. Griffith, "The Innovation Premium to Soft Skills in Low-Skilled Occupations," unpublished manuscript, 2019, figure 1.

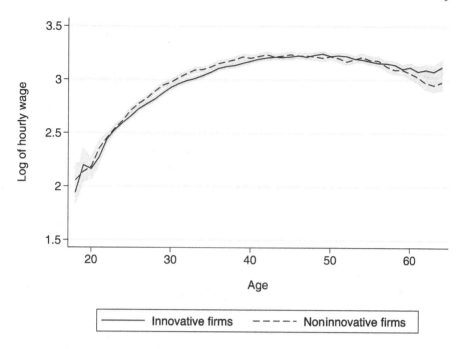

FIGURE 5.8. Average wage of workers in high-skilled occupations.

Reformatted from P. Aghion, A. Bergeaud, R. Blundell, and R. Griffith, "The Innovation Premium to Soft Skills in Low-Skilled Occupations," unpublished manuscript, 2019, figure 3a.

innovative if it invests at least one euro in R&D. We first observe that at all ages, the wages of an unskilled worker are noticeably higher in an innovative firm than in a noninnovative firm. The second observation, less surprising, is that wages increase with age, whether the worker is employed by an innovative or a noninnovative firm: this reflects gains resulting from the experience the worker has acquired within the firm. However, wages increase less with age in an innovative firm than in a noninnovative firm. In other words, innovative firms indeed function as social ladders for the least skilled workers, as the firms invest in those workers for the long run.

What about skilled workers (such as managers, engineers, and researchers)? Figure 5.8 shows that they also benefit from an experience premium that increases over time. However, this premium increases in the same manner whether they are employed by an innovative or a noninnovative firm. In other words, there is no extra premium for high-skilled workers from working in an innovative firm.

Finally, Figure 5.9 depicts the average hourly wage of workers in high-, intermediate-, and low-skilled occupations as a function of the innovation-intensity

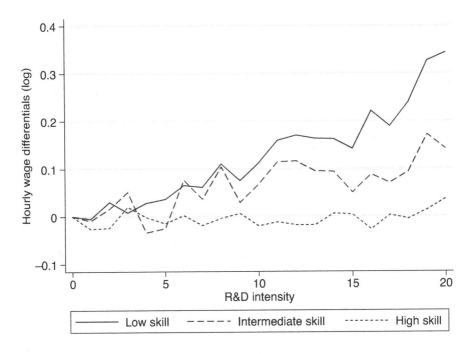

FIGURE 5.9. Wages of different occupational categories according to the firm's innovation intensity.

Data source: P. Aghion, A. Bergeaud, R. Blundell, and R. Griffith, "The Innovation Premium to Soft Skills in Low-Skilled Occupations," unpublished manuscript, 2019.

of the firm, measured by the firm's investment in R&D. We again see that wages of the highest skilled workers do not vary much with the degree of innovativeness of the employing firm (the dotted curve is almost flat), whereas the wages of the least skilled workers increase sharply with the degree of innovativeness of the firm.

How should we interpret these evolutions? The explanation developed in the study is that the highest skilled workers are evaluated above all on the hard skills manifested in their diplomas and their resumes. By contrast, the least skilled workers are remunerated largely on the basis of the soft skills they have acquired over time spent in the firm, which makes these workers more and more indispensable to the firm's success. And the more innovative a firm is, the more important it is for its low-skilled workers to have strong soft skills, especially workers who are seen as perfectly reliable. This type of firm has much to lose if the employee does not perform his or her tasks perfectly. This is because the more innovative a firm is, the more complementarity there is between an individual worker and the firm's other assets. This explains the high premium for a low-skilled worker in an innovative firm compared to a low-skilled worker in a noninnovative firm. It also explains the strong incentive for the manager of an innovative firm to increase the skills of his low-skilled employees, in particular through training.

Overall, the relationship between innovation and social mobility is reflected in a very concrete manner in the wage trajectories of workers in low- or middle-skilled occupations within innovative firms. And the state has a tool to motivate innovative firms to function as social ladders: subsidizing professional training.

4. Barriers to Entry as Another Source of Top Income Inequality

Steve Jobs vs. Carlos Slim

If the increase in income going to the top 1 percent derives not from innovation but rather from the construction of new barriers to entry by incumbent firms, it will not necessarily have the positive effects discussed above. By impeding the entry of new innovators, entry barriers block the process of creative destruction. As a consequence, they may also reduce social mobility. Finally, insofar as entry barriers increase the share going to the top 1 percent and reduce social mobility, it is highly probable that they also lead to an increase in overall inequality.

We can contrast Steve Jobs, cofounder of Apple, who exemplifies building a fortune through innovation, with Carlos Slim, a Mexican businessman with close ties to political power. Slim made a large fortune in the early 1990s from the privatization of the state telecommunications operator Teléfonos de México (Telmex) and its transformation into a private monopoly. Slim benefited from the fact that the telecommunications sector was subject to little regulation and in particular was exempt from regulation by Mexico's Federal Economic Competition Commission.

The Effects of Lobbying on Growth and Inequality

Incumbents rely heavily on lobbying to protect their rents by limiting the entry of new firms. Initially, the term "lobby" referred to the lobbies or antechambers of the British House of Commons, where in the nineteenth century representatives of various interest groups came to interact with parliamentarians. According to the Gallup annual survey of Honesty and Ethics in the Professions for 2017, 58 percent of Americans rated the ethical standards of lobbyists as "low" or "very low," compared to 21 percent for bankers.[10]

Who engages in lobbying, and how extensive is it? In the United States, lobbying represents approximately 3 billion dollars each year, whereas lobbying in

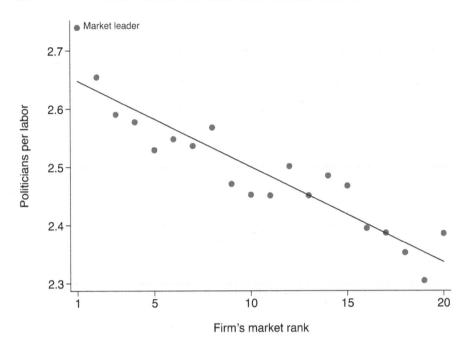

FIGURE 5.10. Market share and political connection.

Extracted and reformatted from U. Akcigit, S. Baslandze, and F. Lotti, "Connecting to Power: Political Connections, Innovation, and Firm Dynamics" (NBER Working Paper No. 25136, National Bureau of Economic Research, Cambridge, MA, October 2018), figure 5.

the European institutions accounts for 1.14 billion euros per year. As Konstantinos Dellis and David Sondermann showed, the largest firms as measured by sales (turnover) are those that utilize lobbying the most intensively. Furthermore, the firms that spend more on lobbying are less productive and have higher profit margins than other firms. Finally, firms in highly competitive sectors spend more on lobbying than firms in less competitive sectors.[11]

A study based on Italian data by Ufuk Akcigit, Salomé Baslandze, and Francesca Lotti again revealed the connections between firms and politicians.[12] As Figure 5.10 shows, the larger a firm's market share—the farther left it is on the graph—the greater the fraction of its employees who also hold political office at the local, regional, or national level.

The following question naturally comes to mind: do lobbies provide useful and enriching expertise to political decision makers, or do they merely exercise pressure to prevent the entrance of new competitors on the market? Using the public archives of the US Senate and the Federal Election Commission, a study by Marianne Bertrand, Matilde Bombardini, and Francesco Trebbi identified lobbyists active in the United States between 1999 and 2008, and tallied the amount of their gifts to electoral campaigns.[13] The authors looked in particular at the individual profiles of these lobbyists in order to determine if they were "specialized" or "connected." According to their terminology, a "specialized" lobbyist is one who concentrates his assignments on a limited number of fields, from which one can infer that the lobbyist has real expertise in those fields. A lobbyist is "connected" if he has privileged access to a political decision maker, either because they belong to the same party or because the lobbyist has contributed to one or more of the politician's electoral campaigns.

The authors showed that the share of connected lobbyists increased during the period from 1998 to 2008. Furthermore, in 2008, more than three-quarters of the lobbyists were not specialized, nearly 54 percent were clearly connected, and less than one out of seven lobbyists was specialized without being connected. Finally, the authors showed that lobbyists who were connected to GOP politicians earned on average 25 percent more than other lobbyists when the Republicans controlled the White House and the Senate, that is, between 2002 and 2007. Overall, even if some lobbyists are specialized and contribute information that is potentially useful to society, this study underscored that a large majority of them are politically connected and not specialized. In addition, even if lobbyists receive a financial premium from specialization, this premium is smaller than the premium from being connected.

What is the impact of lobbying, which we now know is for the most part connected, on inequality? Figure 5.11 depicts the relationship between the top 1 percent's share of income and the intensity of lobbying in the various American states during the period 1998 to 2008. We can see that the share of the top 1 percent increases sharply when lobbying becomes sufficiently intense. This outcome confirms that lobbying is indeed another source, distinct from innovation, of inequality at the top.

It is not at all surprising that lobbying contributes to the increase in the top 1 percent's share of income. Connected lobbyists enable incumbent firms to maintain their market power and thus their rents. In particular, lobbying helps incumbents not only to protect their sector from competition by instituting customs tariffs, but also to win procurement contracts, to have easier access to bank credit, to pay less tax, and to obtain more public subsidies.

The impact of lobbying on corporate taxes is particularly interesting. We can demonstrate that firms that engage in lobbying pay less tax, especially those with the highest levels of debt, have greater capital intensity, and report greater R&D spending. Lobbying enables these firms to obtain tax credits on their R&D expenditures and more favorable tax depreciation schedules for certain types of equipment.[14]

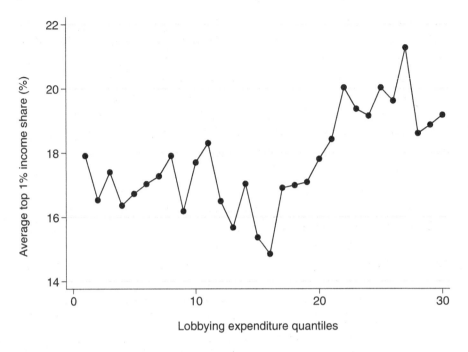

FIGURE 5.11. Lobbying expenditures and the top 1 percent, 1998–2008. *Note:* Each point on the *x*-axis corresponds to a specific level of lobbying expenditure, and the same state can move to the left or to the right from one year to the next.

Data source: P. Aghion, U. Akcigit, A. Bergeaud, R. Blundell, and D. Hémous, "Innovation and Top Income Inequality," Review of Economic Studies 86, no. 1 (2019): 1–45.

Figure 5.12, which derives from the same data, shows that overall income inequality, as measured by the Gini coefficient, in an American state varies with the intensity of lobbying in that state.[15] Overall inequality increases sharply when lobbying becomes sufficiently intense. This situation contrasts with the effect—or rather the absence of effect—of innovation on overall inequality (Figure 5.5). This is precisely the result we would expect: insofar as lobbying is mainly connected, it prevents the entry of new firms into the market, thereby reducing social mobility and at the same time increasing top income inequality. In contrast, innovation enhances social mobility, which is why it has no significant impact on overall inequality.

We now turn to the impact of lobbying on innovation and growth. Figure 5.13 supplements Figure 5.10 with a curve showing the intensity of innovation in the firm as a function of the firm's sales. The higher the firm's sales,

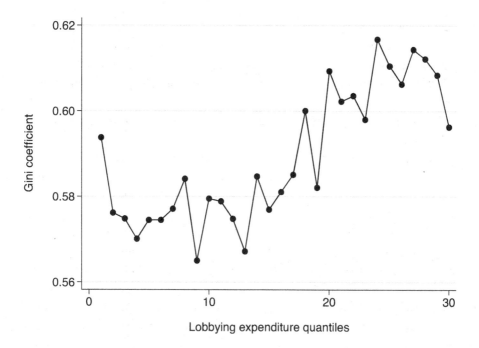

FIGURE 5.12. Lobbying expenditures and the Gini coefficient.

Data source: P. Aghion, U. Akcigit, A. Bergeaud, R. Blundell, and D. Hémous, "Innovation and Top Income Inequality," Review of Economic Studies *86, no. 1 (2019): 1–45.*

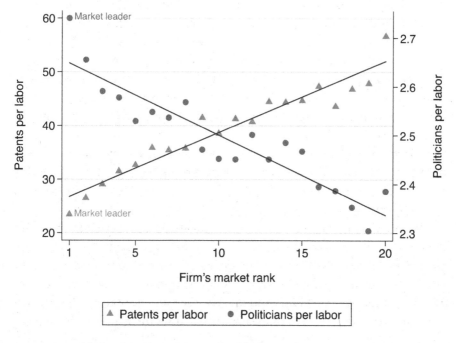

FIGURE 5.13. Market share, innovation, and political connection.

Reformatted from U. Akcigit, S. Baslandze, and F. Lotti, "Connecting to Power: Political Connections, Innovation, and Firm Dynamics" (NBER Working Paper No. 25136, National Bureau of Economic Research, Cambridge, MA, October 2018), figure 5.

the lower its innovation intensity. This figure strongly suggests that as a firm gains greater market power and moves toward market dominance, it focuses its efforts less and less on innovation and more and more on political connections and lobbying.

The same study shows that the rate of productivity growth of Italian firms is negatively correlated with their investment in political connections. In contrast, employment growth is positively correlated with that investment. The explanation is that political connections help these firms save on red tape, but at the expense of innovation, which constitutes the primary source of productivity growth.

Overall, investing in lobbying is bad for growth for two reasons: first, as incumbent firms grow, they invest more and more in lobbying at the expense of innovation, and second, collusion between firms and politicians increases the costs of entry into the market and therefore discourages creative destruction. The higher the proportion of politically connected firms in an industry, the less dynamic the industry is: fewer firms enter the market, fewer existing firms exit, and the average age of firms is higher.

What have we learned from analysis thus far? Our first conclusion is that, although innovation may be a source of top income inequality, it nevertheless has virtues that do not accompany other sources of inequality, such as lobbying and the resulting barriers to entry. First, innovation is a source of productivity growth and business dynamism, which is not true of political connections. Second, innovation, especially by new entrants, is positively correlated with social mobility, whereas lobbying reduces entry and therefore reduces social mobility. Finally, innovation does not seem to be correlated with overall inequality, whereas lobbying aggravates overall inequality. Therefore, if our goal is to reduce top income inequality, we must not treat all sources of top income inequality the same. In particular, we should not treat innovators in the same way we treat politically connected incumbent individuals or firms. Tackling top income inequality in a way that discourages innovation amounts to shooting ourselves in the foot by reducing social mobility with the likelihood of aggravating overall inequality at the same time we reduce growth.

The second conclusion is that we must nonetheless concern ourselves with the wealthy, including those who became wealthy through innovation, because yesterday's innovators often become today's entrenched incumbents. As they grow, they invest increasingly more resources in lobbying and political connections, at the expense of innovation. How then can we both reward innovation and prevent yesterday's innovators from using their innovation rents to prevent the entry of competitors? How can we encourage the emergence of new innovators like Steve Jobs while minimizing the likelihood that they will later resemble Carlos Slim? Is it sufficient to rely on taxation tools and to impose higher taxes on capital, or must we find different ways to tax and use other tools?

5. How to Utilize Taxation

The Swedish Example

In 1991, Sweden radically reformed its tax system by creating a dual taxation of capital income and labor income.[16] The two pillars of this reform were radical cuts in the highest marginal tax rates, which decreased from 88 percent to 55 percent, and the introduction of a 30 percent flat tax on capital income. Prior to 1991, capital income was taxed progressively, with a marginal rate above 72 percent and an average rate of 54 percent. This tax reform coincided with a clear takeoff of growth of Sweden's per capita GDP after 1993: between 1994 and 2007, Sweden's per capita wealth rose an average of 3.4 percent per year, compared to 2.4 percent in the eurozone and 2.7 percent in the European Union. Furthermore, in Figure 5.14 we see an explosion of the number of patents per resident after 1991, indicating that innovation also took off.[17]

These empirical facts are suggestive and do not demonstrate any causal effect of the tax reform on growth and innovation. In particular, the 1991 tax reform was accompanied by a currency devaluation as well as a reform of the government system that granted greater autonomy to administrative agencies and municipalities and provided for more rigorous control of public spending. It is thus difficult to isolate the specific impact of the tax reform. Nevertheless, there was clearly trend disruption in the evolution of innovation and productivity growth before and after the reforms went into effect.

Did the 1991 Swedish tax reform have an impact on inequality? Figure 5.15 shows a limited increase in the share of income going to the top 1 percent,[18] and Figure 5.16 shows a slight increase in overall inequality, but small enough that Sweden still has less inequality than other European nations (Germany, France, Italy, Great Britain, and Portugal).

All in all, Sweden's 1991 tax reform coincided with an acceleration of growth and innovation, without substantially aggravating inequality. In fact, the Swedish reforms were intended to stimulate innovation in order to adapt to the globalizing economy while preserving the social model characterized by an equitable redistribution of income and by strong public investment, especially in education

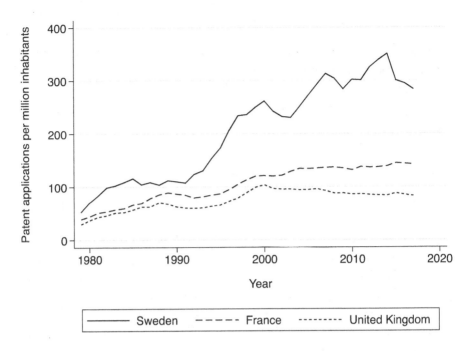

FIGURE 5.14. Evolution of the number of patents per million inhabitants.

Data source: Eurostat.

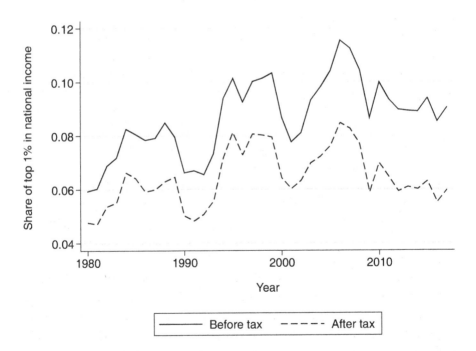

FIGURE 5.15. Evolution of the top 1 percent share in Sweden.

Data source: T. Blanchet, L. Chancel, A. Gethin, "Why Is Europe Less Unequal Than the United States?" unpublished manuscript, 2020.

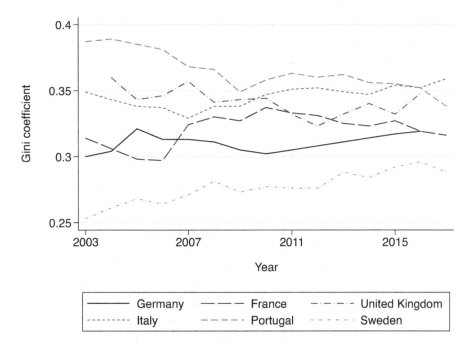

FIGURE 5.16. Evolution of the Gini coefficient in European countries.

Data source: World Bank.

and health care. In this way, Sweden sought to move toward a system that better responds to this double requirement of equity and effectiveness.[19]

BOX 5.2. CAPITAL INCOME TAX AND INCOME MOBILITY IN FRANCE

We have seen earlier that innovation and innovative firms can act as levers of social mobility, and that the state can activate these levers with appropriate policy measures. However, increasing taxation of capital income from an already high starting point does not seem to be an effective lever for social mobility, at least in the short term. One way of measuring change in income mobility between two dates is to compare the "rank" of an individual, meaning the individual's position in the income scale between those two dates. The correlation between the individual's rank at date 1 and the rank at date 2 on average for all individuals in the country is an inverse measure of income mobility at the national level. The stronger the correlation (that is, the closer it is to one), the less income mobility there is in the nation. A recent study shows a weak income mobility on average in France for the period from 2006 to 2017, with a correlation of 0.69 between an individual's rank in 2017 and the same individual's rank in 2006. Even more surprising, income mobility is nearly identical between 2006 and 2011 and between 2012 and 2017: the correlation between a given individual's rank in 2011 and in 2006 is 0.78, while the correlation between a given individual's rank in 2017 and in 2012 is 0.80.[1]

Yet numerous tax reforms were implemented between 2011 and 2013, in particular aligning the tax on capital with the tax on wages in 2013, modifying wealth tax brackets, and introducing an additional 45 percent bracket for income tax in 2012. These reforms were much debated, but until now we did not have data showing the evolution of income reported by individual taxpayers in different income brackets.[2]

Some might argue that the period from 2013 to 2017 following the alignment of taxation of capital income with taxation of labor income is too short to evaluate the effects of this alignment. But this completely flat electrocardiogram of income mobility over the entire period from 2006 to 2017, as well as the absence of any discontinuity before and after the reforms of 2012 and 2013, lead us to question the effectiveness of overtaxation of capital income as the primary means of stimulating social mobility in the short run.

1. See Philippe Aghion, Vlad Ciornohuz, Maxime Gravoueille, and Stefanie Stantcheva, "Reforms and Dynamics of Income: Evidence Using New Panel Data," unpublished manuscript, July 1, 2019, https://www.college-de-france.fr/media/philippe-aghion/UPL8158439681301526632_Tax_Reforms.pdf.

2. This panel data—i.e., longitudinal data where each individual or household is observed over time—allow us to measure trajectories of individual incomes in France with great precision. They come from anonymized data on income taxes and are made available to researchers by the Directorate General of Public Finance through the Secure Data Access Center (CASD).

Lessons from Recent Research on the Relationship between Taxation and Innovation

Several recent studies have demonstrated the causal effect of taxation on innovation. First, taxation has an impact on inventors' geographic mobility. Ufuk Akcigit, Salomé Baslandze, and Stefanie Stantcheva have analyzed the effect of taxation on the brain drain.[20] More specifically, the authors look at the extent to which this phenomenon pertains primarily to "top-quality" inventors, that is to say, those in the top 25 percent according to the patent impact index. This index is constructed from the number of patents filed by an inventor, each of which is weighted by its citations in future innovations. This approach gives greater importance to patents with the most citations, which thus contributed more to later patents than those with fewer citations. The authors use international data on

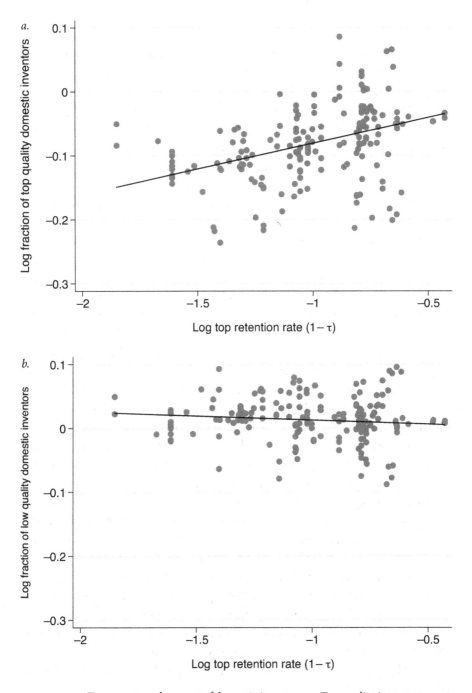

FIGURE 5.17. Top tax rate and percent of domestic inventors. *a.* Top-quality inventors. *b.* Low-quality inventors. *Note:* The *x*-axis shows the percentage of income that is not taxed at the highest marginal rate (in logarithm). For example, if the highest marginal rate is 40 percent, the percentage of untaxed income would be 60 percent. The farther a point is to the right, the lower the highest marginal tax rate.

Reformatted from U. Akcigit, S. Baslandze, and S. Stantcheva, "Taxation and the International Mobility of Inventors," American Economic Review *106, no. 10 (2016): 2930–2981, figure 4 panels A, B.*

patents filed with the US Patent and Trademark Office and the European Patent Office between 1977 and 2003. They first examine the correlation between the marginal tax rate of the highest income bracket and the fraction of inventors that remain in their native country. This correlation is strongly negative for top-quality inventors, whereas it is essentially zero for inventors in the bottom 50 percent of the patent impact index (Figure 5.17). These other inventors constitute a valid counterfactual, as they are less likely to have very high incomes and thus to fall in the highest tax bracket.

Akcigit, Baslandze, and Stantcheva made use of two natural experiments. The first is the collapse of the Soviet Union, as a result of which Russian scientists became internationally mobile. Figure 5.18 shows that prior to the collapse of the Soviet Union, migration of Russian inventors was unrelated to tax considerations because inventors were prohibited from emigrating. By contrast, after the collapse, there is a strong negative correlation between the highest marginal tax rate in a country and the percentage of Russian inventors who emigrate to that country: Russian scientists choose to emigrate primarily to countries with lower tax rates.

The second natural experiment capitalizes on Ronald Reagan's 1986 tax cut. Reagan lowered the highest marginal rate from 50 percent to 28 percent, as shown in the curve with circle markers in Figure 5.19. What effect did this reform have on the immigration of inventors? There is a distinct increase in the number of foreign top-quality inventors moving to the United States (solid curve). By contrast, if, using information from other developed countries, we construct a counterfactual United States not subject to the 1986 tax cut, we observe no particular change in the number of immigrant inventors in that counterfactual United States (dashed curve).

Having looked at the effect of taxation on inventor mobility, we next ask how taxation affects innovation. Ufuk Akcigit, John Grigsby, Tom Nicholas, and Stefanie Stantcheva created a new dataset that combines an exhaustive list of American inventors who had filed patents since 1920, the content of their patents, and the amount of corporate and individual income tax paid.[21]

The authors used two estimation methods to establish a causal relationship between taxation and innovation. The first method was to make use of differences in tax rates across US states to see how the state tax affected inventors' behavior. The second method was to compare the effect of a change in federal tax rate in two neighboring counties, located on opposite sides of the boundary between two US states.

The two methods gave similar results, showing the causal effect of taxation on innovation. In particular, a 1 percent increase in the highest marginal personal income tax rate is associated with a 4 percent drop in the number of patents filed, the number of inventors, and the number of citations. A 1 percent increase in the highest marginal corporate tax rate leads to a 6–6.3 percent decrease in the number

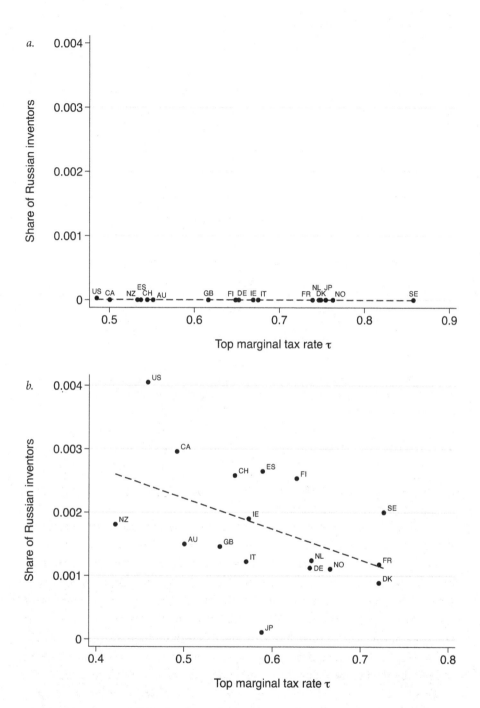

FIGURE 5.18. Top tax rate and percent of Russian inventors. *a.* Pre-Soviet Union collapse. *b.* Post-Soviet Union collapse.

Reformatted from U. Akcigit, S. Baslandze, and S. Stantcheva, "Taxation and the International Mobility of Inventors," American Economic Review *106, no. 10 (2016): 2930–2981, figure 6 panels A, B.*

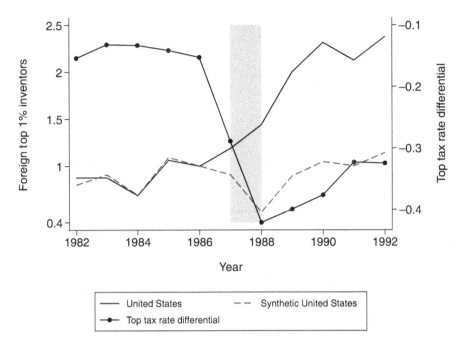

FIGURE 5.19. The 1986 tax reform and foreign inventors in the United States. *Note:* The 1986 tax reform was adopted during the tax year shown in gray. Top 1 percent inventors are those in the top 1 percent according to the patent impact index.

Reformatted from U. Akcigit, S. Baslandze, and S. Stantcheva, "Taxation and the International Mobility of Inventors," American Economic Review 106, no. 10 (2016): 2930–2981, figure 8 panel A.

of patents, a 5.5–6 percent decrease in the number of citations, and a 4.6–5 percent decrease in the number of inventors.

Looking now at taxation and innovation at the state level over time, Figure 5.20 shows the evolution of the rate of innovation, measured by the logarithm of the number of patents, in the state of Michigan following the enactment of a state income tax in 1967 at a rate of 2.6 percent, increased to 5.6 percent in 1968. We observe a pronounced decline in innovation. The dotted line represents a synthetic, or counterfactual, Michigan, which is a reconstruction, on the basis of data from other US states, of Michigan if there had been no change in taxation. In this counterfactual Michigan, we find no drop in the rate of innovation. The results are similar if we consider the number of inventors rather than the number of patents.

These studies confirm the negative impact of taxation on innovation. It is important to bear in mind, however, that the analysis assumes a fixed level of public spending, in other words, of public investment. Yet, as we will see in Chapters 11 and 12, public investment fosters innovation through public funding of research

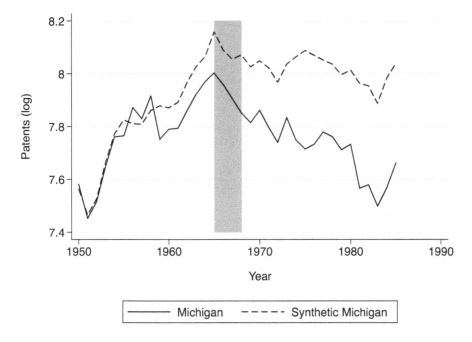

FIGURE 5.20. Case study of a tax reform: Michigan, 1967–1968.

Extracted and reformatted from U. Akcigit, J. Grigsby, T. Nicholas, and S. Stantcheva, "Taxation and Innovation in the 20th Century" (NBER Working Paper No. 24982 National Bureau of Economic Research, Cambridge, MA, September 2018), figure A10.

and an effective education system, investment in health care and infrastructure, and an active policy in the labor market. Given that taxation is necessary to finance these investments, it is important to verify that the state actually uses tax revenues to finance investments that support growth (such as education, health care, flexicurity, and industrial policy), and not to satisfy politicians and interest groups that are close to them.

Another recent study by Philippe Aghion, Ufuk Akcigit, Julia Cagé, and William R. Kerr analyzed the relationship between taxation, innovation-led growth, and the degree of governmental corruption.[22] To measure the tax burden, the authors use the highest marginal corporate tax rate. To measure corruption, they rely on the corruption index from the International Country Risk Guide. They define two sets of countries: "corrupt" countries, or those whose corruption index was greater than the median; and "democratic" countries, or those whose corruption index was less than the median. In the "corrupt" countries, the relationship between tax burden and growth is negative, whereas it is significantly positive in "democratic" countries.

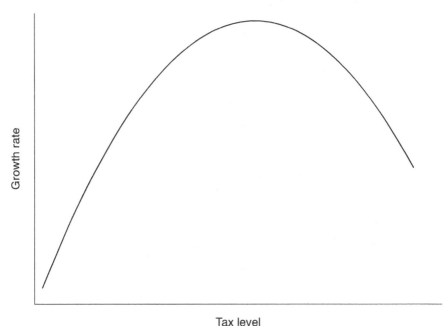

FIGURE 5.21. The inverted U relationship between taxation and growth.

Reformatted from P. Aghion, U. Akcigit, J. Cagé, and W. R. Kerr, "Taxation, Corruption, and Growth," European Economic Review 86 (2016): 24–51, figure 1.

To demonstrate causality with greater rigor, the authors focused on the United States, comparing different US states over time, then the different counties within these states. They assess the level of corruption in a state by the number of civil servants or state employees who have been convicted, and they measured taxation by income tax revenues.[23] The first finding is that of a Laffer curve, which is an inverted U relationship between taxation and growth (Figure 5.21). Up to a certain level of taxation, raising taxes increases growth, but after that threshold, "too much tax kills tax." This inverted U relationship is the result of the two antagonistic effects of taxation on growth mentioned earlier: on one hand, tax revenues enable the government to fund investments that make firms and workers more productive, thereby fostering growth; on the other hand, for a given amount of public spending, taxes disincentivize innovation by reducing the net profit from innovating. Up to a certain tax rate, the positive effect outweighs the negative effect; beyond that level, the negative effect dominates. It is thus not a good policy to lower taxes at all costs under the pretext of stimulating growth, just as it is not a good policy to raise taxes excessively.

The most interesting finding, however, is how corruption interacts with the above results and modifies the inverted U-curves. Analyses at the state and county level in the United States showed that the more corrupt the government, the lower the threshold at which taxation begins to have a negative impact on growth.

6. Conclusion

In this chapter, we have analyzed the link between innovation, inequality, and tax policy and reached several conclusions. First of all, there are various ways to measure inequality: the share of income going to people at the top levels of the income distribution (for example, the top 1 percent); the Gini coefficient, which measures overall inequality, comparing the situation in a country as a whole to a situation where all individuals have equal income; and finally, the correlation between parents' income and the income of their children, which is a dynamic measure of inequality reflecting the absence of social mobility.

Second, although innovation increases inequality at the top of the income distribution, there are other sources of top income inequality, in particular barriers to entry and lobbying. While innovation has undeniable positive effects—it stimulates growth, correlates positively to social mobility, and does not significantly affect the Gini coefficient—lobbying is an entirely different story: it discourages innovation and growth and increases overall inequality.

We have discussed the role of innovative firms as social ladders, in particular for unskilled workers. In turn, the state can stimulate social mobility by encouraging firms to create good jobs and to invest in their employees' professional training in a meaningful way, especially for the lowest-skilled workers.

Taxation thus constitutes an indispensable tool to stimulate growth and make it more inclusive, both because it enables the state to invest in growth levers such as education, health, research, and infrastructure and because it enables the state to redistribute wealth and insure individuals against idiosyncratic risks (job loss, illness, and skill obsolescence) and macroeconomic risks (war, financial crises, and pandemics).[24] But this tool must be used prudently. Apart from the fact that its short-term effects on social mobility are not proven, as we saw in Box 5.2, excessive taxation can discourage innovation and consequently inhibit growth.[25]

One final remark: in this chapter we set aside the question of unequal access to the activity of innovating. In particular, to what extent does an individual's likelihood of becoming an innovator depend on social origin and on parental income, education, and socioprofessional category? We will return to this question in Chapter 10, where we also explore the complementarity between education policy and innovation policy as levers of growth and social mobility.

▼

6

THE SECULAR
STAGNATION DEBATE

In their book *Good Economics for Hard Times: Better Answers to Our Biggest Problems,* Abhijit Banerjee and Esther Duflo contrast Joel Mokyr's optimistic vision of innovation and long-term growth with the pessimistic view of Robert Gordon.[1] For Gordon, the era of great innovations (such as the steam engine, electricity, and the combustion engine) is over, and innovation has entered a phase of sharply decreasing returns, with the corollary that we will experience a lasting decline in growth.[2] For Joel Mokyr, on the other hand, the revolution in information technologies (IT), combined with the globalization of trade, has created the conditions for innovation and growth to prosper more than ever before.

In this chapter, we will attempt to reconcile Gordon and Mokyr by explaining why, in an economy as innovative as that of the United States, productivity growth has declined over the past two decades.

We present our readers with several different explanations, but in the end the one we find the most convincing is that firms that have become leaders or superstars have a discouraging effect on innovation by other firms.

1. Introducing the Secular Stagnation Debate

In 1938, the economist Alvin Hansen explained, in his presidential address to the American Economic Association, that he believed the United States was doomed to weak growth in the future, a condition he dubbed "secular stagnation."[3] The country had just emerged from the Great Depression, and Hansen did not anticipate the coming of World War II with the resulting rebound in public spending and thus of aggregate demand.

Since then, we have gone through another major financial crisis, in 2007–2008, which led Larry Summers and other economists to revive the term *secular stagnation* to describe a situation they saw as similar to that portrayed by Hansen in 1938.[4] Summers contended that investment demand was so weak that only with negative interest rates could we return to full employment.

For Robert Gordon, however, the risk of secular stagnation reflects a "supply side" problem rather than a "demand side" problem. Gordon, using the metaphor of a fruit tree, argued that the great innovations have already occurred: the best and juiciest fruits are the low-hanging fruits; after we have harvested them, we have to climb higher in the tree to find fruits of lower quality. By way of example, the Boeing 707 brought an exponential decrease in travel time when it was introduced in 1958; since that date, travel time has not declined further and in fact has increased because of the need to conserve fuel.[5]

Joel Mokyr and the Schumpeterian economists are more optimistic about the future than are Summers and Gordon, for at least two reasons. First, the IT revolution has not only improved the production of goods and services but has also durably and radically improved the technology for producing ideas.[6] Second, globalization, contemporaneous with the IT wave, substantially increased the potential gains from innovating, due to a market size effect, and at the same time it has increased the potential losses from not innovating, due to a competition effect.

We have indeed witnessed an acceleration in both the quantity and quality of innovation over recent decades, manifested in the number and the impact of patents. Why doesn't this acceleration in innovation show up in the observed evolution of productivity growth?

One explanation, raised in Chapter 3, is based on the observation that the benefits of technological waves are belated and incomplete in many countries, notably because of structural rigidities or inappropriate economic policies. The example of Sweden and Japan is informative. Since the early 1980s, productivity growth accelerated in Sweden while it slowed in Japan. Sweden implemented significant reforms in the beginning of the 1990s (see Chapter 5). On the contrary, Japan, after strong growth until the end of the 1980s, got stuck in a phase of weak growth, which we attribute to the aging of the population and the dominance of large conglomerates (the *keiretsu*) that bridle the economy and stifle innovation and the entry of new firms.[7] Between the period 1985–1993 and the period 1994–2007, the annual growth rate of overall productivity, as measured by the OECD, increased by 1.5 points in Sweden but fell by 1.1 points in Japan. Japan's delay in instituting reforms and its resulting inability to benefit fully from the new technological waves undoubtedly partially explain the weak growth in Japan and some other developed countries. It nonetheless does not suffice to explain the decline in growth in the United States since the beginning of the 2000s.

A second explanation points to the easing of credit conditions starting in the 1990s, accentuated by the highly accommodating monetary policies adopted in response to the 2008 financial crisis. Figure 6.1 traces the continuous decrease in long-term interest rates. According to this explanation, this easing of credit terms enabled inefficient firms to remain in the market, which in turn hindered innovation by new entrants and hence productivity growth. By way of illustration, since 2008 there has been a strong increase in the number of "zombie" firms—firms that are more than ten years old but are so unprofitable that their income cannot cover their interest costs for three consecutive years. According to a study published in 2018 by the Bank of International Settlements, the percentage of zombies in fourteen OECD countries grew from 1 percent in 1990 to 12 percent in 2015.[8] In Chapter 4, we mentioned the perverse effect of relaxing credit constraints on incumbent firms on aggregate productivity growth by using a natural experiment, namely, Mario Draghi's ACC program in 2012. What happened is that relaxing credit constraints on incumbent firms allowed even the least productive incumbent firms to remain in the market, which in turn discourages new, potentially more productive firms from entering the market.

Were credit conditions truly loosened? Remember that firms must bear the weighted average cost of capital in order to obtain financing. A firm's capital consists of debt owed to lenders—mostly banks—and the equity held by its shareholders. The cost of capital thus depends on two parameters: the cost of borrowing and the cost of equity. Although the former is easy to determine, the second depends on investors' expectations of return on their investment. If the activity is risky, investors will demand a greater risk premium and a higher return; if the activity is not risky, they will require a low risk premium. Therefore, we estimate the cost of equity as the risk-free cost—typically the rate for ten-year sovereign debt—to which we add the risk premium. Since the 1980s, and even more since the 2008 financial crisis, the cost of bank credit and the risk-free rate have undeniably fallen (Figure 6.1). However, risk premiums have risen.[9] As a result, the total cost of capital that firms must bear has not actually changed over the past twenty or thirty years.

The remainder of this chapter examines three additional explanations. The first, similar to Robert Gordon's view, maintains that new ideas are increasingly difficult to find. The second holds that we cannot measure growth accurately, and our measurements do not reflect the true contribution of new innovations. The third explanation highlights the role of superstar firms that have developed thanks to

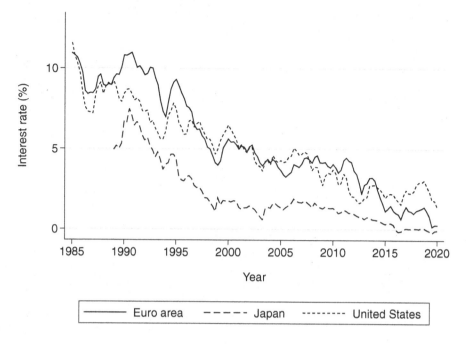

FIGURE 6.1. Long-term interest rates.

Data source: OECD.

the new technological waves (IT and digital technology) but that now obstruct the entry of new, innovative firms.

2. New Ideas Are Harder to Find

In an article published in 2020, Nicholas Bloom, Charles I. Jones, John Van Reenen, and Michael Webb defended the idea of a secular decrease in the productivity of research: more and more researchers are necessary to attain a given level of productivity growth or a given amount of innovation.[10] A precursor article by Charles Jones had already shown that the number of researchers and engineers employed in the R&D sector had increased continuously since 1953, without producing any significant takeoff of productivity growth.[11]

Figure 6.2 reinforces this observation for the period from 1930 to 2000. The solid curve represents the evolution of total factor productivity (TFP) growth, and the dashed curve represents the evolution of the number of researchers. We can see that the number of researchers grew increasingly quickly over time, while productivity growth did not take off over this period. The authors conclude that at

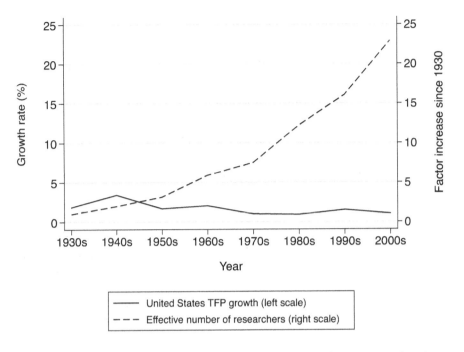

FIGURE 6.2. Number of researchers and productivity in the United States. *Note:* The values correspond to ten-year averages.

Reformatted from N. Bloom, C. I. Jones, J. Van Reenen, and M. Webb, "Are Ideas Getting Harder to Find?" American Economic Review *110, no. 4 (2020): 1104–1144, figure 1.*

the level of the economy as a whole, the return to research in terms of productivity growth seems to decrease with time.

But Bloom and his coauthors went beyond analyzing research and growth at the level of the economy as a whole; they also looked in detail at specific sectors, focusing on semiconductors, agriculture, and health.

Take the example of semiconductors. Moore's law predicts that the number of transistors on a computer chip doubles every two years, which corresponds to annual growth of approximately 35 percent (Figure 6.3). Moore's law is not scientifically grounded; it derives only from observation of data on semiconductors, which manifest a remarkably regular pattern since 1970. This continuous increase in the number of transistors per chip gives rise to a constant improvement in the performance of chips, measured, for example, by the number of tasks per second the chip can execute. And since chips are at the heart of computers, robots, and smartphones, increasing their performance also improves the quality of these products.

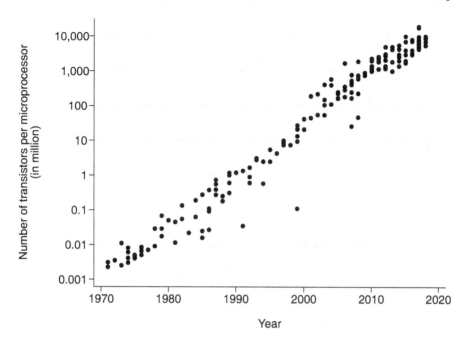

FIGURE 6.3. Moore's law.

Data source: Wikipedia.

With this in mind, if we now look at the number of researchers in large semiconductor firms (such as Intel, Fairchild, National Semiconductor, Texas Instruments, and Motorola) and at the increase in the number of researchers it took to fulfill the predictions of Moore's law, the verdict is clear: the number of researchers required to double the number of transistors on a chip is eighteen times higher than it was at the beginning of the 1970s. One might interpret this result as a reflection of the increased difficulty of advancing the technological frontier for semiconductors.

Similarly, in the pharmaceutical sector, research productivity, measured by the number of new compounds approved by the FDA compared to the research effort, declined while the number of researchers hired by pharmaceutical companies increased consistently over time, as shown in Figure 6.4.

These facts are striking, and the argument is quite appealing, yet it raises a number of questions. First of all, should we characterize a business sector by a specific technology, or rather by a group of technologies that fulfill a given purpose? Photography provides an example of this problem: Kodak suffered severely diminishing returns as the digital camera and then the smartphone replaced the

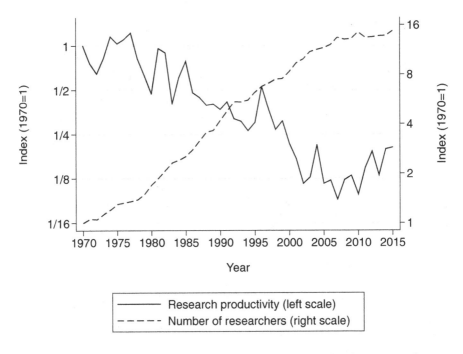

FIGURE 6.4. Research productivity and number of researchers in the pharmaceutical sector.

Data source: N. Bloom, C. I. Jones, J. Van Reenen, and M. Webb, "Are Ideas Getting Harder to Find?" American Economic Review 110, no. 4 (2020): 1104–1144.

film camera. Each of these inventions corresponds to a major technological wave followed by a series of incremental secondary innovations, as shown in Figure 6.5.[12]

Second, semiconductor manufacturers do far more than produce computer chips. For example, Intel develops software, makes computers, and organizes data centers. In 2010 only 8 percent of its patents related to inventions in semiconductors, compared to 75 percent in 1971, demonstrating how much Intel has broadened the scope of its activities. Consequently, it may be misleading to look at the total number of researchers at Intel when analyzing its productivity as a manufacturer of semiconductors. A steadily increasing number of researchers at Intel focus on fields other than semiconductors.

Even among researchers working on semiconductors, not all of them concentrate on increasing the number of transistors on a chip. Beyond the density of transistors, new chips cost less than older ones and can execute more tasks. This can be due to a more efficient arrangement of the transistors on the chips, which improves performance by dissipating heat more quickly.[13] Thus

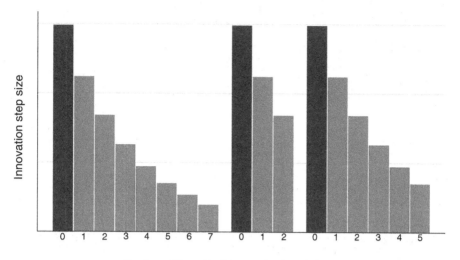

FIGURE 6.5. Primary and secondary innovations.

Reformatted from U. Akcigit and W. R. Kerr, "Growth through Heterogeneous Innovations," Journal of Political Economy *126, no. 4 (2018): 1374–1443, figure 6.*

the variety of products and services even within the narrow category "semi-conductors" has grown continuously over time. If we want to measure research productivity in this sector by the ratio of productivity growth to the number of researchers, we must deflate the number of researchers by a factor reflecting the variety of services provided by computer chips. In doing so, we may find that the returns to research are not diminishing as much as it appears at first sight.

Third, certain R&D expenses seem large because they are duplicated by several competing firms engaged in a race to be the first innovator for a certain type of product, such as batteries for electric vehicles.

Finally, some R&D expenditures are actually defensive investments by incumbent firms to preserve their market share. The economist John Sutton, in *Sunk Costs and Market Structure,* explains how a part of the expenses supposedly allocated to research and innovation serves in reality to prevent the entry of new firms.[14] The accumulation of defensive patents is one of the protective strategies incumbent firms use to protect their rents.

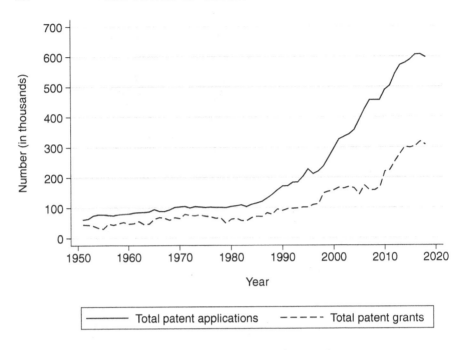

FIGURE 6.6. Patent applications and granted patents in the United States.

Data source: World Intellectual Property Organization.

In sum, the view that the increasing difficulty of producing new ideas explains the decline in growth can be challenged, even if it is clear that innovation advances by successive waves, with decreasing returns for each wave.

3. Productivity Growth Is Mismeasured

Over the past forty years, the pace of innovation in the United States, as measured by the number of patents, has accelerated (Figure 6.6). Why hasn't productivity growth fully reflected this acceleration of innovation? One natural explanation is that the divergence between the rate of innovation on the one hand and the rate of productivity growth on the other reflects a measurement problem. This measurement problem has grown worse over recent decades, especially since the 2000s.

The Role of Digitization and IT

First of all, the measurement problem is inherent in the method of calculating GDP, which is defined as the value generated by the production of goods and services—valued at market price—in a given country over a given period of time. Thus, GDP is basically a measure of production. It is well adapted to economies where the production of physical goods is dominant, but it is less effective at reflecting the increasing importance and variety of services in a digital economy.

In particular, GDP as traditionally defined fails to account for changes in the ways that products and services are used. The photography market offers a good example of this, as Hal Varian, Google's chief economist, has shown.[15] In 2000, 80 billion photographs were taken in the world. The introduction of the smartphone transformed the landscape: the number of photos grew by a multiple of twenty to reach nearly 1.6 trillion in 2015. At the same time, the marginal cost of a photograph fell from approximately fifty cents to nearly zero. Sales of film and cameras declined dramatically. In addition, photo development plummeted because photos today are generally shared and not sold; they have essentially become a nonmarket good. Photography has by no means disappeared. Indeed, today's cameras perform better than ever. But since people essentially produce their own pictures, photography is no longer part of the productive economy and accordingly does not show up in GDP and productivity measures.

More generally, digital technology has stimulated the emergence of nonmarket goods and services. Open-source software and free websites like Wikipedia provide access to free content but are not integrated into measured GDP. They nonetheless often replace paying goods and services such as encyclopedias or paid software.

Measured GDP also fails to capture improvements in quality. Hal Varian cites the example of the smartphone: a smartphone serves as a partial substitute not only for cameras but also for GPS devices, video cameras, e-books, audio readers, alarm clocks, internet browsers, calculators, and dictaphones. The integration of all these items in smartphones may have decreased measured GDP by decreasing the sales of the products that smartphones replaced, as well as by failing to capture improvements in the quality of the phones themselves.

Why is it so difficult to measure the contribution of new products like smartphones to the growth of GDP? One noteworthy reason is the internationalization of value chains. For example, the assembly of a smartphone takes place mainly overseas. Even though the design, engineering, and marketing of iPhones occurs in California, the physical assembly takes place in Shenzhen, China, and the components come from twenty-eight different countries. Moreover, the intangible nature of many digital services makes it difficult to associate a particular activity with a specific territory. This, in turn, favors tax optimization by large firms in the sector (the FAMANG: Facebook, Amazon, Microsoft, Apple, Netflix, and Google). The use of optimization techniques such as not billing certain transactions in

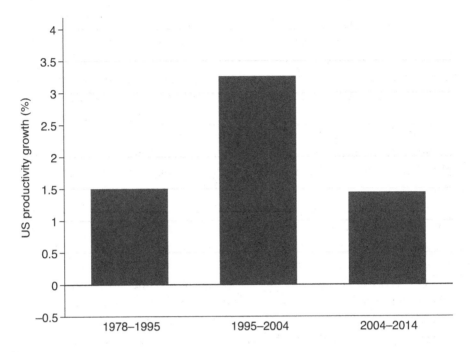

FIGURE 6.7. Evolution of American productivity growth.

Data source: D. M. Byrne, J. G. Fernald, and M. B. Reinsdorf, "Does the United States Have a Productivity Slowdown or a Measurement Problem?" Brookings Papers on Economic Activity 1 (2016): 109–182.

the countries where they truly take place, or manipulating intragroup prices so that subsidiaries in high-tax jurisdictions are in deficit, has a direct impact on GDP.

Does the difficulty of measuring the effect of recent innovations on growth, particularly in IT and digital technology, suffice to explain the decrease in growth? To answer this question, David Byrne, John Fernald, and Marshall Reinsdorf began by observing the evolution of American productivity growth, measured by GDP per hour worked, between 1978 and 2014 (Figure 6.7).[16] For each of the three sub-periods they studied (1978 to 1995, 1995 to 2004, and 2004 to 2014), the height of the bars corresponds to the annual growth rate of GDP per hour worked on average over the period. The figure shows exceptional growth over the period 1995 to 2004, followed by a clear slowdown from 2004 to 2014.

The authors then attempted to correct the measurement of growth by taking into account certain measurement problems related to improvements in the quality of computers, improvements in the quality of software, intangible investments, and lastly internet access and the development of e-commerce (Figure 6.8).

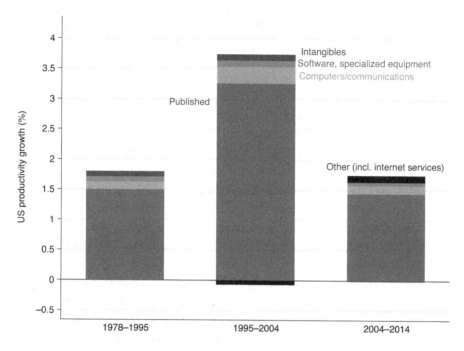

FIGURE 6.8. Adjustments to productivity growth.

Reformatted from D. M. Byrne, J. G. Fernald, and M. B. Reinsdorf, "Does the United States Have a Productivity Slowdown or a Measurement Problem?" Brookings Papers on Economic Activity 1 (2016): 109–182, figure 1.

In sum, although all of these sectors contributed to the underestimation of productivity growth over recent years, their overall contribution remains small. Hence this does not solve the enigma of the decline in growth between 1994 and 2004 or between 2004 and 2014. Finally, the explanation whereby the slowdown in productivity growth is due to a measurement problem is at odds with a recent study by Chad Syverson showing that measurement errors explain only a small part of the growth decline.[17]

The Role of Creative Destruction

The above discussion suggests that the difficulty in measuring digital activity does not suffice to explain why productivity growth has declined to its current low level. A study by Philippe Aghion, Antonin Bergeaud, Timo Boppart, Peter J. Klenow, and Huiyu Li published in 2019 offers an alternative explanation for why we currently observe low productivity growth.[18] The idea is that the contribution to growth of innovations involving creative destruction (that is, innovations leading to new products that replace existing products) is hard to measure. It indeed turns out that innovation, measured by the number of patents, is strongly correlated with productivity growth in US states where creative destruction is low. By contrast, innovation does not correlate strongly with productivity growth in US states where creative destruction is high.

A simple example can explain why creative destruction makes it harder to factor in the contribution of innovation when measuring productivity growth. Suppose that yesterday and today you see the same typewriter in a store, but between yesterday and today its price has increased. This price increase corresponds purely to inflation, because it is the exact same typewriter. Now imagine that between yesterday and today, the quality of the machine has improved marginally, for example by making the type characters more aesthetically pleasing. Imagine, again, that the price has increased between yesterday and today. In this case you can easily disentangle the part of the price increase that is due to the improvement in the typewriter's quality from the part that reflects pure inflation. You simply compare the price of the new typewriter to today's price of other typewriters. But now imagine that there has been an innovation with creative destruction, so that overnight the typewriter has been replaced by a personal computer. The computer fills, among other things, the typewriter's function of producing text, but in a more efficient and user-friendly manner, and its price is higher than that of the typewriter. This time it will be extremely difficult to separate the quality improvement component from the inflation component in the price increase involved in moving from the typewriter to the computer. How should we proceed in this case?

All statistical agencies, including in the United States, resort to what is known as *extrapolation* or *imputation*: for each category of good, they compute the average rate of inflation, ignoring those products in the category that are subject to creative destruction.[19] This typically leads to underestimating productivity growth, to the extent that quality improvements generated by innovations with creative destruction are likely to be greater than quality improvements associated with incremental innovations (Box 6.1). For example, the gain in productivity was greater when we moved from old-fashioned cell phones to smartphones (an innovation with creative destruction) in the late 2000s than when we switched from one old model of cell phone to another, slightly better model, such as the flip phone (an incremental innovation) in the mid-2000s.

BOX 6.1. IMPUTATION AND MISSING GROWTH

The following numerical example, drawn from a 2019 paper by Philippe Aghion, Antonin Bergeaud, Timo Boppart, Peter J. Klenow, and Huiyu Li, illustrates how imputation leads to underestimating productivity growth.[1] Suppose that: (1) 80 percent of products in the economy are like the first typewriter, which experiences no change between yesterday and today, but they are subject to a

4 percent inflation rate; (2) 10 percent of products are like the second type-writer, which experienced an incremental change between yesterday and today, with their quality-adjusted prices falling by 6 percent (that is, an inflation rate of −6 percent); and (3) 10 percent of products experience quality improvement due to creative destruction between yesterday and today, like the typewriter replaced by the personal computer, leading to quality-adjusted prices also falling by 6 percent.

The true average inflation rate in this economy is then 2 percent:

$$\frac{80}{100} \cdot 4\% + \frac{20}{100} \cdot (-6\%) = 2\%.$$

Suppose also that nominal output grows at 4 percent, so that the true growth rate of real GDP is equal to 2 percent (2 percent corresponds to 4 percent minus the 2 percent true inflation rate).

What happens if the statistical agency resorts to imputation when computing the average inflation rate? Imputation implies that the statistical agency will ignore the goods subject to creative destruction when computing the inflation rate for the whole economy, and consider only the products that were not subject to innovation plus the products for which innovation did not involve creative destruction.

Hence the statistical agency will take the average inflation rate for the whole economy to be equal to

$$\frac{8}{9} \cdot 4\% + \frac{1}{9} \cdot (-6\%) = 2.9\%.$$

Assume that the statistical agency correctly evaluates the growth in nominal GDP to be 4 percent. It will then (incorrectly) infer that the growth rate of real output is

$$4\% - 2.9\% = 1.1\%$$

This in turn implies that the statistical agency underestimates the rate growth by:

$$2\% - 1.1\% = 0.9\%$$

1. Philippe Aghion, Antonin Bergeaud, Timo Boppart, Peter J. Klenow, and Huiyu Li, "Missing Growth from Creative Destruction," *American Economic Review* 109, no. 8 (2019): 2795–2822.

Table 6.1 shows measured productivity growth (second column), true productivity growth (third column), and missing productivity growth (first column). Missing growth is simply the difference between true growth and measured growth. In the United States, measured growth increases strongly during the

Table 6.1. Missing Growth and True Growth in the United States

Years	Missing Growth	Measured Growth	True Growth	Percentage of Growth Missed
1983–2013	0.54	1.87	2.41	22.4
1983–1995	0.52	1.80	2.32	22.4
1996–2005	0.48	2.68	3.16	15.2
2006–2013	0.65	0.98	1.63	39.9

Source: P. Aghion, A. Bergeaud, T. Boppart, P. J. Klenow, and H. Li, "Missing Growth from Creative Destruction," *American Economic Review* 109, no. 8 (2019): 2795–2822.

period 1996–2005 before falling sharply during the period 2006–2013, whereas missing growth increases between the periods 1996–2005 and 2006–2013. Yet, even correcting for this, missing growth does not explain the decline in growth, since even true growth declines sharply between the periods 1996–2005 and 2006–2013. The same method, applied to France, provides missing growth estimates that are remarkably close to those for the United States: 0.47 percent per year on average for the period 1996–2005, and 0.64 percent per year on average over the period 2006–2013.[20]

Thus the underestimation of productivity growth by statistical agencies explains only a small part of the observed decline in growth since the beginning of the 2000s. We must look elsewhere for the explanation of this growth decline.[21]

4. Leader or Superstar Firms Discourage New Entrants

In Chapter 4, we referred to the work of Thomas Philippon, who hypothesized that the main reason growth slowed in America was the weakening of antitrust policies.[22] According to his argument, weaker antitrust policy led to greater concentration in many sectors of the economy and to a decline in business dynamism, and especially in the creation of new firms. Even though Philippon's thesis has implications for the dynamics of innovation and technological progress, it does not place technology and innovation at the heart of the explanation of the decline. However, two facts call Philippon's analysis into question: First, the growth decline and the decreasing share of labor in income seem to be concentrated in the sectors that produce or use IT. Second, even though rents and concentration may increase due to barriers to competition, they may also increase as a result of innovation.

In our view, a better approach is to put innovation at the heart of the analysis. In the remainder of this chapter, we discuss two attempts to explain both the increase in rents and the decrease in growth by using the Schumpeterian analytic framework. In this framework, rents come at least partly from innovation, firms decide how much to innovate based on the rents they anticipate, and new innovations render existing technologies obsolete. The two attempts we examine share the assumptions that rents result from past innovations, and that yesterday's innovators, once they become leaders or superstars in certain economic sectors, discourage innovation by other potential actors in the same sectors.[23]

Discouragement by the Leader

Ufuk Akcigit and Sina Ates start with a series of empirical facts showing a decline in dynamism of the American economy since the beginning of the 2000s.[24] They emphasize an increase in industrial concentration and in markups, as well as an increase in the difference in productivity between "leader" firms and "laggard" firms in the various sectors of the economy. Furthermore, the firms that have become leaders in a given sector—having already accumulated the most patents—are the ones that continue to file the most patents. These same firms purchase the greatest number of patents for defensive purposes, that is, to discourage new innovation by potential entrants in their respective sectors.

When explaining these facts, the authors have in mind a world where leader firms in each sector innovate and laggard firms catch up. This is the same paradigm we used in Chapter 4 when analyzing the relationship between competition and innovation. In this paradigm, a laggard firm must first catch up to the leader before it can surpass it.

The plausible argument made by the authors is that it has become harder over time for the laggards to catch up with the leaders. One reason is that the leaders have become better at preventing the diffusion of their accumulated knowledge, for example by acquiring patents for defensive purposes. Leaders are then more inclined to invest in innovation in order to increase their technological lead over the laggards, knowing that the laggards will then have less chance of catching up with them and thereby reducing their rents. The result is that the gap between leader and laggard firms has widened on average. In addition, production ends up being more concentrated in the hands of the leaders, whose rents consequently increase. Innovation by laggards is then discouraged. And to the extent that a new entrant in the market starts as a laggard, the end result is that the entry of new firms is also discouraged.

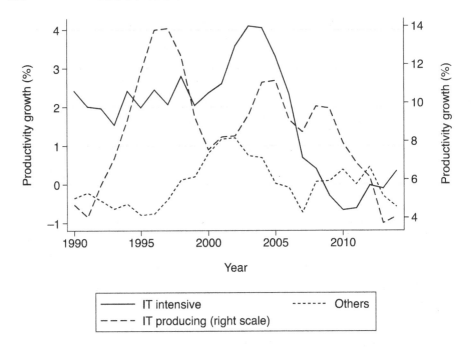

FIGURE 6.9. Productivity growth by IT intensity.

Reformatted from P. Aghion, A. Bergeaud, T. Boppart, P. J. Klenow, and H. Li, "A Theory of Falling Growth and Rising Rents" (NBER Working Paper No. 26448, National Bureau of Economic Research, Cambridge, MA, November 2019), figure 5.

The IT Revolution and Discouragement by Superstar Firms

Aghion, Bergeaud, Boppart, Klenow, and Li have highlighted other empirical observations.[25] The first observation is that the surge and subsequent decline in productivity growth (Figure 6.9) were stronger in sectors that produce or use IT than in other sectors. Second, the share of labor in income decreased more prominently in sectors that produce or use IT (Figure 6.10). Even more importantly, the decline in labor share is due not so much to the fact that within firms the labor share has decreased over time; rather, it reflects a composition effect: namely, "superstar" firms, which typically have a lower share of labor relative to the income they generate, have acquired a greater weight in the economy over time. Mirroring this decline in the share of labor in income, the average share of profits in income has increased over time. Once again, this increase is due to a composition effect: it is not so much that within-firm markups have increased over time; it is more the fact that superstar firms, which typically are the firms with higher markups, have acquired a greater weight in the economy over time.[26]

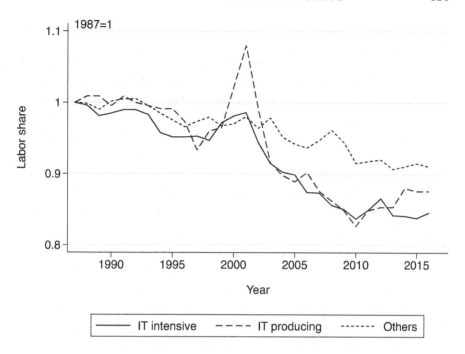

FIGURE 6.10. Labor share by IT intensity.

Reformatted from P. Aghion, A. Bergeaud, T. Boppart, P. J. Klenow, and H. Li, "A Theory of Falling Growth and Rising Rents" (NBER Working Paper No. 26448, National Bureau of Economic Research, Cambridge, MA, November 2019), figure 6.

The following parable helps us understand these three empirical observations. Imagine that there are two types of firms in the economy: superstar firms and nonsuperstar firms. The superstars are firms that have accumulated social capital and know-how that is difficult to imitate. They may also have developed strong networks. For example, firms like Starbucks and Walmart have implemented business models and logistical processes that are extremely difficult to copy and even more difficult to surpass.

Each firm can have several product lines, that is, sell a variety of products, and innovate on each of these products, which yields an innovation rent. Thanks to innovation, the firm can also extend the number of product lines that it controls.

What prevents a single firm from controlling all the product lines in the economy? The answer is time constraints, plus the fact that the fixed costs of doing business increase more than proportionally with the number of products that the firm produces. Because of this time constraint, the CEO is forced to limit the firm to a certain number of product lines; beyond that number, the cost of doing business becomes infinite.

Then the IT revolution arrives. This revolution enables the CEO to save time and to extend the scope of the firm's activities, that is, to increase the number of product lines it controls. But superstar firms are more efficient than the others, so the increased profitability from extending the scope of their activity is greater than for other firms. It follows that superstar firms will extend the scope of their activities to the detriment of other firms.

In the short term, the IT revolution will thus stimulate growth by enabling superstar firms to control a larger fraction of sectors in the economy. This explains the observed increase in the rate of productivity growth between 1995 and 2005, especially in IT sectors. In the longer term, however, the IT revolution can have a negative effect on growth because superstars have a discouraging effect on other firms. For each product line controlled by a superstar firm, other firms will not have an incentive to innovate. The reason is that in order to dethrone a superstar firm, a nonsuperstar will have to drastically reduce its prices and thus its innovation rents. Consequently, as superstars control an increasing number of product lines, nonsuperstars are increasingly discouraged from innovating. But nonsuperstars represent the vast majority of firms. The end result is that by increasing the number of product lines controlled by superstars, the IT revolution can end up reducing innovation and growth in the overall economy in the long run.

What about the effect of the IT revolution on the share of labor in income and on firms' markups? Superstar firms generally have higher markups and lower labor income shares than nonsuperstar firms. By increasing the hegemony of superstars, the IT revolution tends, on average, to increase markups and lower labor share, but this is due to a composition effect. Indeed, if we look within firms, a firm will see its markup on a particular product line decrease and not increase, because it is more likely over time to face a superstar as a direct competitor on that product line. Nevertheless, the average markup economy-wide increases, because superstars end up controlling a higher fraction of product lines, and their markups are intrinsically higher than those of nonsuperstars.[27]

This story has important implications for economic policy. In particular, policies favorable to mergers and acquisitions help superstar firms grow and control ever more sectors. In the short term, they stimulate growth, but in the long term, they hamper both innovation and growth. It is thus imperative to rethink competition policy, and in particular antitrust policy regulating mergers and acquisitions, so that technological revolutions, such as IT and artificial intelligence, increase growth in both the short run *and* the long run. We thus concur with the thesis of Richard Gilbert in his recent book *Innovation Matters: Competition Policy for the High-Technology Economy* (Box 6.2).[28] Thus, the same technological revolution can have very different effects on long-term growth depending on whether it is accompanied by appropriate competition policies. A technological revolution means nothing in the abstract; it is the revolution combined with institutions and economic policies that determines a country's growth prospects.

BOX 6.2. ADAPTING COMPETITION POLICY
TO THE DIGITAL ECONOMY

In his book *Innovation Matters: Competition Policy for the High-Technology Economy,* Richard Gilbert observes that American competition policy did not prevent the emergence of superstar firms that managed to acquire or eliminate their potential competitors and discourage the entry of new firms.[1] On the basis of this observation, he recommends moving from a static competition policy, focused on prices and market shares, to a competition policy focused on innovation. To succeed in this transition, we first have to solve a number of problems. First, the predominant approach in antitrust regulation relies on defining the relevant market and defining market shares. By prohibiting mergers that enable firms to approach a monopoly situation, this approach seeks above all to protect against rising prices.

The authorities do not, however, evaluate the extent to which a merger could discourage the entry of new innovative firms, discourage R&D investment by competitors, or threaten competition in nascent markets. In other words, antitrust regulation neglects the dynamic implications of market concentrations. A main dynamic implication is the emergence of superstar firms. To the extent that superstar firms discourage innovation and the entry of other firms, these firms have contributed to the decline in US productivity growth.

How can we move away from a purely static approach to competition policy? Richard Gilbert believes it is not necessary to rewrite American antitrust law, but its application can be adapted to foster "dynamic competition," by which he means innovation, the entry of new firms, and the creation of new markets. In particular, the antitrust authorities should not use the definition of existing markets as their lodestar. In addition, when they analyze the costs and benefits of a merger, they should consider its anticipated impact on innovation and the creation of new markets. It seems to us that European competition policy suffers from the same defects as those that Gilbert criticized in the United States, and the same recommendations are relevant.

---

1. Richard Gilbert, *Innovation Matters: Competition Policy for the High-Technology Economy* (Cambridge, MA: MIT Press, 2020).

5. Conclusion

Should we share Joel Mokyr's optimism or Robert Gordon's pessimism regarding our prospects for innovation and long-term growth? Our analysis in this chapter suggests that although Joel Mokyr is right to be optimistic about the future of science and our ability to innovate in the future, Robert Gordon's pessimism is justified by the real economic and political resistance that inhibits necessary institutional changes. In particular, so long as competition policy does not take innovation into account, the IT and artificial intelligence revolutions will hinder innovation and growth rather than stimulate them. Another implication, based on our analyses in this chapter and in Chapter 5, is that competition policy integrating innovation will not only stimulate growth but also increase social mobility. It is thus as important as—indeed, complementary to—progressive taxation to make growth more equitable and inclusive.

▼

7

CONVERGENCE, DIVERGENCE, AND THE MIDDLE-INCOME TRAP

In 1890, Argentina enjoyed a per capita GDP approximately 40 percent that of the United States, which made it a middle-income country. This level was three times the per capita GDP of Brazil and Colombia, equivalent to that of Japan and close to that of Canada. It was even slightly higher than France's per capita GDP. Argentina sustained this relative level through the 1930s: to be precise, Chow's test (a statistical test) shows a break around 1938 (Figure 7.1), after which Argentina's per capita GDP declined relative to American per capita GDP.[1]

What explains this drop-off? Argentina's growth came mainly from the development of large-scale agriculture, requiring the import of machinery and foreign capital to finance the necessary infrastructure.[2] Unfortunately, this specialization aimed at the production and export of agricultural products made the Argentinian economy vulnerable to any fluctuation in global demand for these products. Thus the Great Depression coincided with the beginning of the Argentinian drop-off. To ward off this decline, Argentina should have diversified its production, industrialized to a greater extent, and invested in innovation. Instead, it withdrew within its borders and adopted a policy of import substitution rather than developing exports and confronting international competition. In a word, Argentina failed to adapt its institutions to move from an agricultural economy based on accumulation to an industrial economy based on innovation.

Argentina is not the only country that got caught midstream: other countries saw growth take off with the promise of converging to the standard of living of the wealthiest nations, only to stall along the way. These countries remained middle-income countries, failing to enter the group of countries with advanced

FIGURE 7.1. Per capita GDP in Argentina compared to the United States.

Reformatted from P. Aghion, Repenser la croissance économique *(Paris: Fayard, 2016), figure 5.*

economies, thus giving rise to the expression "middle-income trap." The existence of this trap suggests that the transition from a middle-income country to an advanced economy is by no means a straightforward process. To avoid this trap, countries must find a new growth strategy and fix their bearings on production with higher value added, grounded in innovation, a step that Argentina failed to take.

The enigma of the middle-income trap gives rise to other enigmas. What are the underpinnings of convergence or nonconvergence of less-advanced countries toward the standard of living of countries with advanced economies? What are the levers of innovation-led growth, as opposed to accumulation- and imitation-based growth? Why do some countries fail to adapt their institutions to escape from the middle-income trap? This chapter will explore these questions. In closing, we use the example of South Korea to illustrate our analysis. The 1997–1998 Asian crisis led this nation, which had initially been pursuing a catch-up strategy, to implement institutional transformations that enabled it, at least for a time, to change its growth model and escape the middle-income trap.

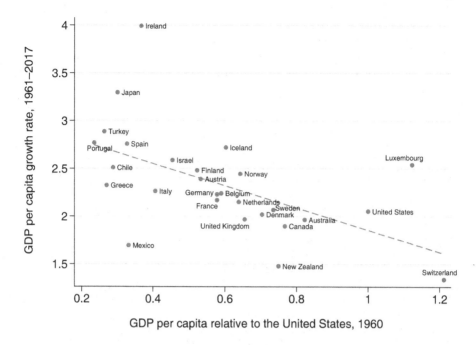

FIGURE 7.2. Per capita GDP growth rate between 1961 and 2017 as a function of 1960 standard of living, OECD countries. *Note:* The graph covers twenty-seven OECD countries for which data post-1960 is available.

Data source: Penn World Table version 9.1.

1. The Variables Favoring Convergence or Nonconvergence

Convergence on Average . . .

Does standard of living tend to converge among countries? Figures 7.2 and 7.3 provide an initial response to this question. These two figures depict the average annual growth rate of per capita GDP from 1961 to 2017 as a function of the initial level of development, measured by per capita GDP in 1960. Each point corresponds to a specific country: countries on the left of each figure have a low initial level of per capita GDP in 1960, whereas those on the right of each figure have a high initial level of per capita GDP. To capture the relationship between initial per capita GDP in 1960 and the average rate of growth between 1961 and 2017, we trace the "ordinary least squares line," which minimizes the sum of the squares of the distances between this straight line and the various points. This line is distinctly downward-sloping in both cases: in other words, on average, countries with lower initial per capita GDP—that is, the least advanced countries—grow faster than countries that

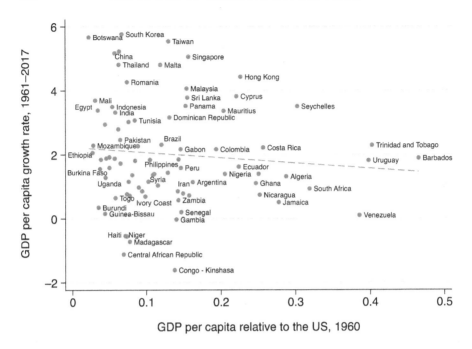

FIGURE 7.3. Per capita GDP growth rate between 1961 and 2017 as a function of 1960 standard of living, non-OECD countries. *Note:* The graph covers eighty-four non-OECD countries for which post-1960 data is available. For readability, not all country names are shown on the graph.

Data source: Penn World Table version 9.1.

are initially more advanced. On average, therefore, the less-advanced countries converge toward the standard of living of the more-advanced countries. But the least squares line is steeper when we restrict our attention to OECD countries (Figure 7.2). This illustrates the fact that convergence is stronger between more similar countries, a phenomenon we refer to as *club convergence*. In contrast, among non-OECD countries, convergence is weaker due to the high heterogeneity across these countries: on the one hand, emerging market economies, such as the Asian tigers (Thailand, Malaysia, Indonesia, and the Philippines) and dragons (South Korea, Taiwan, Hong Kong, and Singapore), are rapidly converging toward the standard of living of advanced nations; on the other hand, the least advanced African countries are stagnating or experiencing sluggish growth.

. . . but Divergence at the Extremes

It is important to note, however, that convergence is only true on average. Not all countries converge toward the standard of living of the most advanced nations.

Table 7.1. Divergence of Per Capita GDP

	1870	1960	2016
GDP per Capita in the United States (A) in dollars ppp	3,736	18,058	53,015
GDP per Capita of the Poorest Country (B) in dollars ppp	247	514	619
Poorest Country	North Korea	Lesotho	Central African Republic
Ratio A / B	15.1	35.1	85.6

Note: Poorest country is determined from the countries for which data is available for the year given.

Data source: Maddison Project Database (2018).

In particular, the ratio of per capita GDP of the United States—the most advanced country—to per capita GDP of less-advanced countries has increased continuously over time. If convergence is a reality, it is indeed "club convergence," with some countries converging to the standard of living of the advanced countries and others lagging behind. In particular, Table 7.1, inspired by Lant Pritchett and constructed using Maddison's historical data on the evolution of per capita GDP, shows an explosion of this ratio between 1897 and 2016, rising from 15.1 in 1870 to 85.6 in 2016.[3]

This growing divergence between the poorest and the richest countries does not result solely from a growth differential between poor and rich countries. In fact, in some countries the standard of living actually declined between 1961 and 2017, with negative growth rates of per capita GDP (Figure 7.4).

By contrast, some countries experienced high growth rates, above 8 percent. The nations with the strongest growth were China and India: since the end of the 1990s, the GDP of these two countries rose sharply compared to the growth of GDP of the G7 nations (Figure 7.5).

How Does World Income Distribution Evolve?

How is this convergence on average and divergence at the extremes reflected in the dynamic evolution of the world income distribution? Xavier Sala-i-Martin has reconstructed the evolution of income distribution in 138 countries between 1970 and 2000.[4] He relies on World Bank household surveys to reconstitute income distribution country by country. He first examines inequality in each country, by comparing income distribution in 1970 with income distribution in 2000. In China and India, income distribution spreads out between 1970 and 2000, reflecting growing income inequality within these two countries. In the United

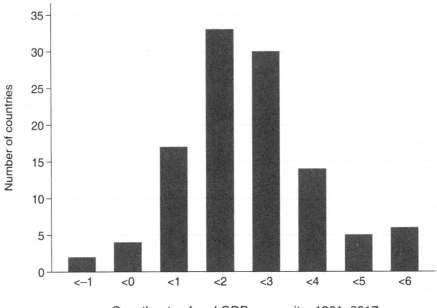

FIGURE 7.4. Distribution of growth rates, 1961–2017.

Data source: Penn World Table version 9.1.

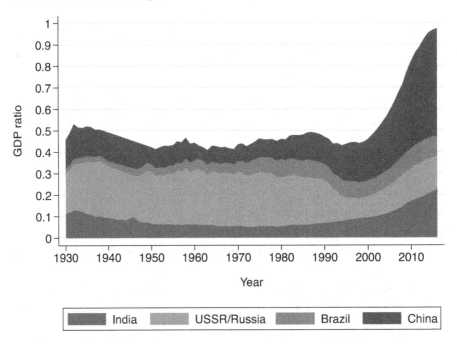

FIGURE 7.5. Ratio of G7 nations' GDP and BRIC GDP.

Data source: Maddison Project Database (2018), Groningen Growth and Development Centre, University of Groningen.

States, dispersion within high incomes also increases between 1970 and 2000, which is consistent with the increase in the top 1 percent's income share that we discussed in Chapter 5.

Sala-i-Martin went further and compared the evolution of poverty and inequality, as measured by the Gini coefficient, between countries.[5] For this purpose, one method would be to compare the evolution of per capita GDP in the various countries, assuming that each country has the same weight regardless of its size, as in Table 7.1. Doing so leads to the conclusion that the disparity between the richest country and the poorest country increased continuously over time, so that global inequality also increased. This method has a drawback: if countries with very low incomes and countries with very high income are very small countries, the growing disparity between rich and poor countries does not tell us much about the evolution of the world income distribution.

Sala-i-Martin thus chose to use an alternative method to study the individual income distribution worldwide. He ran into a problem: the income of a person living in one country is not directly comparable to that of a resident of another country. To overcome this problem, Sala-i-Martin "corrects" individual income for purchasing power parity (PPP), which is a conversion factor, calculated for each country, that allows us to express in a common unit the purchasing powers of different currencies in order to make international comparisons. Thus, one can compare the purchasing power of an individual in country A to the purchasing power of another individual in country B. One can then construct the world income distribution, with each individual having an equal weight regardless of where they live (Figure 7.6).

At first sight, the shift of income distribution to the right over time corresponds to an increase in income for the majority of individuals in the world, with a continuous decrease in the percentage of the population living below the extreme poverty line (vertical line). According to the World Bank, which defines the poverty threshold as corresponding to an annual income of $495, the poverty rate fell from 15.4 percent of world population in 1970 to 5.7 percent in 2000. When we calculate the Gini coefficient, measuring global inequality, we find a decrease in the coefficient. This reduction in the Gini coefficient corresponds to a 4 percent decrease in global interpersonal inequality from 1979 to 2000 (Figure 7.7). This decrease in global inequality is mainly driven by China. If we exclude China from the analysis, the global Gini coefficient rises over the same period. Therefore, overall, worldwide interpersonal inequality has decreased between 1970 and 2000, whereas, if we had focused on the ratio of per capita GDP levels between the richest and the poorest countries, we would have concluded that worldwide inequality had increased between 1970 and 2000.

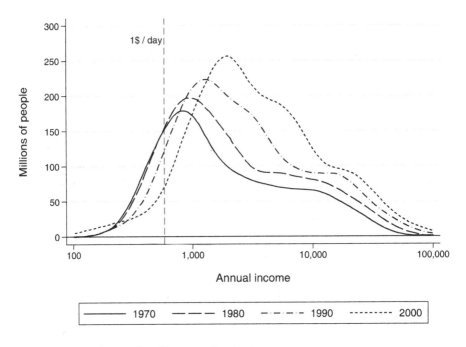

FIGURE 7.6. Evolution of world income distribution.

Reformatted from X. Sala-i-Martin, "The World Distribution of Income: Falling Poverty and . . . Convergence, Period," Quarterly Journal of Economics *121, no. 2 (2006): 351–397, figure IV.*

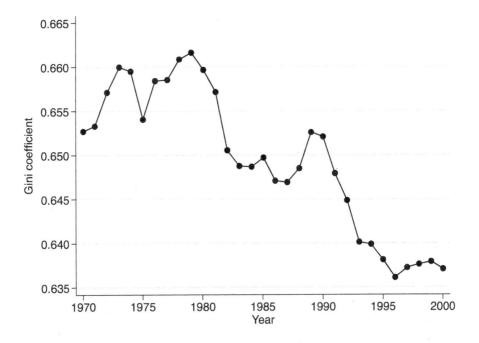

FIGURE 7.7. World income inequality: Gini coefficient.

Reformatted from X. Sala-i-Martin, "The World Distribution of Income: Falling Poverty and . . . Convergence, Period," Quarterly Journal of Economics *121, no. 2 (2006): 351–397, figure VIII.*

What explains convergence on average? And what explains the phenomenon known as *club convergence,* which refers to the fact that the standard of living in certain countries converges toward those of more-advanced countries, whereas for other countries, the standard of living falls farther and farther behind those of advanced countries, in some cases even declining in absolute terms?

Two Possible Explanations

Growth economists offer two explanations for convergence.

The first explanation centers on the diminishing returns from capital accumulation. The underlying idea of this approach, based on Robert Solow's model[6] and further explored by Robert Barro and Sala-i-Martin in 1995,[7] is that the production of consumer goods requires physical capital but the marginal returns on that capital decrease with capital accumulation. In other words, if we start with no equipment (zero machines), the addition of one machine boosts output sharply; by contrast, if we start with 100 machines, one additional machine will increase output only a small amount. According to this approach, growth in an advanced country, with a large stock of machines, will be weaker than that of a less-advanced country that has only a small stock of physical capital.

This explanation, attractive because of its simplicity, does not hold up to a more rigorous confrontation with empirical facts. First of all, if returns on capital are much higher in countries with little initial capital, these countries should always grow more quickly than wealthy countries. The explanation based on diminishing returns thus does not account for the deterioration in the standard of living in the poorest countries relative to the richest countries. Nor does it account for the phenomenon of club convergence. This point echoes what economists call the *Lucas paradox.* In a 1990 article, Robert Lucas observed that since the return on capital is supposed to be higher in less-advanced countries, we should see a flow of capital from rich countries to poor countries. But in fact the opposite happens.[8]

Furthermore, this approach based on diminishing returns from capital does not account for the *Argentine paradox,* that is, the fact that some countries enter a period of strong growth, holding the promise of convergence to the standard of living of the wealthiest countries, but then experience a reversal. Neither does it explain why some nations are overtaken by countries that are initially less advanced. For example, Australia's per capita GDP was far ahead of Canada's at the beginning of the twentieth century, but today the opposite is true.

Finally, taken literally, the Solow model of growth through capital accumulation predicts that a nation's economy will grow more and more slowly the more developed it becomes. Yet when we look at two consecutive decades selected randomly, the probability of faster annual growth of per capita GDP in the later decade was 50 percent greater in the OECD countries for the period 1700 to 1978.[9]

These considerations lead us to examine a second explanation for convergence, namely technological catch-up, more Schumpeterian than the theory based on diminishing returns. According to this paradigm, growth comes from innovation, but specifically the type of innovation consisting of firms in a less-advanced country "imitating" or "adapting" the cutting-edge technologies invented in the more advanced countries. In other words, convergence comes from less-advanced nations catching up to advanced nations by investing in technological imitation.

A number of authors have emphasized the importance of the diffusion of knowledge across national boundaries for the growth of productivity. International data for the period from 1971 to 1990 show in particular the beneficial impact on growth in one country of R&D investments in other countries.[10] A more recent study by Philippe Aghion, Antonin Bergeaud, Timothee Gigout, Matthieu Lequien, and Marc Melitz using patent data confirms the importance of knowledge diffusion across countries.[11] Figure 7.8 shows the evolution of the rate of citation of patents of a French firm that exports to a new country by non-French firms operating in that country. The date $t=0$ corresponds to the arrival of the French firm in the new foreign market. The graph shows clearly that citations of the French firm's patents by non-French firms operating in the new market start increasing after $t=0$. In other words, the intensity of technology transfer from this firm toward the foreign market increases when the firm enters this market.

We now examine whether this alternative approach, based on technological catch-up, accounts for the empirical facts mentioned above. First, with respect to the question of convergence "on average," the farther a country is behind the leader in terms of per capita GDP, the farther the firms in that country are from the technological frontier in the corresponding sector. As a result, the technological leap that these firms take when they imitate the frontier technology is all the greater. This is what we call the "advantage of backwardness." China grows faster than France because the technological leap Chinese firms make when they catch up with the technological frontiers is greater than the leap by French firms that innovate—the Chinese firms start farther behind than do the French firms.

What about club convergence? Innovation, whether imitation or frontier innovation, is a costly activity, especially in less-advanced countries where it is harder to hire researchers and skilled workers and to find funding for R&D investments. Innovation will thus not occur unless the rents from innovation are sufficiently high to compensate for these higher costs. In countries without ade-

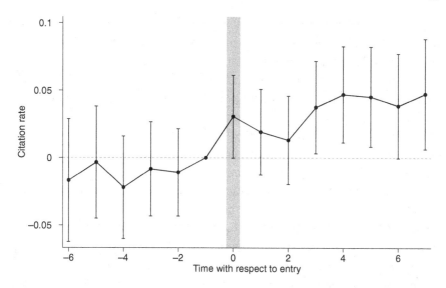

FIGURE 7.8. Citation rate of patents of a French firm exporting to a new country by non-French firms operating in the country.

Data source: P. Aghion, A. Bergeaud, T. Gigout, M. Lequien, M. Melitz, "Spreading Knowledge across the World: Innovation Spillover through Trade Expansion," unpublished manuscript, March 2019.

quate protection of property rights, the anticipated rents from innovation are too low to stimulate innovation. Excluded from club convergence, these nations are typically among the poorest. So even though the technological leap from each innovation tends to be greater in these less-advanced countries, their growth rate may end up being lower than the growth rate of advanced countries. Instead of converging toward levels of per capita GDP of advanced countries, poor countries with weak property-right protection end up stagnating.

2. Technological Catch-Up and Middle-Income Traps

Explaining the Middle-Income Trap

Why do some emerging countries start to grow rapidly toward the richest countries only to derail at some point and slide backward from the technological frontier? Our explanation is a variant of the technological catch-up model discussed earlier. In this variant, firms in all countries can choose between technological catch-up and frontier innovation, that is, innovating upon themselves. In less-advanced countries, where most firms are far below the technological frontier, catching up is the main source of growth because firms make a substantial technological leap whenever they catch up with the frontier. By contrast, in more advanced countries where most firms are initially close to the frontier in their sectors, frontier innovation becomes the main source of growth, because technological catch-up permits only a slight step forward for these firms.[12]

We can represent this argument graphically, as shown in Figure 7.9. The "catch-up policy" is represented by the line labeled "investment-based growth," and the policy that favors frontier innovation is represented by the line labeled "innovation-based growth." Figure 7.9 shows which policy gives rise to maximum growth and to the fastest convergence of a country to the technological frontier. The farther to the right a country is on this graph, the closer it is to today's technological frontier; the higher a country is, the closer it is to the technological frontier of tomorrow. The "investment-based growth" line shows the extent to which a country gets closer to the technological frontier between today and tomorrow if this country adopts the catch-up strategy. The "innovation-based growth" line shows the extent to which a country gets closer to the technological frontier between today and tomorrow if this country adopts the frontier innovation strategy. As long as a country is sufficiently far below today's technological frontier, namely below the "â" threshold, shown as a vertical line in the graphs, then the growth-maximizing strategy is the catch-up strategy, whereas if a country is sufficiently close to today's technological frontier, namely above the "â" threshold, then the growth-maximizing strategy is the innovation strategy. Thus, overall, the growth-maximizing strategy is represented by the bold segments in Figure 7.9a, with a kink at â. Unfortunately, many emerging countries begin by adopting technologies for catching up. But when the time comes to change course and adopt policies favoring innovation at the frontier—that is, to move from the investment-based growth line to the innovation-based growth line—instead these countries maintain pro–catch-up strategies and continue to follow the "catch-up" line (Figure 7.9b).

Why does this happen? The explanation is that frontier innovation policies may go against the interests of incumbent firms. A case in point is competition policy, which we analyzed in Chapter 4. Typically, firms that prospered during the catch-up phase want to preserve their rents and do not want to face increased competition. Accordingly, they will use some of their accumulated wealth to pressure politicians and judges to prevent the introduction and implementation of new, procompetitive rules. A very good example is Japan, where competition has always been strictly controlled by the state: the powerful METI (Ministry of the Economy, Trade, and Industry, formerly MITI), founded in 1949, limits the number of import licenses, and the state subsidizes investments by the large industrial-financial consortia known as *keiretsu*. Given the tight interpenetration of political power, administrative authorities, and the financial and industrial mi-

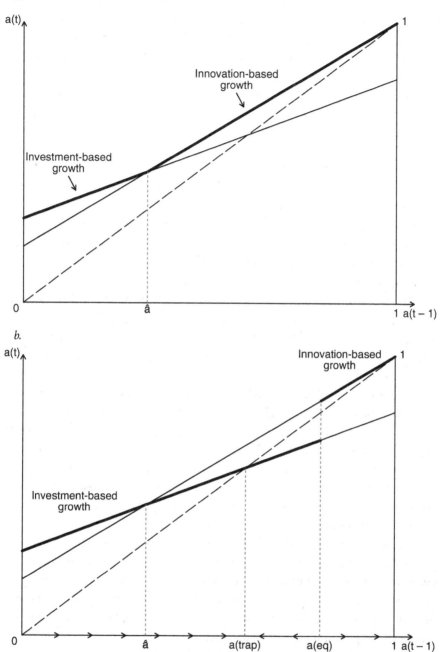

FIGURE 7.9. Distance from the frontier and growth. *a.* Growth-maximizing strategy.
b. Trap.

Reformatted from D. Acemoglu, P. Aghion, and F. Zilibotti, "Distance to Frontier, Selection, and Economic Growth,"
Journal of the European Economic Association *4, no. 1 (2006): 37–74, figures 2, 3.*

lieus, it is not surprising that Japan went from very strong growth, the envy of other developed nations between 1945 and 1985, to very weak growth since 1985.

Another striking example is South Korea, where the government deliberately promoted exports by supporting the growth of large conglomerates, the *chaebols*. But the decline of the *chaebols* with the 1998 financial crisis stimulated the entry of new innovative firms, and at the same time opened a path to structural reforms, which enabled South Korea to return to substantial growth after a brief slowdown, at least until 2003.

Frontier Innovation Policies and Catch-Up Policies

What are the policies that favor catch-up and what are the policies that favor frontier innovation?

We first examine the levers that foster frontier innovation. Frontier innovation comes above all from the knowledge economy, in particular from basic research and postgraduate education: no Silicon Valley without Stanford University. Indeed, the closer a country is to the technological frontier and thus the higher its standard of living, the greater the impact of investment in postgraduate education on productivity growth in that country.[13] By contrast, less-advanced countries should give priority to investment in primary and secondary education. This principle applies just as well between different regions within a country as it does between different countries. Thus Figure 7.10 shows that in American states close to the technological frontier, like Massachusetts and Connecticut, productivity growth is strongly stimulated by investment in basic research and postgraduate education. On the other hand, in less-advanced American states, such as Alabama and Mississippi, productivity growth is more strongly stimulated by investment in undergraduate education. And in fact, one can show that the closer an American state is to the technological frontier, the more investment in postgraduate education stimulates innovation, measured by the number of patents produced in that state.[14]

A second lever of growth "at the frontier" is competition on the market for goods and services, for at least two reasons. First of all, greater competition induces frontier firms to innovate in order to escape competition (see Chapter 4).[15] But the wealthier a country is, the more frontier firms it has; it follows that competition is a stronger growth lever in more advanced countries. Second, frontier innovation requires more creative destruction than does imitation: the exploration of new ideas is risky, and it is critical to facilitate the exit of those who do not succeed in order to make way for other potential innovators. Like Figure 7.2 above, Figure 7.11 looks at convergence "on average" but separates countries where competition is weak because barriers to entry are higher than average from coun-

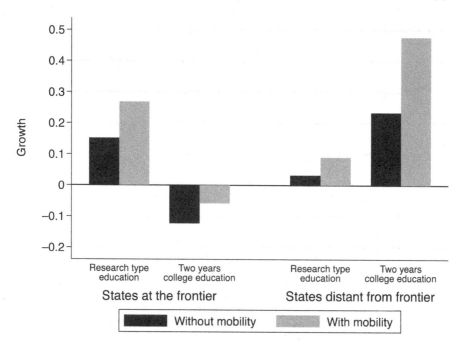

FIGURE 7.10. Growth and investment in education. *Note:* Effects on long-term growth of expenditure of USD 1,000 per person in education.

Data source: P. Aghion, L. Boustan, C. Hoxby, and J. Vandenbussche, "The Causal Impact of Education on Economic Growth: Evidence from U.S.," unpublished manuscript, 2009.

tries with strong competition because barriers to entry are lower than average.[16] The strength of entry barriers in a given country is measured by the number of days it takes to register a new firm in that country. Figure 7.11a focuses on countries with high entry barriers, and Figure 7.11b focuses on countries with low entry barriers. Within each graph, less-advanced countries are on the left, and more-advanced countries are on the right. Comparing the two graphs, we see that among the most advanced countries, those with high entry barriers (in Figure 7.11a) have substantially lower growth than advanced countries with low entry barriers (in Figure 7.11b). But this is not true for the least advanced countries: those with high entry barriers do not experience lower growth than those with low entry barriers.

One significant consequence of this interaction between the degree of development and the impact of competition on a nation's growth concerns corruption. The more corruption there is, the greater the ability of incumbent firms to pressure politicians to reduce competition and prevent the entry of new firms. We would thus expect corruption to inhibit growth more in advanced countries. That result is indeed what Figure 7.12 shows.[17]

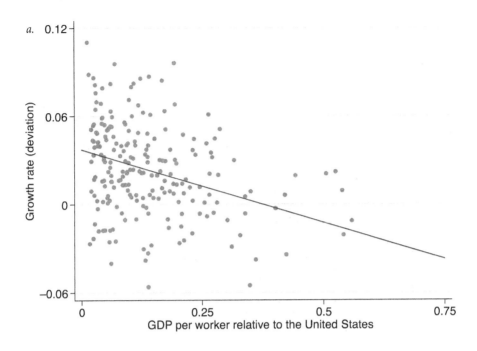

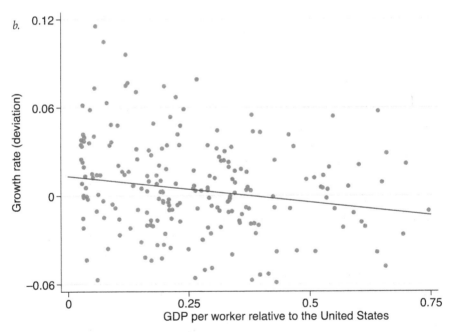

FIGURE 7.11. GDP per worker and GDP growth rate as a function of competition intensity. *a.* High entry barriers. *b.* Low entry barriers.

Reformatted from F. Zilibotti, "Growing and Slowing Down Like China," Journal of the European Economic Association 15, no. 5 (2017): 943–988, figures 5a, b.

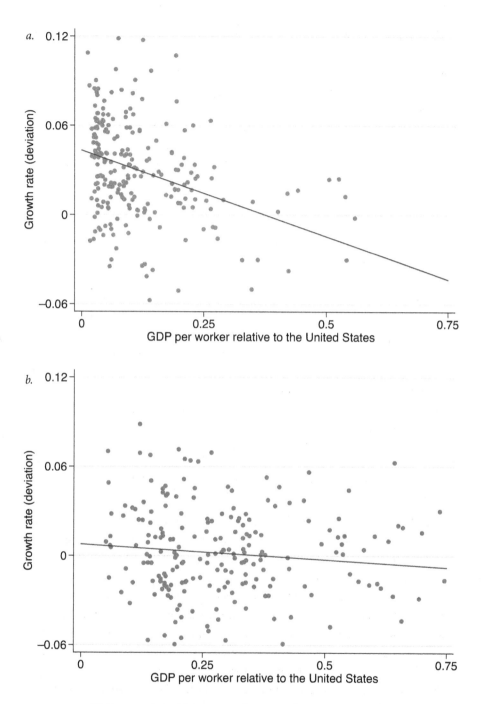

FIGURE 7.12. GDP per worker and GDP growth rate as a function of degree of corruption. *a.* High degree of corruption. *b.* Low degree of corruption.

Reformatted from F. Zilibotti, "Growing and Slowing Down Like China," Journal of the European Economic Association *15, no. 5 (2017): 943–988, figure 6a, b.*

A third lever of innovation-led growth relates to the organization of the financial system. The more advanced a country is—that is, the more its growth relies on frontier innovation—the more stock markets, private equity, and venture capital stimulate growth in that country. By contrast, in less-advanced countries that give priority to imitation, growth depends more on bank financing.[18]

We now turn to the levers of imitation-driven growth. A first lever is to promote technology transfers from more-advanced countries. In China, for example, the average level of education is far higher than that of comparable countries, such as Brazil or India. According to United Nations statistics from 2018, 78.6 percent of the Chinese population over the age of twenty-five has completed a secondary education, as compared to 59.5 percent of Brazilians and 51.6 percent of Indians. China achieved this degree of education by investing massively and over a long period in primary and secondary education and then again in the equivalent of the undergraduate level of education. In addition, Chinese authorities encouraged foreign direct investments and conducted tough negotiations to make sure they would have access to the knowledge embodied in the technologies developed in the context of these investments. China thus progressively gained access to cutting-edge Western technologies, which led to a substantial improvement in the quality of their patents, as demonstrated by recent developments in gene sequencing. This being said, China seems to have remained in an imitation mindset and is struggling to cross the threshold to frontier innovation (see Box 7.1).

BOX 7.1. GENE SEQUENCING: INTERNATIONAL DIFFUSION OF TECHNOLOGY

Cyril Verluise and Antonin Bergeaud relied on recent progress in machine learning, in particular "automated patent landscaping," to take a detailed look at gene sequencing.[1] The researchers' approach was to define the technology they are focusing on with reference to a small core of representative patents called a "seed" of patents. The next step was to "learn" the specific semantics of the seed by means of automated language processing. Finally, they carried out an automated exploration of the worldwide corpus of patents to find inventions with descriptions indicating tasks similar to those described in the "seed." Using this approach, Verluise and Bergeaud were able to follow a technology over time and space. In particular, they applied this method to gene sequencing. From a seed of 300 patents, they identified close to 16,000 patents published between the beginning of the 1990s and 2019 by the patent offices of the G7 nations and the large emerging nations. Although it is still too early to deduce

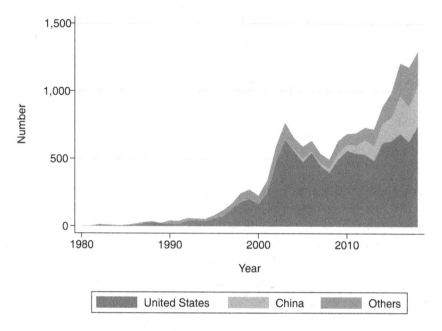

FIGURE 7.A. Main countries of origin of applicants for patents relating to gene sequencing.

Data source: C. Verluise and A. Bergeaud, "The International Diffusion of Technology: A New Approach and Some Facts," unpublished manuscript, 2019.

stylized facts about the international diffusion of a technology, this approach nonetheless reveals several pertinent facts in the case of gene sequencing.

Their first observation is that patents relating to gene sequencing are highly concentrated in a small number of countries and actors. Since the early 1990s, nearly 70 percent of patents on this technology have been granted by the US Patent Office (USPTO), with China a distant second (11 percent), followed by Japan (8 percent), and Canada (6 percent). In addition, although the number of patents granted by the USPTO took off in the beginning of the 2000s, this technology did not spread to China until the 2010s. From that time on, China caught up swiftly: in 2018 China represented nearly 20 percent of patents issued in the field (Figure 7.A). However, when we look at the origin of the inventors and patent agents, the picture looks quite different. Although the German, French, and British patent offices taken together delivered less than 3 percent of relevant patents over the entire period of the study, nationals of each of these countries were responsible for 2 to 3 percent of patents each year worldwide. They are thus overrepresented in relation to the patents registered in their countries of origin. Conversely, Chinese nationals are underrepresented. This contrast suggests that the dynamics at work behind the objective diffusion of patents internationally may be at odds with the real ability of domestic actors to appropriate a technology and expand its frontiers.

---

1. Cyril Verluise and Antonin Bergeaud, "The International Diffusion of Technology: A New Approach and Some Facts," unpublished manuscript, 2019. The quotation "automated patent landscaping" refers to Aron Abood and Dave Feltenberger, "Automated Patent Landscaping," *Artificial Intelligence and Law* 26, no. 2 (2018): 103–125.

A second lever of growth in less-advanced countries is the reallocation of resources. In China, firms that invest in R&D grow at the same rate as those that do not invest in R&D, regardless of their initial level of productivity. By contrast, in Taiwan, firms that invest in R&D experience stronger growth than those that do not, especially for the firms that are initially more productive. This comparison between China and Taiwan suggests that the allocation of R&D investments in China somewhat inhibits growth of the Chinese economy on the whole.

A third lever of imitation-based growth is the improvement of management skills. The best managers are those who can lead their firms to grow by identifying new activities and new technologies that they can import and adapt to local needs. The World Management Survey provides information on management practices from a wide sample of firms across the globe. The best-ranked countries with regard to managerial practices are the United States, followed closely by Japan, Germany, and Sweden (Figure 7.13). At the very bottom of the ranking are the African countries such as Tanzania, Ghana, or Ethiopia. Figure 7.13 shows that the least-advanced countries are those with the least effective management practices. This correlation suggests that investing in better management practices might stimulate growth.

Figure 7.14, produced by our colleagues Chang Tai Hsieh and Pete Klenow, depicts the distribution of productivity of Indian and American plants. The distribution of plant-level productivity appears to be more widely dispersed in India than in the United States, and the fraction of plants with low productivity is far greater in India than in the United States.[19] In Figure 7.15 we revisit data shown in Figure 1.5, which depicts the evolution of the average size of a plant as a function of its age for several countries. American plants continue to grow longer than Indian plants.[20]

These two graphs tell a story with significant consequences for the Indian economy as a whole. They suggest that the inability of Indian plants—even the most productive and innovative—to grow beyond a certain size allows unproductive

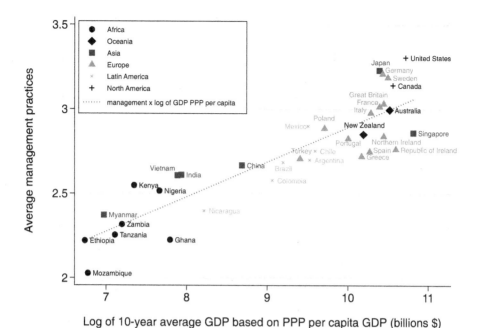

FIGURE 7.13. Growth and management practices.

Data source: World Management Survey (April 2013 version).

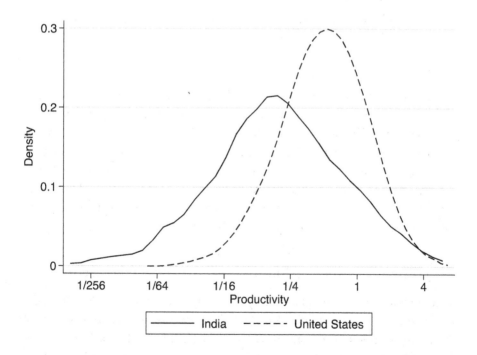

FIGURE 7.14. Distribution of plant productivity in India (1994) and the United States (1997).

Data source: C. T. Hsieh and P. J. Klenow, "Misallocation and Manufacturing TFP in China and India," Quarterly Journal of Economics 124, no. 4 (2009): 1403–1448.

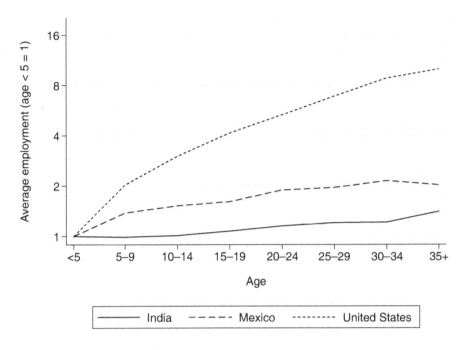

FIGURE 7.15. Plant size as a function of age.

Reformatted from C. T. Hsieh and P. J. Klenow, "The Life Cycle of Plants in India and Mexico," Quarterly Journal of Economics 129, no. 3 (2014): 1035–1084, figure IV.

plants to survive. But the net result is that there is less innovation in the aggregate, and therefore less productivity growth for the Indian economy as a whole. What hinders the growth of Indian plants? One reason might be that in most Indian firms, management remains within the family, because it is hard to find reliable managers. Thus the firm stops growing when the founding family runs out of family members capable of running new establishments. The thinness of the managerial market in India may in turn have to do with the low average level of education in India, flawed infrastructure, and the imperfections of the Indian credit market.[21]

3. The 1998 Crisis in South Korea: A Blessing in Disguise?

South Korea is an example of a country that escaped, at least for a while, from the middle-income trap syndrome.[22] Paradoxically, it was the Asian crisis of 1997–1998 that acted as a full-scale natural experiment, enabling South Korea to start transforming its growth model. The Korean model prior to the 1998 crisis, based on imitation, can be summarized in a few sentences. After emerging from the Korean

War in the late 1950s with a very low per capita GDP, South Korea grew at the exceptional rate of nearly 7 percent annually between 1960 and 1997.

Its imitation-based growth was structured around the creation of large industrial and financial conglomerates, the *chaebols*. The government supported the *chaebols* through a variety of means: preferential and subsidized access to credit, trade protectionism by means of currency devaluation, export subsidies, and explicit and implicit bailout guarantees. Above all, the government sought to limit competition and restrict the entry of new firms by limiting their access to the financial markets, by maintaining high costs of establishing new businesses, by regulating the entry of new foreign investors, who could not hold more than 26 percent of the shares of a Korean firm, and by very lax enforcement of antitrust regulations.

At the height of their prosperity, at the beginning of the 1990s, the thirty largest *chaebols* in terms of sales produced 16 percent of South Korea's GDP, and the five largest *chaebols*—Hyundai, Samsung, LG, Daewoo, and SK Group—accounted for 10 percent of GDP. These conglomerates, supported by the government, were the vectors of the rapid growth of the Korean economy from 1960 until 1995. Had it not made a deliberate choice to create a national industry by providing the *chaebols* with financial support and commercial and monetary protection, South Korea would have remained an agricultural economy. Instead, in the space of barely thirty years, South Korea became a world leader in electronics and in telecommunications.

Then came the Asian financial crisis of 1997 and 1998. The crisis led to the bankruptcy of some *chaebols,* such as Daewoo, and weakened those that managed to survive. This was a consequence both of the crisis and the resulting contraction of credit, and of the policies imposed by the IMF as a condition for its aid to South Korea. In particular, the IMF required South Korea to liberalize foreign direct investments. Accordingly, the maximum shareholding of foreigners in Korean firms increased from 26 to 50 percent in 1997, then to 55 percent in 1998. The IMF also insisted on a radical strengthening of antitrust laws as well as their meaningful enforcement: by 1998–2000, the number of corrective orders increased threefold from the level prior to the crisis, and the financial penalties for anticompetitive behavior increased by a factor of twenty-five, opening the Korean economy to national and international competition.

How did the 1997–1998 financial crisis affect productivity growth, innovation, and firm dynamics in South Korea? With respect to innovation, we note that at the beginning of the 1990s South Korea filed eight times fewer patent applications with the US Patent and Trademark Office (USPTO) than did Germany. In 2012, it filed 30 percent more applications than Germany despite having only half the population. Furthermore, whereas the number of patent applications filed by *chaebols* with the USPTO before the crisis grew slightly faster relative to their non-*chaebol* counterparts, the opposite was true after the crisis, when the number of patents filed by *chaebol* firms stopped growing, while patenting by non-*chaebol* firms accelerated.

With respect to productivity, whereas before the crisis productivity was stagnating or even falling, rapid productivity growth resumed after 1997–1998—both in *chaebol* and non-*chaebol* firms. This rebound in productivity and therefore in growth was particularly impressive in industries previously dominated by *chaebols*, which is unsurprising because these are the industries that were the most affected by the crisis and the subsequent reforms. In addition, the crisis significantly stimulated entry of non-*chaebol* firms in all industries.

All told, the 1997–1998 crisis, because it limited the influence of the *chaebols* and opened the economy to competition, seems to have stimulated productivity growth by encouraging innovation in non-*chaebol* firms, which until then had been inhibited by the complicity between the government and the *chaebols*. Thus the crisis generated an acceleration of productivity growth, essentially due to the entry and innovative activity of non-*chaebol* firms.[23]

4. Conclusion

In attempting in this chapter to explain why some developing countries converge to the standard of living of advanced countries while others stagnate, we revealed the phenomenon of club convergence: some countries have policies and institutions that foster technological catch-up and imitation—these are emerging countries—while others fail to take off. Among the countries that converge, some get stuck midstream. This is the case in particular for countries that are too slow—or fail altogether—to adapt their institutions to transform their economies from catch-up economies to frontier innovation economies. The reason for this is that vested interests and incumbent firms block not only the entry of new competitors but also any reform that would increase competition and more generally help the country move from imitation-led growth to growth driven by frontier innovation. The occurrence of a crisis as well as international economic competition helps nations to escape the middle-income trap syndrome by compelling the government to undertake the appropriate structural reforms. Thus, by weakening incumbent firms, the financial crisis of 1997–1998 opened Korean firms to competition and helped South Korea to enter the club of innovative countries.

CAN WE BYPASS INDUSTRIALIZATION?

The economic, territorial, and social landscape has undergone a radical transformation over the past two centuries. As we saw in Chapter 2, the takeoff of growth coincided with the successive transformations of England, France, and the United States from agricultural to industrial economies. More recently, however, manufacturing was in turn replaced by the services sector. In Napoleon's France, two out of three people in the French labor force worked in agriculture; in 2018, more than three-quarters worked in services. This creative destruction at the broad sectoral level is called *structural change*. The economist Simon Kuznets explained in his 1971 Nobel Lecture, "the rate of structural transformation of the economy is high. Major aspects of structural change include the shift away from agriculture to non-agricultural pursuits and, recently, away from industry to services."[1]

Figure 8.1 shows the evolution of the share of employment in the United States in agriculture, manufacturing, and services between 1840 and 2000. We see that the relative size of the agricultural sector decreased continuously after 1840, the share of the manufacturing sector increased until 1950 then declined, and the share of services increased continuously, with an acceleration after 1950. These structural changes in sectoral shares during the process of development are known as the Kuznets facts.

Paradoxically, these successive paradigm changes did not modify certain major economic variables that have remained astonishingly constant over time. The Kaldor facts—named after the economist Nicholas Kaldor—set out the principle of quasi-invariance of the shares of labor and capital in national income, as illustrated by Figure 8.2 for the United States between 1948 and 2012.

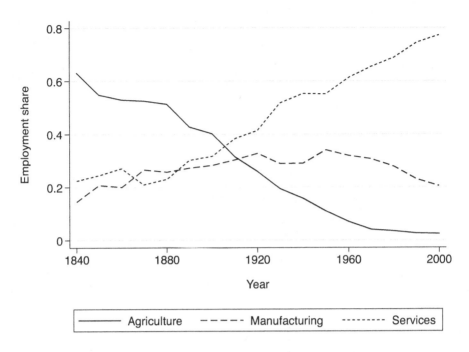

FIGURE 8.1. Share of US employment in agriculture, manufacturing, and services, 1840–2000.

Data source: B. Herrendorf, R. Rogerson, and A. Valentinyi, "Growth and Structural Transformation," in Handbook of Economic Growth, *ed. P. Aghion and S. Durlauf (Amsterdam: Elsevier, 2014), vol. 2, 855–941.*

FIGURE 8.2. Shares of labor and capital in US GDP.

Data source: Bureau of Labor Statistics (2014).

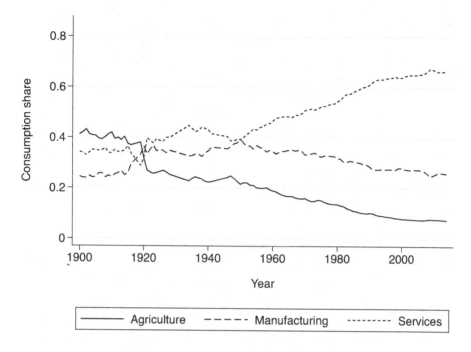

FIGURE 8.3. Sectoral composition of consumption spending in the United States.

Reformatted from S. Alder, T. Boppart, and A. Müller, "A Theory of Structural Change That Can Fit the Data," CEPR Discussion Paper No. 13469, Center for Economic Policy Research, January 2019, figure 1d.

How can we reconcile the Kuznets facts and the Kaldor facts? Is large-scale industrialization a necessary intermediate step in the process of development? These are the main questions we will address in this chapter.

1. Kuznets Facts and Kaldor Facts

Structural Change: The Kuznets Facts

Simon Kuznets (1901–1985) was one of the pioneers of national accounting, as we saw in Chapter 2. He is also known for his work on growth, business cycles, and economic development, among other subjects. In his Nobel Lecture, Kuznets summarized six characteristics of modern economic growth that had emerged from his analysis based on conventional measures of national product and its components. These six empirical regularities are known as the Kuznets facts. The third Kuznets fact is of particular interest to us here, namely that structural change entails an immutable process: first a transition from agriculture to industry, then a transition from industry to services. Furthermore, an important lesson from

Kuznets's work is that structural change in the process of development appears whether we take a historical approach, looking at the evolution within a country over time, or a comparative approach, looking at cross-country comparisons of per capita GDP.

According to the historical approach, three sectors successively gained economic prominence over time: agriculture, manufacturing, then services. Figure 8.3 confirms the structural change depicted in Figure 8.1, with the difference that Figure 8.3 shows the share of each of the three sectors in aggregate consumption rather than in employment.[2] This graph suggests that structural change is related to consumers' preferences and to their evolution over time. Figures 8.4 and 8.5, showing the evolution of the shares of the three sectors in French and British GDP since 1840, again confirm the Kuznets facts.[3]

Figure 8.6 takes a comparative approach. It shows the evolution of the shares of agriculture, manufacturing, and services in total employment, as a function of the standard of living in ten industrialized nations (Belgium, Spain, Finland, France, Japan, South Korea, the Netherlands, Sweden, the United Kingdom, and the United States). The standard of living is measured by per capita GDP using Maddison's data. In all of these countries, the share of agricultural employment declines as the standard of living rises (Figure 8.6a), and the share of the services sector in total employment rises continuously with the standard of living (Figure 8.6b). If we now focus on manufacturing employment as a share of total employment, we observe an inverted U curve: as the standard of living improves, the share of manufacturing employment in total employment rises at first, then declines (Figure 8.6c). A country with a low standard of living will thus have a large agricultural sector, but its manufacturing and services sectors will be far less developed. Conversely, in a country with a high standard of living, the majority of people will work in the services sector, hence once again the size of the manufacturing sector will be small, relatively speaking.

The Kaldor Facts

Nicholas Kaldor (1908–1986) became one of the leading post-Keynesian economists, after having adhered to neoclassical doctrine earlier in his career. As a professor at the University of Cambridge and an advisor to post–World War II Labour governments, he contributed to the development of economic theory on multiple subjects, ranging from imperfect competition to capital theory. Among other things, he won renown for his work on growth, productivity, and income distribution. In 1961, he published six stylized facts in which he observed that, over the long term, there is a quasi-invariance of the rate of

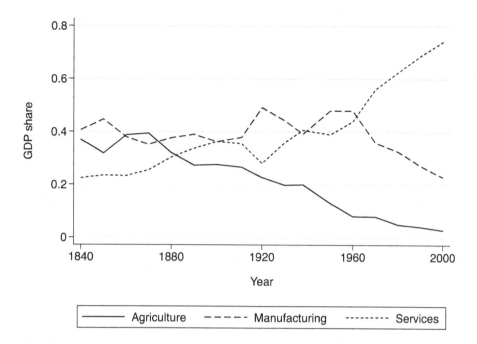

FIGURE 8.4. Sectoral composition of French GDP.

Data source: B. Herrendorf, R. Rogerson, and A. Valentinyi, "Growth and Structural Transformation," in Handbook of Economic Growth, *ed. P. Aghion and S. Durlauf (Amsterdam: Elsevier, 2014), vol. 2, 855–941.*

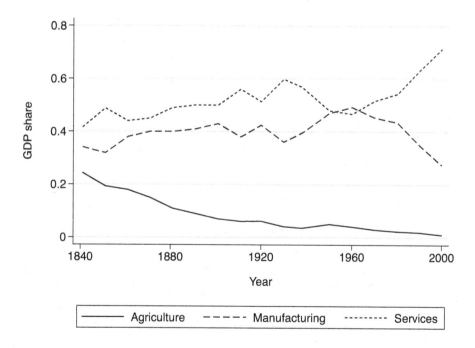

FIGURE 8.5. Sectoral composition of UK GDP.

Data source: B. Herrendorf, R. Rogerson, and A. Valentinyi, "Growth and Structural Transformation," in Handbook of Economic Growth, *ed. P. Aghion and S. Durlauf (Amsterdam: Elsevier, 2014), vol. 2, 855–941.*

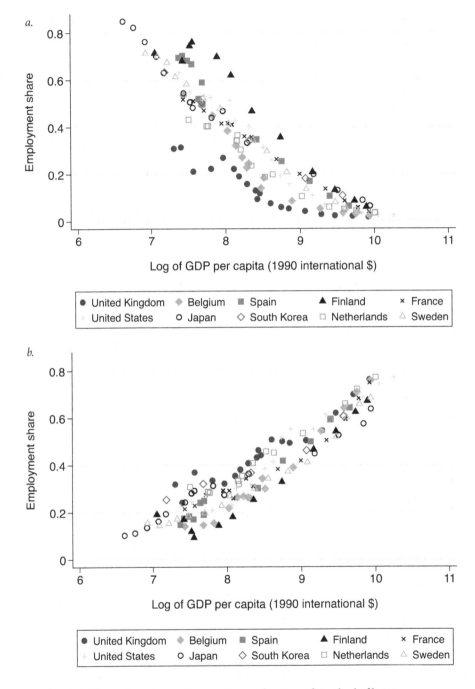

a.

Employment share

b.

Employment share

Log of GDP per capita (1990 international $)

● United Kingdom   ◆ Belgium   ■ Spain   ▲ Finland   × France
⁺ United States   ○ Japan   ◇ South Korea   □ Netherlands   △ Sweden

FIGURE 8.6. Share of employment per sector as a function of standard of living.
a. Agriculture. *b.* Services. *c.* Manufacturing.

Extracted and reformatted from B. Herrendorf, R. Rogerson, and A. Valentinyi, "Growth and Structural Transformation," in Handbook of Economic Growth, *ed. P. Aghion and S. Durlauf (Amsterdam: Elsevier, 2014), vol. 2, 855–941, figure 6.1.*

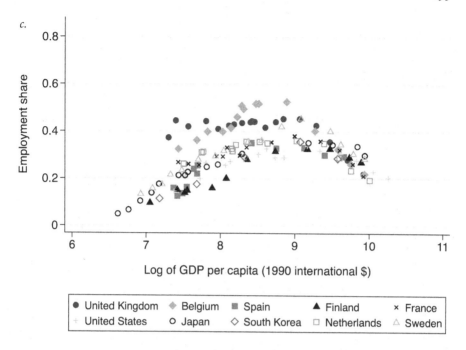

FIGURE 8.6. (*continued*)

return on capital, of the share of capital in GDP, and of the shares of capital and labor in national income.[4] In 1955, he wrote, "No hypothesis as regards the forces determining distributive shares could be intellectually satisfying unless it succeeds in accounting for the relative stability of these shares in the advanced capitalist economies over the last 100 years or so, despite the phenomenal changes in the techniques of production, in the accumulation of capital relative to labor and in real income per head."[5] Thus, Figure 8.7 and Figure 8.8 show the quasi-invariance of the rate of return on capital in the United Kingdom between 1770 and 2010 and in France between 1820 and 2010.[6] Figure 8.9 shows the quasi-invariance of the share of capital in GDP in the United States between 1948 and 2012.

Finally, we see a slight increase in the share of labor and a slight decline in the share of capital in national income, both in the United Kingdom between 1770 and 2012 (Figure 8.10a) and in France between 1820 and 2010 (Figure 8.10b). This observation is in line with Figure 8.2, which showed the quasi-invariance of the shares of labor and capital over the long term in the United States.[7]

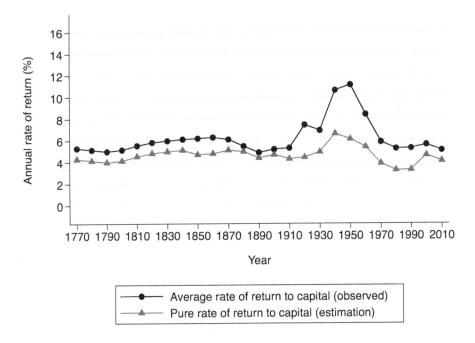

FIGURE 8.7. Return to capital in the United Kingdom, 1770–2010.

T. Piketty, Capital in the Twenty-First Century (Cambridge, MA: Harvard University Press, 2014), figure 6.3. Copyright ©
2014 by the President and Fellows of Harvard College.

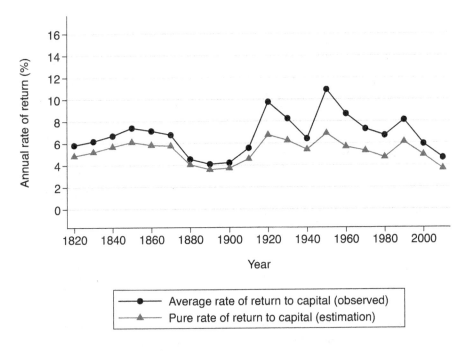

FIGURE 8.8. Return to capital in France, 1820–2010.

T. Piketty, Capital in the Twenty-First Century (Cambridge, MA: Harvard University Press, 2014), figure 6.4. Copyright ©
2014 by the President and Fellows of Harvard College.

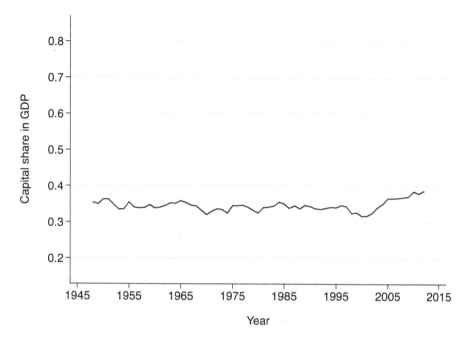

FIGURE 8.9. Share of capital in US GDP.

Data source: Bureau of Labor Statistics (2014).

2. Explaining the Kuznets Facts

In Chapter 2, we sought to explain the transition of economies from the agricultural phase to the industrial phase. In particular, we cited Joel Mokyr and his analysis of the role of industrial innovation, made possible by the conjunction of three factors: the Enlightenment and the improved diffusion of knowledge, especially due to more efficient postal services, an expansion of the press, and a better codification of knowledge with Diderot's *Encyclopédie*; improved protection of property rights, in particular the appearance of patents; and competition among European countries that stimulated innovation in order to surpass the neighbors and that also enabled any inventor experiencing abusive constraints in his own country to seek refuge in a neighboring country. This institutional explanation emphasizes the "supply" side of the market, in other words the conditions that favor innovation by making it easier and less costly. It disregards, however, a second, equally important pillar, namely the role of demand and consumption.

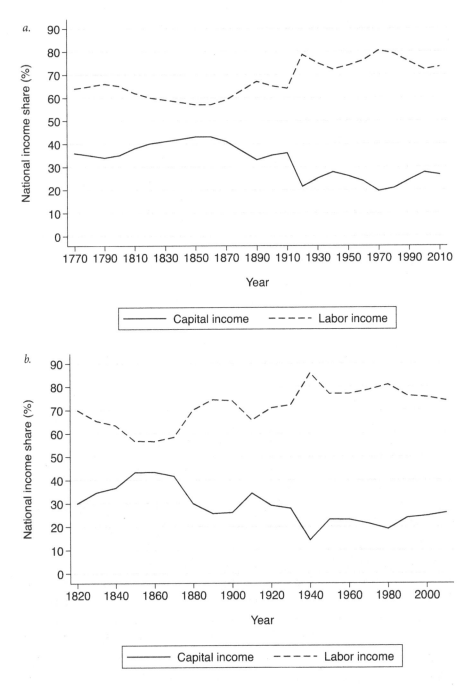

FIGURE 8.10. Shares of labor and capital in national income in the United Kingdom and France. *a.* United Kingdom. *b.* France.

T. Piketty, Capital in the Twenty-First Century *(Cambridge MA: Harvard University Press, 2014), figures 6.1, 6.2.*
Copyright © 2014 by the President and Fellows of Harvard College.

Demand Side and Supply Side

What explains the emergence of the services sector, which resulted in a decline in both agricultural and manufacturing production since the 1950s? The answer lies in both the "supply" and the "demand" sides of the market, and the leading reference on this subject is Timo Boppart's 2014 study.[8]

Boppart examines the evolution of the consumer market basket over time. In other words, he looked at the choices that households make between consuming agricultural and manufactured goods on the one hand and services on the other. Two forces contribute to consumers spending a greater share of their income on services over time. On the demand side, consumers enjoy an "income effect": as a household's standard of living increases, the percentage of income that it devotes to essential goods, food in particular, decreases. On the supply side, there is a "substitution effect": costs of production of agricultural and manufactured goods drop more quickly than those of services. Since firms pass these savings on by lowering prices, prices of agricultural and manufactured goods tend to decrease more than those of services. As a result, households spend more and more on services.

Three Empirical Facts to Be Explained

Timo Boppart demonstrates three significant empirical facts.[9] First, the share of agricultural and manufactured goods in household spending decreases at a constant rate over time (Figure 8.11a); this fact remains valid within each income quintile taken separately (Figure 8.11b). The price of goods relative to the price of services also decreases at a constant rate over time (Figure 8.11c). Finally, at every point in time, poor households spend a bigger portion of their budgets on goods than do wealthy households (Figure 8.11b).

The empirical facts described in these graphs relate to the United States, but the other developed nations experience similar trends. To interpret them, Timo Boppart looks to two major economic forces: Baumol's law on the supply side, and Engel's law on the demand side.

The Supply Side and Baumol's Law

William Baumol (1922–2017) was an American neoclassical economist whose prolific research pertained to numerous fields, including entrepreneurship and competition. One of his most famous contributions is known as Baumol's law, or Baumol's cost disease.[10] To understand this law, consider two products, A and B, the supply of which does not grow at the same rate over time, perhaps because labor productivity grows faster in the sector that produces A than in the sector that produces B. Due to a scarcity effect, the price of B, the product whose supply

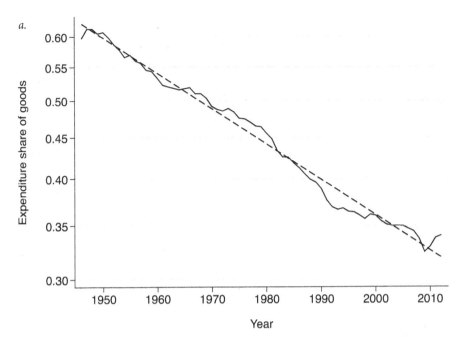

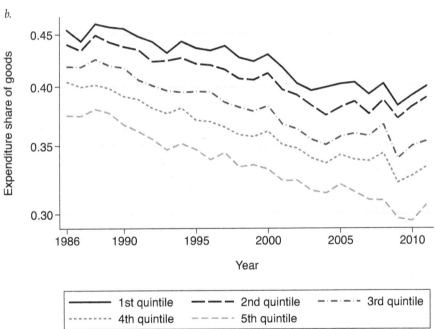

| ── 1st quintile | ─ ─ ─ 2nd quintile | ─ · ─ · ─ 3rd quintile |
| · · · · · · 4th quintile | ─ ─ ─ 5th quintile | |

FIGURE 8.11. Three empirical facts. *a.* Expenditure share of goods. *b.* Expenditure share of goods as a function of household income. *c.* Relative price of goods and services.

Reformatted from T. Boppart, "Structural Change and the Kaldor Facts in a Growth Model with Relative Price Effects and Non-Gorman Preferences," Econometrica 82, no. 6 (2014): 2167–2196, figures 1, 4, 2.

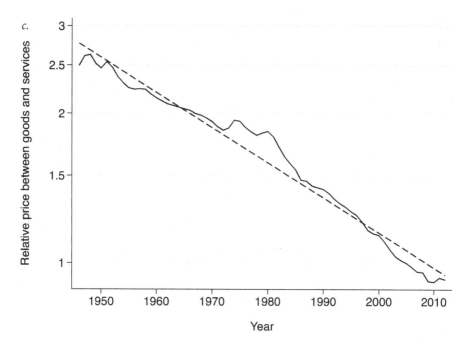

FIGURE 8.11. (*continued*)

grows slowly, will necessarily increase relative to the price of product *A*, the product in faster-growing supply. Accordingly, even if economic actors—households or firms—decide to consume greater amounts of product *A*, the share of their income allocated to product *B* will not necessarily decrease and may even increase, because of the increase in the relative price of product *B* compared to *A*. In other words, faster growth of productivity in sector *A* may lead to a greater share of income going to the purchase of product *B*.

We now return to our examination of the agricultural and manufacturing sectors on the one hand and the services sector on the other. Thanks to economies of scale and to automation, the agricultural and manufacturing sectors have experienced substantial gains in productivity over time. By contrast, the services sector has not had the same gains in productivity because these activities—such as culture, leisure, real estate services, education, and childcare—are less able to benefit from economies of scale. In addition, labor remains the preponderant input in these activities. To illustrate the weak productivity of labor in services, we look to an example in the field of art: a Schubert quartet. The number of musicians needed to perform this piece has not changed from the nineteenth century through today. Furthermore, the "return" on a violinist who performs this quartet cannot be increased. In the same way, there are limits to a theater company's ability to reduce the number of actors needed to perform a Shakespeare play so as to increase productivity. Hence, labor productivity in classical music and in theater has barely increased, as the human factor remains essentially irreducible.[11]

At the same time, to continue to attract the labor force, employers in the services sector have had to increase wages at the same rate as those in the goods-producing sectors. The resulting growth in wages combined with slower productivity growth in the services sector has led to an increase in the cost of production of services relative to the cost of production of goods. Since the costs of production are passed on to prices, the relative price of services has increased compared to the price of goods (Figure 8.11c). To return to the example of the Schubert quartet, the salaries of musicians have increased in real terms since the nineteenth century with no increase in their productivity. As the increase in labor costs cannot be offset by an increase in productivity, and the human factor remains indispensable, the result is a continual increase in the price of tickets. Art and culture thus suffer from Baumol's cost disease.

But this reasoning, based on supply and Baumol's law, does not explain why the share of household budgets allocated to goods decreases over time (Figure 8.11a), nor does it explain why, at any point in time, wealthier households devote a smaller fraction of their budgets to consuming goods than do poorer households (Figure 8.11b). This is where the demand side and Engel's law come into play.

The Demand Side and Engel's Law

Engel's law is an empirical regularity pointed out in 1857 by the German statistician Ernst Engel (1821–1896) based on his observation of the behavior of Belgian families.[12] This law states that the higher a family's income, the smaller the share of its budget allocated to food. Indeed, goods, in particular agricultural goods, are essential for survival and will therefore necessarily be included in the market basket, regardless of the size of the household's budget. Services, on the other hand, are less essential, and will not be in the market basket unless the household's budget exceeds a certain threshold. Consequently, the wealthier the household, the smaller the fraction of its budget allocated to essential goods (such as food and clothing) and the greater the fraction allocated to services (such as culture and travel).[13] Figure 8.12, like Figure 18.1c, illustrates the decrease in the share of household income allocated to food as income increases. Data from French surveys confirm Engel's law.

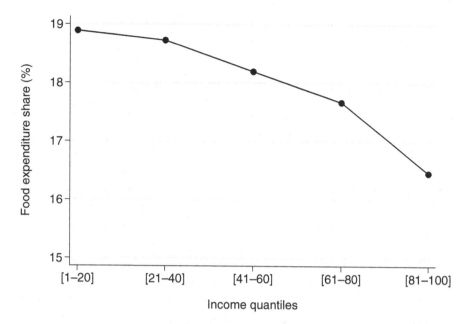

FIGURE 8.12. Share of household spending allocated to food in France, as a function of income quintile.

Data source: Insee survey Budget de famille, *2010–2011.*

Solving the Kuznets Facts Enigma

Why does the share of household budgets devoted to consumer goods decrease over time? First of all, Baumol's law shows that the price of goods decreases over time relative to the price of services, which should encourage people to purchase more goods; on the other hand, the increase in the relative price of services should automatically increase the fraction of household budgets spent on services. Which of these two effects dominates?

The combination of Engel's law and Baumol's law allows us to solve this enigma. First, Baumol's law implies that the price of goods relative to the price of services should decrease over time since productivity in the goods sector increases faster than productivity in the services sector. This decrease in the price of goods relative to services should encourage households to purchase more goods, everything else remaining equal. However, the decrease in the price of goods increases households' purchasing power; in other words it makes households wealthier. This is the income effect. Being wealthier, households can consume more of both goods and services. But then Engel's law comes into play: it implies that the income effect increasingly favors the consumption of services as purchasing power rises. Thus, over time, the share of spending devoted to services increases.

3. Reconciling Structural Change with the Kaldor Facts

How can we reconcile the Kuznets facts—which state that there is more intense technological progress in the manufacturing sector than in the services sector and that consumption evolves toward services—with the Kaldor facts, which show that the shares of capital and labor in total income remain constant? This question also arises with respect to technological revolutions, for example artificial intelligence: how can we reconcile the occurrence of these revolutions with the observation that capital and labor represent near-constant shares of income?

Indeed, in both cases, structural change leads to the substitution of capital for labor in existing production (production of agricultural and manufactured goods in the first case and the automation of existing tasks in the second case), and the potential introduction of new, more labor-intensive activities (the production of new services in the first case and potential new tasks in the second case).

We will examine two solutions to this enigma. The first relies on the notions of market size and directed technical change; the second once again makes use of Baumol's law. We begin by introducing the notion of technical change *directed* toward skilled workers, then apply this notion to attempt to reconcile structural change and the Kaldor facts.

Market Size and Directed Technical Change

The central idea can be summarized as follows: when the size of a market grows, firms find it profitable to direct innovation toward this market in order to respond to the increased demand.[14] Several examples illustrate this idea.

The baby boom and wage inequality provide a first example. In the beginning of the 1970s, the baby boom generation entered the labor market in the United States. This generation was more educated than the preceding generation, largely due to Lyndon Johnson's Higher Education Act, which provided massive federal support to a variety of programs helping Americans of all income levels to obtain college degrees. As a result, the supply of skilled workers increased rapidly in 1970. In the short term, this overabundance of skilled labor led to a decrease in the skill premium, that is, the ratio between the wages of individuals with college degrees and those of individuals with only a high school degree.[15] In other words, in 1970 there was a decrease in the gap between the wages of skilled and unskilled workers, which continued until the end of the 1970s (Figure 8.13). But why did the skill premium explode starting in the early 1980s?

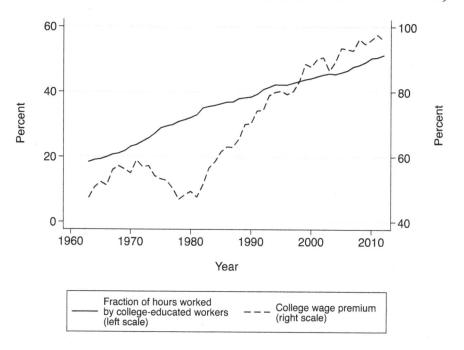

FIGURE 8.13. Supply of skilled labor and skill premium.

Extracted and reformatted from D. Autor, "Skills, Education, and the Rise of Earnings Inequality among the 'Other 99 Percent,'" Science 344, no. 6186 (2014): 843–851, figure 3.

Daron Acemoglu proposes the following explanation: The sudden increase in the supply of skilled labor in 1970 expanded the size of the market for machines used by skilled workers. This in turn increased the rents from innovating on these machines. As a consequence, innovation became targeted more toward improving the quality of machines used by skilled workers, thereby increasing the productivity of skilled labor relative to the productivity of unskilled labor. This would explain the increased wage inequality between skilled and unskilled workers as of the early 1980s in the United States.[16]

A second illustration involves the carbon tax and green innovation. We will see in Chapter 9 that firms do not spontaneously direct innovation toward green technologies, such as producing electric cars. The more a firm has innovated in polluting activities in the past, the more it tends to innovate in the same activities today. This phenomenon is known as path dependence. However, various studies have shown that an increase in carbon price, for example due to an increase in the carbon tax, redirects innovation toward green technologies.[17] The explanation is simple: an increase in carbon price increases consumer demand for environmentally friendly products, thereby increasing the size of the market for those products. This in turn increases the rents from innovation on environmentally friendly products; therefore firms will innovate more in these products.

Directed Innovation and the Kaldor Facts[18]

How does the concept of directed innovation enable us to reconcile structural change—the Kuznets facts—with the Kaldor facts?

We have seen that the growth in labor productivity is stronger in the sectors of agricultural and manufactured goods than in the services sector because of greater automation in the production of goods than in the production of services. The substitution of capital for labor frees up the labor force and at the same time pushes wages downward. All other things being equal, this means the share of labor in income decreases, as labor becomes a less indispensable input to production.

However, this effect is offset by a *directed innovation* effect, which can be understood as follows. The decline in labor cost due to the substitution of capital for labor in the goods sectors increases the rents from innovation directed at new services: the production of services relies more on labor, so that a decline in wages increases the profitability of a new service activity. As a result, there will be more innovation directed toward creating new services. This innovation will itself have two implications. The first is that the services sector will grow. This is an alternative—or complementary—explanation of the Kuznets facts, one that does not rely on Engel's law. The second is that the expansion of the services sector will increase the demand for labor. This increase will in turn push wages upward, thereby restoring the share of labor in income.

The Explanation Based on Baumol's Law

Another way to reconcile the Kuznets facts with the Kaldor facts starts with the idea that labor is an indispensable input in the production of goods and services.[19] Suppose, for example, that the production of consumer goods utilizes multiple different inputs, all of which are indispensable. Each input is produced either by labor, if the corresponding production activity is not automated, or by capital if it is automated. Further suppose that, thanks to the digital revolution, automation affects the production of an increasing number of inputs over time. More precisely, suppose that at each moment in time a constant fraction of inputs previously produced with labor are now produced with capital, thanks to automation.

Two offsetting effects are at work in this type of economy. On the one hand, in volume, capital constitutes an ever-increasing fraction of production inputs with the expansion of automation. As a result, all other things being equal, the share of capital in income will increase over time. This is the *quantity effect*. On the other hand, the accumulation of capital increases the relative scarcity of labor. However, labor remains an indispensable factor of production, since there is always a portion of inputs whose production requires labor, and furthermore all inputs are indispensable to the production of consumer goods. As a result, over time the price of labor will continually increase relative to the price of capital. This is Baumol's cost disease effect; it is a *price effect*. As a result of these two offsetting effects, the shares of capital and labor in income may well remain constant over time despite structural change induced by automation.

4. Is Industrialization a Necessary Phase in the Development Process?

Is two-step structural change—from an agricultural economy to a manufacturing economy and then from a manufacturing economy to a service economy—the archetype of any development process? Or rather is it possible to skip the industrialization phase? This question is especially crucial for nations whose economies are still predominantly agricultural. These nations might thus bypass the industrialization phase, thereby inaugurating a new model of development.

Ghana and South Korea

In a 2012 article, the economist Joseph Stiglitz used the comparison between Ghana and South Korea to extol the virtues of industrialization as a pillar of economic development.[20] In 1960, both of these nations were essentially agricultural with very similar levels of per capita GDP: $944 in South Korea and $1,056 in Ghana, in 2010 dollar equivalents. What accounts for the fact that in 2010 the per capita GDP in South Korea had grown by a factor of nearly twenty-three, reaching $22,087, while Ghana's per capita GDP had not exceeded $1,298?[21]

Stiglitz's response is that South Korea would have experienced the same evolution as Ghana if it had focused on its comparative advantage in 1960, namely rice production. In other words, without the proactive policy of successive governments over sixty years to develop a national industrial sector, South Korea would perhaps be the most efficient producer of rice in the world today, but its per capita GDP would not have taken off. South Korea would not have become a world leader, first in electronics and then in semiconductors. We will, however, return to the example of Ghana, which has experienced strong economic development since 2010.

Why Does Industrialization Favor Economic Development?

Does the comparison between Ghana and South Korea suffice to establish that industrialization is an indispensable phase in economic development? Other factors can explain the Korean success story, in particular the establishment of inclusive institutions that foster growth by technological catch-up.[22] Thus the protection of property rights, massive investment in education, and a proactive policy to support the development of large national leaders by means of subsidized credit, state procurement contracts, and export subsidies played a key role in the South Korean takeoff.

Why should a nation look to manufacturing, rather than the agricultural or services sectors, to accelerate growth in order to converge more rapidly toward western standards of living? Several arguments support the view that industrial development is an unavoidable step in the development process.

One argument is that manufacturing, more than other sectors, is at the heart of the value chain. More specifically, industrialization in one sector stimulates growth in related sectors, both upstream and downstream. An example of an upstream linkage is a plant manufacturing DVDs, which induces the development of an industry for DVD players and a multimedia industry more broadly. An example of a downstream linkage is the construction of a milk-processing plant that induces the development of ice cream factories.

A second argument is that industrialization can generate the production of knowledge through learning by doing, and this knowledge can then spread to the other sectors of the economy, namely the agriculture and services sectors, thereby fostering growth in the economy as a whole. In particular, industrial progress leads to the modernization of agriculture, whereas progress in agriculture has little impact on productivity growth in manufacturing.

These technological externalities between industry and the other branches of a nation's economy are what led Joseph Stiglitz and other economists to return to the arguments of Friedrich List on "educational protectionism."[23] In the nineteenth century, List argued for temporary protectionist policies against foreign competition to allow national infant industries to develop. Protecting domestic industries in the initial stages of their development enables them to catch up with the world frontier in terms of economies of scale or productivity. They can thereby enrich and increase their knowledge and their domestic expertise, which can then spread to nonindustrial sectors of the economy.[24] This reasoning implicitly assumes that the other sectors—agriculture and services—do not have the same capacity to generate knowledge and expertise, and that the knowledge they generate does not have the same capacity to spread throughout the economy.

A third argument is that exports are a powerful lever of growth because foreign demand motivates domestic firms to grow, as we will see in more detail in Chapter 13. But in countries like South Korea and the Southeast Asian tigers, foreign demand has been essentially for industrial products.

A fourth argument is that industrialization induces better institutional development. For example, the development of the Korean *chaebols* facilitated the development of credit institutions, the construction of infrastructure, and the establishment of procurement policies and policies promoting exports. These institutions and policies in turn contributed greatly to the takeoff of the Korean economy and to its technological catch-up, even if they subsequently became an obstacle to growth, as we discussed in Chapter 7.

Finally, advocates of industrialization point out that industry promotes urbanization, and urbanization in turn induces faster catch-up- and innovation-led growth. In particular, urbanization makes it possible to take advantage of scale economies in the creation of new infrastructures and new institutions; it also enables economic actors to interact more intensely, which fosters the exchange of ideas and the emergence of new ideas.

There is abundant empirical evidence supporting industrialization as a factor of growth and development. In addition to the example of the developed countries, all of which went through an industrialization phase, we have the example of the Southeast Asian dragons and more recently the tigers. And China provides another example: its economic takeoff since the end of the 1970s closely coincided with its industrial development. Nonetheless, is industrialization truly indispensable for economic development?

Service-Led Growth: The Singular Example of India

The comparison of the two heavyweights, India and China, is interesting on a number of counts. These economies are of comparable size, and both are experiencing strong growth rates, even if China has grown nearly twice as fast as India: between 1990 and 2018 the annual growth rate of China's per capita GDP reached an average of 8.8 percent, compared to 4.7 percent in India, according to World Bank figures. Yet there is a significant difference between these two nations: again according to the World Bank, in 2018 the manufacturing sector represented 41 percent of China's GDP and only 27 percent of India's GDP.

Is India's weak level of industrialization compared to China responsible for its slower growth? There are many indications that India's fate is far from a lost cause.[25]

First of all, the increase in India's per capita GDP coincided with stagnation of the share of manufacturing in total employment and a significant increase in the share of services. These empirical findings are consistent with the idea that India's current development relies more on services than on manufacturing. This view is reinforced by the two figures below. Figure 8.14 allows us to refine the analysis by district. Indian districts are divided into four categories according to their average per capita GDP. The first quartile (Q1) corresponds to the quarter of districts with the lowest per capita GDP, and the fourth quartile (Q4) corresponds to the quarter of districts with the highest per capita GDP. This figure shows how the employment shares of agriculture, manufacturing, services, construction, and utilities in total employment compare between 1987 (Figure 8.14a) and 2011 (Figure 8.14b). Services account for most of the difference between the wealthiest districts (Q4) and the poorest (Q1) in both of these periods. Furthermore, the comparison between 1987 and 2011 shows that in 2011 services were dominant in the wealthiest districts, unlike in 1987, when agriculture dominated.

Finally, this research shows a positive correlation between the growth rate of per capita GDP and the growth rate of the share of services in GDP. What explains this relationship? One possible explanation is based on Engel's law but takes innovation into account. The increase in the standard of living as development progresses induces an expansion in the demand for services and therefore an expansion of the services sector. The resulting growth of the size of the market for services increases the potential rents from innovation in the services sector. Consequently, there is an acceleration of innovation in services, which stimulates per capita GDP growth in the district.

Overall, although we continue to believe in the virtues of industrialization, services also constitute a potential lever of growth that should not be overlooked. If further empirical analyses confirm this conclusion, it would be a source of hope for many poor nations that have remained predominantly agricultural and wish to progress without necessarily traversing an intensive phase of industrialization. It would also be favorable from an environmental standpoint, in light of the impact of increased industrialization on global warming: indeed, current estimates suggest that if we exclude transport, CO_2 emissions by the services sector are four times lower than CO_2 emissions by the manufacturing sector worldwide.

We began this section with a historical comparison between South Korea and Ghana, to South Korea's advantage. However, since 2010, the annual growth rate of Ghana's GDP has been extremely high, reaching 11 percent in 2011. In the late 2000s and the early 2010s, most of Ghana's development was in the services sector. Once again, we find an example of a country that seems to be able to follow a service-led development strategy, thereby avoiding the need for a mass industrialization stage. Why did Ghana do better in the late 2000s than in the 1960s? One major difference between these two periods relates to globalization, which accel-

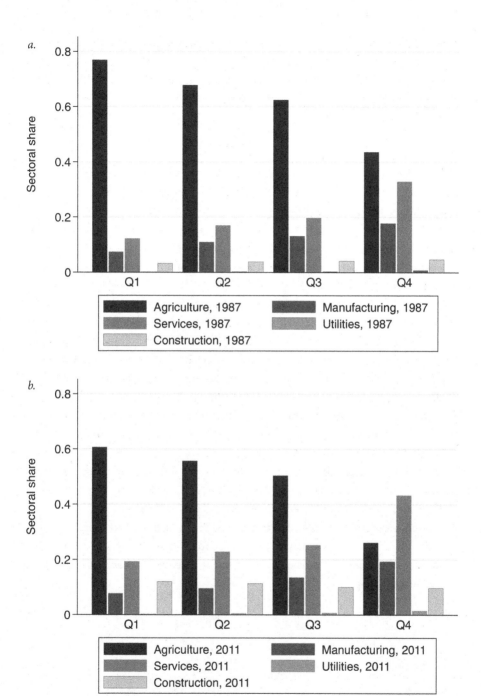

FIGURE 8.14. Employment share by sector in India as a function of income. *a.* 1987. *b.* 2011.

Data source: T. Fan, M. Peters, and F. Zilibotti, "Service-Led or Service-Biased Growth? Equilibrium Development Accounting across Indian Districts," unpublished manuscript, August 2020.

erated during the 1980s. Today, globalization and the international division of labor enable services-producing countries to import more manufactured goods and, in exchange, to export services or services bundled with goods. This creates a stronger incentive to innovate in the services sector.

5. Conclusion

Kuznets described the structural change of an economy over the course of its evolution as a two-step sequence. In the first step agricultural development gives way to industrial development. In the second step, industry is succeeded by services. We saw that in order to understand this process we must take into account supply factors—namely, changes in relative prices between goods and services—as well as demand factors induced by the evolution of income and consumer preferences over time.

Is the industrial phase unavoidable? On the one hand, some economists, such as Dani Rodrik, stress the role of manufacturing in the development of institutions, in urbanization, and in the transmission of technological knowledge throughout the economy.[26] On the other hand, India provides an interesting counterexample of a nation that based its development on services, thereby offering an alternative model of development that potentially enables countries that are still predominantly agricultural to avoid the mass industrialization phase. The future will tell us if this alternative model, with the benefit of globalized trade, the digital revolution, and innovation in services, will truly succeed. A further virtue of this model of direct transition to a service-led economy is the effect on the environment. As we saw above, if we exclude the transportation sector, services generate four times fewer CO_2 emissions than manufacturing worldwide. As a result, enabling nations or continents to skip the mass industrialization phase is undoubtedly an effective way to reconcile growth and protection of the environment at the global scale. The environment and green innovation are precisely the subject of Chapter 9.

GREEN INNOVATION AND
SUSTAINABLE GROWTH

As early as the 1970s, the depletion of natural resources had become a significant concern for economic observers and decision makers. The Meadows report, which presented the findings of a group of MIT researchers commissioned by the Club of Rome in 1970, concluded that it was imperative to end the period of growth sparked by the Industrial Revolution in 1820 and to resign ourselves to a path of zero growth: "Given the finite and diminishing stock of nonrenewable resources and the finite space of our globe, the principle must be generally accepted that growing numbers of people will eventually imply a lower standard of living—and a more complex problematique."[1]

More recently, attention to another phenomenon has reinforced the view that stagnation is unavoidable. This phenomenon is global warming due to greenhouse gas emissions. In his inspiring work *Le climat après la fin du mois,* Christian Gollier explains with clarity that until the beginning of the nineteenth century, the concentration of carbon in the atmosphere was stable, at levels below 280 parts per million (ppm).[2] The oceans and plant photosynthesis were able to absorb the carbon dioxide generated by human activity. But the industrial takeoff starting in 1820 and the massive exploitation of coal that followed destabilized this balance: from 280 ppm at the outset of the last century, the atmospheric concentration of carbon dioxide has grown steadily, reaching 410 ppm in 2018. This rapid increase in CO_2 levels created a greenhouse effect, which has caused substantial global warming. Global warming has multiple consequences for the environment: more frequent and more severe droughts, wildfires, and floods, as well as a significant decrease in biodiversity. Global warming also has an impact on human activity, with increased mortality from climate-related natural disasters as well as a significant decrease in productivity during heat waves.

The depletion of natural resources and the necessity of combating climate change raise numerous questions. Do the limited stock of natural resources and the constraints of climate change doom our economies to stagnation or even negative growth? How can we design the transition to clean energies? What are the main levers available to governments to combat climate change while continuing to promote qualitative and sustainable growth?

These are the questions we are about to explore.

1. Sustainable Growth: Schumpeter vs. Malthus

In Chapter 2, we discussed the Malthusian trap: long-term growth is impossible in this model because every gain in productivity generates a demographic expansion that brings GDP per capita back to subsistence level. This paradigm may seem extreme but in reality many of our fellow citizens are Malthusians without realizing it, like Monsieur Jourdain of Molière's *Le Bourgeois gentilhomme* [The Middle-Class Gentleman], who speaks in prose without knowing it. This is in any case true of those who advocate for "antigrowth" as the only possible response to the constraints of limited natural resources and the urgency of climate change. Their viewpoint can be expressed as follows.

Consider an economy whose growth comes entirely from capital accumulation, in which the final production of consumer goods (known as final production) requires both capital and the extraction of natural resources. The accumulation of capital—investment—is equal to savings, and savings represents part of final production, the remainder being devoted to consumption.[3] Suppose that the stock of natural resources is limited. We can prove two propositions that remain valid whether returns to capital accumulation increase or decrease with the amount of accumulated capital. First, the economy is bound to stagnate in the very long term; second, a slowdown of growth in the short term will prolong the economy's lifespan.

To prove that the economy is bound to stagnate in the very long term, one reasons by contradiction. Suppose that the economy were to continue to grow indefinitely at a positive rate. It follows that final production would not converge toward zero over time. For this to be the case, the flow extraction of natural resources must continue above a certain level. But then the stock of natural resources will end up being depleted in a finite time. Once the stock is depleted, final production falls to zero, which contradicts the initial assumption of ever-increasing final production. Therefore, the only possible rate of growth over the long term is zero.

The second proposition—that slowing growth in the short term prolongs the lifespan of the economy—results directly from the fact that any slowdown of the economy in the short run saves natural resources, thereby making it possible to extract those resources over a longer period, which prolongs the time during which final goods can be produced.

It was this very logical and persuasive reasoning that inspired the champions of zero growth in the 1970s. The same reasoning drives the advocates of anti-growth. Can we escape this logic? Just as in the case of the Malthusian trap, the answer can be summed up in a single word: innovation. Only innovation can push back the limits of what is possible. Only innovation has the potential to improve quality of life while using fewer and fewer of our natural resources and emitting less and less carbon dioxide. Only innovation will enable us to discover new and cleaner sources of energy. For example, the introduction of nuclear power plants enabled France to reduce its CO_2 emissions, and the development of renewable energies amplified this movement.

Creative destruction is a very powerful engine of change. Not only does it enable a new technology to replace an older one, it can also open the path to a radical change in production processes. And environmental urgency calls for radical change in some fields; for example, modifying the mix of energy sources to rely more on renewables requires the entire energy industry to change models. A critical question is whether innovation will be directed spontaneously toward less polluting technologies or toward technologies that use fewer natural resources, or whether, on the contrary, governmental intervention is necessary. We now turn our attention to this question.

2. Green Innovation, Path Dependence, and the Role of the State

Do firms always spontaneously choose green innovation (Box 9.1)? On the basis of an analysis of the automobile sector, a recent study shows that the answer to this question is distinctly negative.[4] The authors use data for patents filed by automobile companies from eighty countries between 1978 and 2005. They distinguish between "green" innovations, which support the development of electric vehicles, and polluting innovations, which support the development of combustion engines.[5] Using these data, they analyze which factors determine a firm's propensity to make green innovations rather than polluting innovations, examining the firm's past innovations. Will a firm that has innovated in the past in polluting technologies continue on the same path, or will it instead change course and innovate in green technologies?

BOX 9.1. GREEN INNOVATION

Green innovation, also known as eco-innovation or environmental innovation, refers to new products, processes, or methods that, over the course of their life cycles, reduce environmental risks, pollution, and the negative impacts of consuming resources.

These innovations can come not only from firms whose main activity is protection of the environment, such as recycling or producing and storing renewable energy, but also from firms whose activities are *a priori* quite far from ecological concerns, such as the construction, automobile, or chemical industries. In addition, green innovation is not necessarily technological; it can be organizational, institutional, or marketing-related.

Green innovations that improve recycling play a crucial role: they go further than incremental innovations—for example those that make an existing machine more energy-efficient—and constitute a breakthrough innovation. Recycling is a true change of model: it breaks with the linear economic model—extract, manufacture, consume, discard—in favor of a circular model—extract, manufacture, consume, recycle, manufacture, etc.—in an uninterrupted virtuous process.

One might think that a firm that has innovated on combustion engines in the past but is faced with decreasing returns on this type of innovation would decide that it is more profitable to turn to electric vehicles. But the authors show that this is not the case. The more a firm has innovated in combustion engines in the past, the more it continues to innovate in combustion engines today. In other words, firms persevere in the fields where they have already acquired a comparative advantage. This *path dependence* implies that, left to their own choices, firms that have acquired experience in combustion engines will not spontaneously choose to focus on electric vehicles. Governmental intervention is necessary to incentivize these firms to redirect their innovative activity from polluting technologies to green technologies.

To determine whether a patent, and thus an innovation, is green or polluting, the authors use the International Patent Classification (IPC), reproduced in Table 9.1, focusing on patents representing a significant advance in knowledge. For this purpose, they examine triadic patents, that is, those registered in the USPTO, the European Patent Office (EPO), and the Japanese Patent Office (JPO). Figure 9.1 shows the evolution of green and polluting triadic patents in the automotive industry in eighty countries from 1986 to 2005. After a long period with virtually no green innovation, we observe a takeoff starting in the mid-1990s, although they do not catch up with polluting innovations.

Table 9.1. Classification of Patents as Green or Polluting

Description	IPC Code
GREEN PATENTS	
Electric vehicles	
Electric propulsion with power supplied within the vehicle	B60L 11
Electric devices on electrically propelled vehicles for safety purposes; monitoring operating variables, e.g., speed, deceleration, power consumption	B60L 3
Methods, circuits, or devices for controlling the traction–motor speed of electrically propelled vehicles	B60L 15
Arrangement or mounting of electrical propulsion units	B60 K1
Conjoint control of vehicle subunits of different type or different function / including control of electric propulsion units, e.g., motors or generators / including control of energy storage means / for electrical energy, e.g., batteries or capacitors	B60W 10 / 08, 24, 26
Hybrid vehicles	
Arrangement or mounting of plural diverse prime movers for mutual or common propulsion, e.g., hybrid propulsion systems comprising electric motors and internal combustion engines	B60K 6
Control systems specially adapted for hybrid vehicles, i.e., vehicles having two or more prime movers of more than one type, e.g., electrical and internal combustion motors, all used for propulsion of the vehicle	B60W 20
Regenerative braking	
Dynamic electric regenerative braking	B60L 7 / 1
Braking by supplying regenerated power to the prime mover of vehicles comprising engine-driven generators	B60L 7 / 20
Hydrogen vehicles / fuel cells	
Conjoint control of vehicle subunits of different type or different function; including control of fuel cells	B60W 10 / 28
Electric propulsion with power supplied within the vehicle—using power supplied from primary cells, secondary cells, or fuel cells	B60L 11 / 18
Fuel cells; manufacture thereof	H01M 8
POLLUTING PATENTS	
Internal combustion engine	
Internal combustion piston engines; combustion engines in general	F02B
Controlling combustion engines	F02D
Cylinders, pistons, or casings for combustion engines; arrangement of sealings in combustion engines	F02F
Supplying combustion engines with combustible mixtures or constituents thereof	F02M
Starting of combustion engines	F02N
Ignition (other than compression ignition) for internal combustion engines	F02P

Source: P. Aghion, A. Dechezleprêtre, D. Hémous, R. Martin, and J. Van Reenen, "Carbon Taxes, Path Dependency, and Directed Technical Change: Evidence from the Auto Industry," *Journal of Political Economy* 124, no. 1 (2016): 1–51.

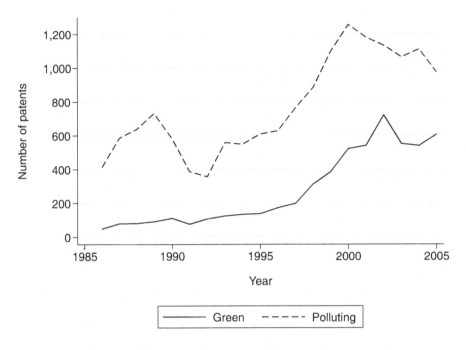

FIGURE 9.1. Evolution of the number of green and polluting triadic patents in the automobile sector, 1986–2005.

Extracted and reformatted from P. Aghion, A. Dechezleprêtre, D. Hémous, R. Martin, and J. Van Reenen, "Carbon Taxes, Path Dependency, and Directed Technical Change: Evidence from the Auto Industry," Journal of Political Economy 124, no. 1 (2016): 1–51, figure 4.

For each innovator, whether a firm or an individual, and for each year from 1978 until 2005, we know not only the number of green and polluting patents obtained by the innovator that year, but also the history of patents that have been granted to the same innovator. This information enables us to analyze the extent to which a firm's propensity to innovate in green or in polluting technologies depends on whether the patents it has accumulated in the past were green or polluting.

The authors find that the probability that a firm would produce a green patent increased by 5 percent if more than 10 percent of its past patents were green. In a symmetrical fashion, a firm that has registered more polluting patents in the past has a higher probability of producing a polluting patent today. Firms thus exhibit path dependence when choosing what innovation to pursue, and we cannot rely solely on the private sector to redirect innovation toward green technologies without the intervention of the state.

The good news is that public policy can be effective in redirecting innovation toward green technologies. The authors show that a 10 percent increase in fuel price that a firm faces increases by 10 percent its likelihood of innovating in green technologies. This redirection results from the same type of market size effect discussed in Chapter 8. An increase in fuel prices reduces the demand for cars running on combustion engines. Lower demand reduces the profitability of polluting innovation, which in turn redirects firms to green innovation.

The authors simulate the effects of different policies for increasing the price of gasoline in 2005 on the number of green patents (solid line) and polluting patents (broken line) through 2028. Figure 9.2a shows the evolution of the two curves with no increase in gas prices; Figures 9.2b, c, and d show the evolution of the curves if gas prices had increased by 10, 20, and 40 percent respectively in 2005. With a 40 percent increase, the curves would have converged in 2020. In this scenario, firms would spontaneously choose green innovation after that date, because by then that is where they would have the most accumulated expertise.

The reader will undoubtedly object, and rightfully so, that a 40 percent increase in gasoline prices is unrealistic because it places an exorbitant cost on current generations. Implementing a punitive ecological tax aimed at modifying behavior is a highly inflammatory idea with potential public repercussions, as demonstrated by the Yellow Vest movement in France, a group who staged violent protests triggered in part by an increase in the price of fuel.[6] The carbon tax is not the only tool available, however. We must enlarge the debate and look at several levers to redirect research toward green innovation.

3. Which Policies Foster Green Innovation?

William Nordhaus vs. Nicholas Stern

To study the impact of global warming on growth, as well as the costs and benefits of various environmental policies, economists began by integrating climate change into classical growth models.[7] One example is William Nordhaus's Dynamic Integrated Climate-Economy model—the DICE model—which examines an economy in which final goods are produced with labor and capital.[8] The productivity of both of these factors increases over time with improvements in technology coming from technical progress. In addition, productivity is positively correlated with the quality of the environment. The environment is negatively affected by the increasing temperatures that result from aggregate economic production. The model implicitly assumes that production generates CO_2, which in turn generates global warming.

The only source of inefficiency in this economy comes from the fact that individual producers do not take into account the negative effect of their activity on

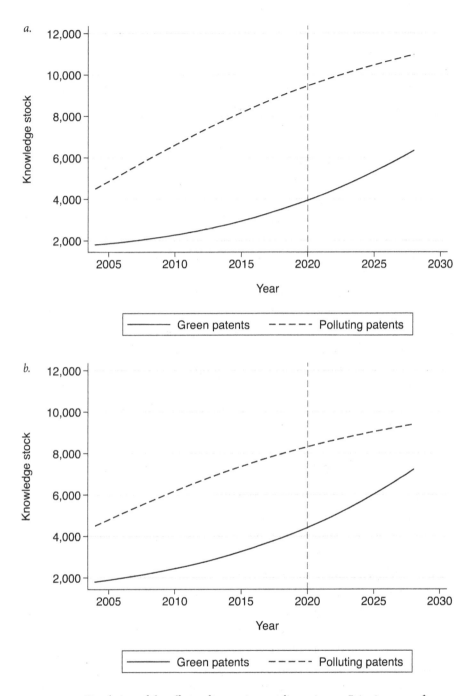

FIGURE 9.2. Simulation of the effects of increasing gasoline prices. *a.* Price increase of 0 percent. *b.* Price increase of 10 percent. *c.* Price increase of 20 percent. *d.* Price increase of 40 percent.

Reformatted from P. Aghion, A. Dechezleprêtre, D. Hémous, R. Martin, and J. Van Reenen, "Carbon Taxes, Path Dependency, and Directed Technical Change: Evidence from the Auto Industry," Journal of Political Economy 124, no. 1 (2016): 1–51, figures 6a, b, c, e.

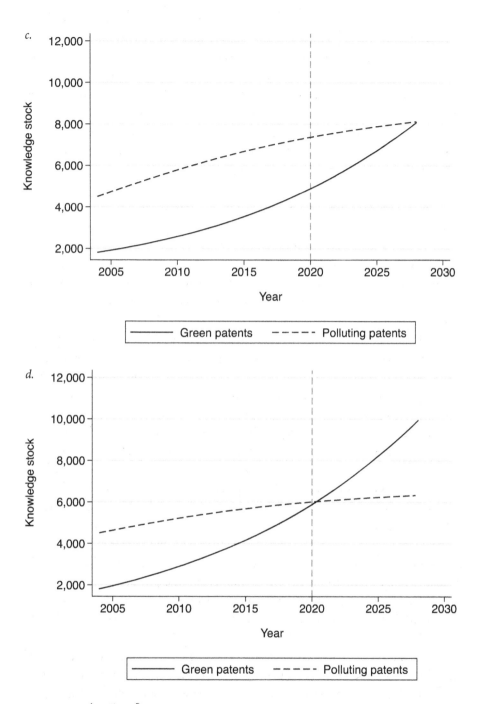

c.

d.

FIGURE 9.2. (*continued*)

the production of CO_2 emissions and thereby on productivity. These emissions constitute a negative environmental externality. In economists' language, individual producers do not internalize the environmental externality. How can we remedy this problem? Since there is only one externality, a single instrument of economic policy suffices to put the economy back on the path of efficiency. That instrument is a carbon tax, that is, a tax on fossil fuels proportionate to their carbon content. The main question for economists who use this model is how to allocate the burden of environmental policies between the current generation and future generations.

Is it best to set a high rate for the carbon tax from the outset, which will have a strong impact on the current generation, or rather to increase the tax more gradually to better distribute the sacrifices between current and future generations? The answer depends largely on how you evaluate the discount rate between the present and the future. This is what gives rise to the difference between the optimistic approach of William Nordhaus and the pessimistic approach of Nicholas Stern regarding global warming.

Nicholas Stern is a British economist and a professor at the London School of Economics who served as senior vice president of the World Bank from 2000 to 2003. He is a world-renowned expert on environmental issues and development and is especially known to the general public for his Report on the Economics of Climate Change.[9] This report, published by the British government in 2006, was the first report led by an economist and not a climatologist: for the first time, expertise in economics was mobilized to attempt to estimate the magnitude of the economic cost of climate change. The report's conclusion is unambiguous: only strong and prompt action to reduce emissions of greenhouse gases will enable us to avoid the worldwide loss of between 5 and 20 percent of GDP per year.

William Nordhaus is an American economist and a professor at Yale. He pioneered the modeling of climate change with Martin Weitzman and is especially known for his research on environmental economics, in particular the DICE model mentioned above, which integrates the factors affecting economic growth, CO_2 emissions, the carbon cycle, climate change, climate damage, and climate policies.

Nordhaus believes that an increase of three degrees Celsius in global temperatures would result in a 2.1 percent drop in worldwide GDP by 2100, and that an increase of six degrees Celsius would result in an 8.5 percent drop.[10] The impact of global warming would thus be very small, because a drop of 8.5 percent in global GDP over more than a century is equivalent to worldwide growth declining by a little less than 0.1 percent per year! Numerous climatologists criticize this optimistic vision and assert that it substantially underestimates the severe impacts of climate change.

Nordhaus assumes a high discount rate, thereby giving lower weight to future generations compared to current generations. His optimism stems from the idea that growth will make future generations much wealthier than the present generation, so that they will be in a better position to cope with climate change. He therefore proposed a more gradual carbon tax than Stern, who assumed a lower discount rate and therefore advocates strong and immediate action.

Environment and Directed Innovation[11]

Consider an economy that produces both polluting goods like combustion vehicles and nonpolluting goods like electric vehicles.[12] Only the production of polluting vehicles increases the atmospheric concentration of CO_2, thereby contributing to global warming. The direction of technical progress toward polluting or nonpolluting goods is endogenous: it depends on firms' decisions to direct innovation either to polluting technologies or to green technologies.

In this economy, characterized by endogenous technical progress, there are two types of externalities. There is first an environmental externality associated with the production of polluting goods and the CO_2 emissions this production entails. But there is another type of externality that has to do with the phenomenon of path dependence in innovation: namely, when a firm decides to innovate in polluting technologies rather than in green technologies, it does not take into account that this decision will motivate it to continue to innovate in polluting technologies even more in the future. We all spontaneously innovate in activities where we are already very good. If you are better at cooking than at dancing, you will spontaneously innovate in cooking rather than in dancing.

Introducing directed innovation as a source of technical progress enriches the analysis and modifies the nature and terms of the debate on environmental economic policy.

One implication is that, even accepting Nordhaus's discount rates, we might want to act immediately to redirect innovation toward nonpolluting technologies. To understand this point, imagine that initially the technology for producing combustion engines is much more advanced than for electric vehicles. Because of path dependence, in the absence of any state intervention, firms will continue to innovate in combustion engines because that is where they are the strongest. It follows that the differential between combustion engine technology and electric engine technology will increase in favor of combustion engines. As a result, future policies aimed at redirecting innovation toward electric vehicles will become longer and more costly. A toothache provides a useful analogy: if one puts off going to the dentist, the cavity worsens and will require longer and more painful treatment in the future.

What is the cost of delayed state intervention? It is substantial, whether we use Stern's discount rate or Nordhaus's rate. Applying reasonable values for the parameters, with either discount rate, the best policy is to redirect research toward green innovation immediately.

A second implication is that state intervention is temporary: once the technology for electric vehicles has caught up to the technology for combustion vehicles, firms will spontaneously continue to innovate on electric vehicles, once again due to path dependence, which now favors green innovation.

A third implication is that two instruments of economic policy are needed because there are two sources of inefficiency in this economy: the negative environmental externality and path dependence. The main purpose of a carbon tax is to correct for the environmental externality, while subsidizing green innovation helps deal with path dependence. Although it is true that setting a high carbon tax would, as we saw above, also discourage polluting innovation, utilizing both instruments—a carbon tax and subsidizing green innovation instead of only a carbon tax—reduces the increase in the carbon tax necessary to fight effectively against global warming.

Diffusion of Green Innovation

Because the environment is a global public good, one country's unilateral investment in environmental policies benefits the entire planet, since the decrease in CO_2 emissions is worldwide. Consequently, every country is tempted to be a free rider and let the others bear the burden of the ecological effort. Does this mean that there is no hope for meaningful international cooperation to combat climate change?

We live in a time where emerging countries increasingly make their voices heard, and they express a legitimate aspiration for economic development. Their position— after all quite justified—is that developed nations, having benefited from two centuries of polluting growth, should not now deny emerging nations the right to follow the same path in order to catch up with them. As a result, emerging countries are reluctant to commit formally to objectives for lowering CO_2 emissions.

The introduction of green innovation, however, changes the terms of the debate on how to combat climate change in a coordinated, global manner.[13] While some emerging countries such as Brazil and China contribute to innovation at the global level, the vast majority of developing countries seek mainly to imitate or adapt technologies invented in the developed world (see Chapter 7).

Imagine that developed countries decided collectively to redirect innovation toward green technologies, then to make these new, green technologies accessible in order to facilitate their diffusion to less-developed countries. Imagine that firms in the developing countries could choose between investing in the adaptation of green technologies and the adaptation of polluting technologies. In this scenario, we can easily show that once green technologies are sufficiently advanced compared to polluting technologies in developed countries, it becomes profitable for firms in developing countries to stop adapting the old, polluting technologies and turn to adapting new, green technologies. For example, China has become a world leader in solar panels and is currently making huge investments in batteries and electric vehicles.

In sum, it is not necessary that all countries in the world coordinate from the outset. Unilateral coordination among developed countries to redirect innovation toward green technologies, combined with a resolute policy to disseminate these technologies to less-developed countries, would suffice to successfully combat global warming.

Nonetheless, our reasoning up to this point has not fully integrated globalization, and in particular free access of emerging countries to international trade. In fact, taking free trade into account adds a caveat to this optimistic scenario. In the context of a globalized economy, if a group of virtuous countries has decided unilaterally to invest in green innovation by blocking polluting innovation—for example by taxing carbon or heavily subsidizing green innovation, some countries outside this group can decide to become "pollution havens." This term refers to countries that either specialize in polluting production activities or attract multinational firms specialized in polluting production and innovation. These firms, no longer able to operate in the virtuous countries, can nevertheless continue their activities in the pollution havens. Then, taking advantage of free trade, they will export their products throughout the world, including to the virtuous countries. Ultimately, not only will the environment deteriorate worldwide in the short term, but in addition the redirection of technical change toward green innovation will be slowed or even thwarted.

Precisely in order to avoid this perverse effect of virtuous climate policies, nations must adopt joint policies aiming to disseminate green technologies and to subsidize their adaptation by less-developed countries. These policies must also include carbon tariffs applicable to countries that, despite having access to green technologies, choose to become pollution havens. It is important to bear in mind that disseminating green technologies to other countries is a very costly invest-ment for the countries where these technologies originated. It implies a loss of revenue for the innovators, who are dispossessed of rents when their inventions can be imitated in other countries. The countries of origin must therefore com-pensate this loss of revenue, which represents a cost.

This combination of incentives (the carrot) plus the threat of carbon tariffs (the stick) gives credibility to unilateral climate policies that then spread to other coun-tries in order to combat global warming effectively worldwide.

4. Consumers, Competition, and Green Innovation

If we ended our analysis here, our main message would be that state interven-tion is indispensable to redirect technical change toward green innovation and thereby avoid environmental catastrophe. Without state intervention, firms will choose spontaneously to innovate in polluting technologies, and because of path dependence, they will do so more and more intensely over time. In consequence, pollution will worsen and global warming will accelerate.

This being said, is the state the only relevant actor in the ecological transition? Doesn't civil society also have a role, in particular through corporate social re-sponsibility (CSR)? Milton Friedman and, before him, Arthur C. Pigou came down unequivocally against the notion of CSR.[14] Their idea was that firms should pursue a single objective—maximizing profits—and let the state deal with sources of inefficiency, such as transaction costs, asymmetric information, and negative externalities, as well as with inequalities, by means of redistribution. Partisans of both ultraliberalism and strong state power share Friedman's point of view, since these groups have in common a desire to minimize the role of civil society.

There are, however, limits as to what the state can achieve, as explained by Ro-land Bénabou and Jean Tirole.[15] One limitation is that government officials are often subject to lobbying by various interest groups, as discussed in Chapter 5. A second limitation is that climate change is a global problem that cannot be re-solved by any single country. Why not rely on civil society as well, and in particular on consumers, who increasingly take social and environmental considerations into account when making their choices?

Consumers indeed have the power to influence corporate decisions.[16] Thus, in countries where consumers are truly concerned about the environment, height-ened competition on the automobile market led manufacturers to innovate more in green technologies, such as electric vehicles. The basic idea is intuitive. We saw in Chapter 4 that competition motivates firms to innovate to improve their products' value in order to get ahead of the competition. We can apply this concept to an economy with directed innovation and pro-environment consumers. In this context, heightened competition will motivate firms to innovate to reduce the ratio between price and the environmental impact, which means they will pursue greener innovations to escape competition. Conversely, in an economy where consumers are more concerned with the price of goods than with their environmental impact, increased competition will not stimulate green innovation and will instead aggravate the environmental problem. This is the "Chinese syndrome": heightened competition lowers prices and increases consumer demand, leading to increased production and thus more pollution.

Figure 9.3 shows the evolution of concern for the environment versus economic growth in the United States between 1984 and 2019, based on a Gallup poll.[17] Concern for the environment decreased between 2000 and 2010, but the trend reversed after 2010.

To measure the importance of environmental concern across countries, the authors use data from surveys by the International Social Survey Programme (ISSP) conducted in 1998 to 2002 and again in 2008 to 2012, as well as data collected by the World Value Survey. Consumers in all of the countries covered by the survey received an identical questionnaire, with questions such as "How willing would you be to pay much higher prices [or taxes] in order to protect the environment?" or "Would you be willing to give up some of your income if you were certain the money would be used to reduce pollution?" The surveys covered forty-two countries, including the major developed countries.

To measure the degree of competition faced by firms, the authors use the degree to which countries are open to international trade—a World Bank index—as well as the degree to which the state regulates product markets in the different countries—which is the inverse of the OECD's competition index.

The study focuses on the automobile industry and analyzes the impact of competition and of societal pro-environment attitudes on the likelihood that firms would innovate in combustion or in electric engines. The main finding is that product market competition combined with consumers' concern for the environment constitutes a powerful lever to motivate firms toward green innovation, in addition to the carbon tax. This result is especially interesting because it suggests another avenue for combating climate change that is complementary to a carbon tax and direct subsidies of R&D. This avenue is to implement educational policies to increase consumer awareness of environmental issues, and to intensify competition, in particular by opening product markets and regulating lobbying.

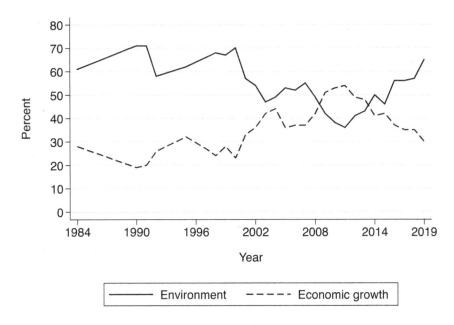

FIGURE 9.3. Americans' preference for environmental protection vs. economic growth.

Data source: Gallup.

5. Intermediate Energies and Energy Transition

How should we approach the transition to renewable sources of energy when intermediate sources are also available—less polluting than coal or oil, but more polluting than renewable energies? Natural gas is a case in point. Although it is a fossil fuel, it is considered the cleanest hydrocarbon, as its combustion emits 30 percent less CO_2 than oil and 50 percent less than coal. Thus, shale gas, an unconventional form of natural gas, has elicited renewed interest as an intermediate form of energy.[18] Without entering the substantive debate over the exploitation of shale gas, we use this example to elucidate the tradeoffs entailed in utilizing an intermediate energy source.[19]

The shale gas boom was a game changer for the American market for natural gas. Figure 9.4 shows the evolution of shale gas production in the United States. We observe a sharp acceleration beginning in 2008—the shale gas boom—with a 50 percent increase in production between 2008 and 2018. Figure 9.5 shows that natural gas started displacing coal at a much faster rate starting in 2008.

What are the effects of the transition from coal to natural gas on emissions of CO_2? Figure 9.6 shows a sharp drop in CO_2 intensity, which means CO_2

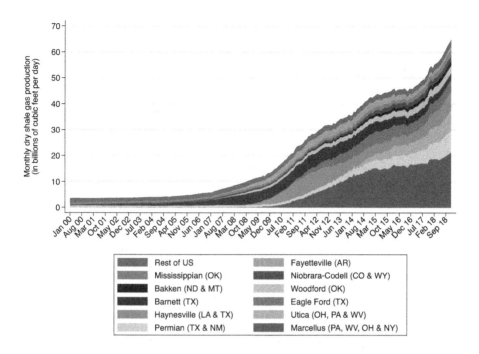

FIGURE 9.4. The shale gas boom.

Reformatted from D. Acemoglu, P. Aghion, L. Barrage, and D. Hémous, "Climate Change, Directed Innovation, and Energy Transition: The Long-Run Consequences of the Shale Gas Revolution," unpublished manuscript, February 28, 2019, figure 1.

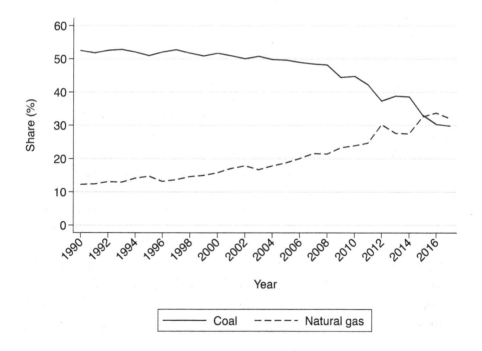

FIGURE 9.5. Share of coal and natural gas in electricity generation.

Reformatted from D. Acemoglu, P. Aghion, L. Barrage, and D. Hémous, "Climate Change, Directed Innovation, and Energy Transition: The Long-Run Consequences of the Shale Gas Revolution," unpublished manuscript, February 28, 2019, figure 2 panel A.

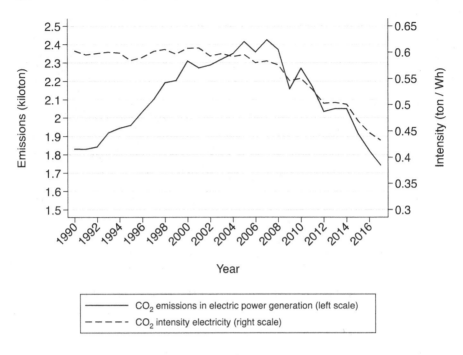

FIGURE 9.6. Emissions and CO$_2$ intensity in electricity generation.

Reformatted from D. Acemoglu, P. Aghion, L. Barrage, and D. Hémous, "Climate Change, Directed Innovation, and Energy Transition: The Long-Run Consequences of the Shale Gas Revolution," unpublished manuscript, February 28, 2019, figure 2 panel B.

emissions per unit of energy produced (dashed curve). This drop is due to a substitution effect: pollution per unit of energy decreases as a result of the partial replacement of a highly polluting energy source (coal) by a less-polluting one (shale gas). This effect could however be more than offset by a scale effect: the introduction of shale gas as a supplemental source of energy increases the overall supply of energy, thereby lowering the cost of energy and therefore in firms' production costs. This encourages firms to produce more and potentially to emit more CO$_2$. Figure 9.6 shows that total CO$_2$ emissions declined after 2008 after having continuously risen until that time (solid curve). Thus the substitution effect predominated.

Setting aside criticism relating to its polluting effects, can we conclude that we should not hesitate to exploit shale gas massively? Once again, if we consider the effects on innovation, we must reevaluate this reasoning. Thus, a recent study looks at an economy where the production of consumer goods requires three sources of energy: coal, shale gas, and a renewable energy.[20] Coal pollutes more than shale gas, which in turn is more polluting than the renewable source. Firms can invest in technical progress either in fossil fuels—coal or natural gas—or in renewable energy. What are the short and long-term effects of the shale gas boom on CO_2 emissions?

In the short term, thus with existing technologies, the introduction of shale gas has the two opposite effects we have already described: a substitution effect, which reduces pollution, and a scale effect, which increases pollution, all other things being equal. As Figure 9.6 shows, the substitution effect tends to predominate. What happens over the long term, when we introduce innovation and take into account firms' choices between two types of innovation—fossil fuels and renewables? The boom in fossil fuels incentivizes firms at least temporarily to direct innovation away from renewables, because the size of the market, and thus the rents from fossil fuels, increases. Indeed, Figure 9.7 shows that the number

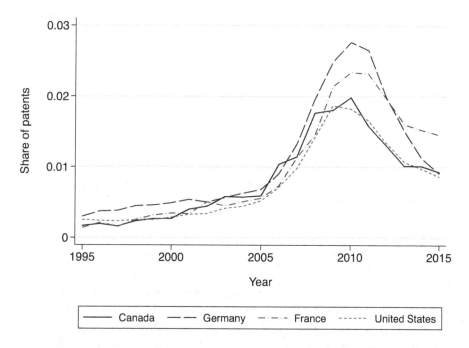

FIGURE 9.7. Number of patents in renewable energies as a proportion of total number of patents.

Data source: D. Acemoglu, P. Aghion, L. Barrage, and D. Hémous, "Climate Change, Directed Innovation, and Energy Transition: The Long-Run Consequences of the Shale Gas Revolution," unpublished manuscript, February 28, 2019.

of patents in renewables as a proportion of the total number of patents began to drop sharply in the United States in 2008, after having risen continuously until then.

Thus, the shale gas boom will either delay the switch to green innovation or block it entirely because of path dependence. As a consequence of the shale gas boom, the accumulation of expertise in fossil fuel technologies incentivizes firms to continue innovating in these technologies indefinitely. We can call this an intermediate energy trap. In both instances, the introduction of shale gas leads to an increase in CO_2 emissions in the long term and to a possible climate catastrophe that could have been avoided without the boom.

Does this mean we should ignore these intermediate energy sources, or is there rather an optimal way to use them, taking advantage of their positive effects in the short term and minimizing their long-term negative effects on innovation? The authors show that for reasonable values of the parameters of their model, the optimal policy is to accompany the shale gas boom by strong subsidies of innovation in renewables, together with a substantial but not excessive increase in the carbon tax on the order of 2 or 3 percent. This policy avoids the intermediate energy trap and accelerates the transition to green innovation.

6. Conclusion

Four main ideas emerge from our analyses in this chapter. The first idea is that innovation is what makes possible the continuous improvement of our standard of living and quality of life despite the constraints of limited natural resources and the necessity of combating global warming. The second idea is that innovation is not spontaneously environmentally friendly; on the contrary, firms whose production and innovation have been in polluting technologies in the past prefer to innovate in polluting technologies in the future (path dependence). Hence the need for state intervention to redirect innovation toward green technologies. Yet the state should not try to take the place of firms; it should act through incentives. We have identified several levers to motivate firms toward green innovation: a carbon tax, subsidies for green innovation, technology transfers to developing countries, and carbon tariffs to discourage pollution havens. The third idea is that using intermediate sources of energy, such as natural gas, may reduce CO_2 emissions in the short term but can hinder the transition to clean energy by trapping innovation in these intermediate sources. Here again, it is the role of the policy maker to choose the right policy mix to prevent our countries from being trapped in the middle of the energy transition. The fourth idea is that civil society has an important role to play to persuade firms to innovate in green technologies. We have mentioned the role of consumers, but all of the components of corporate social responsibility are relevant. We will return to the synergy between the state and civil society in Chapter 15.

INNOVATION

Behind the Scenes

Until now, we have treated innovation like a black box: individuals who invest in R&D produce, with a probability that depends on the nature of the investment, innovations that can be patented and exploited. The reality is more complex.

First, not every individual has the same opportunity to become an innovator: family and social environment, and in particular parents' income, level of education, and professions, affect the individual's propensity to innovate. Intrinsic innovative abilities and talents, which are not distributed equally among individuals, also play a role. Can we identify the factors that have the greatest influence on the likelihood of an individual becoming an innovator? In addition, to what extent does innovation benefit others—such as employees and managers—in the same firm?

Second, innovation is not just a matter of investing in R&D at a given moment with a given probability of a successful outcome in the future. It is an entire process that occurs over several stages. The first steps are usually basic research—the "R" in "R&D." This research is not necessarily patentable, and its protagonists act on motivations that are not necessarily financial. Then come the stages of applied research and of development—the "D" in "R&D." What are the engines of basic research, and how does basic research tie in with applied research, which is more directly marketable? What institution is best for each of the stages in the innovation process? These are the questions we will address in this chapter.

1. Who Becomes an Inventor?

To what extent is the likelihood that an individual will become an inventor influenced by social and familial factors? For the purposes of this section, we are defining an inventor as someone who has obtained at least one patent over the course of her life.[1] Figure 10.1a illustrates how the likelihood for a person living in the United States to obtain a patent from the USPTO between 1996 and 2014 is correlated to his or her parents' income.[2] Parental income is plotted along the x-axis and divided into hundredths (centiles). For each centile of parental income, the figure shows the percentage of children who will obtain at least one patent during their lifetime. This J-shaped curve indicates that the probability of inventing is very low and increases very little with income when parental income is low. By contrast, the probability of inventing starts increasing sharply with parental income when we get to the upper deciles of the income distribution, in particular the highest 20 percent.

Figure 10.1b, based on historical American data, shows the same J-curve relationship between parental income and the probability of inventing over a longer and earlier period, from 1880 to 1940.[3]

Finally, Figure 10.1c, using Finnish data over the period from 1988 to 2012, again shows this J-curve relationship between the father's income and the likelihood of inventing.[4] This resemblance is all the more remarkable because access to education is far more egalitarian in Finland than in the United States. The quality of primary and secondary education is excellent, judging by Finland's PISA scores: Finland ranked seventh out of seventy-seven countries on the 2018 PISA reading tests, whereas the United States and France were in thirteenth and twenty-third place, respectively.[5] Furthermore, education in Finland is entirely free, from kindergarten through Ph.D., and thus universally accessible.

What explains the J-shaped curve in the United States, and why do we find the same curve in a much more egalitarian country such as Finland?

Social and Family Barriers to Innovation in the United States

To explain the J-curve in the United States (Figure 10.1a), two considerations come to mind. First, parental income affects the individual's abilities from the outset: inherited differences, which are manifested in both aptitude and penchant for a career involving innovation. In addition, having parents with higher incomes helps the child surmount different types of entry barriers to becoming an innovator.

Figure 10.2 looks at the probability that an individual will invent during her lifetime, with the vertical axis showing the number of inventors per thousand individuals, as a function of her intrinsic abilities, represented on the horizontal axis by scores on standardized math tests in third grade. The shaded curve models this relationship for children whose parents' income is in the top 20 percent, and the black curve models the same relationship for all other children. We see that in both cases, the likelihood of becoming an inventor as a function of intrinsic abilities takes the form of a J-curve. In other words, children of normal ability

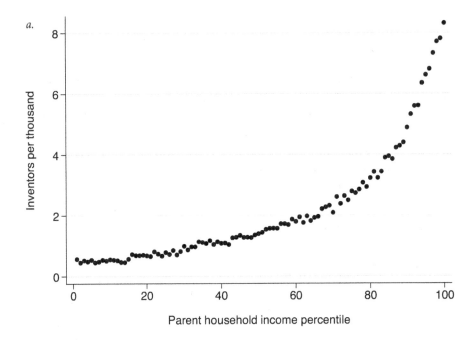

a.

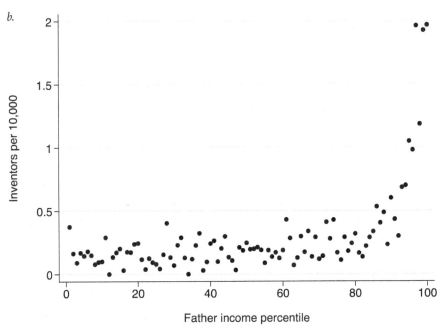

b.

FIGURE 10.1. (*continued*)

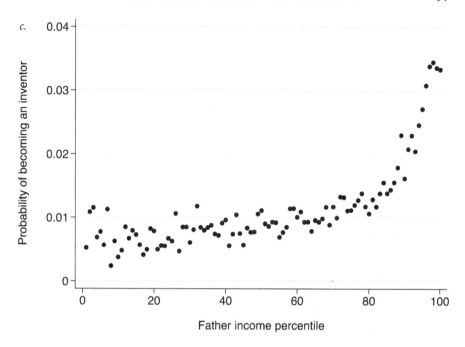

FIGURE 10.1. Parental income and probability of inventing. *a.* United States (1996–2014). *b.* United States (1880–1940). *c.* Finland (1988–2012).

a. *Reformatted from A. Bell, R. Chetty, X. Jaravel, N. Petkova, and J. Van Reenen, "Who Becomes an Inventor in America? The Importance of Exposure to Innovation,"* Quarterly Journal of Economics *134, no. 2 (2019): 647–713, figure 1 panel A ;*
b. *Reformatted from U. Akcigit, J. Grigsby, and T. Nicholas, "The Rise of American Ingenuity: Innovation and Inventors of the Golden Age" (NBER Working Paper No. 23047, National Bureau of Economic Research, Cambridge, MA, January 2017), figure 8 panel A ; c. Reformatted from P. Aghion, U. Akcigit, A. Hyytinen, and O. Toivanen, "The Social Origins of Inventors" (NBER Working Paper No. 24110, National Bureau of Economic Research, Cambridge, MA, December 2017), figure 1 panel C.*

have a low probability of becoming inventors; but if they have exceptional ability, the probability increases significantly. The gap between the shaded and black curves at the extreme right of the graph demonstrates that for children with equivalent, very high intrinsic abilities, the probability of innovating is far greater if their parents have substantial financial means. The difference is less striking for children of ordinary ability. All told, this figure confirms the importance of intrinsic abilities, and at the same time underscores the importance of parental income in enabling above-average intrinsic abilities to bear fruit.

To separate the effect of intrinsic abilities from that of the family environment on the probability of inventing, Alex Bell and his coauthors start by distinguishing between two groups: families in the top 20 percent of the income distribution and the remaining 80 percent.[6] On this basis, they construct a (fictitious) scenario in

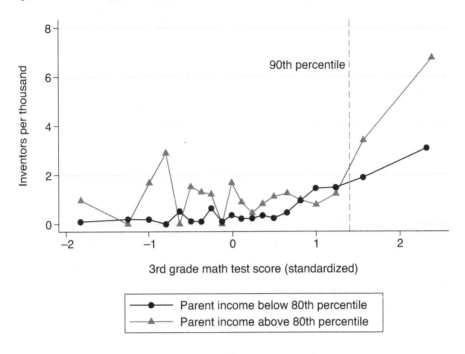

FIGURE 10.2. Probability of inventing and third-grade math test scores.

Reformatted from A. Bell, R. Chetty, X. Jaravel, N. Petkova, and J. Van Reenen, "Who Becomes an Inventor in America? The Importance of Exposure to Innovation," Quarterly Journal of Economics 134, no. 2 (2019): 647–713, figure IV panel A.

which the abilities of third graders were evenly distributed in the two groups. In other words, they use the working hypothesis that social environment has no influence on the abilities of children in third grade. Under this hypothesis, they show that social milieu explains more than two-thirds—68.8 percent—of the innovation differential between the two groups. It is important to note that this hypothesis is too strong, and so 68.8 percent is a lower bound. The impact of social environment on children's probability of inventing is undoubtedly much greater.

We can speculate on different types of social barriers to innovation. First, there is a financial barrier: parents' limited financial resources prevent children with disadvantaged backgrounds from pursuing their studies. Second, there is the barrier of knowledge: more affluent parents most often have a higher level of education and therefore more knowledge to transmit to their children. Finally, there is also a cultural and aspirational barrier: children are influenced by the goals that their parents envision for them, as well as by their parents' professional choices.

We can illustrate the impact of environment and social background along a variety of dimensions. From a geographic perspective, we observe that the more innovative the employment zone in which a child grows up, the greater the child's chance of innovating later on. From the perspective of the parents' professions, the more innovative the sector in which the parents work, the higher the child's rate of innovation. Finally, we observe a replication between parents and children in the field of innovation: if an inventor's child innovates, it is almost always in the same field as the parent.

What have we learned from the American data about the social and familial antecedents of invention? First, there is a clear connection between parental income and children's likelihood of innovating, especially when the parents' income is high. This relationship is due in part to the influence of family background on children's intrinsic abilities, but above all it is due to the various barriers to entry that limit access to innovation for children from disadvantaged families. Finally, there is a significant cultural barrier coming from the difference in children's goals depending on their family origin.

The Finnish Enigma

When we look at Finland rather than the United States, we find a similar relationship between parental income and the probability that the child will innovate. Yet inequality in Finland is much lower than in the United States. What explains this paradox? A study of Finnish data attempts to answer that question, using three databases for the period from 1988 to 2012.[7] Investigators use Finnish administrative data on income, socioprofessional status, and parental education; EPO data on 12,575 Finnish inventors over the period; and data from Finland's mandatory military service that provides the intelligence quotient (IQ) of all male Finnish citizens, which includes inventors. Although this measure of IQ is sometimes contested, it provides, like the third-grade test scores mentioned above, a measure of individuals' abilities.

Figure 10.3 shows the relationship between the likelihood that an individual will innovate and the educational level of his parents (the father in Figure 10.3a and the mother in Figure 10.3b). The higher the education level attained by the father and mother, the greater the probability that the child will innovate. In particular, individuals whose fathers or mothers have obtained a PhD in a scientific field have a substantially higher likelihood of innovating than the others.

We now return to our Finnish enigma. When we estimate the probability of innovating in Finland as a function of paternal income (Figure 10.1c), we find the familiar J-shaped curve: the probability of inventing increases with paternal income. From this basic relationship we model a nearly identical relationship: the probability of inventing as a function of the position of the father's income in the national income distribution (Figure 10.4, solid curve). The difference is that

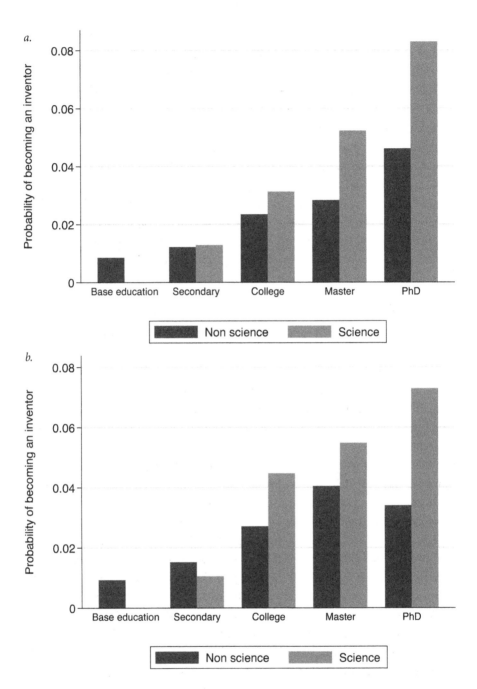

FIGURE 10.3. Parental education status and probability of inventing. *a.* Father's education status. *b.* Mother's education status.

Reformatted from P. Aghion, U. Akcigit, A. Hyytinen, and O. Toivanen, "The Social Origins of Inventors" (NBER Working Paper No. 24110, National Bureau of Economic Research, Cambridge, MA, December 2017), figures 5A, 5B.

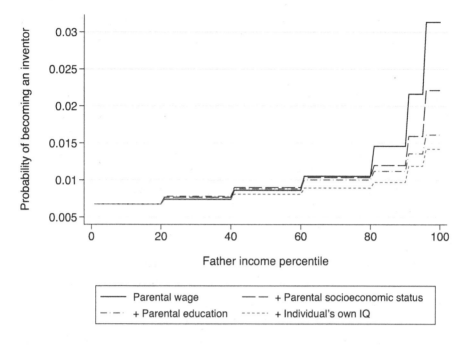

FIGURE 10.4. Decomposing the impact of father's income.

Reformatted from P. Aghion, U. Akcigit, A. Hyytinen, and O. Toivanen, "The Social Origins of Inventors" (NBER Working Paper No. 24110, National Bureau of Economic Research, Cambridge, MA, December 2017), figure 7.

paternal income is measured not continuously but by brackets. Lower income brackets are on the left of the graph, and higher income brackets are on the right.

We then regress the probability of inventing on the father's income bracket. We find the same pattern as in Figure 10.1c: the probability of inventing increases with each increase in paternal income. Starting from the basic solid curve, we study how the relationship between probability of inventing and paternal income changes when we control for parental socioeconomic status (dashed curve).[8] We observe a small flattening of the curve, indicating that parental socioeconomic status affects the probability of inventing.

We next control for parental education (dashed and dotted curve): the curve is substantially flattened, especially at high levels of parental income. This result confirms the importance of education in explaining the J-shaped curve in Finland: one of the main reasons children of wealthier families are more likely to invent is that the parents in these families tend to be more highly educated, which has an influence on the children. Even though the Finnish educational system is highly egalitarian and of high quality, parental influence remains a decisive factor. This influence is undoubtedly channeled through the transmission of knowledge but also through the goals that parents do or do not impart to their children: on average, parents who have PhDs in scientific fields stimulate stronger ambitions and goals in their children.

Lastly, we consider the individual's IQ (dotted curve): the J-curve flattens even more. This implies a positive relationship between parental income and children's IQ. What could explain this relationship? Here we are walking on shifting sands, and sociologists and psychologists are certainly more qualified than economists to answer this question.[9] One possible explanation is that children in more affluent families are better prepared for IQ tests. Another explanation could be that more affluent parents are higher skilled, and there tends to be a positive correlation between parents' skill level and IQ, and also between parents' IQ and their children's IQ.

In short, the Finnish enigma can be explained to a large extent by the fact that higher income parents have pursued higher studies, which in turn influences the probability that their children will innovate.

Compared to the American study, the Finnish study, explicitly using data on parental education level, confirms the importance of education and goals in nurturing innovation. In addition, however, it suggests another factor: the correlation between IQ and parental income.

The Finnish data also allows us to ponder a further question: can the family environment be an obstacle to the emergence of new Einsteins? And it tells us that the answer is yes. Consider two brothers, A and B, whose father's income is in the lowest 20 percent of the income distribution. Individual A's IQ is close to average, and individual B has a very high IQ. If we replace this father with one with a very high income, the data show that the probability of innovating increases three times more for individual B than for individual A. More generally, the probability that individuals with high IQs will innovate increases much more sharply with parental income than that of other individuals. In other words, having poor parents, *a priori* less educated and less well connected, inhibits the innovative potential of a high-IQ child: family disparity causes us to lose potential Einsteins.

Complementarity between Education Policy and R&D Subsidies

Taking into account the disparities in individuals' access to cutting-edge knowledge, attraction to research careers, and intellectual abilities has direct implications on growth policy choices. As Ufuk Akcigit, Jeremy Pearce, and Marta Prato explain in a 2020 paper, there are at least two reasons individuals turn away from research and innovation careers: either they do not have the material resources and human capital necessary for such a career, or they have those resources but prefer to pursue other paths.[10]

The main effect of R&D subsidies is to motivate qualified individuals to choose a career in research and innovation over other careers by making the former more lucrative (in particular by lowering the cost of access to laboratory equipment and by increasing researchers' salaries). Public investment in education, on the other hand, enables talented individuals from modest backgrounds to pursue higher education that will give them the chance to become researchers and innovators. These two policies—public R&D subsidies and public investment in education— thus have complementary positive effects on innovation and growth because they direct different segments of the population toward research careers.

When a government is operating within a limited budget, it will maximize innovation-led growth by investing most of its resources in education. By contrast, if it has greater budgetary resources, the optimal innovation policy will combine public investment in innovation and R&D subsidies, without sacrificing the former to the latter. Only when a sufficient number of "*a priori* talented" individuals reach the knowledge frontier and thus have the option of deciding whether to pursue a research career can public R&D subsidies have a significant effect on innovation and growth.[11]

Who Benefits from Innovation within Firms?

When analyzing the impact of different types of institutions and economic policies on innovation, we have until now treated the innovator as an individual entrepreneur who reaps the entirety of the innovation rents. In practice, innovations are often produced within a firm, which raises the question of how innovation rents are distributed between the innovator and other stakeholders in the firm.

A recent study by Aghion, Akcigit, Hyytinen, and Toivanen attempts to answer this question, again relying on Finnish data. This study analyzes the employer-employee relationship on the basis of detailed information about the firms employing each individual, the type of job held by the individual (for example, blue collar vs. white collar), and salary.[12] The authors utilize this data for the period from 1988 to 2012 and match it with patent data from the EPO. An inventor is again defined as an individual who has obtained at least one patent from the EPO between 1988 and 2012. One can see immediately from the data whether the individual works alone or within a firm. The study focuses solely on inventors working in firms, as well as on white-collar employees, blue-collar employees, and entrepreneurs.[13] The authors look at individuals in firms who had just obtained a patent from the EPO on a new invention. How does that occurrence affect their income and that of other stakeholders in the firm?

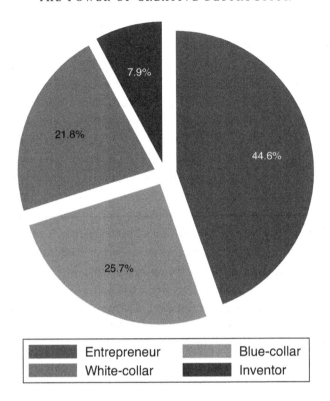

FIGURE 10.5. Share of innovation returns captured according to socioprofessional category.

Reformatted from P. Aghion, U. Akcigit, A. Hyytinen, and O. Toivanen, "On the Returns to Invention within Firms: Evidence from Finland," AEA Papers and Proceedings *108 (2018): 208–212, figure 2.*

The authors break down the total revenues generated by the innovation during the period from five years before until ten years after the innovation, among four types of actors within the firm (entrepreneur, inventor, white-collar employee, and blue-collar employee). Figure 10.5, which shows this decomposition, indicates that entrepreneurs take the lion's share with 44.6 percent of the returns from innovation. They are followed by blue-collar employees, who, because they are more numerous than other types of employees, receive 25.7 percent of returns; then white-collar employees with 21.8 percent, and lastly, the inventor, with only 7.9 percent of returns. Overall, employees receive nearly 47 percent of returns on innovation. Is this result unique to Finland?

A parallel study by Patrick Kline, Neviana Petkova, Heidi Williams, and Owen Zidar relies on tax data for US firms and employees, matched with patent data from the USPTO for the period from 2000 to 2014.[14] Their analysis is focused on

US firms for which tax and patent data are available. They study firms that obtained a patent for the first time for a patent of high potential value.[15] This sample represents approximately two thousand firms in all. These firms tend to be smaller than the average firm filing patent applications in the United States: they have an average of sixty-one employees over the period studied. The authors' objective was to understand how the income shock caused by the new patents affected the remuneration of the firms' employees. To do so, the authors compare firms whose patent applications were granted by the USPTO to similar firms in the same technology field whose applications were denied.

They first observe that approximately 30 percent of the gains generated by the patent go to employees in the form of wages. This percentage is smaller than in Finland, where it was 47 percent. In addition, the increases in earnings are heterogeneous across different types of employees. Thus, new patents have no effect on the remuneration of newly hired employees; only more senior employees benefit from the innovation. Furthermore, among these more senior employees, males benefit the most from the innovation, meaning that the innovation widens the gender gap in remuneration. Finally, the impact of a new patent on remuneration is strongly concentrated among the firm's top 25 percent highest earners (the fourth quartile). This result echoes the finding of higher innovation returns per employee for white-collar employees in Finnish firms.

Thus the overall lesson of this section is that innovation rewards not only the inventor within a firm, but also the employees and entrepreneurs of the firm, with notable differences according to their socioprofessional category, seniority, and gender. A potentially interesting implication of this analysis concerns the effects of taxation on innovation: we should not limit our attention to the effects of income taxation on the inventor alone, but rather we should consider the effects of income taxation on the net incomes of all stakeholders in the firm. To understand this point, suppose that the inventor belongs to the top 5 percent of the income distribution while the entrepreneur is in the top 0.1 percent. An overly simplistic reasoning would surmise that raising taxes on the top 0.1 percent without changing tax rates for the top 5 percent will have no impact on innovation. However, this reasoning disregards the importance of entrepreneurs in the innovation process. Typically, entrepreneurs sacrifice a large part of their earnings to invest in innovation. Discouraging them would jeopardize the whole innovation process.

2. The Impetus for Basic Research

At the heart of the Schumpeterian paradigm as it has unfolded in the preceding chapters are entrepreneurs and innovators who, building on knowledge generated by others before them, invest in research and development in order to enhance their chances of innovating.[16] Why do they innovate? Because innovation is marketable and consequently yields monetary rents. Intellectual property rights thus play the crucial role of protecting innovators and their monetary rents from imitation. This paradigm offers an extremely useful lens for understanding a number of facts and empirical enigmas raised in preceding chapters. Nevertheless, like all paradigms in economics, it masks a more complex reality.

We begin with the process of accumulation of knowledge: in reality, innovation is based not only on prior innovations, but also and above all on basic research, which does not obey the logic and incentives of R&D in firms. Academic researchers and those working in independent research labors are often paid less than researchers with equivalent qualifications in firms.[17] Why would a researcher who has a choice between a university position and a better-paid job in a firm choose the university? This question can be answered in two words: academic freedom. The academic researcher can determine her own research agenda. She can delve into a new project, then abandon it midstream and set out on a new path. She can freely undertake projects that fail or projects whose results do not necessarily lead to marketable applications. In addition, she can communicate freely with other researchers, she is free to decide with whom she wishes to collaborate, and she is free to disseminate the results of this research—hence the trade-off between remuneration and freedom.

Academic Freedom at the University; Focused Research in Firms

Why do we need both basic research and applied research? Why is basic research carried out mainly in universities, where academic freedom is the rule, while applied research and commercial innovation take place mostly in firms? To simplify, imagine that all innovation occurs not in a single step, as we have assumed until now, but in two steps, as illustrated in Figure 10.6.[18] The first stage is a discovery in basic research, for example, a new theorem, a new molecule, or a new bacterium—this is Stage 0 of basic research. Then, grounded on this idea or initial discovery, a second discovery completes the innovation process and gives rise to a marketable product—for example, a vaccine or a new medication. This is Stage 1 of applied research.

Each of these stages is uncertain: whether it be Stage 0 (basic research) or Stage 1 (applied research), research is never sure to yield results. In particular, if Stage 0—basic research—does not come to a successful conclusion, there is no Stage 1. *A priori*, each stage can proceed either in the academic setting, where researchers enjoy freedom to choose their projects and to diffuse their results as they wish, or in firms, where the research agenda and the diffusion results are strictly monitored. Why, then, is basic research most often carried out in universities?

| Basic research | Applied research | |
| Stage 0 | Stage 1 | Commercialization |

FIGURE 10.6. Schema of the R&D process.

© The Authors.

The explanation is as follows.[19] Basic research is particularly uncertain, proceeding by trial and error: the researcher explores new territory without knowing what might lead to a concrete application. Permitting the researcher to choose her research strategy freely is doubly advantageous. The first advantage is informational: a researcher conducting basic research knows better than anyone else how to move forward—which paths to pursue and which to abandon to maximize the chances of success. Second, there is a financial advantage: in exchange for academic freedom, academic researchers generally accept lower remuneration than researchers in firms. It would undoubtedly be too costly to pay private-sector salaries for all stages of the research process, including those that do not lead to more applied, marketable research. Finally, there is the third advantage of open exchange of ideas among researchers. Basic research advances largely thanks to open communication among researchers and to the fact that researchers can freely elaborate projects based on the past research of their colleagues. Researcher *A* can launch an idea that she is not able to see through to the end, but it so happens that Researcher *B* knows how to transform *A*'s embryonic idea into one that may become marketable in a later stage (Stage 1). Limiting the open exchange of ideas at Stage 0 can only reduce the flow of ideas that pass the threshold of Stage 1 with the potential of coming to fruition in an innovation.

Although basic researchers do not always know *a priori* which avenue of research they should pursue—asking the right questions is just as important as solving them—the path forward is clearly traced for Stage 1 of applied research. In order for Stage 1 to succeed in producing a marketable innovation, teams of researchers must focus exclusively on that specific innovation. The firm's role is to know in advance in which product line it wants to invest and then to convey extremely precise instructions to the researchers it employs. These researchers are thus not free to determine their own research agendas. Nor do they have the freedom to communicate with other researchers about their work, because the firm must protect itself against the risk of expropriation of its innovation. This risk becomes especially acute the closer one gets to a marketable innovation. This double loss of freedom is compensated by higher salaries in firms than in academia.

In short, academic research has three specificities: it is less costly than private sector research, it leaves researchers free to determine their own research agendas, and it allows researchers to make use of their academic freedom to exchange ideas openly with other researchers.[20] Hampering the academic researcher's freedom can only impair the innovation process and ultimately reduce the flow and diversity of new ideas. In addition, it hinders the entry of new researchers who may choose other careers.

Imagine for an instant a world in which every step forward in research and every new theorem is strictly protected by IP rights in the form of patents. Applied researchers would face huge financial and administrative costs if they had to pay royalties to all of the basic researchers involved in Stage 0, which would create a strong deterrent for Stage 1. For example, multiple patent holders could block a line of research on a new drug. This phenomenon has been labeled by Michael Heller as the "tragedy of the anticommons": the excessive fragmentation of property rights in common goods obstructs potential new innovations.[21] Even though patents are justified to protect property rights in commercial innovation and the applied research that leads to it, they can nevertheless become counterproductive if used to excess in the basic research stage. Another implication of this paradigm is that the most groundbreaking commercial innovations are more likely to see the light of day in more unfettered institutional environments.

"Of Mice and Academics"

What is the impact on innovation of more open access to the results of basic research? In an article entitled "Of Mice and Academics," Fiona Murray, Philippe Aghion, Mathias Dewatripont, Julian Kolev, and Scott Stern analyze the effect on innovation of a natural experiment reducing property rights in basic research—in other words increasing openness—in the field of biology in the United States.[22]

For over a century, experimentation on mice has played a key role in the advancement of the life sciences. Thirty years ago, however, a veritable scientific revolution occurred: the ability to create genetically engineered mice. It became possible to introduce or delete a gene that causes cancer or diabetes.[23] This genetic experimentation was conducted on over 13,000 mice, each experiment giving rise to an initial publication in the scientific literature. We refer to each of these initial publications as a "mouse-article pair." This technological revolution went through two important steps. In the first step, researchers at Harvard University developed the Onco technique, which was used to create the OncoMouse (from *onkos,* the Greek word for tumor), a transgenic mouse that had received an oncogene giving it a high probability of developing a particular form of cancer.[24] The purpose of this genetic manipulation was to advance cancer research. In 1988, this invention was patented with the USPTO. Because of its partial funding of the research, DuPont Corporation gained exclusive control over the patents. In the second step, DuPont subsequently developed the Cre-lox technology that made it possible to create mice in which specific genes could be turned on or off.

The natural experiment was the following. The US National Institutes of Health (NIH) required DuPont to sign Memoranda of Understanding (MoUs) relating to the Onco and Cre-lox techniques with the US government and Jackson Labs, a mouse repository in Bar Harbor, Maine. The effect of these MoUs was to diminish DuPont's property rights, which in turn gave academic researchers easier access to the Onco and Cre-lox techniques and to the mice created with them. The Cre-lox and Onco MoUs were signed in 1998 and 1999 respectively. Therefore, by observing what happened before and after their signatures, we can infer whether easier access to the technologies had a positive effect on basic research.

In light of our analysis of the relationship between basic and applied research, this natural experiment should generate first a bigger flow of new ideas in basic research and second more diversity and novelty in research ideas. That is exactly what the study finds. More precisely, the authors look at all publications through the year 2006 that cited one or more "mouse-article pairs" published between 1983 and 1998. There are a total of 2,171 mouse-article pairs and more than 432,000 citations of these pairs. After the implementation of the Cre-lox MoU, the authors observe two phenomena. First, the number of citations of mouse-article pairs involving a Cre-lox mouse increases by nearly 20 percent. Second, the increase concerns mostly citations by articles with novel content,[25] or articles by new authors, by authors from institutions that had never before cited these mouse-article pairs, or by newly established scientific journals. The conclusions are similar for the Onco MoU. It follows that increasing openness of basic research fosters innovation.

Gene Sequencing

The sequencing of the human genome provides another example of the negative effects of IP protection on discoveries in basic research. Heidi Williams published the seminal article on this topic in 2013.[26] Genome sequencing means figuring out the order of DNA bases that constitute genes. A gene is a piece of DNA that gives instructions to produce one or more proteins. These proteins determine all of the observable characteristics of an individual, called a phenotype. The genotype is the genetic constitution of an individual that gives rise to the individual's specific phenotype. Thus, an "abnormal" gene will give instructions for an abnormal protein and provoke a pathology as a result of the link between the genotype and the phenotype.[27] For example, hereditary illnesses such as cystic fibrosis, hemophilia, or Huntington disease are determined by the sick person's genes. Why is it

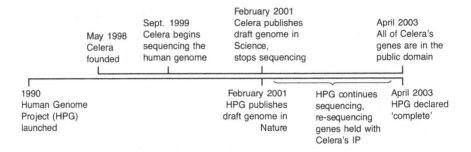

FIGURE 10.7. Timeline of key events.

Reformatted from H. L. Williams, "Intellectual Property Rights and Innovation: Evidence from the Human Genome," Journal of Political Economy *121, no. 1 (2013): 1–27, figure 1.*

useful to sequence DNA? It can show us the relationships between genotype and phenotype, enabling us to detect illnesses and potentially to develop genetic therapy, in other words to attempt to replace the gene responsible for the illness by a healthy gene.

Heidi Williams constructed a database tracking the sequencing of the genome over time. As shown in Figure 10.7, the two main protagonists were the Human Genome Project (HGP), a publicly funded project coordinated by the NIH, and Celera Corporation, a private company specialized in genetic sequencing. Celera, founded in 1998, owned the IP rights on certain genes; it began working on sequencing the human genome in 1999 and interrupted its efforts in 2001, having sequenced only certain genes (the "Celera genes"). The HGP started in 1990, with the objective that all of the sequenced genes would be placed in the public domain. The project continued until 2003, when the HGP had sequenced all of the genes in the human genome, including the Celera genes. In April 2003, information on the sequencing of all of the genes, including Celera's, had become freely accessible to the public, when resequenced by the HGP.

Between 2001 and 2003, Celera used its IP rights to protect the gene sequences it had produced but that had not yet been sequenced by the HGP. Imagine that another firm, for example Pfizer, had discovered a diagnostic test for a genetic disease based on a gene for which Celera owned the IP rights. In a contractual setting with no transaction costs, Pfizer and Celera would end up agreeing on a mutually beneficial licensing agreement such that the cumulative process of research leading to the test would be unhindered. But in a setting with transaction costs, for example, asymmetric information about R&D costs, Pfizer and Celera might never reach an agreement, in which case the genetic test would never be developed.

How did Celera's ownership of IP rights affect scientific publications relating to the corresponding genes? Heidi Williams's research showed that R&D on the Celera genes, for which the information did not become public until resequenced by the HGP in 2003, was 20 to 30 percent lower than R&D on the genes sequenced by the HGP but not by Celera and immediately placed in the public domain. Furthermore, the Celera genes generated 40 percent fewer publications between 2001 and 2009 than the other genes. Finally, the Celera genes had 38 percent less chance of being used in a diagnostic test. Overall, Celera's ownership of IP rights on basic research had a negative impact on both basic research and applied research.

Basic Research and Applied Research in Private Firms

Our model of research as a multistep process sought to explain why basic research is carried out at universities while applied research occurs mostly in firms. In reality, the distinction between basic and applied research is not as clear-cut as this model suggests. First, between the two extremes, there is a continuum of research that is more or less applied or more or less basic. Between the university, which gives researchers total freedom, and firms that completely direct their activity, there are firms like Google, which allow their researchers partial freedom. Finally, even within a firm, there is often some research that is more on the basic side and some that is more on the applied side.

A recent study differentiates basic research from applied research within firms.[28] Many firms have multiple establishments, often corresponding to different product lines. These product lines can be part of the same business sector or several different business sectors. The study finds that the greater the number of business sectors in which a firm operates, the more the firm invests in basic research. The underlying idea is that basic research plays the role of Stage 0 for applied research in multiple sectors, whereas applied research is sector-specific from the outset. Once again we see that basic research enhances diversity in innovation. But since basic research generates more positive externalities than applied research, and these externalities also benefit a firm's competitors, firms will always tend to underinvest in basic research.[29] For this reason, the state and universities have a critical role to play.

3. Conclusion

In Chapter 5, we put forth the idea that innovation increases social mobility. However, as we have shown in this chapter, there is deep inequality in individuals' access to becoming innovators. In particular, parental education and parental socioeconomic status are key determinants of the probability that children will innovate. Accordingly, schools play an important role in equalizing opportunities, particularly by effectively transmitting knowledge and inspiring students to become future innovators.

In this chapter we also described innovation as a multistep process that begins with basic research and continues with more applied stages, leading to the marketing of a new product. We emphasized the role of the university as the guardian of the academic freedom and openness that are necessary to basic research, whereas the applied steps are more naturally carried out within firms. The governance of universities and their interaction with the rest of the economy so as to maximize their potential for innovation remains largely an open question.[30]

▼

11

CREATIVE DESTRUCTION,
HEALTH, AND HAPPINESS

Since the election of Donald Trump in November 2016, not a month has gone by without a new book or article being published on the rise of populism in developed nations. Without seeking to compete with those contributions, which address the very essence of the phenomenon and propose highly convincing explanations, we will introduce an additional variable into the equation: creative destruction and the individual's experience of creative destruction. Modern growth, grounded in innovation, is often berated because of the new type of risk it imposes on individuals: the risk that comes from the creation and destruction of firms and activities. "The problem with all the innovation," state Anne Case and Angus Deaton, "is that Schumpeterian creative destruction is not only creative but destructive. It eliminates jobs that used to exist, accelerated by the cost of health insurance, throwing workers into an increasingly hostile labor market, and with an inadequate safety net; the lives and communities that were supported by those jobs are put at risk, at the worst leading to despair and death."[1]

The era of secure employment, when people could spend their entire professional lives in one occupation and one firm, is over. Creative destruction eliminates existing jobs at the same time as it creates new ones, forcing individuals to continually re-examine themselves, to accept that nothing is ever settled once and for all, and to reassess their professional paths again and again.

To what extent does innovation increase the risk of loss of status through job loss, wage stagnation, or obsolescence of educational degrees? What are the consequences of this risk on health and happiness? What can be done so that the increased mobility that innovation imposes on activities and workers does not lead to insecurity and unemployment for the majority of people? Which labor market policies are the most likely to reconcile innovation-led growth and individual happiness? In this chapter, we attempt to bring answers to these questions.

1. Creative Destruction, Unemployment, and Loss of Status

We start by analyzing the extent to which creative destruction increases the probability of job loss, leading to the obsolescence of acquired knowledge and educational degrees.

Creative Destruction and Unemployment[2]

Does innovation through creative destruction—that is, the replacement of old activities by new ones—increase or decrease the probability that an employed worker will lose her job? From a theoretical perspective, the answer to this question is ambiguous.[3] On one hand, by making certain activities obsolete, innovation destroys jobs and pushes the people who held them back into the job market. Given that the job market is frictional, and job seekers thus don't find new jobs immediately, the unemployment rate will increase. There is, however, a countervailing effect: employment creation. Innovation creates new jobs, which tends to reduce the unemployment rate. Finally, there is a third effect known as the "capitalization effect," which can be summarized as follows. A higher innovation rate implies a higher growth rate.[4] But any investment aimed at creating a new activity is rewarded by future profits, and these future profits will grow faster as the economy as a whole grows faster. In other words, the higher the growth rate, the more lucrative it will be to create a new activity that will in turn generate new jobs and thus reduce unemployment. Note that these three effects are not simultaneous: the job destruction effect plays out in the short run, whereas the job creation effect and the capitalization effect are more long term. As we will see below, it is indeed in the short run that individuals experience the negative effects of creative destruction, according to opinion polls.

We now turn to the empirical analysis of the effect of creative destruction on unemployment. Directly inspired by the work of Steven Davis and John Haltiwanger on the creation and destruction of jobs and firms in the United States, a recent study by Philippe Aghion, Ufuk Akcigit, Angus Deaton, and Alexandra Roulet examines the correlation between creative destruction and unemployment within US employment zones.[5,6] The study uses local employment data from the US Bureau of Labor Statistics. Data on the rate of creative destruction comes from Business Dynamics Statistics, which provides local-level data on the rate of job creation and destruction as well as on the entry and exit of establishments. The

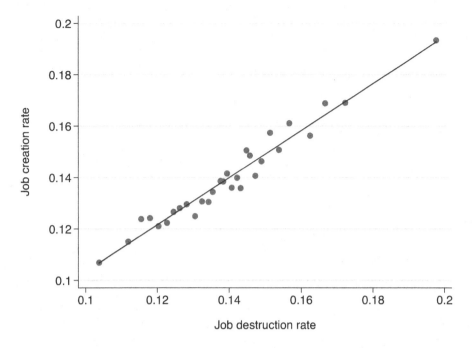

FIGURE 11.1. Relationship between creation and destruction of jobs in the United States.

Data source: P. Aghion, U. Akcigit, A. Deaton, and A. Roulet, "Creative Destruction and Subjective Well-Being," American Economic Review 106, no. 12 (2016): 3869–3897.

rate of creative destruction is measured by adding the rate of job creation and the rate of job destruction in the corresponding employment zone.[7] These rates are computed using information on all American firms in the Census Bureau's Longitudinal Business Database. Figure 11.1 highlights a strong positive correlation between job creation and job destruction over the period from 2005 to 2010 in the United States: the areas with the highest rates of job destruction are the same as those with the highest rate of job creation. This is indeed what creative destruction is all about: a strong connection between job destruction and job creation.

Figure 11.2 depicts the correlation between the rate of creative destruction and the unemployment rate. On average, between 2005 and 2010, the employment zones with the highest rates of creative destruction are also the ones with the highest unemployment rates. In other words, an individual living in an employment zone with a high rate of creative destruction has greater chances of experiencing unemployment at some point. Nevertheless, this transition through unemployment is not destined to be long-lived: indeed, as we saw in Figure 11.1, job creation is also more intense in this type of employment zone. Yet, creative

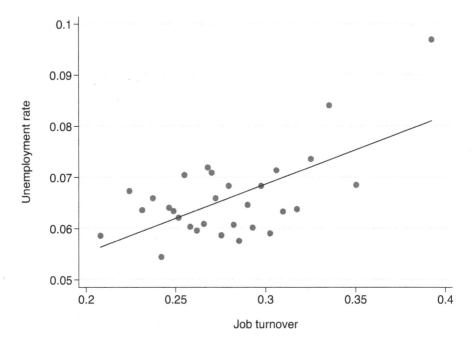

FIGURE 11.2. Relationship between creative destruction and unemployment rate in the United States.

Data source: P. Aghion, U. Akcigit, A. Deaton, and A. Roulet, "Creative Destruction and Subjective Well-Being," American Economic Review 106, no. 12 (2016): 3869–3897.

destruction is associated with a greater probability of job loss at some point in time. Later in this chapter we will discuss the consequences of transiting through unemployment on health and well-being.

Innovation and Obsolescence of Educational Degrees

How does innovation affect the value of degrees and acquired skills? To answer this question, Philippe Aghion, Ufuk Akcigit, Ari Hyytinen, and Otto Toivanen merged databases on individual incomes, firm-level accounting, and patents in Finland between 1988 and 2012.[8] The authors start with their prior work on the distribution of innovation rents within the firm employing the inventor (see Chapter 10). We see that innovation rents are not uniformly distributed within the firm. It turns out that a blue-collar worker loses an average of 1 percent of his wages over the five years preceding the innovation, then realizes a monetary gain of 2.3 percent after the innovation, whereas a white-collar worker experiences no drop in wages before the innovation, then enjoys a monetary gain of 2 percent after the innovation. Thus, innovation introduces uncertainty in employees' wages, particularly for the least-skilled workers, whose income drops in the years preceding the innovation, on average.

The same authors examine another source of heterogeneity, namely an individual's age and the time elapsed since they earned their most recent academic degree. At first sight, age seems to be a decisive factor: only younger workers seem to benefit from innovation. Furthermore, on average, innovation is positively correlated with workers' chances of losing their jobs. This is in line with our previous findings of a positive correlation between creative destruction and unemployment in aggregate US data. The correlation between innovation and the probability of job loss appears stronger for older workers. Nonetheless, the conclusions change dramatically when we introduce an additional element, namely the time elapsed since the employee earned her last degree, which reflects the individual's "distance to the knowledge frontier." The longer this interval, the lower the individual's innovation revenue: each additional year since the degree reduces innovation revenue by five percentage points and increases the probability of job loss by 0.4 to 0.6 percentage points. In other words, innovation induces loss of status for individuals with older degrees.

In sum, innovation generates unemployment and loss of status. Now let us look at how that fact impacts health, before examining more generally the relationship between creative destruction and happiness.

2. Creative Destruction and Health

Health and Innovation: The Bright Side

In Chapter 2, we examined innovation's central role in explaining the takeoff of per capita GDP growth at the global level, and we observed a coincidence between this takeoff and the takeoff of life expectancy. This concomitance suggests that the two takeoffs had common sources. As it turns out, innovation has contributed more to the increase in life expectancy than to the increase of GDP per capita, as we see from a quick look at Table 11.1.[9] This table shows the evolution of GDP per capita and life expectancy respectively in developed countries and developing countries. Between 1961 and 2017, on average developing countries converged toward developed countries, in terms of both standard of living and life expectancy. However, the convergence of life expectancy was much stronger: life expectancy in developing countries grew twice as fast as in developed countries, whereas the growth of GDP per capita between 1961 and 2017 in developing countries was slightly greater than in developed countries (377 percent compared to 324 percent).

Table 11.1. GDP per Capita and Life Expectancy in Developed and Developing Countries

	1961	2017	Variation between 1961 and 2017	Growth Rate between 1961 and 2017
DEVELOPED COUNTRIES				
GDP per Capita	10,585	44,901	+34,316	324%
Life Expectancy at Birth	68.5	81.5	+13.0	19%
Number of Countries	27	27		
DEVELOPING COUNTRIES				
GDP per Capita	2,346	11,195	+8,849	377%
Life Expectancy at Birth	49.2	69.2	+20.0	41%
Number of Countries	84	84		

Note: The developed countries sample covers twenty-seven OECD countries while the developing countries covers eighty-four non-OECD countries for which data after 1960 is available.

Data sources: Robert C. Feenstra, Robert Inklaar, and Marcel P. Timmer, "The Next Generation of the Penn World Table," *American Economic Review* 105, no. 10 (2015): 3150–3182, available for download at www.ggdc.net/pwt; World Bank.

The fact that convergence of life expectancy was stronger than that of per capita income between 1961 and 2017 is directly related to innovation. In particular, we can credit the discovery of penicillin and antibiotics in the late 1920s, and the dissemination to less-developed countries of these drugs and medical advances resulting from their discovery. Focusing on the history of developed countries, Angus Deaton brings to light that prior to 1900, life expectancy was greater at fifteen years of age than at birth because of the high infant mortality rate.[10] At the beginning of the twentieth century, however, the introduction of new vaccines, among other things, reversed this comparison. Similarly, before 1950, the increase in life expectancy mainly affected children, whereas after 1950 life expectancy after age fifty increased substantially. Although this improvement was partly due to changes in lifestyle, especially the decline in cigarette smoking, innovation again played a major role. For example, the introduction of diuretics to treat hypertension reduced cardiovascular-related deaths beginning in the 1970s in the United States and then in other developed countries.

All told, innovation has given rise to a spectacular increase in life expectancy throughout the world over the last century, as well as to a convergence of life expectancy between rich and poor countries and within developed countries. However, this bright side of innovation is tempered by the existence of a darker side, which we will now address.

Innovation and Health: The Dark Side

In a 2017 article entitled "Mortality and Morbidity in the 21st Century," Angus Deaton and Anne Case pinpoint a recent and worrisome phenomenon: after a long period of decline, mortality within the middle-aged (aged fifty to fifty-four), non-Hispanic white population in the United States began to rise in the early 2000s, with a distinct acceleration since 2011–2012, as shown in Figure 11.3.[11]

The other striking fact emphasized by Anne Case and Angus Deaton is the increase in so-called "deaths of despair," meaning deaths resulting from suicide or substance abuse. Figure 11.4 shows the evolution of deaths of despair among American non-Hispanic whites aged fifty to fifty-four compared to the average mortality rate for the same age range in other developed countries. The rapid increase in deaths of despair in this population has no equivalent in other developed countries. Anne Case and Angus Deaton show that this rapid increase primarily affects unskilled individuals. As we have already seen, these are the same people whose jobs and earnings are the most destabilized by innovation.

The authors' explanation for this trend reversal in the mortality of non-Hispanic whites is their heightened job insecurity, one consequence of which is increased family instability. Thus we have moved from a world where people could expect to spend their entire careers doing the same job in the same company, with the certainty of an upward trajectory, to a world where creative destruction is the norm. Creative destruction threatens especially the "working class aristocracy" of the 1970s with an increased risk of unemployment and of loss of status accompanied by earnings loss. The anxiety that results from the perception of this risk leads to increased consumption of antianxiety medication, opioids, and alcohol, thereby increasing the risk of overdose, ethylic coma, and liver disease, as well as of suicide, which accounts for the observed increase in mortality.

Thus, a 2009 study by Daniel Sullivan and Till von Wachter finds a significant impact of job displacement on mortality in the United States.[12] This study utilizes administrative data on employment and income of Pennsylvania residents in the 1970s and 1980s, matched to death records between 1980 and 2006. The authors focus on those who had worked at least three consecutive years with the same employer before losing their jobs. These workers' mortality during the year following job loss increases by over 75 percent and then stabilizes over the long term at 10 to 15 percent more than if they had not lost their jobs. The authors next look at the factors potentially responsible for this increase. In the short run, increased mortality results mainly from the drop in average earnings (50 to 75 percent) and the greater instability of earnings (20 percent) caused by dismissal. In the long run, the drop in earnings remains the main source of increased

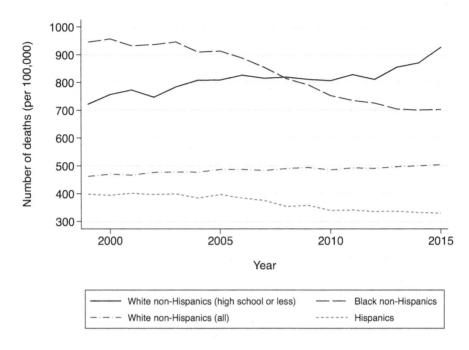

FIGURE 11.3. Mortality by race and ethnicity in the United States for ages 50–54.

Reformatted from A. Case and A. Deaton, "Mortality and Morbidity in the 21st Century," Brookings Papers on Economic Activity *1 (2017): 397–476, figure 1.*

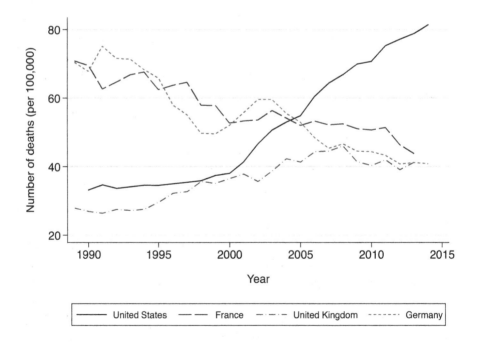

FIGURE 11.4. Deaths of despair by country for ages 50–54.

Extracted and reformatted from A. Case and A. Deaton, "Mortality and Morbidity in the 21st Century," Brookings Papers on Economic Activity *1 (2017): 397–476, figure 5.*

mortality, the consequences of which are lower individual investments in health and more chronic stress.

The Danish Miracle

Is it possible to break the vicious circle between unemployment and health risk and to enable individuals to traverse periods of unemployment with greater serenity? An interesting study by Alexandra Roulet in 2017 on the effects of job displacement on health in Denmark provides some hope.[13] She shows that when a country adopts good safety nets to protect people in the event of job loss, being laid off has no negative effect on health.

A noticeable difference between Denmark and the United States is that in 1993, Denmark introduced a new system called *flexicurity* to regulate its labor market. This system has two pillars. First, the labor market was made more flexible by simplifying dismissal procedures for firms. For example, severance pay is limited and litigation is rare.[14] To offset this flexibility, there are two forms of security: unemployment benefits equal to 90 percent of salary—subject to a ceiling—for a maximum of three years, and a massive government investment in professional training to give workers the skills they need to reenter the labor market quickly.

To conduct her study, Alexandra Roulet relies on several Danish administrative databases from the period 1996 to 2013, including individual tax records, firm-level data matched with information on workers, data from unemployment insurance organizations, and death records. To measure negative impact on an individual's health or the emergence of addiction following job loss, the author uses indicators such as the purchase of antidepressants or pain medication, and alcohol consumption. Additional indicators of deteriorated health are hospital admissions and diagnosis of an illness by a doctor. The author compares the state of health of workers whose place of employment closed between 2001 and 2006 with workers identical in all respects (such as age, experience, and skills), but whose employing firm did not close. Firm closure does not seem to impact the various indicators of health status, in particular consumption of antidepressants or pain medication, or consulting a general practitioner. Similarly, the study finds firm closure has no significant effect on mortality of workers in the firm.

This contrast between Denmark and the United States suggests that institutions—in particular the existence or nonexistence of safety nets on the labor market—play a decisive role with respect to the effects of creative destruction on health and life expectancy. We will now see that the same is true of the relationship between creative destruction and happiness.

3. Creative Destruction and Happiness

Per capita GDP is a useful indicator, as it provides a concise and objective measure of a nation's standard of living and degree of development. But why should our primary focus be per capita GDP, and why should its growth be our primary objective? The answer to this question is by no means clear. It is true that international comparisons suggest that happiness in a given country increases with per capita income.[15] At the same time, however, as Richard Easterlin has shown, there were not more "very happy" Americans in 1970 than in 1942, relative to the total population.[16] At one end of the spectrum are those who believe that we must pursue the objective of growth of per capita GDP because it is a source of prosperity and employment for all. At the other end of the spectrum are the partisans of de-growth. For them, growth of per capita GDP and the policies supporting such growth are a source of unhappiness: they degrade the environment, increase inequality, and generate stress and insecurity in the daily lives of most citizens.

Between these two extremes lie the views of our colleagues Jean-Paul Fitoussi, Amartya Sen, and Joseph Stiglitz, who maintain that in addition to per capita GDP, we should factor in other indicators of development, in particular those that reflect the quality of the environment, education, and health, and containment of unemployment and inequality.[17]

In earlier chapters as well as the present chapter, we have examined how innovation and creative destruction contribute to reconciling growth of per capita GDP with these other objectives. But we can go further: new databases based on opinion surveys enable us to analyze directly how growth by creative destruction is related to indicators of happiness and life satisfaction. As always, however, before delving into the data, it is best to start by looking through the lens of theory.

What Does Theory Predict?

A first effect of creative destruction is to eliminate jobs, thereby increasing a worker's probability of becoming unemployed. This, in turn, is detrimental to happiness, at least in the short run, especially if unemployment entails an immediate and substantial drop in earnings in the short term and increased uncertainty about earnings in the longer term. The best way opinion polls can capture the short-term impact on satisfaction is by asking about the amount of stress the individual is experiencing.

A second effect of creative destruction is to create new jobs, thereby increasing the chances of finding new employment in the future. Creative destruction creates jobs but also new activities, new goods, and new production processes leading to better value for money for consumers. This "creation" side of creative destruction, which takes place mostly over the long term, tends to increase life satisfaction.

Finally, a third effect, also long term, involves the fact that innovation by creative destruction generates growth and, as a consequence, improves future earnings prospects.

This theoretical reasoning gives rise to at least four predictions that can be empirically tested. On one hand, creative destruction increases stress or anxiety, largely because it heightens the chances that an individual will experience unemployment. On the other hand, creative destruction implies growth and the creation of jobs, which has a positive effect on life satisfaction. The negative impact predominates in the short run, and the positive impact is more visible over the longer term. Finally, the effect of creative destruction on satisfaction is on the whole more positive when unemployment benefits are more generous.

Theory Put to the Test

We can measure creative destruction objectively by calculating the job turnover rate (replacement of old jobs by new jobs) or the establishment turnover rate (replacement of old establishments by new establishments). To measure life satisfaction, however, we rely on opinion surveys carried out by Gallup-Healthways between 2008 and 2011. Based on telephone interviews of approximately 1,000 randomly selected Americans, Gallup collects more than 350,000 responses to its questionnaire, on the basis of which it computes life satisfaction measurements.

A first measure, which is inverse to the degree of satisfaction, corresponds to the degree of worry reported by the respondent. It is measured by the binary response to this question: "Did you experience worry during a lot of the day yesterday?" A second measure relies on the Cantril ladder, named after Albert Hadley Cantril, an American psychologist working at Princeton University who was known for his research on public opinion.[18] The Cantril ladder is based on the following questions: "Imagine a ladder with steps numbered from 0 at the bottom to 10 at the top; the top of the ladder represents the best possible life for you and the bottom of the ladder represents the worst possible life for you. On which step of the ladder would you say you personally feel you stand at this time? And which level of the ladder do you anticipate to achieve in five years?" The answers to the first question form the basis of the current Cantril ladder, and the answers to the second question form the basis of the future Cantril ladder.

How do these measures of satisfaction react to creative destruction?[19] Figure 11.5 shows that creative destruction increases anxiety, but to a lesser extent if we

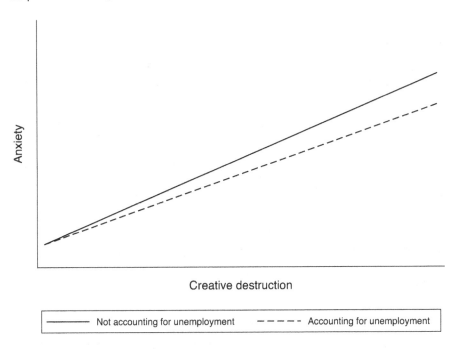

FIGURE 11.5. Creative destruction and anxiety.

© *The Authors.*

control for the effect of creative destruction on unemployment (dashed curve). In other words, unemployment is one channel whereby creative destruction increases anxiety, but it is not the only one. In light of the foregoing discussion, we might conclude that obsolescence of educational degrees and more generally loss of status within the firm also play a role.

Figure 11.6a shows that the overall effect of creative destruction on the current Cantril ladder is nil when we take into account the effect on unemployment (solid curve). In other words, the negative effect associated with the destruction of jobs is offset by the positive effects associated with the creation of jobs and with growth. However, when we ignore the negative effects on unemployment, creative destruction has a positive effect on the current Cantril ladder (dashed curve). This result tends to validate our first prediction.

Figure 11.6b repeats the same exercise but uses the future Cantril ladder as the measure of satisfaction. We find that a higher rate of creative destruction increases the future Cantril ladder even more than it increased the current ladder; both curves are steeper than the equivalent curves in Figure 11.6a. In fact, the impact of creative destruction is positive even if we take into account the effect of

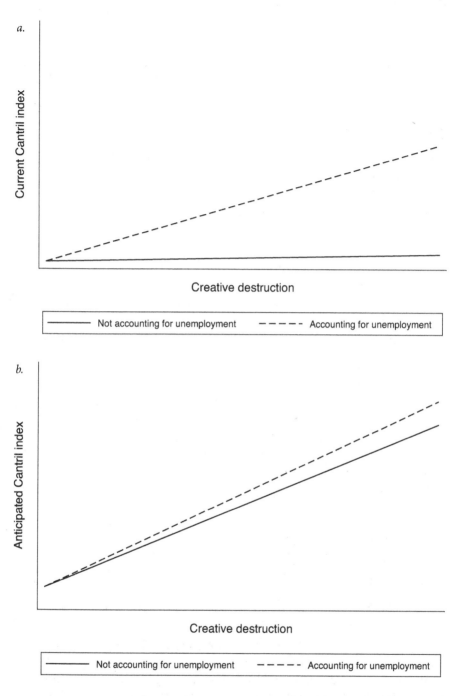

FIGURE 11.6. Creative destruction and anxiety. *a*. Current Cantril ladder. *b*. Anticipated Cantril ladder.

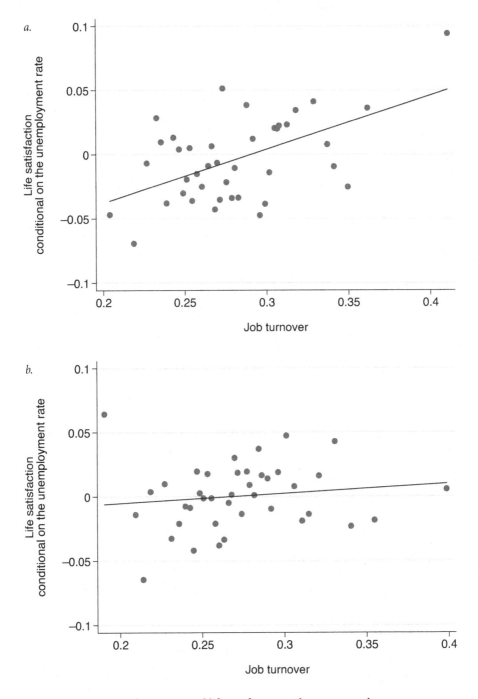

FIGURE 11.7. Creative destruction and life satisfaction, with generous and not generous unemployment benefits. *a.* Generous unemployment benefits. *b.* Not generous unemployment benefits.

Data source: P. Aghion, U. Akcigit, A. Deaton, and A. Roulet, "Creative Destruction and Subjective Well-Being," American Economic Review *106, no. 12 (2016): 3869–3897.*

creative destruction on unemployment (solid curve). In other words, when individuals project five years into the future, they tend to minimize the negative effect of creative destruction—namely, unemployment—and focus more on the positive effects—namely, job creation and growth.

Finally, Figure 11.7 compares employment zones in American states where unemployment benefits are generous (Figure 11.7a) with employment zones in American states with less generous unemployment benefits (Figure 11.7b). These figures show that the positive effect of creative destruction on life satisfaction—measured by the present Cantril ladder in this case—is stronger in employment zones with more generous unemployment benefits. This strengthens the case in favor of an unemployment or flexicurity system closer to the Danish model.

Making Flexicurity Work

The Danish model of flexicurity presents a double advantage: It reduces the rigidity of the labor market, rigidity that can hinder the process of creative destruction.[20] At the same time, it ensures individuals of some security in their professional paths and enables them to manage periods of unemployment with greater serenity, minimal loss of earnings, and the perspective of a rapid return to employment. For the worker, flexicurity means moving from "job security" to "employment security" or "employability," facilitating professional transitions that have become more frequent due to innovation. According to the European Commission, flexicurity "involves flexible and reliable contractual arrangements . . . ; comprehensive lifelong learning strategies; effective active labour market policies; and modern social security systems."[21]

As the European Commission notes, professional training and skills training are a critical element of successful career transition. To emphasize this point, two Danish researchers, Ove Kaj Pedersen and Søren Kaj Andersen, devised the concept of "mobication," combining the words "mobility" and "education."[22] The idea behind this concept is that the development of skills promotes both mobility within the labor market and the ability to meet challenges, such as the AI revolution discussed in Chapter 3.

4. Conclusion

How does creative destruction translate into individuals' real-life experience? In this chapter, we have shown that creative destruction increases the probability of joblessness and more generally of loss of status. In addition, it has a negative impact on health in the United States but not in Denmark. Finally, it has contradictory effects on individuals' life satisfaction: on one hand it increases anxiety, but on the other it improves their expectations of future employment and growth. On the whole, creative destruction does not necessarily entail worse health or less happiness; everything depends on the institutional environment. To win support and avoid a drift toward populism, safety nets are imperative to accompany creative destruction. The first such safety net, as we have seen with the 2020 pandemic, is high-quality health care accessible to all. The second safety net is a system of minimum income to eliminate poverty traps. The third safety net is a system of flexicurity that gives innovative firms the necessary flexibility to hire and terminate employees but also provides individuals with security in their professional paths. This security depends on the combination of generous unemployment insurance and effective lifelong professional training to enable people to find new employment more easily. This is where the state has a role to play as an insurer against the risks associated with creative destruction and job loss, and as an investor in education and innovation. We will return to this last point in greater detail in Chapter 14 and in the Conclusion, which concerns the future of capitalism.

FINANCING CREATIVE
DESTRUCTION

In Chapter 2, we described the misfortunes of the printer David Séchard, the protagonist of Balzac's *Lost Illusions*. Séchard has invented a new and cheaper way to make paper, but he is forced to sell the rights to his invention to the Cointet Brothers in order to repay his debts. A modern-day David Séchard could have turned to a bank or to venture capitalists to finance his invention, and the bank or venture capitalist would have repaid the debt once the invention appeared sufficiently profitable.[1]

Although it is easier for an inventor to find financing today than at the outset of the industrial era, very few countries manage to generate truly disruptive innovations. What are the sources of funding for groundbreaking discoveries and revolutionary ideas? The time frame of the basic research that leads to these discoveries and innovations is most often very long. In addition, the path is strewn with obstacles, because inventing entails clearing unexplored territory. The most disruptive projects are usually pursued by new entrants, for a number of reasons.

First, incumbent firms are marketing the products of their past innovations and do not want those products to be pushed out of the market by new innovations; in other words, they do not wish to replace themselves.[2] Second, existing innovators and firms are influenced by what they have done in the past. This is the path dependence syndrome we discussed in Chapter 9. This syndrome is more ingrained in large firms.[3]

In this chapter, we follow an innovation through its successive stages, from basic research through marketing, and attempt to identify the levers of financing at each stage.[4] Is funding from governmental research agencies and universities sufficient to create fertile ground for revolutionary discoveries? Why is venture capital indispensable to fund new firms capable of generating and implementing disruptive innovations? How can we foster greater risk-taking and motivate large firms to undertake more sweeping innovation? How can the state encourage innovation? In this chapter we will try to shed light on these issues.

1. Financing New, Revolutionary Ideas

Why are universities and governmental research agencies necessary but not sufficient to generate new, revolutionary ideas?

Universities and Governmental Research Agencies as a Lever of Innovation

In Chapter 10, we saw how universities stimulate basic research by ensuring academic freedom and openness. But funding is critical to basic research. Figure 12.1 illustrates the connection between average spending on higher education per student in each OECD country and the country's rank in the Shanghai Ranking, which measures the research performance of higher-education establishments. There is a strong positive correlation between expenditure per student and ranking.[5] Another source of funding for basic research is grants from governmental research agencies. In the early 1960s, at the height of the Cold War, the United States created three federal research agencies: the National Science Foundation (NSF), the National Institutes of Health (NIH), and the National Aeronautics and Space Administration (NASA).

One might think that funding supplied by these research agencies replaces funding from the university. On the contrary, the American example shows a strong positive interaction between university funding and researchers' access to additional funding from a research agency.[6] One explanation of this complementarity could be that competing with other universities for grants stimulates innovation. But other factors undoubtedly play a role, such as the substantial fixed costs of disruptive research, especially in certain fields such as physics, chemistry, and biology. The problem is that there are far too many promising projects for universities and research agencies to be able to finance the fixed costs for all of them.

The Role of Foundations

In the absence of adequate financing from universities and governmental research agencies, "disruptive" researchers can look to private firms. But as we saw in Chapter 10, by partnering with a firm, the researcher may accept certain tradeoffs: the firm will be tempted to restrict the researchers' academic freedom so that they will concentrate on the firm's commercial objectives. Furthermore, the

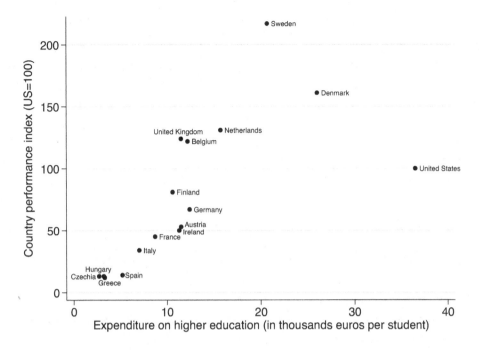

FIGURE 12.1. Relationship between expenditure per student and Shanghai ranking.

Reformatted from P. Aghion, M. Dewatripont, C. Hoxby, A. Mas-Colell, and A. Sapir, "Why Reform Europe's Universities?" Policy Brief 34, Bruegel, Brussels, September 2007, figure 1.

firm will want to limit researchers' contacts with other researchers out of a concern for losing the property rights to the work.

In addition, the firm could redirect the researcher away from novel avenues of research. Gustavo Manso developed this idea on the basis of Bengt Holmström and Paul Milgrom's 1991 work on "multitask agents" within a firm.[7] Their idea is that "agents" (employees or borrowers) may have several different tasks to perform for the "principal" (firm or investor), in which case the principal will tend to provide work incentives that encourage the agents to focus on the least uncertain and most routine tasks, because they have the most predictable and easily measurable returns, and are thus the least risky for the principal.[8] Researchers are seen as multitask agents who always have a choice between devoting themselves to *exploitation* research or to *exploration* research. Exploration consists of starting an entirely new and untested line of research, whereas exploitation consists of pursuing a line of research that is already well defined. The theory of multitask agents predicts that the firm or investor will tend to push researchers

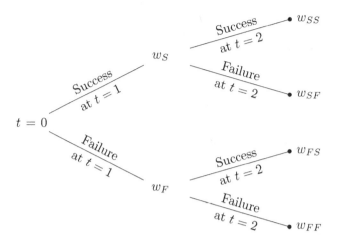

FIGURE 12.2. Possibilities of success and failure and associated salary in the two periods.
© *The Authors.*

toward exploitation rather than exploration because the returns are more predictable and less risky.

Gustavo Manso incorporates the time dimension into this reasoning. Suppose that the research is carried out over two periods. In each period, the probability of success depends on the researcher's efforts, whether she chooses to pursue exploration or exploitation research. Further suppose that exploration has a lower probability of success than exploitation before the first period begins, but a successful result at the end of the first period leads to exploration with higher chances of success in the second period. Figure 12.2 shows the set of possibilities of success and failure at the end of each period, with the bonus w associated with each step. The bonuses that the principal pays to the agent at the end of the first period in case of success and failure are denoted by w_S and w_F, respectively. After a success in the first period, w_{SS} and w_{SF} are the bonuses paid in the respective cases of success and failure in the second period. After a failure in the first period, w_{FS} and w_{FF} denote the bonuses paid in the respective cases of success and failure in the second period.

A principal (firm or investor) taking a short-term perspective will be inclined to "punish" any failure by the researcher in the first period in order to motivate the researcher to increase her efforts and to focus on exploitation research, which is less risky in the short term (Figure 12.3a). In a nutshell, the principal will give the researcher a zero bonus in the case of failure at the end of either the first or the second period ($w_F = 0$, $w_{FF} = 0$, $w_{SF} = 0$). However, a principal who values experimentation and the information it can provide for the second period will adopt a radically different strategy (Figure 12.3b). In order to motivate the re-

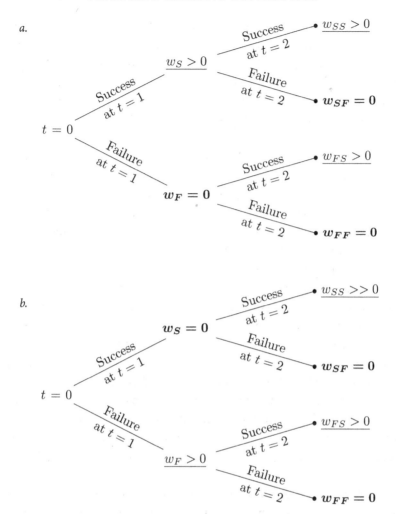

FIGURE 12.3. Contract offered by a principal seeking to encourage exploitation or exploration. *a.* Encourage exploitation. *b.* Encourage exploration.

© *The Authors.*

searcher to pursue exploration research during the first period, this principal will not punish a failure in this period. On the contrary, the principal will guarantee a positive bonus in the first period in the case of failure ($w_F > 0$) but a zero bonus in the case of success ($w_S = 0$), to discourage the researcher from employing the conventional work method. If the exploration leads to failure in the first period, the principal can still encourage the researcher to fall back on exploitation research and avoid shirking in the second period. It will thus offer the researcher a positive bonus in the second period if the initial failure is followed by success ($w_{FS} > 0$). But if exploration leads to success in the first period, the principal will induce the researcher to pursue exploration because, conditional upon success of exploration in the first period, exploration will also be more profitable in the second period. The principal will thus offer a very large bonus in the second period if success in the second period follows the initial success ($w_{SS} \gg 0$).

As a practical matter, how can we encourage exploration? Within firms, one option is to protect agents' compensation and employment from the uncertainty of the firm's short-run performance. This is what institutional investors do, as we will see below. It is also an objective of bankruptcy law, such as the well-known Chapter 11 of the US Bankruptcy Code, which protects debtors from the risk of premature liquidation under pressure from creditors.[9]

Until now, we have been considering the question from within the firm. But how can we encourage exploration by scientists outside a firm when their research entails high fixed costs? Let's look at the example of the Howard Hughes Medical Institute (HHMI), which is the largest source of private funding for academic biomedical research in the United States. One of HHMI's programs is the Investigator Program, which selects young scientists they believe are capable of making fundamental discoveries that will push the bounds of knowledge in biomedical research. In all, the Investigator Program selected seventy-three scientists over the years 1993, 1994, and 1995. Unlike the NSF or the NIH, HHMI bets on people rather than on projects. In addition, whereas the NSF and the NIH fund projects for only three years, HHMI funds most of its researchers for at least five years.[10]

What are the results of this funding strategy? First of all, more than twenty HHMI Investigators have been awarded the Nobel Prize. But most importantly, this funding has had a striking effect on the number of publications, as shown in Figure 12.4. The solid curve represents the evolution of the number of publications written by the "treatment" group, meaning the recipients of HHMI funding, and point 0 corresponds to the year the investigator received the funding. The dashed curve shows the same evolution for the control group of scientists, meaning those who did not obtain HHMI funding but had nearly identical characteristics to the recipients (age, academic institution where they worked, research field, and results) and had received another research grant early in their careers (scholarships from the Pew, Searle, Beckman, Packard, and Rita Allen Foundations).

Before the HHMI funding, the solid and dashed curves are very close: the non-recipient "control" scientists are thus comparable to the recipients prior to HHMI funding. However, the two curves diverge starting at that date, and estimations

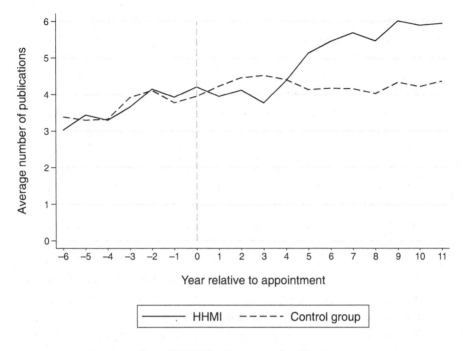

FIGURE 12.4. Dynamic effect of HHMI funding on total publications.

Extracted and reformatted from P. Azoulay, J. S. Graff Zivin, and G. Manso, "Incentives and Creativity: Evidence from the Academic Life Sciences," RAND Journal of Economics 42, no. 3 (2011): 527–554, figure 4A.

indicate that the rate of publication increases an average of 39 percent for recipients compared to *a priori* similar nonrecipients.

2. Financing Disruptive Firms: The Role of Venture Capital

Firms Backed by Venture Capital: What Theory Says

What is venture capital? An investor acquires an equity interest in a startup with the intention of selling it down the road and making a profit. But why are startups the most common type of entity to make use of venture capital financing?

Let us first take a look at financial structure and control rights. Until recently, economists specialized in corporate finance focused on how a firm's revenues were distributed between the firm's owners and investors. Thus, debt was defined as a contract that entitled a lender to a fixed amount, with the firm taking the remaining revenues.[11] Equity financing was defined as a contract entitling shareholders, the firm's owners, to a fraction of the firm's revenues.

An alternative theory of corporate finance emphasizes control rights.[12] In a nutshell, we can understand this theory by considering the case of an entrepreneur (or a family-run business). The business needs external funding—in addition to its own assets—to finance a new, innovative project. This firm will look for an investor. The entrepreneur and the investor both want the project to succeed, even though their objectives may differ. The investor is seeking monetary returns and therefore seeks to maximize the firm's monetary profits. The entrepreneur, however, is more of an empire-builder and has the ambition of establishing a reputation as an innovator. These motivations may lead the entrepreneur to try to keep the firm in business at all costs, even at the expense of short-term monetary returns. In a world of "incomplete contracts," where it is impossible to predict what will happen in every possible contingency, the allocation of control rights between the entrepreneur and the investor becomes a key component of the contract between these two actors. Thus the different financing techniques differ above all by how they allocate control between the parties, rather than by the manner in which they distribute the firm's income. Philippe Aghion and Patrick Bolton examine three principal ways of allocating control.

First, issuing voting equity can be seen as a contract that forces the entrepreneur to share control rights with the investor, who can impose decisions that the entrepreneur would not otherwise have made—such as closing down the firm in the event of financial difficulties. Second, issuing nonvoting equity enables the entrepreneur to fund her project without sharing control with the investor. Investors, however, often refuse this type of contract, particularly if the entrepreneur does not have personal funds or tangible assets (equipment, buildings, land) that the investor can recover if the firm faces financial difficulties. Lastly, debt financing allocates control in a contingent manner between the two parties. As long as all goes well, the entrepreneur retains full control; if things go badly, she will lose control to the investor. Bankruptcy is a mechanism for transferring control in the event of serious deterioration of the firm's financial condition.

Let's return to our start-up firm attempting to fund a new, innovative project. To retain control, the firm will seek, to the extent possible, to issue nonvoting equity. But if the investor refuses, perhaps because of inadequate financial or tangible assets to serve as collateral, the entrepreneur will have no choice but to turn over some control to the investor. This is where venture capital comes in.

Venture capital is a multistage financing contract. At first, the contract grants the investor a large share of the firm's revenues and a veto right over firm decisions. But at each successive stage, the investor progressively hands control rights to the entrepreneur.

Building on the approach of Aghion and Bolton, Steven Kaplan and Per Strömberg explain why this type of financing is particularly well adapted to young, innovative firms.[13] These firms generally start with low shareholders' equity and little tangible capital upon formation. For at least minimal protection, the investor will thus insist on having a share of the pie—including when the firm is successful—and will also insist on a veto right over firm decisions in order to prevent the firm from going down a path that would result in the investor losing too much of its investment. The investor will thus rule out nonvoting shares as well as debt financing and will prefer voting equity. This type of contract induces the investor to get involved in the firm's decisions, not only to block decisions that it views as too risky, but above all to share its experience, knowledge, knowhow, and network with an entrepreneur who in many cases is inexperienced and little knowledgeable about how the market works. However, as the firm grows and accumulates retained earnings, the investor can afford to yield control rights back to the entrepreneur and reduce its share of dividends, since the retrained earnings serve as a guaranty, should difficulties arise. The faster retained earnings—or other external funding—increase, the more quickly the investor will agree to transfer its control rights to the entrepreneur.

Based on information covering 213 investments in eleven American firms by fourteen venture capitalists, Kaplan and Strömberg confirm their theory empirically. They first show that venture capitalists accept a reduction in their dividends and voting rights when the firm's financial performance is good but insist on greater voting rights if performance is poor. Second, it appears that venture capitalists give up voting rights when they are in possession of indicators reflecting that the firm is in good health, including in particular when the firm has secured a sufficient number of satisfied customers; in the case of the pharmaceutical industry, when the FDA has approved a new drug or when a patent has been approved. Finally, Kaplan and Strömberg show that the venture capitalist gives up some control as the firm grows. All of these empirical findings reflect the investor's willingness to grant the entrepreneur more control rights as the firm's financial condition evolves positively.

Firms Backed by Venture Capital: What the Data Says[14]

A recent study by Ufuk Akcigit, Emin Dinlersoz, Jeremy Greenwood, and Veronika Penciakova underscores the importance of venture capital in funding young, innovative firms.[15] This study merges several datasets of US firms and establishments: the Longitudinal Business Database of the US Census Bureau, which provides information on employment, salaries, and the age of firms and establishments; Thomson Reuters' VentureXpert Database of US firms that have

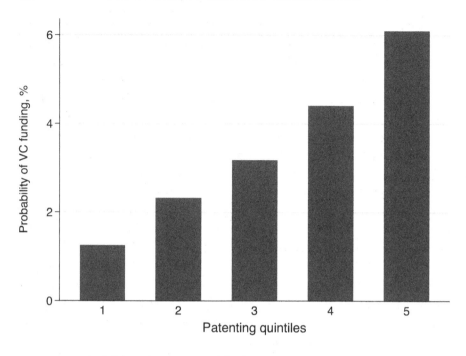

FIGURE 12.5. Probability of venture capital funding and innovation.

U. Akcigit, E. Dinlersoz, J. Greenwood, and V. Penciakova, "Synergizing Ventures" (NBER Working Paper No. 26196, National Bureau of Economic Research, Cambridge, MA, August 2019), figure 3.

received venture backing together with the dates and amounts of the venture investments; and finally a database of the USPTO showing the patents granted to US firms and citations of these patents.

The authors first show that venture capital financing was concentrated on new firms: 42 percent of US venture-backed firms receive their first funding in the year that they first hire employees, and 15 percent of them receive their first funding before they hire their first employee. Furthermore, venture capital (VC) funding is concentrated on firms with a high growth potential, meaning firms whose employment growth grew very rapidly during their first three years of existence. Similarly, venture capital funding targets firms that are the most innovative in their first years of existence (Figure 12.5).[16] Firms in the lowest quintile of innovative activity have only a 1 percent likelihood of receiving venture capital funding, compared to about 6 percent—six times higher—for the highest quintile.

Overall, venture capitalists look for new firms with strong growth and innovation potential. What is the impact of venture capital funding on innovation?

Figure 12.6 compares the evolution of total employment (Figure 12.6a) and innovative activity (Figure 12.6b)[17] respectively for firms with venture backing (solid curves) and for similar firms without venture backing (dashed curves). The figure shows clearly that the former grow much faster than the latter starting from the date they receive venture capital funding. In other words, firms that benefit from venture capital have distinctly better chances of growing in size and of increasing their innovative activity. This fact reflects the skill of venture capitalists both in selecting firms with high innovation and growth potential and then in providing guidance to these firms.

The Contrast Between the United States and France

Ghizlane Kettani identifies the main differences in venture capital activity in France and in the United States, beginning with the characteristics of venture capitalists in these two countries.[18] In the United States, the typical venture capitalist started out as an innovative entrepreneur who received venture capital funding. The royal road is for the entrepreneur to sell her firm by means of an IPO. She uses the proceeds of this IPO to become a venture capitalist herself. Her personal experience as an entrepreneur has provided her with the expertise and know-how necessary to select the most promising projects and to advise newer entrepreneurs pursuing those projects. These venture capitalists, who are themselves entrepreneurial, passionate about creating new firms, and willing to invest their personal wealth to foster the development of startups, are known as business angels.

By contrast, in France, venture capitalists are most often finance professionals whose career has been in banking or insurance and who, therefore, have neither the practical entrepreneurial experience nor the technological knowledge necessary to advise a startup. This explains in part why, in 2009, French venture capitalists invested only 353 million euros in young innovative firms, compared to 4.5 billion euros in the United States. Of course, this description of American and French venture capitalists is deliberately simplified and exaggerated. Some French venture capitalists are former entrepreneurs, and some American venture capitalists are finance professionals.

A second difference is that the equity markets are much more developed in the United States than in France. As a result, an IPO rewards American venture capitalists more than their French counterparts. Finally, institutional investors play a much greater role in the United States than in France, in particular because of the importance of pension funds, and these institutional investors participate in venture capital financing.[19] Another virtue of institutional investment is that it encourages innovation in large firms, as we will see below.

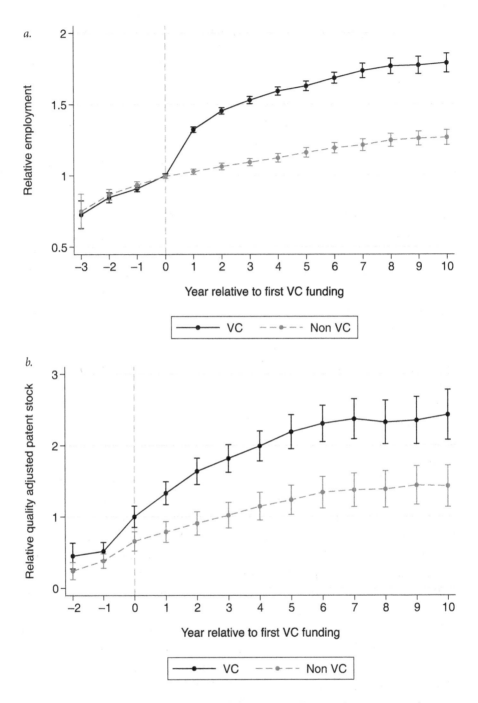

FIGURE 12.6. Evolution of employment and innovation in firms with venture capital backing and without venture capital backing. *a.* Employment. *b.* Innovation.

Reformatted from U. Akcigit, E. Dinlersoz, J. Greenwood, and V. Penciakova, "Synergizing Ventures" (NBER Working Paper No. 26196, National Bureau of Economic Research, Cambridge, MA, August 2019), figures 4, 6.

3. Disruptive Innovation in Large Firms:
The Role of Institutional Investors

If venture capital plays a decisive role in financing innovation in new firms, who takes over once these firms have become mature enough to be listed on a stock market? The United States has seen a surge in the importance of institutional investors over time: their ownership of the capital of publicly traded firms grew from 9.4 percent in 1970 to 61 percent in 2005.[20]

What is the impact of this spectacular increase in the role of institutional investors on innovation in the firms in which they invest? Our initial hypothesis was that the impact must be negative: we perceived the institutional investors as short-termist and fickle, not supportive of innovation and even less of disruptive innovation. But empirical data toppled our preconceptions: we found a positive correlation between the percentage of a firm's capital held by institutional investors and the intensity of innovation in the firm.[21] What explains this positive effect?

The Theory of Career Concerns[22]

The basic idea of the theory of *career concerns* is that the manager of a business seeks to signal her ability in order to secure her position in the firm and strengthen her reputation (and thereby her "price" on the market for managers). The first indication of ability is the performance of the firm in which she works. However, the firm's performance only imperfectly reflects the manager's skill. It depends both on her ability and on luck: regardless of the manager's ability, there is always a risk her project will fail. In this context, a manager will hesitate to take on a disruptive project because it will be riskier, with a higher probability of failure, than a nondisruptive project. She will be all the more hesitant if she is risk averse and fears losing her job and her reputation on the market for managers. How does the strong presence of an institutional investor in the firm's ownership counterbalance the manager's reluctance to innovate?

The answer is that the institutional investor can directly obtain information about the manager's ability. Doing so, however, is costly, and accordingly only an institutional investor with a large shareholding in the firm will find it profitable to invest the fixed costs of acquiring this information. If the information turns out to be positive, in other words if the institutional investor finds out that the manager is competent, then the manager will be shielded from the risks inherent in innovation. Consequently, the manager will not hesitate to undertake an innovative project: if the project fails, the institutional investor will protect her job, thereby minimizing the downside risk, and if the project succeeds, her reputation will be enhanced.[23]

The greater the institutional investor's financial stake in the firm, the more it will protect the manager if an innovative project fails, and therefore the stronger the manager's incentive to undertake disruptive projects. This explains the positive correlation we observe between the weight of institutional investment and the firm's innovation intensity.

Putting the Theory to the Test

To verify this theory empirically, a 2013 study by Philippe Aghion, John Van Reenen, and Luigi Zingales looks at a sample of 803 publicly listed US firms covered in the Compustat database for the period from 1991 to 1999.[24] Information on the number and quality of these firms' patents comes from the USPTO. Finally, information about the percentage of shares held by institutional investors in these firms comes from the Compact Disclosure database.

Several observations emerge. The percentage of shares held by institutional investors has a positive impact on the number and quality of the firm's patents. Furthermore, the degree of competition that the firm faced reinforces this positive effect. Thus, Figure 12.7 shows that institutional investment has a stronger effect on innovation in firms facing intense competition.[25] The explanation is that competition increases the losses the firm will incur if the project fails; it exacerbates the risks induced by innovation—in particular the risks of imitation and of creative destruction. But institutional investors are there precisely to protect the manager from the risk of job and reputation loss in the event the project fails. This protection is all the more valuable to the manager when the firm faces more intense competition.

Another result also in line with the theory of career concerns is that the impact of institutional investors on innovation should be weaker when the managers have alternative protection, for example in American states where hostile takeovers are subject to greater regulation. The idea here is that these regulations are a substitute for the protection of institutional investors. Finally, the theory of career concerns predicts that institutional investors will decrease the risk of job loss for the manager in the event the firm performs poorly, and this is indeed what the data says. Overall, contrary to our initial conjecture, institutional investment stimulates innovation in publicly traded firms, because it protects managers from the potential career risks associated with innovation.

Comparing the weight of institutional investors in France and the United States, we find that the United States once again is far ahead, due to the importance of pension funds. In 2017, pension fund assets represented 145 percent of US GDP,

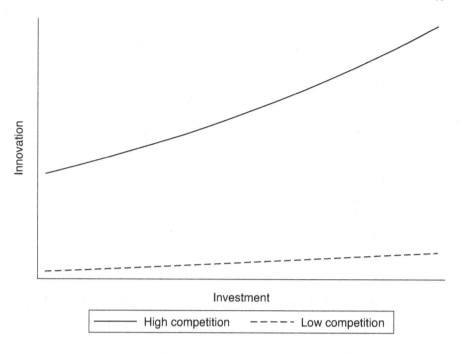

FIGURE 12.7. Innovation and institutional investment by degree of competition.

Data source: P. Aghion, J. Van Reenen, and L. Zingales, "Innovation and Institutional Ownership," American Economic Review 103, no. 1 (2013): 277–304.

compared to only 10 percent for France.[26] Moreover, US institutional investors finance young innovative firms in the amount of 56 billion euros in 2018, compared to 665 million for French institutional investors—an amount eighty-four times less than their American counterparts.[27]

4. Innovation in Firms and Tax Incentives for R&D

How can the state contribute to funding innovative activity by firms? Tax incentives are a logical response. Tax incentives for R&D can take the form of a tax deduction that reduces taxable income; this is the mechanism used in the United Kingdom. It can also take the form of a tax credit, as in France.[28]

In the United Kingdom, the tax incentive for R&D, introduced in 2000, was initially available only to small- and medium-sized enterprises (SMEs). In 2002, it was extended to large firms. However, it continued to provide more generous relief to SMEs: until 2007, firms with fewer than 250 employees, assets under 43 million euros, and annual sales (turnover) under 50 million euros benefited from a more generous tax deduction on R&D expenditures than did larger firms. In 2008,

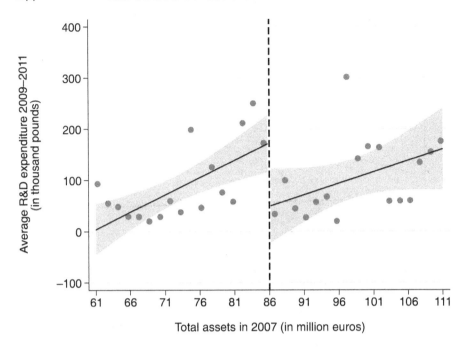

FIGURE 12.8. Average R&D expenditure between 2009 and 2011 as of a function of firm total assets.

Reformatted from A. Dechezleprêtre, E. Einiö, R. Martin, K.-T. Nguyen, and J. Van Reenen, "Do Tax Incentives for Research Increase Firm Innovation? An RD Design for R&D," unpublished manuscript, 2020, figure 2.

the United Kingdom reformed the mechanism, raising the threshold for qualifying as a SME: the allowance now applies to all British firms with fewer than 500 employees, assets under 86 million euros, and sales under 100 million euros. What effect did this reform have on innovation?

Figure 12.8 depicts average annual R&D expenditures between 2009 and 2011 as a function of firm size measured by the value of its assets. Generally speaking, there is a positive correlation between a firm's annual R&D spending and the amount of its assets, reflecting the fact that large firms with more assets can spend more on R&D. However, there is a clear discontinuity at the eligibility threshold of €86 million. Average R&D spending was greater for firms just below the threshold, who benefited from more generous tax relief, than for firms just above it. The evolution of the number of patents obtained between 2009 and 2013 is similar to that of R&D expenditures. We again observe a discontinuity: whereas the relationship between the number of patents and the firm's assets increased both above and below the threshold, there was a distinct drop at the threshold.[29]

As mentioned above, the British system of R&D incentive targets SMEs. This choice makes sense insofar as SMEs innovate more—as measured by the number of patents per 1,000 employees—in France (Figure 12.9a) and in the United States (Figure 12.9b).[30] In addition, innovations produced by SMEs are more radical and significant. However, this virtue of the British system is nonetheless not shared by other developed countries, including France (Figure 12.10). Thus, in 2018, the rate of tax subsidies on R&D expenditures was very high in France and was identical for SMEs and for large firms (43 percent).[31] In Great Britain, the rate was lower overall, and it was greater for SMEs (27 percent) than for large firms (11 percent).

In France, the thresholds to qualify for a tax credit are not defined in terms of firm size but rather of the amount of R&D spending: R&D expenditures up to 100 million euros are eligible for a 30 percent subsidy and for a 5 percent subsidy beyond that threshold. Yet very few firms spend more than 100 million euros on R&D, and almost all firms conducting R&D thus obtain the 30 percent subsidy. We can reasonably expect, however, that even without an R&D tax credit, the very large firms—whose R&D expenditures exceed 100 million euros—would have in any event invested tens of millions of euros in R&D. In other words, the tax credits on the first several million in spending are a pure windfall for these firms, with no effect on their R&D investment. Nevertheless, in 2014, the 100 largest firms received 34 percent of total R&D tax credits.

To make the R&D tax credit less biased in favor of large firms, a radical solution would be to emulate the British system by setting thresholds that are contingent on the size of the firm. An intermediate solution would be to create a marginal subsidy rate that increases with the intensity of the firm's R&D, defined as the ratio between R&D spending and the size of the firm.[32]

5. Conclusion

What is the best way to finance the different stages of innovation, especially disruptive innovation? We have seen that at the basic research stage, funding from research agencies and universities is often insufficient to stimulate revolutionary discoveries, and the involvement of private foundations betting on promising researchers also plays an important role. At the development stage, we have shown that beyond the purely financial dimension, the degree of involvement of the investor in the firm's project makes all the difference. In the early stage, venture capital funding modulates control over firm decisions over time and thus constitutes a key mechanism for stimulating disruptive innovation and firm growth. Once the firm has grown in size, institutional investors take over this role: by protecting managers who undertake innovative projects, they motivate them to take more

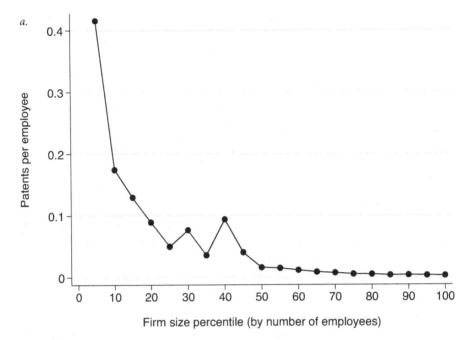

a.

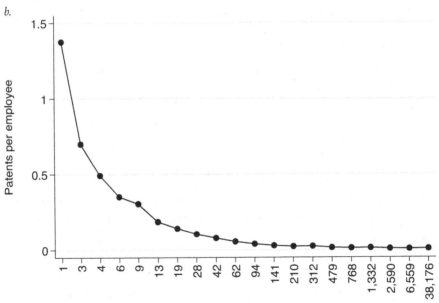

b.

FIGURE 12.9. Innovation intensity by firm size in France and in the United States.
a. France. *b.* United States.

a. *Data source: Matched employer-employee data (DADS) and Patstat; b. Reformatted from U. Akcigit and W. R. Kerr,*
"Growth through Heterogeneous Innovations," Journal of Political Economy *126, no. 4 (2018): 1374–1443, figure 2.*

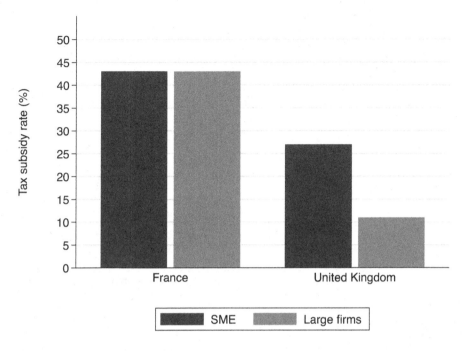

FIGURE 12.10. Subsidy rate on R&D spending by country and by type of firm.

Data source: OECD.

risks. Finally, the state has a role to play in financing innovation, in particular by means of tax incentives for R&D, but also by means of procurement contracts and more generally through its industrial policy (see Chapters 4 and 14).

In sum, the financial ecosystem has a major influence on innovation. The United States benefits from the existence of a powerful network of research foundations, institutional investors, and venture capitalists with the experience necessary to guide new firms to grow successfully. This network contributes to the US predominance in innovation. Nonetheless, finance must be regulated to prevent it from becoming an obstacle to growth. We will return to this point in Chapter 14 and in Box 12.1.

BOX 12.1 THE PITFALLS OF FINANCE

Chapter 12 describes the different means of financing innovation. But financing comes with some dangers.

Investors (the public sector, venture capitalists, and institutional investors) are facing two types of potential errors when they have to decide whether or not to fund an innovative project. They can make a Type I error, which consists

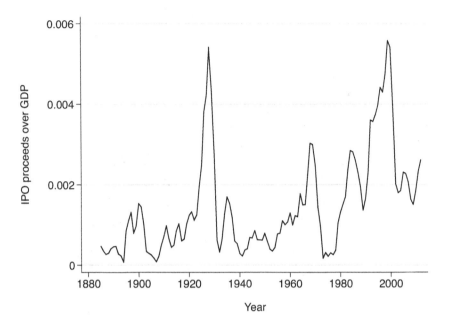

FIGURE 12.A. Share of IPO proceeds in GDP.

Extracted and reformatted from T. Philippon, "Has the US Finance Industry Become Less Efficient? On the Theory and Measurement of Financial Intermediation," American Economic Review *105, no. 4 (2015): 1408–1438, figure 13.*

of not financing a good project, or a Type II error, which consists of financing a project that is not good. As we know, the Schumpeterian innovator has a high probability of failure, which implies the failure of the project, and a low probability of success, which comes with a very substantial payoff. In the context of funding innovation, it is thus not uncommon to make Type II errors. The real problem for an investor is the risk of making a Type I error, or failing to finance what turns out to be a highly lucrative project. A typical example is the error that an investor would have made by refusing to invest in Facebook or Google at their founding.

But as we saw in Chapter 3, numerous secondary innovations follow the arrival of a major general purpose technology, and their chances of success are greater. Because of investors' fear of committing Type I errors, there is a surge of enthusiasm in the financial sector, as illustrated by Figure 12.A, depicting the evolution over time of the share of IPO proceeds in GDP.[1] There was a peak in the 1920s with the introduction of electricity, and also in the late 1990s with the IT revolution.

Intense competition among investors to avoid missing the good projects leads them to exercise less scrutiny on project quality, inducing them to fund unworthy projects. They will make more Type II mistakes through fear of making Type I mistakes. This tendency explains the emergence of financial bubbles associated with general purpose innovations, of which the Internet bubble of the early 2000s is a typical example.

Another source of inefficiency in corporate finance for innovation is that a firm may get ensnared by the financial markets' expectations, abandoning its own objectives.[2] A firm thus has the choice between either increasing sales or consolidating its existing customer base by lowering its costs and streamlining its production. The firm's manager is concerned about her reputation, as discussed earlier. Since she wishes to signal her ability to the financial markets, she will be inclined to do what financial markets expect of her. If financial markets look to sales growth as an indicator of the firm's success, the manager will tend to concentrate on increasing sales to the detriment of streamlining production. But if financial markets perceive that the firm is pursuing a growth strategy, they will attach greater importance to growth measures. This two-way feedback process becomes a vicious circle, in which firms never make the transition from expansion to streamlining, potentially to the point of provoking a systemic crisis.

---

1. Thomas Philippon, "Has the US Finance Industry Become Less Efficient? On the Theory and Measurement of Financial Intermediation," *American Economic Review* 105, no. 4 (2015): 1408–1438.

2. Philippe Aghion and Jeremy C. Stein, "Growth vs. Margins: Destabilizing Consequences of Giving the Stock Market What It Wants," *Journal of Finance* 63, no. 3 (2008): 1025–1058.

▼

13

HOW TO MANAGE
GLOBALIZATION

As Adam Smith explains in *The Wealth of Nations,* international trade encourages a better division of labor, which facilitates technological progress and can
therefore promote prosperity throughout the world. Why, then, has the globalization of trade recently met with increasing opposition in developed countries?
Part of the answer surely lies in the fact that globalization can lead to widespread
outsourcing and deindustrialization. Indeed, the last fifty years have witnessed
numerous factory closings and massive job losses in the American Rust Belt, the
north of England and Wales, the mining regions of northern France and southern
Belgium, and the steelmaking regions of eastern France and Germany.

First the election of Donald Trump as president of the United States and then
the outbreak of the COVID-19 pandemic in China have renewed debate about
the economic impact of globalization. Trump was elected in November 2016 on
a promise to protect American industry and therefore American jobs by erecting
customs barriers against imports from abroad. In 2018, the United States imposed
import duties and quotas on a long list of foreign products. In January 2018, for
instance, the Trump administration raised tariffs on solar panels and washing machines. In March 2018 additional duties were imposed on aluminum, steel, automobiles, and automotive parts, all in the name of national security. These were
followed by a series of significant tariff hikes targeting Chinese products of all
kinds. In addition, the European Union was hit with tariffs ranging from 10 to
25 percent on $7.5 billion dollars' worth of its exports to the United States (in-
cluding French wines, Italian cheeses, and Scotch whiskeys). Taken together, the
effect of these measures was to slow global growth.[1]

Global growth has also suffered from a more recent scourge: the COVID-19
pandemic. Economic forecasters initially favored an optimistic scenario, antici-

pating that the epidemic would reach its peak in China in the first quarter of 2020 and spread only moderately to other countries. In fact, the disease spread widely, especially in Europe and North America. In April 2020, the IMF predicted a global recession of 3 percent in 2020, with developed countries bearing the brunt: a contraction of 7.2 percent was forecast for France and 5.9 percent for the United States.[2]

In particular, the COVID-19 pandemic highlighted the importance of "value chains," also known as supply chains, which link countries together in multinational production processes. Each country in such a chain produces some raw material, service, or component included in the final product. According to the OECD, approximately 70 percent of international trade currently involves global value chains. China in particular participates as a producer of intermediate goods in a growing number of value chains in the information technology, electronics, pharmaceuticals, and transportation equipment sectors. Hence any slowdown in China will have a very significant impact on aggregate world output. In today's globalized economy, this effect is likely to be particularly strong owing to the widespread adoption of "just in time" production methods in the developed economies.

In this chapter we will focus on the relation between globalization and innovation, touching on questions of international trade and immigration. Specifically, we will look at the effects of growing Chinese imports on employment and innovation in the United States and Europe following China's entry into the World Trade Organization (WTO). Did these effects justify Donald Trump's massive tariff increase? Might the reaction have been different? Why does export market expansion stimulate innovation? How does immigration contribute to innovation? These are among the questions we will try to answer.

1. The Chinese Import Shock

The share of Chinese goods as a fraction of total global imports jumped spectacularly in the first decade of the twenty-first century, rising from 3 percent in 1999 to 10 percent in 2012. Figure 13.1 shows the impressive rise of China's share of total US and European imports between 1980 and 2007, while the share of other low-labor-cost countries remained stable.[3] China's entry into the WTO in 2001 clearly accelerated the process. Should we be afraid of the increased competition from China? And how should we respond to it?

Negative Effects of the Chinese Shock

Effect on employment and wages. How did China's entry into the WTO affect the American labor market? The answer cannot be deduced from theory *a priori*. Consider a specific geographical region of the United States—call it "region *R*."

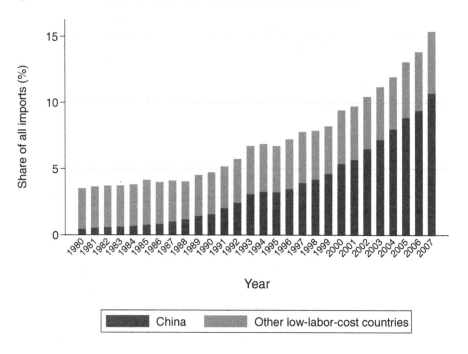

FIGURE 13.1. Share of imports from China and other countries with low labor costs as a percentage of total imports to Europe and the United States. *Note:* The European aggregate is constructed from the following twelve countries: Austria, Denmark, Finland, France, Germany, Ireland, Italy, Norway, Spain, Sweden, Switzerland, and the United Kingdom.

Reformatted from N. Bloom, M. Draca, and J. Van Reenen, "Trade Induced Technical Change? The Impact of Chinese Imports on Innovation, IT and Productivity," Review of Economic Studies 83, no. 1 (2016): 87–117, figure 1.

How would we expect China's entry to affect the labor market in *R*? To answer this question, we need to consider two opposing effects. First, China's entry heightens competition in markets in which *R* sells its output, negatively affecting employment and wages. For concreteness, imagine that China manufactures automobiles and that *R* also specializes in the same product. Then the increase in auto imports from China will decrease demand for *R*'s output, with a consequent negative impact on the region's labor market. But China's membership in the WTO might also increase Chinese demand for automobiles, which could lead to an increase of *R*'s output, with a positive effect on employment and wages.

Now, it so happens that US imports from China vastly exceed US exports to China,[4] which suggests that the negative effect of the Chinese shock should outweigh the positive effect. In fact, as we will see shortly, it turns out that the American manufacturing sector was particularly vulnerable to the Chinese import

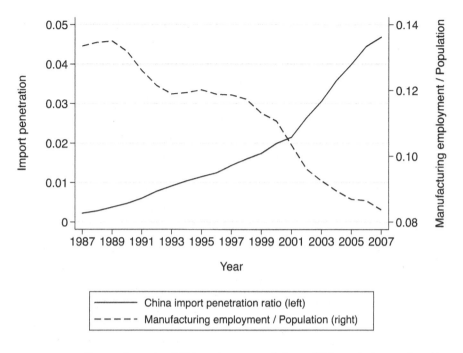

FIGURE 13.2. Penetration ratio of Chinese imports and share of US population employed in the manufacturing sector.

Reformatted from D. Autor, D. Dorn, and G. H. Hanson, "The China Syndrome: Local Labor Market Effects of Import Competition in the United States," American Economic Review 103, no. 6 (2013): 2121–2168, figure 1.

shock, due in part to production outsourcing, in part to layoffs in US-based firms, and in part to decreased wages.[5]

Figure 13.2, drawn from a pathbreaking study by David Autor, David Dorn, and Gordon Hanson, shows the evolution of the penetration ratio of Chinese imports to the United States (indicated by the solid curve in the graph) and of US industrial employment as a percentage of the population (dashed curve).[6] As the graph clearly shows, Chinese import penetration increases steadily throughout the period, rising from 0.6 percent in 1991 to 4.6 percent in 2007, and accelerating in 2001, when China joined the WTO. At the same time, industrial employment decreases from 12.6 percent in 1991 to 8.4 percent in 2007, falling at a faster rate in the first decade of the twenty-first century.

But is this aggregate picture for the United States accurate for the country's regional sub-economies? Put another way, were the regions most affected by the Chinese import shock the ones where manufacturing employment declined the most? To answer this question, the authors of the cited study used an econometric approach known as a "shift-share instrument." This method is based on the construction of a measure of regional exposure to the Chinese import shock that combines information about the sectoral composition of the regional economy with information about sectoral exposure at the national level. More concretely, suppose that the American automobile industry is particularly sensitive to increased auto imports from China. Then regions of the United States where the auto industry is concentrated will be strongly affected by the shock. Conversely, regions in which few people are employed in the manufacture of automobiles will barely be exposed at all. Ultimately, the study found that a high Chinese penetration ratio in a given region led to a significant loss of industrial employment in that region. Of the ensuing job loss, 25 percent was due to increased unemployment and 75 percent to decreased labor market participation.[7]

Adults without higher education are the most likely to have been affected by the loss of industrial jobs. Furthermore, this job loss was not offset by an increase in nonindustrial employment. Lost industrial jobs were more likely to be replaced by service-sector jobs. On average, increased competition from Chinese imports accounts for 21 percent of lost manufacturing jobs in the United States from 1990 to 2007. This translates into 1.5 million workers who lost their livelihoods. It was these workers, among others, whom Donald Trump targeted in his 2016 presidential campaign when he called for the repatriation of American manufacturing.

The loss of industrial jobs was not the only consequence of the Chinese import shock. Wages also fell. Hence the negative effect of Chinese imports on regional economies was even worse, because the fall in wages decreased the demand for local services while increasing the supply of labor available for service-sector jobs.

Effect on innovation. What was the effect of Chinese imports on innovation? A preliminary answer to this question can be found in a recent study of the relation between Chinese imports and innovation as measured by patents.[8] Figure 13.3 compares the evolution of the number of patent applications in the period 1975–2007 with total Chinese imports in the period 1990–2007. Over the period 1991–2001, Chinese imports increased in parallel with patent applications. A naïve interpretation of this graph might lead to the conclusion that Chinese imports encouraged innovation. But a closer look reveals that the pace of Chinese imports accelerated after 2001, when China joined the WTO, at which point US patent applications began to decline.

Note, however, that here we are arguing in terms of the aggregate American economy. What happens when we look at individual firms? Here, the authors find that when the penetration ratio of Chinese imports increases in a given sector of the economy, firms in that sector become less innovative.[9]

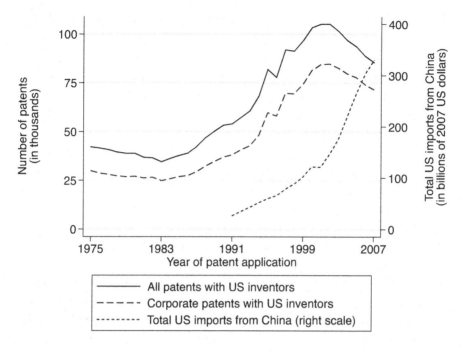

FIGURE 13.3. Evolution of the number of US patents and of total Chinese imports to the United States.

Extracted and reformatted from D. Autor, D. Dorn, G. H. Hanson, G. Pisano, and P. Shu, "Foreign Competition and Domestic Innovation: Evidence from US Patents," American Economic Review: Insights 2, no. 3 (2020): 357–374, figure 1 panel A.

How can we explain the negative effect of the Chinese import shock on the innovativeness of American industrial firms? One natural explanation is that increased competition from China, where labor is cheaper than in the United States, reduces the profit margins of American firms and therefore diminishes their incentive and their capacity to invest, especially in innovation. The authors show that increased Chinese penetration in a sector not only reduces the gross revenues of American firms in that sector but also decreases their investment in research and development. In sum, the study finds that the impact of Chinese imports on innovation by American firms is generally negative. But is that effect uniform across firms, or does it vary with the nature of the firm?

Contrasting Effects of the Chinese Shock

More and less productive firms. In Chapter 4 we saw that increased competition leads firms close to the technological frontier to innovate more in order to beat the competition. By contrast, increased competition discourages innovation in firms far from the technological frontier. We may therefore conjecture that the Chinese shock should have had a particularly negative effect on firms far from the technological frontier but a positive effect on those close to the frontier. Recall the analogy with the arrival in class of a brilliant new student: the other good students will be stimulated by the competition to work harder in order to remain at the head of the class, while struggling students may be so discouraged by the new arrival that they fall even further behind.

This is in fact what we find in France for the period 1995–2007.[10] On average, the effect of the Chinese import shock on gross revenues, employment, and survival probability of French firms is negative, in keeping with the findings of the American studies cited above. But when we distinguish between firms close to the technological frontier and those far away, our conjecture is confirmed: the Chinese shock had a negative effect on innovation in firms far from the frontier (defined as the least productive 10 percent) but a positive effect on those closest to the frontier (defined as the most productive 10 percent). This finding suggests that the right response to the Chinese import shock is not to increase tariffs to reduce competition from China but rather to encourage investment in innovation while reallocating resources and jobs from less productive to more productive firms.

Upstream shock or downstream shock? A second possibility is that the Chinese import shock is in fact a combination of shocks of two different kinds: on the one hand, a shock on the downstream side of a firm's production chain, that is, to the final product market, which directly increases competition in that market; and, on the other hand, a shock on the upstream side, affecting the market for the inputs the firm uses to manufacture its products. Take, for example, the French automobile industry. If an import shock affects the market for automobiles, then an auto firm's incentive to innovate may decrease because the potential rent from innovation is lower: this is a downstream shock. Conversely, if the import shock affects the market for automobile parts, competition in the parts market will increase, and production costs will therefore fall. Innovation rents will then increase, and the firm will have more incentive to innovate: this is an upstream shock, and the anticipated effect is the opposite of a downstream shock. Empirically, we find that Chinese import shocks were more likely to occur on the upstream side of the production chain in France as compared with the United States.[11]

We can decompose the import shock into an upstream shock and a downstream shock in order to analyze separately the effect of each on innovation.[12] Doing so, we find a slightly positive effect of upstream shocks on innovation (Figure 13.4a) but a strongly negative effect of downstream shocks (Figure 13.4b).[13]

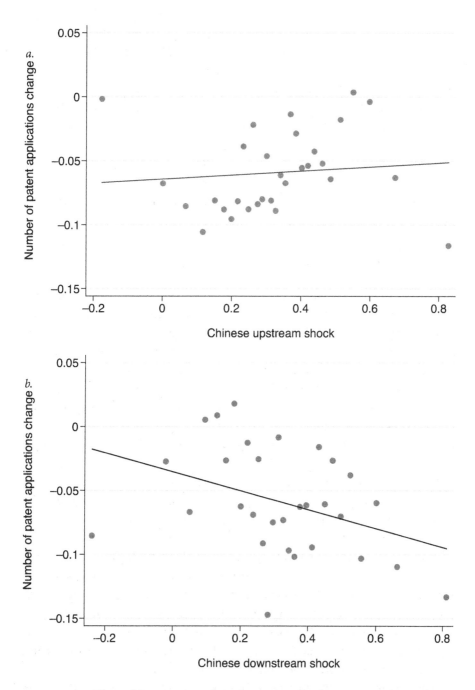

FIGURE 13.4. Effects of downstream and upstream import shocks on innovation. *a.* Upstream import shock. *b.* Downstream import shock. *Note:* The vertical axis corresponds to the change in the average number of patent applications between 1993–2000 and 2000–2007. The horizontal axis corresponds to the change in Chinese imports on the downstream/ upstream market of the firm over these time periods.

Data source: P. Aghion, A. Bergeaud, M. Lequien, M. Melitz, and T. Zuber, "Imports and Innovation: Evidence from French Firm-Level Data," unpublished manuscript, 2020.

Once again, this suggests that a policy of indiscriminate protection is not the best response to foreign import shocks, especially because such a policy can provoke retaliation by the exporting country, as in the case of the US-China trade war of 2018. On March 8, 2018, the United States imposed a 25 percent tariff on steel imports and a 10 percent tariff on aluminum imports from China. On March 22, the United States published a list of additional Chinese products that would be subject to tariff increases, including flat-screen TVs, satellites, medical equipment, automobile parts, and batteries. A few days later, China retaliated by increasing its tariffs on American goods, including soybeans, automobiles, and wine. Yet as we will show now, exports have a clearly positive effect on innovation.

2. Export to Innovate

Our theory of growth suggests that seeking new export outlets stimulates innovation. Why? Because of the "market size effect": if a firm can export its product to a new country, the size of its market increases and so do its innovation rents, because innovations can be sold over a wider area, creating a strong incentive to innovate. A second factor also comes into play: a firm that operates in broader markets will face stiffer competition from other firms operating in those same markets. As we saw earlier, competition stimulates innovation when a firm is close to the technological frontier. Thus, entering new export markets should stimulate innovation, especially in the most productive firms, that is, those closest to the technological frontier.

What do the data tell us? At the end of 1988, the United States and Canada signed a free-trade agreement, which provided an ideal setting for analyzing the impact of new export markets on the productivity of domestic firms.[14] The agreement significantly decreased customs duties between the two countries. For econometricians interested in putting theory to the test, the treaty was a godsend, because it set up a natural experiment that made it possible to observe how firms reacted to a tariff decrease. As Figure 13.5 clearly shows, the treaty increased exports by Canadian manufacturing firms to the US market. The same study shows that the liberalization of trade not only increased the volume of Canadian exports but also had a significant positive effect on the productivity of Canadian firms, implying a further positive effect on innovation.

What about the connection between export markets and innovation? Using French microeconomic data for the period 1994–2012, Philippe Aghion, Antonin Bergeaud, Mathieu Lequien, and Marc Melitz show that exports had an impact on both the number and quality of patents issued to French firms.[15] Figure 13.6 shows the predominance of innovative firms among those that export the most.

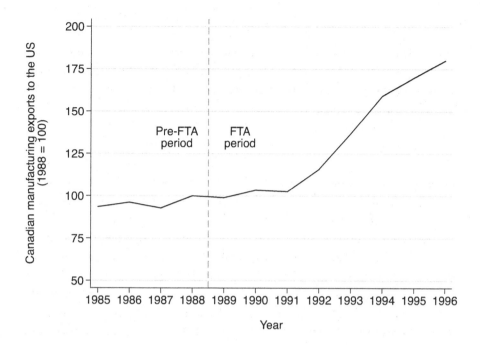

FIGURE 13.5. Effects of the Canadian-American free trade agreement on Canadian manufacturing exports to the United States.

Reformatted from A. Lileeva and D. Trefler, "Improved Access to Foreign Markets Raises Plant-Level Productivity . . . for Some Plants," Quarterly Journal of Economics *125, no. 3 (2010): 1051–1099, figure III.*

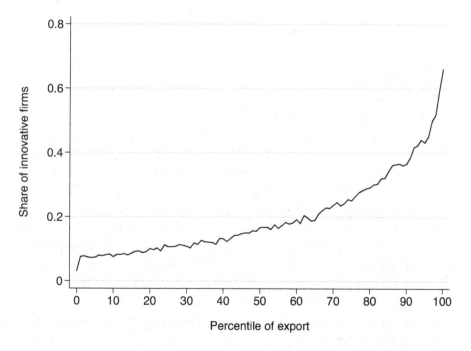

FIGURE 13.6. Share of innovative firms as a function of export percentile.

Reformatted from P. Aghion, A. Bergeaud, M. Lequien, and M. J. Melitz, "The Heterogeneous Impact of Market Size on Innovation: Evidence from French Firm-Level Exports" (NBER Working Paper No. 24600, National Bureau of Economic Research, Cambridge, MA, May 2018), figure 2.

Correlation is not causation, however: just because export and innovation evolve together, it does not follow that one is the cause of the other. The correlation may be due to a third factor that affects the likelihood of both. The authors therefore analyzed the effects of an expansion of a firm's export markets—an export "shock"—on several characteristics of that firm (namely sales, employment, and innovation measured by the number and quality of patents). What they found was, first, that the export shock had an immediate positive effect on the firm's sales and employment. In other words, the export shock yielded a short-term market size effect. Second, the export shock also had a significant positive effect on innovation as measured either by the number of pioneering patents ("prior patents") or the number of citations of patents held by the firm within five years of the granting of the patent. Innovation is a process that takes longer to bear fruit than decisions affecting turnover and employment, so it is natural to expect that there will be a lag between any demand shock and its effects on innovation. Third, the same study also found that, in keeping with the conjecture proposed in Section 1, the positive effect of the export shock on the number of patents and citations was more marked for firms close to the technological frontier than for those distant from it.

To sum up, expanding export markets clearly stimulates innovation. Hence recourse to broad and indiscriminate protectionist policies to cushion competitive shocks does not appear to be the best response.

3. Dealing with Trade Shocks

There are two ways to deal with foreign competition: one is to increase import duties (tariffs); the other is to incentivize domestic firms to innovate more, especially by subsidizing investment in R&D.

Increasing import duties can be risky, for three reasons. First, firms may need to consume intermediate goods upstream of the final product.[16] A uniform increase of import duties, which affects intermediate and final goods indiscriminately, may sharply increase input costs and thus raise the production cost of the final product. To preserve its margins, the firm must then increase the price of its product, leading to a loss of purchasing power by domestic consumers and to a decrease of the size of the firm's market. Consider, for example, an American automobile manufacturer that buys rearview mirrors from a Chinese supplier. If the United States raises import duties on all Chinese imports, both the price of Chinese automobiles and the price of Chinese-made rearview mirrors will be affected. While the tariff on Chinese cars may have a positive effect on the American firm's sales, the tariff on mirrors will penalize the American firm by raising its production costs.

Second, multinational firms can easily deal with tariffs targeted at certain countries by outsourcing production to other countries not affected by the tariff policy. Take, for instance, an American shoe manufacturer that has outsourced most of its production to China. If the United States tries to combat this outsourcing by increasing tariffs on shoes from China, the firm can always move its production to Vietnam, which has yet to be targeted by the US tariff on shoes. The tariff policy thus does nothing to bring shoe production back to the United States.

Third, as we have already discussed, tariffs may have a negative impact on innovation. For one thing, there is a market size effect: punitive tariffs aimed at certain countries can trigger retaliation, and these retaliatory measures will curtail the size of the export market of domestic firms, thereby discouraging innovation. There is also a competition effect: erecting customs barriers reduces competition in both import and export markets. Domestic firms thus lose the incentive to innovate, whether to compete more effectively with imported goods at home or with foreign firms in export markets abroad.

In this respect, the diagram below, proposed by Ufuk Akcigit, Sina T. Ates, and Giammario Impullitti, is illuminating.[17] It is based on a pioneering 2003 article by Marc J. Melitz, who points out that a domestic firm can export what it produces only if it crosses a certain productivity threshold.[18] The underlying idea is that there is a certain fixed cost associated with exporting, which only sufficiently productive firms—generally the largest—can afford to pay.

Consider a firm that produces an intermediate good and sells it to firms that produce a final good. The purchasing firms may be located in the same country as the producing firm or abroad. Furthermore, the producing firm is in competition with foreign firms. Take, for example, a French firm (M), which produces automobile engines that it wants to sell to both French and foreign automobile manufacturers. Suppose that firm M is in competition with foreign engine manufacturers. If M is not very productive (that is, to the left of point I in Figure 13.7), so that its quality/price ratio is low, the auto manufacturers, including French auto manufacturers, to whom it wishes to sell its engines will prefer to buy from a foreign competitor. Point I is therefore labeled "import threshold." If a French firm exceeds this level of productivity, the French auto manufacturer will prefer to buy from the French firm rather than from a foreign competitor.

Moving further to the right along the productivity axis, we come to point E, the point at which firm M has become sufficiently productive that it can begin to export what it produces. In other words, the firm can increase its market size by selling its engines not only to French manufacturers (since it is to the right of point I) but also to foreign manufacturers. Point E is called the "export threshold": it

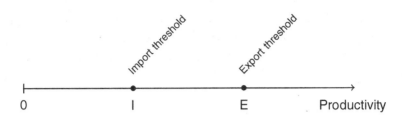

FIGURE 13.7. Capacity to import and export as a function of a firm's productivity.
© *The Authors.*

designates the productivity level above which the intermediate-good producer (in this case the engine manufacturer) has access to foreign markets.

Now consider innovation by the domestic firm. To increase its quality / price ratio, firm M must either innovate to improve its quality or cut its production costs in order to lower the price of its engines. How does the innovation intensity of a domestic intermediate-goods producer vary when its productivity moves from left to right in Figure 13.7? Figure 13.8 answers this question. Starting from the far left, the domestic intermediate-good producer's innovation intensity increases as it approaches the import threshold I. In fact, the closer it comes to the import threshold, the more intensely it must compete with the foreign producer to capture the domestic market for the intermediate good, hence the greater its incentive to innovate. The authors call this "defensive innovation," or innovation aimed at holding on to the domestic market.

Once the firm passes import threshold I, however, its innovation intensity falls because the firm no longer has to compete with foreign producers on the domestic market; hence its incentive to innovate to escape the competition disappears. The closer the domestic firm comes to export threshold E, however, the more intense ("neck and neck") the competition with foreign producers to capture the foreign market. We therefore see a new peak in the domestic firm's innovation intensity. The authors call this "expansionary innovation," that is, innovation aimed at acquiring new foreign markets.

Note that innovation intensity does not fall immediately after a firm passes either the import threshold or the export threshold. Indeed, if the firm were to cease innovating immediately after passing either threshold, it would risk losing the market it had just conquered; a marginal increase in a competitor's quality / price ratio would suffice. Overall, the shape of the innovation intensity curve of a domestic intermediate-good producer resembles a mountain range with two peaks, as shown in Figure 13.8.

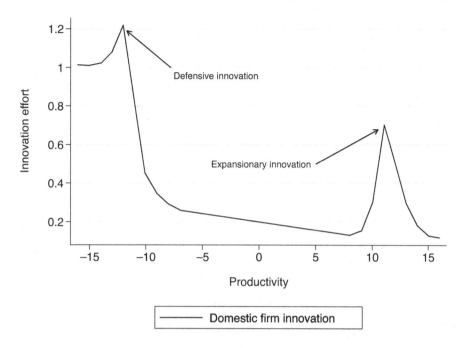

FIGURE 13.8. Innovation intensity as a function of productivity. *Note:* The horizontal axis corresponds to the productivity deviation from o.

Reformatted from U. Akcigit, S. T. Ates, and G. Impullitti, "Innovation and Trade Policy in a Globalized World" (NBER Working Paper No. 24543, National Bureau of Economic Research, Cambridge, MA, April 2018), figure 9A.

With this general pattern in mind, we can now ask how an increase in import duties might affect this curve. Basically, such an increase would shift import threshold *I* to the left, as in Figure 13.9, and transform the solid curve into the dashed curve. Additional import duties would be levied on the foreign-produced intermediate good, increasing its production costs and making it harder for the foreign company to compete in the domestic market. Hence the domestic firm would not need to be as productive as before to capture this market. The effect of the import duty is to reduce competition, thus decreasing defensive innovation, the purpose of which is to ensure the domestic producer a dominant position in the home market. Meanwhile, the need for expansionary innovation would remain unchanged. Thus, the long-term effect of the protectionist tariff is to reduce innovation and productivity growth among domestic intermediate-good producers.

In contrast, subsidizing R&D in domestic firms that produce the intermediate good has virtuous effects. As Figure 13.10 shows, such a subsidy shifts the curve

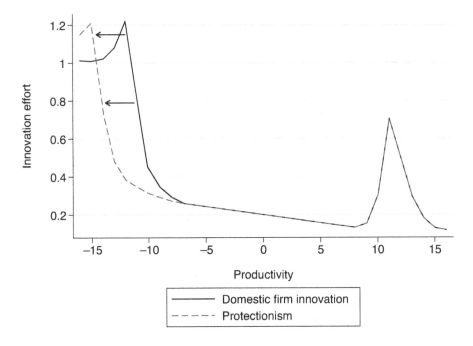

FIGURE 13.9. Deformation of the curve in the wake of a protectionist tariff. *Note:* The horizontal axis corresponds to the productivity deviation from 0.

Reformatted from U. Akcigit, S. T. Ates, and G. Impullitti, "Innovation and Trade Policy in a Globalized World" (NBER Working Paper No. 24543, National Bureau of Economic Research, Cambridge, MA, April 2018), figure 13B.

upward (from the solid to the dashed curve), because it creates an incentive for all firms to innovate. Hence the R&D subsidy increases both defensive innovation and expansionary innovation. The authors show that the resulting gains in productivity growth and in household consumption largely compensate the cost of the subsidies.

This discussion does not imply that protectionist policies must always be rejected. They may be necessary to deal with foreign firms that engage in social or environmental dumping.[19] What emerges from our analysis is rather this: when it is simply a question of responding to competition from foreign producers, and that competition is not unfair, tools such as public investment in the knowledge economy, infrastructure, and industrial policy are more likely to yield productivity gains and long-term prosperity than a drastic increase in import duties.

By way of illustration, let us compare France and Germany with respect to anti-COVID products and facilities. What we find is that Germany maintained

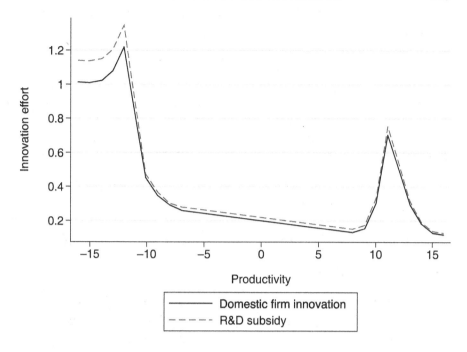

FIGURE 13.10. Shifts due to subsidizing R&D. *Note:* The horizontal axis corresponds to the productivity deviation from 0.

Reformatted from U. Akcigit, S. T. Ates, and G. Impullitti, "Innovation and Trade Policy in a Globalized World" (NBER Working Paper No. 24543, National Bureau of Economic Research, Cambridge, MA, April 2018), figure 16A.

significant control over the value chains necessary for the production of anti-COVID products, including pharmaceuticals (reagents, drugs, active ingredients), medical equipment (especially ventilators), and protective equipment (gloves, masks, etc.).[20] What made such control possible was investment and innovation rather than protectionist measures. Figure 13.11 shows the evolution of imports and exports of these products since 2000 in France (shaded curve) and in Germany (black curve). Starting from a level close to that of France in 2002, Germany saw its exports increase sharply, much more than France. That this was not due to protectionist policies is clear from the fact that German imports of anti-COVID products also increased. The Germans achieved these results by maintaining a high level of competitiveness (that is, a high quality / price ratio) thanks to both massive investment in quality-enhancing innovation and cultivation of social dialogue. The results are indisputable: Germany today is better equipped materially, in terms of both ventilators and tests, than France to cope with the epidemic.

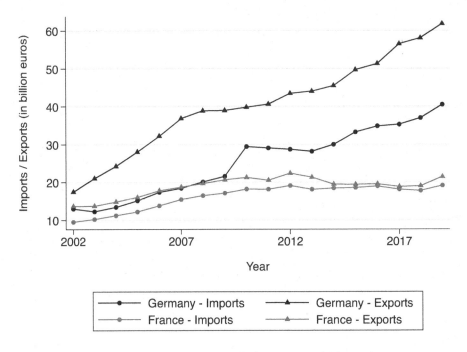

FIGURE 13.11. Evolution of imports and exports of products useful for combatting COVID-19.

Data source: P. Aghion, C. Bellora, E. Cohen, T. Gigout-Magiorani, and S. Jean, "Masques, respirateurs, tests . . . Pourquoi la France doit repenser sa politique industrielle après la crise du coronavirus," Challenges, *April 8, 2020.*

4. Immigration and Innovation-Based Growth

Globalization facilitates the circulation of people as well as goods, especially among technologically advanced countries. In this section we will look at how restricting immigration of skilled individuals affects innovation.[21]

The historic example of European immigration to the United States is particularly illuminating. As Costas Arkolakis, Sun Kyoung Lee, and Michael Peters explain in a recent study, the period 1880–1920 is noteworthy for two parallel evolutions.[22] First, the United States caught up with England and France to become the most technologically advanced country in the world as well as the wealthiest in terms of GDP per capita. Second, the United States welcomed large numbers of immigrants, most notably from Europe. The purpose of the cited study was to demonstrate a causal connection between these two phenomena: in other words, to show that European immigration was responsible for the United States' taking the lead in technology.

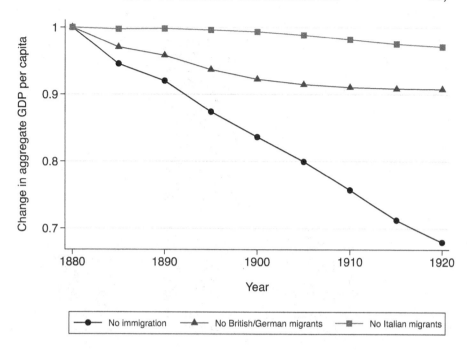

FIGURE 13.12. Impact of border closures on growth.

Data source: C. Arkolakis, S. Y. Lee, and M. Peters, "European Immigrants and the United States' Rise to the Technological Frontier," unpublished manuscript, June 2020.

By matching immigration records, which contain information about immigrants' country of origin and arrival date in the United States, with patent records for the period 1880–1920, the authors are able to evaluate the effect of European immigration on American innovation and growth. Figure 13.12 shows the loss of per capita GDP that the United States would have incurred if it had closed its borders to immigrants from Europe. The graph is based on a growth model in which innovation is estimated from patent and immigration data. More precisely, if the United States had completely closed its borders to all foreign immigrants in 1880, its per capita GDP would have been 30 percent lower than the level actually attained in 1920 (curve with circle markers). The graph also indicates the loss of income if the United States had closed its borders to immigrants from Germany and the United Kingdom (curve with triangle markers) and to immigrants from Italy (curve with square markers).

Why did immigration encourage growth through innovation 150 years ago? European immigrants to the United States turned out to be prolific innovators, but only after they had spent several years in the United States. Figure 13.13,

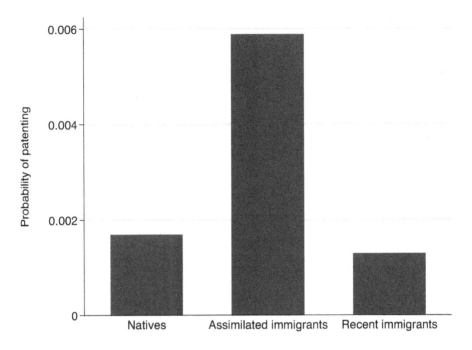

FIGURE 13.13. Probability of patenting within different groups.

Data source: C. Arkolakis, S. Y. Lee, and M. Peters, "European Immigrants and the United States' Rise to the Technological Frontier," unpublished manuscript, June 2020.

based on data from the period 1880–1920, shows that European immigrants living in the United States for ten years or more were more likely to innovate than both native-born Americans and more recently arrived European immigrants. The natural explanation proposed by the authors is that these migrants were able to capitalize on the ideas to which they had been exposed in their native lands so as to innovate once they were truly and permanently settled in the United States.

What can we say about the relation between immigration and innovation today? A study focusing on the period 1976–2012 by Shai Bernstein, Rebecca Diamond, Timothy McQuade, and Beatriz Pousada shows that foreign-born individuals who arrived in the United States after the age of twenty were responsible for 23 percent of total output (Figure 13.14), which was greater than their demographic weight among innovators (16 percent) and even greater than their weight in the population as a whole (10 percent).[23] Thus, both in the recent and not-so-recent past, it is clear that foreign-born individuals contributed substantially to innovation in the United States.

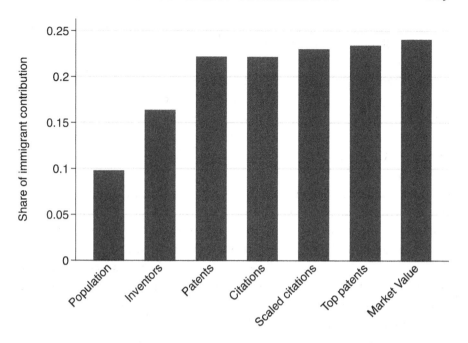

FIGURE 13.14. Proportion of immigrants in various groups.

Reformatted from S. Bernstein, R. Diamond, T. McQuade, and B. Pousada, "The Contribution of High-Skilled Immigrants to Innovation in the United States," Working Paper no. 3748, Stanford Graduate School of Business, November 6, 2018, figure 1.

Furthermore, the same study shows that the unexpected or premature death of an innovator affects the productivity of his or her network of collaborators, measured in terms of numbers of patents filed by the latter. Such an unexpected death can then be interpreted as an unanticipated negative shock on his collaborators.[24] It turns out that such shocks result in larger productivity decreases when the innovator is foreign-born rather than native-born.

Immigrant brains arrive with knowledge and experience garnered in their countries of origin, which may in some domains be in advance of the receiving countries. Consider Israeli innovators who migrate to other countries. Since Israel is a world leader in water-production technologies, countries that absorb a critical mass of Israeli innovators are more likely to achieve breakthroughs in water production.[25] More generally, it is possible to demonstrate a causal link between the immigration of foreign innovators with certain specialties and future innovation in those specialties in the receiving countries: doubling the number of foreign innovators specializing in certain technologies yields a 25 to

60 percent greater likelihood that the receiving country will achieve a break-through in those technologies in the next ten years.[26]

Another important and related idea is that a diverse population—consisting of qualified individuals who do not all come from the same country or region—also encourages innovation. Innovators of diverse backgrounds meld complementary cultures, skills, and forms of knowledge, thereby advancing understanding. In fact, a diverse range of skilled immigrants has a positive impact on productivity growth in the host country, suggesting a positive effect of immigration diversity on innovation.[27]

Why does immigration of skilled individuals stimulate innovation in the host country? One reason has to do with education: for example, William Kerr notes that between 1995 and 2008 immigration accounted for a 29 percent increase in the proportion of the US working population with a college degree.[28] Immigrants were particularly prominent in the so-called STEM fields (science, technology, engineering, and mathematics). Foreign-born individuals residing in the United States were overrepresented among the 250 most-cited authors in STEM fields as well as among recipients of the Nobel Prize.[29]

A second reason, also discussed by Kerr, has to do with the notion of *intrinsic motivation*. The argument relies on two statistical facts. First, immigrants and children of immigrants are not strictly speaking better at STEM fields than the native-born, but they tend to choose these fields in greater numbers and therefore are more likely to excel. Second, given equivalent levels of education, immigrants seem to be more innovative. Taken together, these two observations suggest that immigrants are more enterprising, more determined, and more accepting of risk than native-born Americans. What accounts for this intrinsic motivation? Two things. First, a selection process: only the most enterprising and motivated individuals have sufficient desire and tolerance for risk to become immigrants. Second, the immigration process itself tends to foster a determination to succeed.

Although immigration has positive effects on innovation, there is concern about brain drain in sending countries. Immigration from poor and developing countries to the developed world should not be allowed to deprive the sending countries of the skilled individuals they need to develop their own economies. Ideally, skilled foreign workers should be able to return to their homelands without cutting ties to their host countries. If things do not go well back home, they should be allowed to return to the host countries. Creating such safety nets rather than permanently closing doors is the best way to encourage skilled workers to return to their countries of origin.[30]

5. Conclusion

China's admission to the WTO and the ensuing import shock had an overall negative impact on employment and wages in the United States. Without the increase in US-China trade between 1990 and 2007, there would have been 1.5 million additional American manufacturing jobs in 2007. Does this mean that globalization was a mistake and that the United States would have done better to wage a trade war with China? The answer is no, for at least three reasons. First, the risk of job loss can be dealt with more straightforwardly by establishing a social safety net, as we saw in Chapter 11. Second, the intensification of trade lowered prices and therefore increased the purchasing power of US households by $1,171 per year.[31] Third, launching a trade war risks provoking retaliation, which can shrink export markets for domestic firms and thus discourage innovation.

By contrast, subsidizing R&D by domestic firms has virtuous effects: it stimulates domestic innovation while increasing control over value chains. Indeed, the best way to win the battle of competitiveness is through investment and a true supply-side policy. The German example demonstrates this. At the start of the twenty-first century, Germany and France were roughly equal in the import and export of anti-COVID products (such as masks, ventilators, and tests), but in the ensuing years Germany became a major producer and exporter of these goods while maintaining control of its value chains in the strategic health sector. It accomplished this not through protectionism but through innovation, industrial policy, and social dialogue, which taken together made German producers more competitive.

Finally, although protectionism and trade wars are best avoided, it does not follow that tariffs should not be imposed under any circumstances. They may be necessary to combat social or environmental dumping. In Chapter 9 we showed how carbon taxes levied at international borders can be used as weapons against "pollution havens." But such tariffs must be designed and implemented in a multinational framework (such as the WTO or European Union) and not unilaterally by a single country.

Finally, recent studies show that immigration has a positive effect on innovation in the host country, particularly immigration of skilled or fully integrated individuals.

▼

14

THE INVESTOR STATE
AND THE INSURER STATE

No sooner had the 2008 financial crisis ended than political leaders in developed nations, in particular the United Kingdom and the United States, began to recommend the return to a minimal state. Their reasoning was as follows: Minimizing public spending would make it possible simultaneously to balance the budget and lower taxes. Lowering taxes would allow firms to restore their margins and invest in growth.

This reasoning disregards the fact that a laissez-faire economy, with economic actors—whether individuals or firms—left to their own devices, tends to underinvest in knowledge and innovation. The reason is that they do not take into account the positive externalities of their investments on future innovations. For example, an individual who invests in education does not take into account the positive effect of his education on his coworkers and family. Likewise, a firm that invests in innovation does not take into account the positive effects of the resulting technical progress on future innovations and on economic growth. For this reason, we need an *investor state* that invests in order to stimulate the knowledge and innovation economy.

In the same manner, a laissez-faire economy tends to aggravate inequality, reduce social mobility, and disregard the potentially negative effects of creative destruction—in particular job loss—on health and well-being. This is why we need an *insurer state*: to protect individuals against the risks induced by innovation and creative destruction. The role of the state as an insurer is not limited to idiosyncratic risks. It is also to insure individuals and firms against macroeconomic recessions, especially those brought about by war, major financial crises, or epidemics.

This chapter identifies the forces that have, historically, elicited the emergence of states capable of fulfilling the roles of investor and insurer, which are essential to innovation-led growth.

1. The Threat of War and the Emergence of the Investor State

In his 1918 lecture *Politics as a Vocation,* Max Weber defined the state as "a human community that (successfully) lays claim to the *monopoly of legitimate physical violence* within a particular territory."[1] From this perspective, the state is a political enterprise whose administrative structures are capable, directly or by delegation, of attaining compliance with the law and of levying taxes. It achieves this by maintaining order through use of the army, the judiciary, and the police.

Why Law and Order Is Not Enough to Generate Innovation-Led Growth

If the state's role were limited to maintaining law and order, there would never have been an Industrial Revolution or a takeoff of growth. It is helpful here to recall the three Schumpeterian levers of innovation-led growth, namely: the development of ideas through a cumulative process in which every inventor stands on the shoulders of the giants who preceded her; the protection of innovation rents, in particular by means of patents; and creative destruction, whereby every new innovation destroys the rents of previous innovations, thereby motivating yesterday's innovators to block new innovations.

The absolute power of Chinese emperors or French kings before the French Revolution perfectly fulfilled the sovereign functions described by Weber. It did not, however, favor the development of technological innovations. First, the population at large was uneducated. Second, there was no separation of powers to guarantee the free production and circulation of knowledge. Moreover, there was no protection of property rights, in particular because French kings and nobles could at any moment expropriate the rents of merchants and artisans. Nor was there creative destruction, because it was imperative to prevent individuals from becoming sufficiently rich and powerful to challenge incumbent rulers.

A first step in the evolution of the state occurred in Great Britain with the Glorious Revolution of 1688, then in France with the French Revolution in 1789. It entailed the limitation of the sovereign's power via the growing prerogatives of a Parliament where emerging economic forces, in particular the bourgeois merchant class, could defend their interests.[2] There was thus a progressive movement toward the separation of powers espoused by Montesquieu, making it possible to limit abuses of power so as to protect economic actors, in particular entrepreneurs.[3] The protection of rents and the establishment of patent protections resulted historically from this institutional progress toward less absolutism and increased power-sharing.

A second step, also gradual, involved what Timothy Besley and Torsten Persson have called the state's fiscal capacity, or its ability to collect taxes and then to invest in major public services such as infrastructure, education, and health care.[4] Timothy Besley introduced his lecture in honor of Arthur Lewis with two quotations.[5] The first cited Arthur Lewis himself: "Two conditions of self-sustaining growth are that a country has acquired a cadre of domestic entrepreneurs and administrators, and secondly that it has attained to adequate savings and taxable capacity."[6] The other came from Joseph Schumpeter: "The fiscal history of a people is above all an essential part of its general history. An enormous influence on the fate of nations emanates from the economic bleeding which the needs of the state necessitate, and from the use to which the results are put."[7]

Figure 14.1 depicts the evolution of the fiscal capacity of eighteen nations over time.[8] Each of the curves represents the percentage of countries that adopt a specific tax instrument (income tax, income tax withholding, VAT) over time. For example, the solid curve, which shows the progressive adoption of an income tax in the eighteen countries, is an S-curve, the same form as the curve for adoption of a general purpose technology (Chapter 3). At first, few countries have an income tax, then there is a distinct takeoff from the late nineteenth century through the 1930s until all of the countries in the sample had adopted one. The process is similar for income tax withholding between the 1930s and 1950 (dashed curve) or VAT between the 1970s and 2000 (dotted curve).

Why did nations little by little decide to levy taxes? We now attempt to answer this question.

Competition among Nations and Investment in Public Education[9]

In Chapter 2, we showed that competition among European nations helped spur the industrial takeoff. It also contributed to the evolution of the role and organization of the state. For a long time, military rivalry was the main incentive for states to increase their fiscal capacity and to invest in public services.[10] The development of public education in particular was by no means spontaneous: war or the threat of war provided the impetus for its emergence in many nations worldwide.

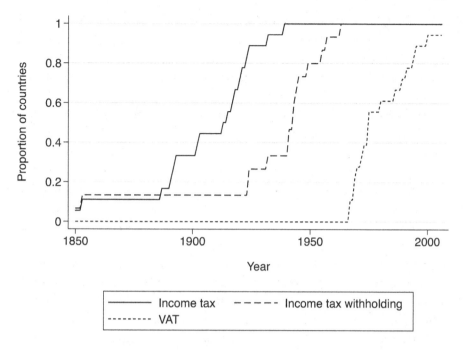

FIGURE 14.1. Historical evolution of fiscal capacity in a sample of eighteen countries. *Note:* The countries included in the data are Argentina, Australia, Brazil, Canada, Chile, Colombia, Denmark, Finland, Ireland, Japan, Mexico, the Netherlands, New Zealand, Norway, Sweden, Switzerland, the United Kingdom, and the United States.

Reformatted from T. Besley and T. Persson, "Taxation and Development," in Handbook of Public Economics, ed. A. J. Auerbach, R. Chetty, M. Feldstein, E. Saez (Amsterdam: Elsevier, 2013), vol. 5, 51–110, figure 4.

The French Example: From Sedan to Jules Ferry

The French educational system evolved following the Battle of Sedan during the Franco-Prussian War. Emperor Napoleon III was imprisoned after the French defeat at that battle in September 1870. In February 1871, Germany seized Alsace and Lorraine. This stinging defeat sparked a revolution in the French educational system. Until 1870, France had lagged behind other European countries, including Germany, with respect to education.[11] The French educational system was mostly private and run by the Church. In a nation that was still mainly rural, the teacher was often the local priest or indeed any villager who knew how to read, with improvised classrooms in farm buildings or courtyards. As a result, the French population was by and large illiterate. In 1863, 7.5 million French citizens, representing one-fifth of the total population, spoke only their local dialect. The governing elite was aware of this educational deficit, and Victor Duruy, whom

Napoleon III had appointed minister of education in 1863, recommended sweeping reforms and massive investment in the educational system. His advice went unheeded, however, until the defeat at Sedan and the fall of Napoleon III, when Duruy's revolutionary reform was implemented by Jules Ferry, minister of education in the nascent Third Republic.

Ferry's reforms were radical: In 1881, school became free; in 1882, it became mandatory for all children from age six to age thirteen; in 1883, it became compulsory for all villages with at least twenty school-age children to establish a school; in 1885, the government instituted a vast plan to invest in teachers' remuneration and the construction and maintenance of schools. The expansion was considerable: 17,320 new schools were built, 5,428 school buildings were enlarged, and 8,381 schools were renovated.[12] The reforms went beyond making school free and mandatory for all French children. The quality of teaching was ensured by the establishment of training programs for teachers. In addition, the content of school programs was completely overhauled to emphasize reading, spelling, history, geography, and civic instruction so as to instill young people with patriotism. As a result, not only did illiteracy decline, but more importantly students were able to read, reason, and communicate in one common French language.

The Japanese Example: From Kanagawa to the Meiji Restoration

From 1603 to 1867, Japan was ruled by shoguns—military lords—of the Tokugawa shogunate. Throughout this period, the regime enforced a deliberate policy of isolationism and maintained a closed economy, with education reserved exclusively for a narrow samurai elite and centered on the study of Confucianism. In 1853, US president Millard Fillmore sent Commodore Matthew Perry to Japan to issue an ultimatum: if Japan did not entirely open to international trade, the consequence would be war. To make this threat credible, the Americans sent gunboats to the Japanese coasts. In 1854, in the face of this threat, Japan signed the Treaty of Kanagawa, authorizing Western ships to enter the Japanese ports of Shimoda and Hakodate to resupply. This humiliation was the catalyst for broad political and educational reforms. In 1868 the Tokugawa shogunate fell and insurgents enthroned the Meiji emperor. The new government decided to invest massively in modernizing the state and the educational system. In 1872, four years of school became compulsory for all children, and a national system of teacher training was established. In addition, teaching Confucianism was deemphasized in order to focus more on the sciences. This reform produced spectacular results: between 1865 and 1910, the literacy rate increased from 35 percent to 75 percent for men and from 8 percent to 68 percent for women.

The French and Japanese examples demonstrate that the existence of military rivalry can bring about an improvement in the educational system. Has this hypothesis been confirmed more generally? The response is affirmative, according to a 2019 study by Philippe Aghion, Xavier Jaravel, Torsten Persson, and Dorothée Rouzet based on annual data from 166 countries between 1830 and 2010: this study shows measurable growth in primary school enrollment in response to war or an increase in military risk, measured by the degree of hostility of speeches by leaders of neighboring countries.[13] This result confirms that a nation's investments in education increase in response to military threats and competition.

Still, is the threat of war indispensable for a state to invest more in public goods? The good news is that competition on the world market for goods and services, induced by trade globalization, can replace military rivalry as a lever of institutional reform and economic development. The existence of transparent, accessible information on national performance, when combined with comparative analysis of indicators such as education and health, is also a lever of institutional change by virtue of yardstick competition. Thus, competition from the Southeast Asian tigers (Thailand, Indonesia, Malaysia, and the Philippines) undoubtedly acted as a catalyst in Deng Xiaoping's reforms in China in the late 1970s, giving greater priority to economic development rather than exclusively to military development. In France, the lackluster performance of French universities in the Shanghai Ranking encouraged a vast reform of the university system, along with a substantial public investment in universities in the framework of the "Investments for the Future" program established in 2010.

Industrial Policy: The Emergence of the DARPA Model

Industrial policy is another lever available to the state to stimulate innovation-led growth. Various factors justify the implementation of an industrial policy, in particular the necessity of coordinating resources and actors in sectors such as aeronautics, where fixed costs are very high and demand is uncertain (see Chapter 4).

In this respect, we can reap valuable lessons from the Defense Advanced Research Projects Agency (DARPA), a research agency within the US Department of Defense responsible for innovations with military applications. The history of DARPA's success demonstrates that a well-managed industrial policy can successfully foster rather than inhibit innovation. DARPA was created after the United States lost a battle in the space race against the USSR: in October 1957, the Soviet satellite Sputnik became the first artificial satellite to orbit the earth. This event had a huge international impact. It substantiated the advance of the Soviet space

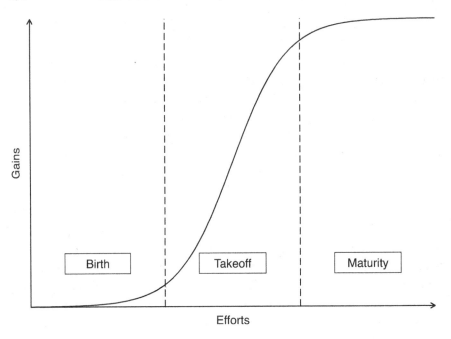

FIGURE 14.2. Development of a disruptive technology.

program and stunned the American public. Then-Senator Lyndon B. Johnson wrote of "the profound shock of realizing that it might be possible for another nation to achieve technological superiority over this great country of ours."[14] Within five months, in February 1958, even before the creation of NASA, President Eisenhower established DARPA as America's primary tool in the military race and the space race against the Soviet Union.

DARPA still exists, and its novel model has been studied in detail.[15] In areas such as defense and space exploration, it is difficult to make the transition from basic research to implementation and marketing. We can see from Figure 14.2 that technologies advance along an S curve. The beginning of the curve represents the origin of a concept to which not much development effort has been devoted because the returns on such efforts are low. The median part of the curve corresponds to the takeoff phase: returns on development efforts are higher, enabling the technology to advance more quickly. Lastly, the phase of maturity implies diminishing returns to development efforts and slower improvements to the technology. Because the initial phase requires substantial efforts, the anticipated social gains from future exploitation must be considerable in order for the project to generate interest and be eligible for DARPA funding. Accordingly, DARPA projects have three characteristics: they are midway between basic and applied research; it is possible to organize research toward a precise objective; and the existence of coordination problems makes large-scale funding and testing of the technology difficult without public intervention.

The DARPA model is especially interesting because it combines a top-down approach with a bottom-up approach.[16] On the top-down side, the Department of Defense funds the programs, selects the program heads, and hires them for a three- to five-year period. On the bottom-up side, the program heads, who come from the academic world or the private sector, or who are investors, have full latitude to define and manage their programs. They can freely organize partnerships between start-ups, university labs, and large industrial firms, and they enjoy great flexibility in recruiting collaborators.

This model of scientific development enabled the United States to catch up steadily with the Soviet Union in the space race. Even though in the initial years after DARPA was created the USSR had a series of successes, thanks to an equally ambitious space program (for example, the first animal in space in 1957, the first man and first woman in space in 1961 and 1963, respectively, and first unmanned lunar landing in 1966), the United States ultimately won the race in 1969, when they first landed humans on the moon.

Today, DARPA's annual budget is over 3 billion dollars, and it funds over one hundred programs. DARPA has played a decisive role in the development of high-risk projects with high social value, such as the internet, originally called Arpanet (at the time DARPA had been renamed ARPA), and GPS. Other nations, including Germany, are considering replicating this model of governance of industrial policy by establishing their own DARPA. One idea would be to create European DARPAs, starting with a bilateral Franco-German institution that would gradually be expanded to other European countries. The primary incentive for a European DARPA would be for Europe to assume greater responsibility for its own defense in the context of the United States' worldwide withdrawal from this role. Another incentive for establishing a European DARPA is that Europe is confronting major technological challenges, in particular in the energy and environment, digital, and health-care sectors. The projects of these European DARPAs would be funded directly from participating nations' governmental budgets. Because they would be outside the European budget, they would escape the "*juste retour*" principle, according to which each member state expects to "get its money back," meaning to receive, in monetary returns, at least as much as it contributes, and also avoid member states' obsession with veto rights.

2. The Emergence of the Insurer State

Insuring against Idiosyncratic Risks:
The Birth and Evolution of the Welfare State

The three decades of growth in France following World War II brought full employment and, for many, an entire career doing the same job in the same firm. In this situation, social policy consisted essentially of complementing low incomes with social, educational, and family-based subsidies. This system stemmed from a long evolution of social safety nets provided by the state.

The "Bismarck model" is widely considered the first example of a welfare state. It was instituted by German Chancellor Otto von Bismarck at the end of the nineteenth century and was based on the idea of insuring workers against a variety of risks—those associated with illness, work-related accidents, old age, and disability—on the condition that they paid into the insurance fund. These laws were promulgated while the first labor unions were coming into existence in Germany, and Bismarck sought to undermine radical socialist alternatives by providing workers with protections.[17] In other words, the political leaders' perception of a threat to their power already played a role in their motivation to establish a welfare state.

The second classic example of a welfare state emerged in the United Kingdom. In 1942, at the request of the government, the economist William Beveridge prepared a report entitled *Social Insurance and Allied Services,* laying the groundwork for another model, with the objective of protecting citizens regardless of whether they were employed.[18] This report was released at the height of hardships caused by the war, with the purpose of ensuring that no one would fall below a minimum standard of living. Once again, we see the important role of a shock, in this case the shock of war, in permitting the emergence of a welfare state.

Although the Beveridge Report laid the theoretical groundwork for this model of social welfare as a matter of national solidarity, public policies along those lines had already been established in the United States during the 1930s in response to the Great Depression and the mass unemployment it generated. As early as 1935, in the context of President Franklin D. Roosevelt's New Deal, Congress passed the Social Security Act, combining insurance mechanisms—a retirement system funded by a payroll tax—and welfare mechanisms such as Aid to Families with Dependent Children, providing welfare payments to children whose parents were unable to support them.

The shock of World War II led France as well to establish a true welfare state as part of the government's determination to rebuild the nation. Against the backdrop of economic planning, nationalizations, and public intervention prompted by the vision of a better economy, the laws of October 4 and 19, 1945, established social security in France. In reality this ambition to enact reforms originated during the war: the 1944 program of the National Council of the Resistance included reforms that would apply upon Liberation, including a complete social security plan, guaranteeing means of subsistence for all citizens.[19] In addition, the war left labor unions with increased bargaining power, and the Communist Party, which was the main party after the Liberation, changed its strategy from one of opposition to one of participating in the government.[20]

Although the modern French system is a mixture of the Beveridge and Bismarck models, it is historically grounded in an insurance model. The creation of social security was above all a remodeling of the pre-war system of social insurance: it protects workers against the risks associated with illness, old age, disability, and work-related accidents and distributed family subsidies. The general system applies to the entire working population but allows special systems to remain in place. Thus, even if the state plays a major role in the new system, the tradition of cooperatives and labor unions remains important. Coverage gradually became more widespread, extending to farmers in 1960 and to medical professionals in 1962. The French model of the welfare state transformed little by little to include more elements from Beveridge, in respect of both benefits—a minimum retirement pension was established in 1956, and a minimum guaranteed income (the *revenu minimum d'insertion*) in 1986—and funding—with a special tax (the *contribution sociale generalisée*) earmarked for funding social security, assessed on all forms of income.

After a legitimacy crisis in the 1980s, with a powerful comeback of the free market ethic, welfare states were able to adapt to a new macroeconomic context.[21] New models emerged, the most noteworthy being flexicurity, implemented in 1997 in the Netherlands, then in Denmark (see Chapter 11). The Dutch and Danish models were not however identical; the former mainly protected the most precarious workers whereas the latter was more universal, based on an active labor market policy. This model thus appeared in very specific national contexts and did not correspond to a pre-established strategy. As with each step in the construction of a welfare state, successive compromises between labor, management, and governmental institutions led to the emergence of a new paradigm. The Dutch example illustrates the role of negotiations between these partners (social dialogue), because the adoption of laws on flexibility and security in 1997 was the result of many months of negotiations between the unions and the government. The importance of social dialogue in the construction of the welfare state is not specific to the late twentieth century and the emergence of flexicurity. The 1930s witnessed the violent repression of the labor movement in Sweden.[22] The emergence of the Social-Democratic movement under a red-green coalition—labeled, not without irony, *Kuhhandel,* or "livestock market"—permitted an honorable exit from this crisis. This coalition, initially composed of workers and farmers, proposed in particular to strengthen the role of the state, but also to endow civil society with checks on state power (see Chapter 15).

Today, flexicurity, the most recent step in the history of the welfare state, appears to be a logical tool to make creative destruction more humane, while inducing individuals to remain active in the labor force. We have also mentioned potential levers to improve the effectiveness of flexicurity. Even with these improvements, however, is it sufficient to protect individuals against the risks that accompany creative destruction? Several considerations suggest we may want to do more. First, there is a limit to individuals' ability to continually change jobs and reinvent themselves during their careers. Yuval Noah Harari, in his book *21 Lessons for the 21st Century,* argues that the artificial intelligence revolution brings about an acceleration in the frequency of job changes as well as in the obsolescence of skills.[23] In his view, this dual acceleration justifies guaranteeing all individuals a minimum income to cover basic needs at a certain life stage regardless of how they spend their time. In addition, Monique Canto-Sperber, in *La fin des libertés,* notes the large number of eighteen- and nineteen-year-olds who have neither the basic professional training nor the resources necessary to find jobs that will enable them to advance and to rebound from one job to another down the road. She believes that they, too, deserve adequate material support.[24]

These considerations led some colleagues to push the idea of an unconditional income, which, in the view of Canto-Sperber, "helps liberate the individual, by enabling him not only to provide for his own needs, but also to position himself to have access to resources such as training, a better job, the ability to determine his life."[25] The vision of the individual and of freedom inherent in this argument is the opposite of the vision espoused by advocates of "less government." For the latter, any benefit payment is a handout and encourages laziness, whereas for Canto-Sperber, we stimulate initiative by giving individuals the means to act.

Various proposals have been advanced as to the optimal form of an unconditional income. One consists of paying a universal basic income to all citizens, rich and poor, young and old. The problem is that this mechanism can be extremely costly from a budgetary and tax standpoint. Another idea, initially formulated by Milton Friedman in 1962, is a negative tax below a fixed threshold of income and assets.[26] Yet another idea is to provide every young citizen with a number of "points" she can use to finance her education, housing, and first steps in the workforce. The debate over whether and how a universal income would be administered is as yet unresolved. It is a debate that raises legitimate questions

that contribute to our reflections on the best way to temper the harsher consequences of creative destruction and new technological revolutions.

Insuring against Macroeconomic Risks: The Role of Countercyclical Policies

How did countercyclical policies come about? For a long time, the dominant doctrine in economic thought was laissez-faire, an economic system in which
market forces would always bring the economy back to equilibrium. John Maynard Keynes later provided a theoretical basis for government intervention and
countercyclical policies. But we cannot fully understand Keynes's policy ideas
without returning to the political and economic context of his time. Beginning
in the 1920s, he observed unemployment was growing rapidly in Great Britain:
in 1922, 2.5 million people—nearly 15 percent of the labor force—were unemployed.
Under Lloyd George, the Liberal Party proposed a program of public works and a
number of measures to combat underemployment. Keynes supported these
measures in an essay he coauthored in 1929 with Hubert Henderson, *Can Lloyd
George Do It?* In this essay, they asserted that every jobless person who finds a
job automatically creates additional jobs.[27] But the true game changer was the
Great Depression in the United States. In the face of deflation and a crisis of such
amplitude, as well as the glaring failure of free-market remedies, it was no longer
possible to remain immobile and wait for price adjustments and actors' behav-
ioral adaptation to restore equilibrium. Beginning in 1933, the United States implemented the New Deal, signaling the beginning of an interventionist government and laying the groundwork for the welfare state.

Only in 1936, with the publication of John Maynard Keynes's most famous
work, *The General Theory,* did state intervention through macroeconomic
policy find a theoretical foundation.[28] This groundbreaking work marked a decisive break with the thinking about government intervention. Its thesis was
that when demand is insufficient, in particular as a consequence of rising unemployment, the primary objective of macroeconomic policies, especially budgetary policy, is to stimulate economic activity by stimulating aggregate demand.
The idea was that each additional dollar of public spending on public employment generates more than one dollar of economic activity because workers
will spend their additional wages, thereby increasing demand for goods and
services. These policies became widespread beginning in the 1960s. They were
also known as "stop-go" policies, as they alternated between stimulating economic activity (go) when economic activity slowed and unemployment rose and
restricting it (stop) in the presence of inflationist trends and a deteriorating
current account.

In the 1970s and 1980s, demand-side policies were criticized, especially because of the appearance of stagflation—simultaneous stagnation and inflation—at the time of the oil shocks.

Above all, it appears that an innovation economy open to globalization is an economy where managing the cycle by stimulating demand is no longer working very well. In an open economy, increasing public spending leads to an increase in imports and a widening of the trade deficit rather than a revival of domestic economic activity. In 2009, Willie O'Dea, then Irish minister of defense, summarized this idea perfectly: "We tried the fiscal stimulus approach in response to the oil shock in the late Seventies. The increased spending power given to the Irish consumer largely leaked out on increased imports and left us in an even worse position. There is absolutely no evidence to suggest that the same thing would not happen again. . . . From Ireland's point of view, the best sort of fiscal stimuli are those being put in place by our trading partners. Ultimately these will boost demand for our exports without costing us anything."[29]

Starting in the early 1980s, developed countries progressively converted to policies more centered on the supply side to manage business cycles. Supply-side policies focus primarily on increasing firms' competitiveness. One objective is to enable firms to maintain their level of investment throughout the business cycle. R&D investment that is interrupted because of a recession would otherwise be irremediably lost.

In a hypothetical world where access to credit is never a problem, firms can always borrow as long as their investment is profitable in the long run, and short-term fluctuations do not affect the amount they can borrow. Consequently, when they pursue R&D and innovation rather than short-term investments, firms are certain their investments will not be vulnerable to swings in the economy. Accordingly, in such a world, the state does not have to intervene to assist firms during recessions.

On the other hand, when firms face credit constraints, their current income rather than their future profits determines the amount they can borrow from banks. In this case, if there is a recession that reduces the firm's current income, the firm will be unable to cope with liquidity shocks and will have to cut back its R&D spending. But in doing so, the firm handicaps itself in the race to innovate.

Consider the initial moment when the firm decides between embarking on an innovative project or instead pursuing more routine projects: the anticipation of recessions that could force it to pull out of the innovation race will lead the firm to refrain from innovation and instead to invest in conventional projects.[30] How can the state counteract this logic, so unfavorable to innovation? The answer lies in countercyclical budgetary and monetary policies. Countercyclical budgetary policy means that the state borrows during a recession in order to finance innovative firms that are confronting a liquidity shock, then repays its debts in periods of expansion. Countercyclical monetary policy means that the central bank lowers short-term interest rates during a recession and, if necessary, engages in quantitative easing in order to relieve innovative firms facing a liquidity shock so they do not have to cut back on R&D spending.[31] In a period of expansion, however, the central bank will increase interest rates and end quantitative easing. All told, the greater the credit constraints facing firms in a given country, the more a countercyclical macroeconomic policy will stimulate innovation in that country.[32]

During the 2008 crisis, governments attempted to apply both supply-side and demand-side countercyclical policies. On the demand side, beginning in 2009, most countries were able to rely on automatic stabilizers, which mitigated the impact of the recession.[33] Furthermore, many nations adopted large-scale fiscal stimulus packages between 2008 and 2010.

On the supply side, in December 2008 European nations adopted a variety of measures to support business, following the example of the European Union's Small Business Act. This act provided for 30 billion euros in loans to SMEs over the period from 2008 to 2011. The quantitative easing measures implemented by a number of central banks starting in 2008 constituted the other pillar of this supply-side policy.

Which countries have pursued the strongest countercyclical policies in the recent past? Focusing on budgetary policies, Figure 14.3 compares fifteen OECD countries according to the intensity of their pro- or countercyclical budgetary policies. A budgetary policy is defined as being more countercyclical when the budget deficit increases more during recessions and decreases more during periods of expansion. The budgetary policies of the Scandinavian countries (Denmark, Sweden, and Finland) are far more strongly countercyclical than that of France. Furthermore, Greece and Italy have clearly procyclical budgetary policies, meaning their budget deficits increase during booms.

Two factors influence the countercyclical nature of budgetary policies. The first is the state's commitment to maintain a number of benefit payments throughout the business cycle, in other words to make use of automatic stabilizers. The countries where automatic stabilizers play a major role are the countries where per capita public spending is relatively high. In other words, minimalist states do not insure their citizens against macroeconomic risks.

A second factor is budgetary discipline, which enables virtuous countries to adopt more ambitious stimulus packages during crises and thus to implement more countercyclical budgetary policies. This is easy to understand: a fiscally

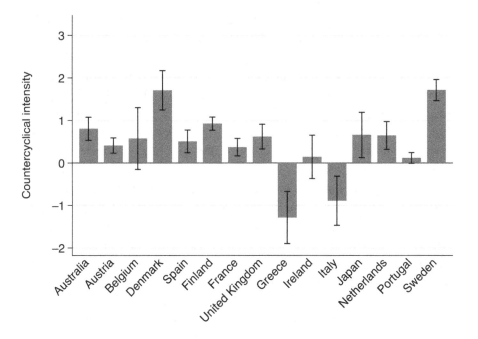

FIGURE 14.3. Intensity of the countercyclical character of budgetary policy, 1980–2005.
Note: A positive value indicates a countercyclical budgetary policy, and a negative value
indicates a procyclical budgetary policy.

*Reformatted and extracted from P. Aghion, D. Hémous, and E. Kharroubi, "Cyclical Fiscal Policy, Credit Constraints, and
Industry Growth," Journal of Monetary Economics 62 (2014): 41–58, figure 2.*

virtuous country will find it easy to borrow on the international markets during
a recession, because lenders will be confident that they will be repaid when the
cycle reverses.

We observed this phenomenon in the 2008 crisis. Italy, for example, whose
public debt exceeded 100 percent of GDP prior to the crisis, implemented a small
stimulus package, which limited the deficit in the short run but aggravated the
recession. Furthermore, the eurozone countries that had imposed austerity measures starting in 2010 in order to reduce their deficit as quickly as possible were
the same ones that had the highest precrisis debt levels, namely Greece, Italy,
Spain, Belgium, and France. The most "virtuous" countries, such as Germany and
the Netherlands, were the ones that were able to prolong the recovery. Greece and
the Scandinavian countries represent opposite extremes: Greece, with its lack of
budgetary discipline prior to the 2008 crisis, appears in Figure 14.3 as the most
procyclical in the figure and was consequently forced to make budgetary cuts at
the low point of the cycle.[34] The Scandinavian countries, however, which subjected

themselves to strict budgetary discipline, appear as the most countercyclical in Figure 14.3.

The COVID-19 crisis also demonstrated the importance of budgetary discipline in confronting macroeconomic shocks. Thanks to its accumulated budget surpluses, Germany's public debt had returned to a level below 60 percent of GDP in 2019. This gave it the latitude to implement a countercyclical policy of unprecedented scope in order to overcome the economic ramifications of the crisis: at the beginning of June 2020, the fiscal stimulus measures and debt rescheduling reached 24.6 percent of GDP compared to 12.3 percent in France.[35]

Finally, we note the major role of banks in countercyclical policy. In the wake of the 2008 crisis, there is a view that banks should be subject to even stricter capital requirements than those imposed by the Basel I and Basel II Agreements, in order to prevent a new financial crisis. Those who hold this view believe that the ratio between the bank's capital and its risk-weighted assets should be substantially increased. The problem with this approach is that riskiness increases during a recession. This type of capital requirement would encourage banks to lend more in periods of expansion than in periods of recession, in other words to adopt procyclical lending policies in order to satisfy regulatory requirements. For this reason, we believe that banks should be subject to countercyclical capital requirements, meaning they could have lower capital in relation to assets during a recession. Such a system would allow banks to lend more to firms during recessions, thereby helping to stabilize the economic cycle. This idea of countercyclical capitalization rules underlies the Basel III Agreements, although the arguments put forward to justify them were not based on growth considerations.[36]

3. Conclusion

Innovation relies above all on the market and on firms, but it also needs the state, both as an investor and as an insurer. Historically, international rivalry, whether military, commercial, or industrial, gave rise to the emergence of the investor state with the requisite fiscal capacity, meaning the ability to levy taxes. Jules Ferry's system of public schools in France would never have existed had France not suffered military defeat against Prussia in Sedan. Similarly, the major economic crises—the Crash of 1929 and the recent COVID-19 crisis—and world wars gave rise to the emergence of the insurer state. Thus, in response to the Great Depression, the United States implemented the New Deal to revive demand and pull the American economy out of recession. Today, governments respond to macroeconomic cycles by adopting strongly countercyclical policies, especially budgetary policies. These policies can be fully effective only if the state has exercised strict budgetary discipline outside periods of crisis.

The state does not, however, act only as an insurer against macroeconomic shocks; it also insures against idiosyncratic risks. This is how the crises and wars of the first half of the twentieth century spurred the appearance of social security and public health care, and of family subsidies, ensuring a minimum level of income and protecting against risks of illness. Yet, the liberalization of the economy and the globalization of trade starting in the 1980s gave rise to an acute new risk in developed nations: the risk of job loss. The flexicurity model introduced in Denmark in the 1990s was intended as a response to the challenge of combining economic liberalism and innovation, on the one hand, with protecting the individual against the consequences of job loss, on the other. This model can be improved both to encourage lifelong professional training and to prevent people from falling below the poverty line. A negative tax may be one way to reduce this risk, which is a particular threat for seasonal or occasional workers.

In the next chapter, we will examine the dangers of a state that is too strong or too omnipresent, as well as the failures and inadequacies of the state. In particular, we will analyze the checks and balances and other safeguards that limit the risk of abuse of power by the executive branch. More specifically, we will explore how the media, labor unions, nonprofits, and more generally all the components of civil society ultimately guarantee the separation of powers and oversight of the executive branch.

▼

15

CREATIVE DESTRUCTION
AND THE GOLDEN TRIANGLE

In the last chapter, we treated the state as a homogenous entity. In reality it is a complex aggregate; it is made up of individuals motivated by a commitment to public service but who, to varying degrees, are also pursuing their own interests and responding to a variety of incentives (such as financial, professional, or related to status). Yet our colleague Jean-Jacques Laffont caused a scandal when he made this common-sense observation in front of the French Council of Economic Analysis shortly after its creation in 1997 by Prime Minister Lionel Jospin.[1]

At the end of the day, the government's action depends less on the personalities of the individuals exercising power than on the safeguards that set limits on their power. In this chapter we will examine in particular the checks and balances that constrain the possibility of collusion between the executive branch and private interest groups. A direct consequence of this collusion is to impede the process of creative destruction and the entry of new firms into the market.[2]

What are the advantages and disadvantages of a strong executive branch? What are the constitutional instruments that make it possible, in theory, to regulate the exercise of executive power? What is the role of the judicial branch as a counterpower, and what limits that role? Why are the media and civil society indispensable to ensure the separation of powers and the effectiveness of limitations on executive power? Why does creative destruction hinge on the existence of a well-proportioned triangle of markets, state, and civil society? These are the questions we will address in this chapter.

1. When the State Blocks Creative Destruction:
The Example of Venice

The state can hinder the process of creative destruction, as Diego Puga and Daniel Trefler illustrated in their historical analysis of the grandeur and the decadence of Venice in the Middle Ages.[3] Venice enjoyed great prosperity as it opened to trade between the end of the twelfth century and the end of the thirteenth century, until it started to close in on itself and began to decline at the beginning of the fourteenth century.

In the first phase, opening to trade was facilitated by three major institutional innovations that made it possible to limit the power of the doge, chief of state of the Republic of Venice. The first and most important innovation from which all others flowed was the establishment of an elected parliament in 1172, the Maggior Consiglio or Great Council, made up of representatives of the aristocracy as well as 100 members renewed each year by a nominating committee. Over the following decades, the Great Council used its power to gradually restrict the doge's power by means of two institutional innovations. The first was to establish an oath of office: in order to assume his duties, the doge had to swear publicly to comply with all the limits imposed by the Great Council. This meant he could not expropriate state assets or preside over judicial disputes against himself. In addition, a second council was established, the members of which were elected by the Great Council. The doge was required to consult this second council before taking any significant decision. These innovations favored the appearance of independent judges, new laws regarding contracts and bankruptcy, and the first modern banking system.

But above all, it was during this period that a new type of contract emerged, the *colleganza,* precursor of modern joint-stock companies.[4] These contracts concerned long-distance trade, as that was the main source of revenue in Venice at the time. In its most simple form, the *colleganza* was an agreement between two parties, the investor and the traveling merchant. The contract provided for the allocation of risks and rewards between the investors who provided the merchandise and the traveling merchants who sold or traded this merchandise in their travels, in particular in the eastern Mediterranean and the Black Sea. This type of contract permitted a large portion of the population to participate in international trade and enabled Venice to reach its zenith.

This contract is similar to the arrangement between investors and innovators that we discussed in Chapter 12. The *colleganza* made it possible to finance long-distance trade with high fixed costs (merchandise, ship) and chances of success

that, albeit low, could potentially bring very substantial gains. This institution offered opportunities for Venetian traveling merchants, often from poor backgrounds, to rise to a higher economic and social class. It gave them the ability to
participate in government alongside the aristocracy. This movement was accompanied by more creative destruction: each new cohort of traveling merchants
enriched by the *colleganza* eroded the profits and political power that had previously been reserved to the elite.

The reaction was not slow to follow. In 1286, the Great Council decreed that
any new candidate would be automatically admitted if his father and his grand-
fathers had already been members of the Great Council. In 1297, it voted that all
those who had served in the Great Council during the previous four years would
be automatically reelected. This institutional retreat, called the *Serrata*, meaning
"closure," gave rise to an economic retreat. First, use of the *colleganza* was restricted
to the most powerful families of the Venetian nobility, and second, in 1314, trade
was partially nationalized and heavy taxes were imposed on aspirants to the merchant profession. Starting in 1297 with the enforcement of the *Serrata*, there was
a sharp drop in the number and percentage of *colleganza* involving commoners
(Table 15.1). In parallel, the median number of seats attributed to the oligarchy
started to increase, reaching a high point in 1339–1342.

Table 15.1. Participation of Commoners in *Colleganza*

	Number of Colleganza Involving Commoners	Percentage of Colleganza Involving Commoners	Median Merchant's Family Seats per Session in the Great Council
1073–1200	27	42	1.5
1201–1220	24	38	1.0
1221–1240	42	53	0.9
1241–1261	30	51	0.8
1310–1323	22	27	3.0
1324	0	0	1.8
1325–1330	1	5	4.8
1331–1338	0	0	5.4
1339–1342	0	0	13.6

Source: D. Puga and D. Trefler, "International Trade and Institutional Change: Medieval Venice's
Response to Globalization," *Quarterly Journal of Economics* 129, no. 2 (2014): 753–821.

It followed that trade became the monopoly of the aristocracy, thereby contributing to the economic demise of Venice, whose population declined continuously between 1400 and 1800.

In their book *Why Nations Fail,* Daron Acemoglu and James Robinson refer to other examples where incumbent public officials blocked growth out of fear that the ensuing creative destruction would jeopardize their power.[5] For example, in the Ottoman Empire, the first printing press was not authorized until 1727, more than 300 years after its invention by Gutenberg. The objective was to limit the diffusion of new ideas by guaranteeing a low literacy rate, which indeed remained below 3 percent of the population until 1800. The authors also cite fifteenth-century Spain, where trade with the new American colonies remained under the strict control of a guild system. Another example is Russia, where the obsession with creative destruction led to a prohibition on new cotton mills and metal foundries in order to prevent the emergence of an organized and concentrated working class and to curb the development of railroads, which could foster a threatening mobility of the population.

2. Innovation Needs Democracy

Why are democratic institutions essential to innovation at the technological frontier? First of all, because in a more democratic political system, vested interests have less influence on public officials, and it is harder to corrupt political power. When there is less corruption, there is more innovation.[6] First, lower corruption facilitates market entrance of new firms and new technologies: Figure 15.1a shows a negative relationship between anticorruption measures in a given country and barriers to entry of new firms in that country.[7] Second, the entry of new firms induces incumbent firms to innovate more in order to survive competition from the new entrants, as illustrated by Figure 15.1b, which shows a positive relationship between anticorruption measures in a country and rate of innovation in that country as measured by patents per capita.

The Hungarian economist Janos Kornai listed the most revolutionary innovations of the twentieth century and showed that they were all produced in democracies.[8] Larry Page and Sergey Brin were able to develop what would become Google as part of their doctoral work at Stanford University, above all because they had broad freedom to choose the direction they wished to explore and did not have to follow their supervisors' orders when choosing the subject of their theses.

Must we conclude that fostering innovation necessarily means imposing strict limits on government power? In the preceding chapter, we saw that a state ca-

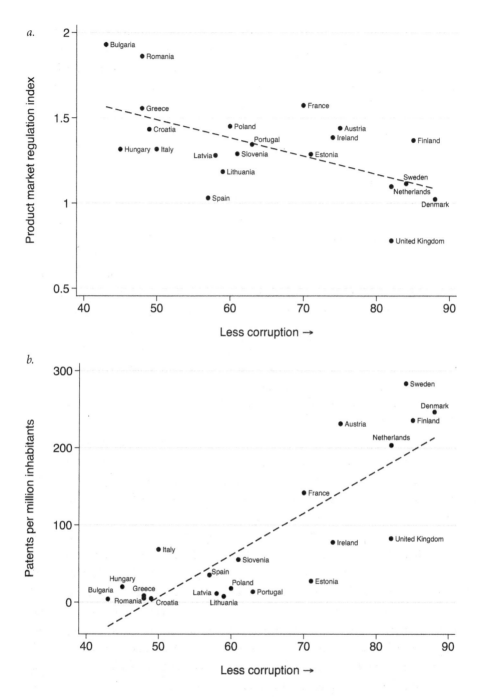

FIGURE 15.1. Relationship between corruption, regulation, and innovation. *a.* Corruption and regulation. *b.* Corruption and innovation.

Data sources: a. *Transparency International and OECD*; b. *Transparency International and Eurostat.*

pable of levying taxes, investing, insuring against individual risks, and implementing countercyclical budgetary policies was essential to innovation. How can we reconcile these prerogatives with the need for safeguards and checks and balances on executive power? Is there a happy medium between an autocratic regime and an executive branch with little power?

3. The Role of Constitutions

The Constitution as an Incomplete Contract[9]

The idea of a necessary balance in order to avoid tyranny between delegating power to public officials and controlling how they use this power is a very old one. In particular it underlies the separation of powers advocated by Montesquieu in 1748, Friedrich Hayek's constitutional theory, James Buchanan's seminal 1960 article, and the 1962 article by James Buchanan and Gordon Tullock.[10] Two citations illustrate this idea particularly well: Alexis de Tocqueville wrote in *Democracy in America,* "Our contemporaries are incessantly racked by two inimical passions; they feel the need to be led and the wish to remain free."[11] Alexander Hamilton, coauthor of an essay defending the unitary executive created by the Constitution (1787–1788), contended that "Taking for granted [. . .] that all men of sense will agree in the necessity of an energetic executive. [. . .] How far can they (the ingredients which constitute this energy) be combined with those other ingredients which constitute safety in the Republican sense?"[12]

By attributing prerogatives among the executive, the legislative, and the judicial branches, a country's constitution sets up the legal framework that simultaneously determines both the breadth and the limits of executive power.[13] To understand why it is important for a constitution to provide for the separation of powers, we must first appreciate that a constitution is an *incomplete contract* among a nation's citizens.[14] What is an incomplete contract? Imagine for a moment that we lived in a world where all possible future events could be perfectly known in advance, and furthermore that the realization of a given event could be verified by a third party—a judge. In such a world, society could decide in advance on a contingent course of action: "if event x occurs, then action y must follow." There would then be no need for a constitution to specify the separation of powers, because everything could be determined in advance, and judges would verify that the action contingent on an event was indeed carried out. In this world, we would be in a "complete contract" environment.

Reality, however, is very different: it is impossible to identify all potential future events in advance; indeed it is even difficult to verify whether a predicted event actually occurred. In these conditions, the best a constitution can do is to establish rules for sharing decision-making power and safeguards limiting abuses of power. In other words, a constitution is an "incomplete contract."

Why is it important to limit the power of the executive, and what are the constitutional tools to do so?

The Balance between Too Much and Too Little Executive Power

The advantage of a strong executive is that it gives political leaders latitude to act quickly in undertaking major transformations and investments. This advantage is especially valuable in wartime or during a crisis, when rapid decisions must be made and military operations must be kept secret.

However, the disadvantage of an overly strong executive is that political leaders can abuse their power to prevent innovations that might threaten their power or to enrich themselves rather than enacting effective reforms, and potentially, in the long term, they may abuse their power in order to perpetuate it. In other words, an overly strong executive can drift toward autocracy, generating corruption to the detriment of innovation, and thus weakening a nation's prosperity.

In the same way that there is an optimal amount of competition that will stimulate innovation and growth, there is an optimal level of executive power. Too little executive power may paralyze the state's ability to carry out reforms; too much executive power can give rise to an "illiberal democracy" or to autocracy. The optimal compromise between too much and too little power depends on considerations such as the importance of reform on the one hand and the risk and cost of expropriation on the other. In times of war, a crisis, or an urgent need for reform, it will be desirable to give the executive greater power. In ordinary times, however, it is preferable to limit the executive's power.[15]

In the absence of limits on the executive's power, incumbent firms are likely to want to use their rents to block the entrance of new, innovative firms, and they will lobby political leaders to that end. The more unbridled the power of officials in the executive branch, the greater the temptation will be for firms to try to influence or even bribe them.

How Can a Constitution Limit Executive Power?

How can a constitution, by means of rules governing decision-making within the state, limit the power of the executive?

One channel involves the voting rules for adopting a law. The constitution can provide that ordinary laws are subject to a simple majority rule—more than half of the votes—but still require lower or reinforced majorities in some instances, thereby increasing or reducing the executive's power. For example, if a parliamentary majority much greater than 50 percent were required to adopt all laws, any reform would be virtually impossible. In France, a supermajority—three-fifths of the MPs and senators sitting together—is required for amending the constitution. This rule intentionally makes it more difficult for the government to change the constitution than to pass an ordinary law. We want to enable the government to make reforms but at the same time avoid a drift to authoritarianism in which the executive would take advantage of the allegiance of a simple majority loyal to him in Parliament to change the constitution so as to perpetuate its power.

Status quo rules in legislative votes also have a bearing on the strength of the executive's power. In France, under the Fourth Republic, when Parliament was unable to agree on a budget, the budget of the preceding year would be implemented again. But with the advent of the Fifth Republic, these *status quo* rules radically changed: if Parliament fails to adopt a budget, the executive decides the budget. This constitutional change obviously shifted the balance of power in favor of the executive. The positive consequence is that this change initiated a modernization of French industry that successive constitutional crises under the Fourth Republic impeded. The negative consequence is that it favored certain practices of corruption like the Garantie Foncière Scandal of the early 1970s, in which people close to inner leadership circles made substantial fortunes from the renovation and modernization of two large neighborhoods in central Paris.

We can cite three additional means of regulating executive power. The first is the ability to amend draft laws. In the United States, when one party controls the House of Representatives, it can control the legislative agenda by invoking so-called "closed rules," under which amendments are prohibited and debate time is limited. When the majority controlling the House is the party of the president, the possibility of resorting to this special rule procedure effectively diminishes Congress's ability to act as a countervailing power.

The type of electoral system is another means of regulating executive power. The majority system gives a comfortable majority to the party that wins legislative elections, because that party receives a proportion of representatives far greater than the proportion of votes it obtained at the national level. By contrast, a proportional system allocates the number of seats according to the number of votes and thus gives greater representation to minority parties. A system with strictly proportional representation makes the executive more fragile and forces it to form coalitions that can be very surprising, as happens in Israel and Italy.

Lastly, the duration of terms of office and the number of terms a political leader can serve are the final means limiting or strengthening the executive's power. The longer a political leader can remain in office, the greater his latitude to reform the nation. However, when the same leader remains in place for a long time, it becomes especially tempting for incumbent firms to invest in lobbying to prevent the entry of new, innovative firms.

A natural question to ask is why constitutions evolve in the real world toward more or less executive power. We will return to this question in the final section of this chapter, which is devoted to the role of civil society in bringing change to state institutions. First, however, we will discuss the role of judges as a constitutional counterweight to executive power.

4. The Role and Limitations of the Judiciary

The Judiciary as a Counterpower

Since Montesquieu, liberal thinkers have insisted on the necessity of establishing an independent judiciary that can check the power of the executive. According to Hayek, the role of judges as a counterpower is grounded above all in the independence of the judiciary.[16] Judges perform two essential functions: first, they interpret the laws and apply them to specific and concrete factual situations, whereas the executive branch enforces the law; and second, they alone have the power of constitutional review, or the authority to interpret the constitution, verify that laws comply with the constitution, and invalidate noncomplying laws.

These two cornerstones turn out to be indispensable to the effective functioning of an innovation economy. Judicial independence is a necessary condition for the protection of private property rights. It limits the executive's ability to expropriate innovation rents, which would discourage innovation. Furthermore, the independence of the judiciary guarantees fair resolution of disputes, in particular when one party benefits from political favor. Constitutional review limits public officials' ability to promulgate laws or regulations that serve their personal interests rather than the public interest, including laws aiming to protect incumbent firms from the entrance of new, innovative firms.

We can compare different international systems by measuring the degree to which the judiciary is independent and empowered to ensure compliance with the constitution.[17] The degree of judicial independence can be computed by combining three indicators. The first two are the duration of term of office of judges sitting on the country's highest courts (such as a supreme court or constitutional court) and the duration of the term of office of administrative judges, the idea being that a judge with life tenure is insulated from political and economic pressures. The third indicator is related to the weight of precedent in rendering decisions, the idea being that when precedent plays a role, the courts are sources of law rather than mere interpreters of the law. To define the degree to which the judiciary has final authority to interpret the constitution, we combine two indicators: the existence of a hierarchy of legal standards and the right to challenge the constitutionality of laws.

France provides a historical example with the October 29, 1974, reform of the rules for invoking the jurisdiction of the Constitutional Council extending the right to challenge the constitutionality of laws. When it was established in 1958, the Constitutional Council could be invoked only by the president of the Republic, the prime minister, the president of the National Assembly, or the president of the Senate. In other words, it was impossible for the political opposition to challenge the constitutionality of a new law. With the 1974 reform, any group of sixty senators or sixty MPs could also invoke the Constitutional Council's jurisdiction, which in practice enabled the opposition to challenge new laws on constitutional grounds. This reform made the Constitutional Council a true counterpower.

In an international comparison of seventy-one countries, Rafael La Porta, Florencio López-de-Silanes, Christian Pop-Eleches, and Andrei Shleifer showed that countries where judicial independence is the most secure are the countries with stronger protection of property rights and fewer administrative formalities for setting up new firms.[18]

The Limits on Judicial Impartiality

The view that the judicial branch constitutes a counterpower is at odds with the existence in the real world of multiple sources of bias in decisions rendered by the courts. First of all, there are political biases: it has been shown, for example, that Democratic judges in the United States render less harsh sentences than Republican judges. All other things being equal, political party affiliation explains 38 percent of the difference in severity of sentences.[19]

Next are media biases. In particular, a recent study by Arnaud Philippe and Aurélie Ouss, carried out on French data, analyzed the extent to which current news affected the decisions rendered in criminal courts, which utilize a mixed tribunal composed of a minority of professional judges and a majority of jurors randomly selected from the population at large.[20] The authors compared verdicts rendered immediately after significant media coverage of criminal matters—unrelated to the case under consideration—with verdicts rendered after a period of less media coverage of criminal matters. They show that greater media coverage of crimes one day before the trial increases the duration of sentences imposed by juries and that only media coverage on that specific day seems to make a difference. In contrast, sentences are more lenient after coverage of judicial errors. It is interesting to note, however, that the authors find that media coverage has no effect on the decisions of the professional judges in criminal cases.

A third type of bias in judicial decision-making is economic. In particular, how does the economic cycle affect judgments rendered in wrongful dismissal cases? A study by Ioana Marinescu based on British data showed that an increase in the unemployment rate and / or the number of bankruptcies considerably reduces the probability that judges will decide in favor of the dismissed employee rather than of the firm that engages in layoffs on economic grounds.[21]

Finally, there is a psychological or reputational bias. For example, a widespread psychological bias is the "gambler's fallacy." It leads to an error of logic: if you play "heads or tails" and land on heads five times in a row, you will undoubtedly think that the probability of landing on tails on the next toss is greater than that of landing on heads. This expectation is false: the probability of landing on tails is always 50 percent because each toss is independent. Applied to judges, those who were more permissive in respect of prior requests for asylum have a greater tendency to deny asylum in subsequent cases.[22] Yet their past decisions should not affect future decisions because no objective factor links the successive cases they adjudicate. This source of bias can be complicated by bias relating to the judge's reputation. If she has often granted asylum in past cases and wants to have a reputation of being strict, she may deny more asylum claims in the future to support that image.

Similarly, fatigue, on the scale of a workday as well as over the span of an entire career, leads to greater leniency in judicial decisions: judges tend to be more lenient before lunch or at the end of the day (Figure 15.2); they also become more lenient with age.[23] Other, more surprising, psychological biases have been demonstrated: in Louisiana, for example, more severe sentences are imposed after unexpected losses by the football team of a prominent state university, and more lenient sentences are imposed if the trial falls on the defendant's birthday.[24]

These deficiencies in the impartiality of judges have led some researchers to wonder whether it might be appropriate to replace judges with artificial intelligence algorithms. In particular, to what extent can machine learning reduce the human biases described above?

Nearly 10 million people are arrested each year in the United States. After they are arrested, judges can order detention of the accused pending trial. As a matter of law, such an order requires that conditions exist that raise doubt as to whether the defendant will appear at trial (meaning that the defendant presents a flight risk) or whether the defendant may cause harm to the community. If the judge considers these risks to be sufficiently high, the defendant is placed in custody, which eliminates the risk of nonappearance but increases the prison population. If the judge considers flight risk to be low, she takes the risk of leaving the defendant at liberty to flee or commit a crime pending trial. Jon Kleinberg, Himabindu

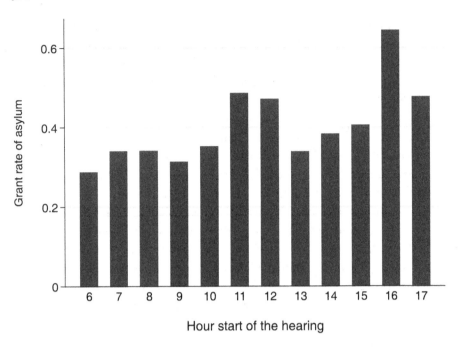

Hour start of the hearing

FIGURE 15.2. Asylum grant rate by hearing hour.

Extracted and reformatted from D. L. Chen and J. Eagel, "Can Machine Learning Help Predict the Outcome of Asylum Adjudications?" Proceedings of the Sixteenth International Conference on Artificial Intelligence and Law (2017): 237–240, figure 1.

Lakkaraju, Jure Leskovec, Jens Ludwig, and Sendhil Mullainathan utilized information covering 750,000 persons arrested in New York City between 2008 and 2013 to create a machine-learning algorithm predicting the probability that an individual released pending trial would fail to appear.[25]

It is thus possible to order pretrial detention of individuals presenting the highest risk according to the algorithm. How do the algorithm's decisions compare to those of judges? The answer is complex. Judges have biases; computers presumably have fewer.[26] The judge, however, has access to information or signals that are not in the file, such as the defendant's behavior in the courtroom. There is a near-perfect correlation between the rate of failure to appear at trial ("nonappearance") predicted by the algorithm and the actual rate of nonappearance of defendants who have been released, which indicates that the algorithm does a good job of predicting risk on the basis of information available in the defendant's file. What about the accuracy of the decisions of New York City judges? They release nearly 50 percent of defendants whom the algorithm gives a 60 percent chance of nonappearance and order custody of 30 percent of defendants who have only a 20 percent risk of nonappearance.

According to this study, ordering custody on the basis of the risk of nonappearance predicted by the algorithm would allow us to either reduce the rate of nonappearance by 25 percent without increasing prison populations or reduce the prison population by 42 percent without increasing criminality. This approach would obviously raise ethical questions. And our natural reluctance to rely on algorithms is in part based on our desire to treat each person as a unique individual, not as just another data point.

To summarize, although an independent judiciary provides greater protection of property rights and free enterprise, in reality judges are subject to a variety of biases—political, media-induced, economic, and psychological—that influence their decisions. Judges' expertise and professionalism enable them to limit the impact of these biases. But beyond the judicial system, it is undeniably civil society above all that has compelled state institutions to evolve, including the judiciary. We thus turn now to civil society.

5. The Role of Civil Society

We discussed above the advantages and disadvantages of a strong executive and then identified a variety of institutional tools to limit and oversee the executive. However, we must remember that constitutions are incomplete contracts and, in reality, nothing guarantees that these tools will be put in place or actually applied. This is where civil society plays a crucial role as a means of ensuring the effective implementation of this incomplete contract.

Incomplete Contracts and Civil Society

As Samuel Bowles and Wendy Carlin explain, when contracts are incomplete—whether between an employer and an employee, a lender and a borrower, or a buyer and a seller—performance depends on both the allocation of rights and duties specified in the contract and on current social norms.[27] The transaction is thus not solely an economic act but also a political and social act. More specifically, social norms and the civil society that incarnates them are there to limit abuses of power by employers and lenders. Figure 15.3 illustrates this idea very clearly. It depicts a triangle whose three vertices are the state, markets, and civil society. The "markets" vertex stands for private actors (entrepreneurs, consumers, employees) and the organizations (markets, firms) within which these actors interact. The closer one is to the "markets" vertex, the more the economy obeys market forces and laissez-faire. The "state" vertex represents the executive branch.

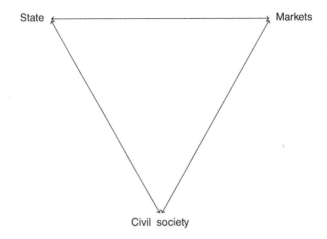

FIGURE 15.3. The triangle of state, markets, and civil society.

© *The Authors.*

The closer one is to this pole, the more the executive branch acts without factoring in markets and civil society. An extreme case is that of a centrally planned and authoritarian regime.[28] Finally, the closer we are to the "civil society" vertex, the closer we get to a self-governing society.[29] An extreme case is that of an anarchical regime.[30] The ideal combination for stimulating innovation and creative destruction lies inside the triangle; in other words it relies on a balance of markets, the state, and civil society.

Just as civil society helps enforce incomplete contracts between employers and employees and between lenders and borrowers, it also helps enforce national constitutions, which are incomplete social contracts. Here, the role of civil society is to give substance to the constitutional safeguards discussed above.[31] In particular, civil society gives effect to constitutional provisions limiting executive power. In other words, civil society takes these safeguards from the realm of theory to the realm of practice.

Two Examples: COVID-19 and the Climate

COVID-19. Bowles and Carlin recently emphasized the role of civil society as a necessary complement to the state-markets pair to curb the COVID-19 pandemic.[32] They acknowledge the decisive role of the markets and competition in fostering the discovery of new treatments and vaccines. They take note of the indispensable role of the state in managing the health crisis in the short term and in restarting the economy in the medium term. But, looking in particular at the example of South Korea, they also call attention to the role of civil society as an essential third pillar of a strategy to stop the pandemic. Their argument is that South Korea's good performance had a lot to do with the self-discipline and civic-mindedness that are prevalent there. These assets enabled the country both to take social-distancing measures very early on, thereby limiting the spread of the virus, and to immediately manage contaminated individuals. The overall public health strategy to contain the virus would not have worked if it had relied solely on the state and on coercion.

Unfortunately, this civic-mindedness is lacking in many other nations. In France, we saw numerous Parisians violate the confinement directives during spring vacation, and in the United States, Donald Trump himself used his Twitter account to champion local demonstrations against confinement, contradicting the advice of his own administration.

Climate. In Chapter 9 we described a number of levers that could be used to foster green innovation. Instruments such as a carbon tax and a subsidy of green innovation make use of the state–markets pair: the state utilizes these two instruments to redirect firms' innovation toward environmentally friendly technologies. The former reduces the incentive to produce and innovate in polluting technologies, and the latter reduces the costs of innovating in green technologies. But we also discussed the role of pro-environment social values and their interaction with competition. This interaction between social values and competition mobilizes the markets–civil society pairing. Civil society harbors these pro-environmental values; markets are the venue for competition and innovation.[33] First, we saw that when citizens express a stronger preference for the environment and a willingness to pay more to promote a greener economy, firms are more motivated to innovate in green technologies in order to cater to consumer preferences. Second, we showed that the degree of competition on the market for goods and services enhances the effect of social preferences on green innovation. In a country where consumers care about the environment, competition pushes firms toward environmental innovation to escape competition from their rivals. Lastly, the state–civil society pair describes the interaction between citizen action and governmental decisions. In the presence of the public's ecological aspirations, the state is pressured to adopt laws or policies in favor of the environment. Overall, the success of a policy combating climate change requires all three pillars: the markets, the state, and civil society.

How Civil Society Gives Substance to Democracy

The Fight for Civil Rights in the United States

The civil rights movement in the United States offers a striking example of the necessary role and galvanizing power of civil society as a lever for obtaining legislative action, bringing litigation, and obliging officials in the executive branch to enforce the law.

After the Civil War, the US Constitution was amended to guarantee equal rights to all races. But authorities in some states undermined those guaranties, denying Black Americans political rights and equality through legally sanctioned segregation in, for example, the military, schools, and public spaces and facilities. Although the Fifteenth Amendment gave Black Americans the right to vote, many states in the South used poll taxes or required Black voters to take unfairly implemented literacy tests, effectively disenfranchising them. Even after the Supreme Court's landmark decision invalidating racial segregation in schools, many schools remained segregated.

The civil rights movement gained momentum in the middle of the century, marked notably by Rosa Parks's refusal on December 1, 1955, to give up her seat on a public bus to a white man in Montgomery, Alabama. Her action prompted a long sequence of events. First, there was a boycott of Montgomery buses, then a series of nonviolent protests against racial discrimination starting in 1957 that were coordinated by leaders such as Martin Luther King, Jr. There was a confrontation between nine black students arriving for the first day of school at a previously all-white high school and the Arkansas National Guard, who had been sent by the governor to block those students from entering the school. This incident was the first of a series in which the US president would subsequently send federal troops to enforce desegregation. Four black college students who refused to leave a "whites only" lunch counter in Greensboro, North Carolina, sparked similar sit-ins throughout the South, and the Freedom Riders—black and white activists—rode buses through the South to protest segregation and were often met with vicious violence. These notable events were supplemented by the activism of a number of organizations such as the Southern Christian Leadership Conference, the National Association for the Advancement of Colored People, and the Student Nonviolent Coordinating Committee. The work of all of these activists culminated in the March on Washington for Jobs and Freedom of August 28, 1963, at which Martin Luther King, Jr., gave the now-famous speech in which he proclaimed "I have a dream" before approximately 250,000 people.

All of these direct actions and many others by members of civil society, together with wide media coverage, were behind the enactment of the Civil Rights

Act of 1964, which prohibits employment discrimination on the basis of race, color, sex, religion, or national origin, and the Voting Rights Act of 1965, which bans voter literacy tests and mandates federal examiners in certain voting jurisdictions.

The goals of the civil rights movement are still a work in progress, and demonstrations, litigation, and other actions by civil society continue with a goal of achieving full social, economic, and political equality.

The Movement of May 1968 and the Ability to Contest the Constitutionality of Laws in France

We referred earlier to the extension of the right to challenge the constitutionality of laws before the Constitutional Council pursuant to the constitutional reform of October 29, 1974. This extension, initiated by the newly elected president, Valéry Giscard d'Estaing, strengthened the parliamentary minority by allowing a group of at least sixty MPs or sixty senators to bring an action before the Constitutional Council. This reform had immediate consequences: the number of cases increased from five over the entire decade preceding the reform to ninety-four during the decade following the reform, hence an increase by a factor of nineteen. Valéry Giscard d'Estaing, when questioned about the reasons for the extension, tied it directly to the student-led riots of May 1968. To prevent future riots of such magnitude, it was necessary to expand the rights of the opposition and increase dialogue between the majority and the opposition. Thus it was once again civil society, set in motion by students in 1968, which led public officials to amend the constitution so as to strengthen the checks on executive power. These examples illustrate the idea that the actions of civil society can impel the executive to yield power, thereby giving substance to the constitutional contract.

Extending the Franchise as a Commitment Device

Daron Acemoglu and James Robinson formalized the idea in a 2000 paper that extending the franchise could be a means of preventing riots or revolutions.[34] Their theoretical framework allows us to understand why, for example, under pressure from civil society, voting rights in the United Kingdom were steadily expanded between 1820 and 1920 (Figure 15.4). Until 1832, only an oligarchical elite had the right to vote. In 1832, the minimum wealth and property thresholds for voting were lowered, extending the franchise to one in seven men. In 1867, the franchise was extended to all men living in urban areas and owning real property. The voting reform of 1884 extended this right to men who owned property in the countryside. In 1919, all men over the age of twenty-one and women over the age of thirty obtained the right to vote.

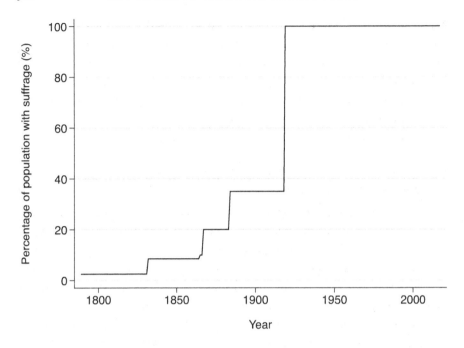

FIGURE 15.4. Share of the population with voting rights in the United Kingdom.

Data source: Our World in Data.

Why did the British elite grant these successive extensions of the right to vote, which led to increased public investments and redistribution, thus ultimately to a decrease of their political power and economic wealth? The answer is that this expanded franchise was a way for the elite to credibly commit to establish public services and a system of redistribution. In this way they avoided major social unrest, perhaps even a revolution. Simply promising redistribution would not have sufficed; in order to make such a promise credible, it was necessary to grant control rights to civil society by extending the franchise.[35] The threat of revolution that emanated from civil society forced the executive to complete the social contract by extending the franchise, thereby lending credibility to its performance of this contract.

A recent study by Toke S. Aidt and Peter S. Jensen tested this hypothesis on twelve European nations for the period from 1820 to 1938.[36] This study analyzed the effects of a threat of revolution on the extension of the voting franchise within a country. The franchise is measured by the fraction of the population having the right to vote in legislative elections. The threat of revolution is measured by the occurrence of revolutionary events in neighboring countries, based on the idea that revolutions are disseminated between countries.[37] The coauthors found that on average the threat of revolution has a significant positive effect on the extension of voting rights. In particular, a revolutionary event somewhere in Europe has the short-term effect of increasing the fraction of the population with voting rights by approximately 2 percent.

Nonetheless, fear of revolt is not the only reason that incumbent powers expand democracy. For example, such a fear did not motivate Nicolas Sarkozy to propose the constitutional reform of 2008. This reform strengthened the powers of the parliamentary opposition, in particular by allowing a law to be submitted for review *a posteriori* by the Constitutional Council—after it has entered into force—at the behest of any French citizen.[38] The motivation was more generally to associate the opposition with an ambitious program of reforms.

Can we nonetheless disregard the risk of major revolts in current times? Are the same processes still relevant today? The Yellow Vest movement in France from November 2018 to March 2019 proved that we must take this risk seriously, and that an overly confident executive can encounter many stumbling blocks.

The Cost of Disregarding Civil Society: The Yellow Vest Movement

Emmanuel Macron, after serving as minister of the economy under François Hollande, won France's 2017 presidential election.[39] His victory was amplified in the legislative elections one month later, in June 2017. The "En Marche" movement, transformed into a new political party, "La République en Marche," won a sweeping majority of seats in the National Assembly, while the traditional left- and right-wing parties emerged greatly weakened. The result was that Macron could rely on a strong majority to make reforms, which he promptly undertook in high gear in the summer of 2017. His goal was to stimulate long-term growth and bring down unemployment by means of a flat tax on capital income, a reform of the labor market and of professional training, and a reform of the educational system.[40] All of these reforms appeared in the candidate's program, with the purpose of giving them political legitimacy if he was elected.

In particular, President Macron's administration made frequent recourse to a constitutional provision allowing the executive branch to bypass Parliament and force the adoption of laws drafted by the administration, unless Parliament votes a measure of no confidence. This procedure circumvents parliamentary debate and thus accelerates the reform process. Under this constitutional provision, Parliament authorizes the administration to enact laws in a specific area for a limited time, relinquishing the ability to weigh in on the contents of these laws.[41] Examples are the reform of the national railway system (the SNCF), and the reform of labor law, which were both adopted under this procedure.

Emboldened by the lack of opposition in Parliament and confident it had marginalized labor unions, the administration in place at the time chose to introduce unpopular measures that were not in the candidate's program: eliminating inflation adjustments on retirement benefits, which hit families with modest pensions hard; reducing housing subsidies for students; lowering speed limits on roads from 90 to 80 kilometers per hour; and most importantly, sharply increasing the carbon tax, which ultimately sparked the crisis.

Although the underlying causes of the revolt go back to the beginning of 2018, the increase in the carbon tax marked the starting point for the Yellow Vest movement, a protest movement that emerged from civil society. In the minds of those who initiated the carbon tax increase, it would achieve two goals: first, it would bring revenues to the state, and second, it would brand the administration as pro-environment. But the artisans of the measure neglected to take into account its redistributive effects. They specifically failed to account for the strong negative impact on suburban populations who have no alternative to automobiles for commuting to work or taking their children to school. The movement began in November 2018, and by December 1, 2018, it had become an urban guerrilla rebellion. Emmanuel Macron watched on television from Argentina, where he was attending a G20 meeting, as the Arc de Triomphe was vandalized and the Champs-Elysées was the scene of violent clashes between demonstrators and police. Only after this urban riot on December 1 did the French president announce, on December 5, 2018, the cancellation of the increase on gasoline taxes. The cost of having disregarded civil society was not only the 18 million euros spent on extinguishing the fire of the rebellion but, critically, the suspension of the reform process for nearly a year.

The Yellow Vest movement nevertheless had a positive consequence: it resulted in greater decentralization and deconcentration of the French political system. In particular, it led to the establishment of the "Citizens' Convention for the Climate," which gathered 150 citizens selected at random to formulate proposals for combating global warming. President Macron promised to submit these legislative and regulatory proposals, without filtering them, either to a public referendum or to the vote of Parliament. Once again, the fear of resurgence of the protest movement became a Sword of Damocles for the French government, both inducing institutional change and guaranteeing that those changes would be substantive and not merely formal.

Another effect of the movement was to validate social media as a real counterpower, especially Facebook, which enabled citizens to coordinate spontaneously, with no prior formal organization. The emergence of social media is a cause for self-examination by the traditional spokespeople of civil society—the media.

The Role of the Media

It is difficult to talk about the role of civil society without also talking about the role of the media because of their role as amplifiers.

A Case Study on Media's Positive Role. One of the virtues of the media is to alert the public to abuse of power by the executive. One powerful illustration is the diffusion of photos or videos exposing the mistreatment of prisoners by American forces in the Abu Ghraib prison under the George W. Bush administration.

In April 2004, CBS News received a file of photos and videos showing in detail the abuse of prisoners at Abu Ghraib in Iraq. The chairman of the Joint Chiefs of Staff, the highest-ranking officer in the US military, then contacted the head of the news network to request that he not broadcast the material at least temporarily in order to protect the US troops present in Iraq. However, three weeks later, CBS News learned that *New Yorker* magazine might be publishing the photos. Unwilling to lose the "scoop" to a competitor, CBS News released the photos: the scandal broke, and in 2006 control of the prisons was handed over to the Iraqi authorities. The revelation of this scandal and specifically of the use of waterboarding led the American administration to prohibit this practice in interrogations by any governmental agency.

Thus, the existence of independent media is a means for civil society to influence the state. In addition, free competition between media outlets plays a role in their action as a counterpower. This double freedom—independence of the media and free competition—gives substance to the social contract.

Media and COVID-19. On December 30, 2019, when Ai Fen, director of the Emergency Department of Central Hospital of Wuhan, China, read a laboratory report analyzing the first cases of COVID-19, she began to disseminate alarming information about the severity and transmissibility of this new virus, but she was rapidly reprimanded by her supervisors. On March 10, 2020, the magazine *Ren Wu*, which belongs to the *People's Daily,* the official newspaper of the Chinese Communist Party, published an interview with Ai. Paper copies of the magazine were immediately confiscated. On December 30, 2019, Li Wenliang, an ophthalmologist at the Wuhan hospital who had also seen the report, alerted his colleagues over the WeChat messaging app. On January 3, 2020, he was summoned by police, who accused him of "making false comments" that had "severely disturbed the social order." He was forced to promise in writing not to violate the law again.[42] This young physician died from COVID-19 on February 7, 2020. The coverup of information on COVID-19, combined with conditioned self-censorship by doctors and local authorities, contributed to China's delay in responding to the appearance of the virus, with dramatic economic and public health consequences worldwide.

In other countries, the COVID-19 pandemic provided a pretext to censor or intimidate the media, to varying degrees. To justify their infringement of freedom of the press, governments pointed to their fight against "fake news," a pretense that authoritarian regimes have invoked for some time to stifle independent media, claiming that they wanted to reassure the population and maintain social order. In other words, the state used the pandemic as a pretext for reinforcing its power to the detriment of civil society.

In mid-April 2020, Turkish president Recep Tayyip Erdogan declared that rather than contributing to the fight against the pandemic, reporters were disseminating false information and untruths and were therefore more dangerous than the virus itself. He accused the opposition's media outlets of "waging a war against their own country." In India, on March 31, 2020, the Supreme Court directed the media to refer to and publish only the official version of developments relating to the pandemic, claiming that this was necessary in order to prevent widespread panic and invoking the media's "sense of responsibility." On March 30, 2020, the Hungarian parliament adopted a law authorizing Prime Minister Viktor Orban to govern by decree, with no time limit, and imposed prison terms of up to five years for spreading "false information" on the virus or on the government's measures. In other words, the public health emergency provided an opportunity for a power grab by authoritarian regimes.

Although the control of information is always eminently political, it is even more so during a pandemic. Control can range from censorship to coercion with direct aggression against individuals (abusive imprisonment or physical violence). Morocco, Jordan, and Syria, for example, prohibited the sale of newsprint on the pretext it could spread the virus. Censorship also coincides with an increase in the number of journalists assaulted, threatened, or imprisoned (for example in Turkey, Jordan, Zimbabwe, and Ukraine). Furthermore, journalists have expressed concern about the use of digital tracing apps. These were initially intended to suppress the spread of COVID-19, but some governments have already employed them to monitor the media. Threats and surveillance intensify the self-censorship that is already the norm in these countries.

6. Conclusion

Limiting executive power is essential to the functioning of an innovation economy. In particular, monitoring the power of the executive limits the scope of collusion between public officials and incumbent firms seeking to maintain their rents. In other words, it supports the entry of new innovative firms and thus stimulates the process of creative destruction.

The first channel for regulating the executive's power is the constitution. In an environment of "incomplete contracts," the constitution establishes a hierarchy of norms and power-sharing rules. Specifically, it sets up the separation of powers between the executive and legislative branches and proclaims the independence of the judiciary. It also determines the electoral system for electing members of the legislature and voting rules within the legislature, the ability to make amendments, the right to invoke the jurisdiction of the supreme court, and the duration of terms of office, all of which directly impact the extent and limits of the executive's power. Nonetheless, all of these constitutional guaranties remain empty words without an active and vigilant civil society.

This leads to the critical triad of the market, the state, and civil society for the proper functioning of an economy of innovation and creative destruction. The market provides incentives to innovate and constitutes the framework in which innovative firms compete. The state is there to protect property rights on innovations, to enforce contracts, and to act as an investor and insurer. Finally, civil society—the media, labor unions, nonprofits—generate or call for the enforcement of constitutional provisions intended to check executive power and ensure greater efficiency, ethics, and justice in the operation of the market.

History shows that a mobilized civil society has contributed greatly to the evolution of capitalism toward a system that is better regulated, more inclusive, more protective of citizens, and a better steward of the environment. However, this evolution has not been linear and has occurred at different rates in different countries. What are the different forms of capitalism today, and what is the ideal system that we should aim for? These are the questions we will address in the next chapter, the conclusion of our exploration of the underpinnings of creative destruction.

CONCLUSION

The Future of Capitalism

Exploding inequality, growth stalled for the past decade and a half, unrelenting climate disturbance, and now the COVID-19 pandemic that has laid bare the deficiencies of our economic and social systems: these very real phenomena are the bread and butter of proponents of isolationism and the end of globalization, of antigrowth partisans, and of those advocating for abandoning capitalism altogether.

Capitalism is thus confronting an unprecedented identity crisis. No one can deny that capitalism, particularly when it is unregulated, has a number of adverse consequences: it exacerbates inequality and enables the strong to fetter the weak; it can fragment society and destroy the sense of community; it makes employment precarious, causing deterioration of individuals' health and increasing their stress; it enables incumbent firms to use lobbying to block the entry of new innovative firms; it aggravates global warming and climate change; it induces financial crises that generate severe recessions such as those of 1929 and 2008.

Nonetheless, the abolition of capitalism is not the solution. The last century witnessed a large-scale experiment with an alternative system—a system of central planning in the Soviet Union and other communist countries of Central and Eastern Europe. This system failed to offer individuals the freedom and economic incentives necessary for frontier innovation, and so these nations were unable to get beyond an intermediate level of development.[1] Henri Weber, a well-known figure of the French movement of May 1968, was a former Trotskyist leader in the 1960s and 1970s but later became a leader of the French Socialist Party and Socialist member of the European Parliament. He explained his personal conversion to the free market economy and social democracy, looking to the Scandinavian experience: "Having witnessed from a front-row seat the disaster of collectivization of agriculture and firms in the Soviet Union, the Scandinavian Socialists were the first to break with the dogma of socializing means of production and managing the economy by a central planning committee. To control and humanize the economy, it is altogether unnecessary to expropriate management, to nationalize firms, or to eradicate the market . . . altogether unnecessary to deprive society of the creativity, knowhow, and dynamism of entrepreneurs. Under certain conditions, entrepreneurial talent can be mobilized to serve the common good."[2] A market economy, because it induces creative destruction, is inherently disruptive. But historically it has proved to be a formidable engine of prosperity, hoisting our societies to levels of development unimaginable two centuries ago. Must we therefore resign ourselves to the serious pitfalls and defects of capitalism as the necessary price to pay to generate prosperity and overcome poverty?

In this book, we have sought to better understand how growth through creative destruction interacts with competition, inequality, the environment, finance, unemployment, health, happiness, and industrialization, and how poor countries catch up to rich ones. We have analyzed to what degree the state, with appropriate control of the executive, can stimulate the creation of wealth while at the same time tackling the problems mentioned above.

We have seen how, by moving from laissez-faire capitalism, with market forces given free rein, to a form of capitalism in which the state and civil society play their full role, it is possible to stimulate social mobility and reduce inequality without discouraging innovation. We have also seen how appropriate competition policies can curb the decline of growth and how we can redirect innovation toward green technologies to combat global warming. We have seen that, without forgoing globalization, a country can improve its competitiveness through innovative investments and put in place effective safety nets to protect individuals who lose their jobs. Lastly, we have seen how, with the indispensable support of civil society, it is possible to prevent yesterday's innovators, in collusion with public officials, from pulling up the ladder behind themselves to block the path of tomorrow's innovators.

Some may accuse us of naivete and excessive optimism about the possibility of reforming capitalism, drawing their arguments from the current rigidities of the systems in place in many countries and from the history of capitalism in the last century, strewed with calamities, injustice, world wars, and colonial wars.

What have we learned by comparing the different forms of capitalism? Should we follow the model of the United States, more innovative, or of Germany and the Scandinavian countries, more protective of their citizens? Are we necessarily facing an "either / or" choice, or can we imagine a "both / and" form of capitalism that takes the positive elements of each?

Those who believe in the "either / or" scenario see the world as divided between "cutthroat capitalism" and "cuddly capitalism."[3] The United States incarnates a more cutthroat form of capitalism, while the Scandinavian countries, and to a lesser extent Germany, are the representatives of a more cuddly capitalism. According to this view, insofar as innovation at the technological frontier relies on strong monetary incentives, the countries that aim for frontier innovation should forgo the goals of insurance and equality: in other words, they should renounce "cuddly capitalism" in favor of a "cutthroat" form of capitalism. As for the countries who choose cuddly capitalism, they would have no alternative but growth by imitation of technologies invented by the frontier countries. The "cuddly" countries provide their citizens with greater equality and insurance, but their growth depends ultimately on the growth of the "cutthroat" countries, which, one might say, work for the benefit of the rest of the world.

Does the comparison between the United States, on the one hand, and Germany and the Scandinavian countries, on the other, confirm this thesis? Let's start by comparing the innovation performance of these countries. Table C.1 shows that, between 2010 and 2017, the United States is far ahead of Germany, France, and the Scandinavian countries with regard to average annual number of patents per one million inhabitants. American supremacy is even more staggering if we focus on the 5 percent of patents that are the most cited.

Table C.2 compares these countries' performance in terms of inequality and poverty. We can see that income inequality—measured by the Gini coefficient[4]—and poverty in the United States are markedly higher than those of Germany, the Scandinavian countries, and France.

What about protecting individuals against macroeconomic shocks?[5] Figure C.1 shows the evolution of the percentage of individuals with no health insurance in Germany and in the United States since 2008. In Germany this fraction is zero because all citizens have health coverage. But in the United States, the fraction is significant. It fell in 2014 thanks to Obamacare (see below), but it has increased sharply with the COVID-19 crisis, due to the dramatic rise in unemployment induced by the crisis. The reason is that Americans very often get their health insurance through their employers and thus lost their employer-sponsored health in-

Table C.1. Number of Patents per Country, Average from 2010–2017

	Patent Applications per Million Inhabitants	Number of Top 5% Patents per Citations	Percentage of Top 5% Patents per Citations
Germany	617.1	170.5	0.4%
Denmark	87.4	0.0	0%
United States	1,186.4	32,678.0	71.7%
France	231.1	5.9	0%
Norway	316.4	0.3	0%
Sweden	129.8	0.3	0%

Data source: Patstat. Author's calculations.

Table C.2. Gini Index and Poverty Rate, 2017

	Gini Index	Poverty Rate
United States	0.390	0.178
Germany	0.289	0.104
Sweden	0.282	0.093
Norway	0.262	0.084
France	0.292	0.081
Denmark	0.261	0.058

Note: Data from 2016 for Denmark.

Data source: OECD.

surance when they lost their jobs. Similarly, Figure C.2 shows the evolution of the share of the population at risk of falling into poverty in Germany and in the United States since 2008. Again, the risk clearly increases more dramatically in the United States than in Germany with the advent of the COVID-19 pandemic.

This comparison of innovation performance, on the one hand, and measures of inequality, poverty, and protection against macroeconomic shocks, on the other, seems at first glance to validate the "either/or" thesis. We emphasize, however, that these international comparisons were made over a limited span of years, 2010–2017, or in a select year, 2017. They do not show the countries' evolution over time. Yet certain evolutions in Scandinavia and in the United States give us reason to hope for a synthesis of these two forms of capitalism.

With regard to Scandinavia, we have discussed the Danish system of flexicurity in Chapters 11 and 14. The idea behind this system was precisely to introduce

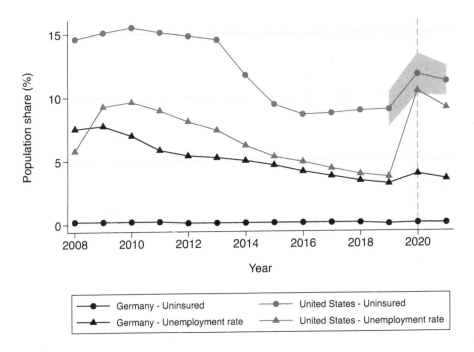

FIGURE C.1. Percentage of uninsured and percentage of unemployed individuals in Germany and in the United States.

Reformatted from P. Aghion, H. Maghin, and A. Sapir, "Covid and the Nature of Capitalism," VoxEU, June 25, 2020, figure 1.

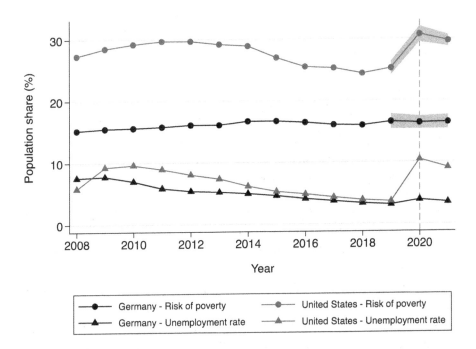

FIGURE C.2. Share of the population at risk of poverty and share of the population unemployed in Germany and in the United States.

Reformatted from P. Aghion, H. Maghin, and A. Sapir, "Covid and the Nature of Capitalism," VoxEU, June 25, 2020, figure 3.

greater flexibility in the labor market in order to encourage innovation and creative destruction while protecting laid-off workers' income and enabling them to retrain and move more easily to a new job. This reform boosted innovation in Denmark but did not compromise the Danish social model: to this day Denmark continues to have the lowest inequality and poverty rates of any nation in the world.

The example of Sweden is equally interesting. In 1991, Sweden undertook a vast reform of its taxation system with the objective of stimulating innovation. The marginal tax rate for the highest income bracket was lowered from 88 percent to 55 percent, and capital income was taxed at a flat rate of 30 percent.[6] In conjunction with a devaluation of the Swedish krona, this tax reform boosted innovation and productivity growth in Sweden: the average annual rate of productivity growth was quadrupled after the reform and innovation took off in 1990. Did this process entail sacrificing redistribution? Although it is true that inequality as measured by the share of total income going to the top 1 percent has materially increased in Sweden since 1990, global inequality measured by the Gini coefficient, as well as the poverty rate, increased only minimally, so that Sweden remains one of the most protective and least unequal countries in the world.[7]

Overall, Denmark and Sweden undertook reforms that stimulated innovation and at the same time preserved the essential preexisting elements of the welfare state. These successes give hope to the "both/and" thesis of a possible synthesis combining the positive aspects of the two types of capitalism. The United States introduced reforms aimed at making capitalism more protective, in particular the Patient Protection and Affordable Care Act, known as Obamacare. This law was intended to make health care accessible to more Americans. One of its main provisions was to prohibit insurance companies from refusing to insure people with preexisting conditions or charging them higher premiums. In spite of vehement opposition, the law was adopted at the end of 2013, and by 2016 the number of uninsured Americans had already been cut in half. There have been numerous attempts by members of the Republican Party to repeal this law, but as of this writing none have succeeded. Obamacare is nonetheless only a first step toward a more humane form of capitalism in the United States, and the road ahead is long.

More generally, the history of capitalism, since its appearance two hundred years ago, is largely the story of a system that was initially cutthroat, even in Sweden until the 1930s. Sweden today is light-years from the violent repression depicted in the film *Adalen 31*, just as France as we know it today is light-years from the France described by Emile Zola in *Germinal*.[8]

But in developed countries, capitalism has become more protective and inclusive over time, thanks above all to the struggles led by civil society (unions, progressive parties, and media). The intervention of visionary individuals to make the state evolve in response to pressure from civil society has also played a role. We can cite Leon Blum (paid vacation leave introduced in France in 1936), Franklin D. Roosevelt (the New Deal in 1930), William Beveridge (the welfare state in Great Britain in 1942), Charles de Gaulle (implementation of the Program of the National Council of the Resistance in 1945), Olof Palme (Social Democratic prime minister of Sweden in the 1970s), and Barack Obama (Obamacare in 2010). Conversely, starting from a protective model of capitalism, reformers such as Poul Nyrup Rasmussen, father of Danish flexicurity in the 1990s, and Assar Lindbeck, artisan of the 1991 Swedish reform, helped make Denmark's and Sweden's economies more innovative.

Despite these evolutions, the United States is by no means a country that protects individuals from job loss, illness, or macroeconomic shocks such as the 2008 financial crisis or the COVID-19 pandemic, or from environmental risks. As for the European countries, they suffer from a different evil: they have failed to create the ecosystem—universities, institutional investors, venture capitalists, philanthropists, DARPA—that would enable them to be leaders rather than followers in future technological revolutions, and they may well be overtaken by China before long.

Nonetheless, we firmly believe in "both / and" for at least two reasons. First, the reforms increasing protection and inclusiveness in the United States did not inhibit innovation and creative destruction, and the reforms facilitating innovation and creative destruction in Germany and Scandinavia did not fundamentally undermine the social systems and public services in those countries. Second, as the analyses developed in this book have shown, innovation and inclusiveness, like innovation and protection, are not a zero-sum game. In fact, the opposite is true. Fostering the entry of new innovative firms and inspiring young people to go into research careers stimulates innovation and growth, and simultaneously makes that growth more inclusive. A well-designed system of flexicurity protects individuals against the negative consequences of job loss and at the same time motivates them to acquire skills that will prepare them for a new job. The consequence is stronger protection of individuals without hindering the process of creative destruction.

Capitalism is a spirited horse: it takes off readily, escaping control. But if we hold its reins firmly, it goes where we wish. In this book, we have brought to light a number of paths in which to direct capitalism, and we have identified levers that can steer it in those paths.

The COVID-19 pandemic has shed a stark light on the weaknesses and inadequacies of different forms of capitalism. In the United States, the pandemic laid bare the dramatic plight of the millions of individuals uninsured or underinsured against unemployment or illness. In France, it showed the vulnerability of an economy that went too far in delocalizing value chains, including in strategic sectors such as health; it also showed the limits of an excessively centralized, overly bureaucratic state that does not put enough trust in civil society and a bottom-up approach. In other countries, COVID-19 revealed the dangers of capitalism without freedom of expression: information retention and self-censorship led to delay in acknowledging the gravity of the novel virus, which in turn greatly contributed to its worldwide proliferation.

This crisis will unavoidably provoke existential debates on how to shape what comes next. Although we cannot predict the exact turn of these debates, we can be sure they will touch on many of the themes and analyses developed in this book. In answer to the question, "What is the future of capitalism?" we respond with the words of Henri Bergson: "The future is not what will happen to us, but what we will do."

Notes

1. A New Paradigm

1. Joseph A. Schumpeter, *Capitalism, Socialism and Democracy*, 3rd ed. (1950; New York: Harper Collins, 2008).

2. This quotation comes from "Theses on Feuerbach," which Karl Marx wrote in 1845 but was not published until 1888 by Friedrich Engels. For a recent translation, see Karl Marx, "Theses on Feuerbach," trans. W. Lough, Marxists internet archive, 2002, https://www.marxists.org/archive/marx/works/1845/theses/theses .htm.

3. Daniel Kahneman and Angus Deaton, "High Income Improves Evaluation of Life but Not Emotional Well-Being," *Proceedings of the National Academy of Sciences* 107, no. 38 (2010): 16489–16493.

4. The essential reference on development indicators is Joseph Stiglitz, Amartya Sen, and Jean Fitoussi, "Report by the Commission on the Measurement of Economic Performance and Social Progress," CMEPSP, Paris, 2009, https://www.uio.no /studier/emner/sv/oekonomi/ECON4270/h09/Report%20in%20English.pdf.

5. See Robert Solow, "A Contribution to the Theory of Economic Growth," *Quarterly Journal of Economics* 70, no. 1 (1956): 65–94.

6. Romer developed a model of innovation-led growth that did not include creative destruction. See Paul Romer, "Endogenous Technological Change," *Journal of Political Economy* 98, no. 5 (1990): 71–102. For a review of the theoretical literature on growth models from the Solow model to the Schumpeterian model, see the works of Gene M. Grossman and Elhanan Helpman, *Innovation and Growth in the Global Economy* (Cambridge, MA: MIT Press, 1991); Elhanan Helpman, ed., *General Purpose Technologies and Economic Growth* (Cambridge, MA: MIT Press, 1998); Charles I. Jones, *Introduction to Economic Growth* (New York: W.W. Norton, 1998); Robert J. Barro and Xavier Sala-i-Martin, *Economic Growth* (New York:

McGraw Hill, 1995); Philippe Aghion and Peter Howitt, *Endogenous Growth Theory* (Cambridge, MA: MIT Press, 1998); Daron Acemoglu, *Introduction to Modern Economic Growth* (Princeton: Princeton University Press, 2009); Philippe Aghion and Peter Howitt, *The Economics of Growth* (Cambridge, MA: MIT Press, 2009); and Philippe Aghion, Ufuk Akcigit, and Peter Howitt, "What Do We Learn from Schumpeterian Growth Theory?" in *Handbook of Economic Growth,* ed. Philippe Aghion and Steven Durlauf, vol. 2, 515–563 (Amsterdam: Elsevier, 2014). The most recent version of the Schumpeterian model incorporates firm dynamics; it was first developed by Tor Jakob Klette and Samuel Kortum (see Tor J. Klette and Samuel Kortum, "Innovating Firms and Aggregate Innovation," *Journal of Political Economy* 112, no. 5 [2004]: 986–1018) and further developed in later work, in particular by Ufuk Akcigit and his coauthors.

7. This model was written during the academic year of 1987–1988 at the Massachusetts Institute of Technology, where Philippe Aghion was starting out as an assistant professor and Peter Howitt was a visiting professor on sabbatical from the University of Western Ontario in Canada. Philippe Aghion and Peter Howitt, "A Model of Growth through Creative Destruction," *Econometrica* 60, no. 2 (1992): 323–351; Aghion, Akcigit, and Howitt, "What Do We Learn from Schumpeterian Growth Theory?"

8. Raghuram G. Rajan and Luigi Zingales, *Saving Capitalism from the Capitalists: Unleashing the Power of Financial Markets to Create Wealth and Spread Opportunity* (New York: Crown Business, 2003).

9. We cannot do justice here to the abundant literature on patents as a measure of innovation. We note the pioneers on this topic, in particular Pierre Azoulay, Ian Cockburn, Zvi Griliches, Bronwyn Hall, Dietmar Harhoff, Adam Jaffe, Jacques Mairesse, Ariel Pakes, Mark Schankerman, Otto Toivanen, Manuel Trajtenberg, and Reinhilde Veugelers, and invite the reader to consult their web pages.

10. U. Akcigit, J. Grigsby, and T. Nicholas, "The Rise of American Ingenuity: Innovation and Inventors of the Golden Age" (NBER Working Paper No. 23047, National Bureau of Economic Research, Cambridge, MA, January 2017).

11. One might think this correlation is fortuitous, but in their paper "The Rise of American Ingenuity," Akcigit, Grigsby, and Nicholas show, using historical data, that the relationship between innovation and growth is indeed causal.

12. J. Haltiwanger, R. S. Jarmin, and J. Miranda, "Who Creates Jobs? Small versus Large versus Young," *Review of Economics and Statistics* 95, no. 2 (2013): 347–361.

13. The reader can refer to the seminal work of Steve Davis, John Haltiwanger, and their coauthors on the creation and destruction of firms and jobs. See, for example, S. J. Davis and J. Haltiwanger, "Measuring Gross Worker and Job Flows," in *Labor Statistics Measurement Issues,* ed. J. Haltiwanger, M. E. Manser, and R. Topel, 77–122 (Chicago: University of Chicago Press, 1998); S. J. Davis and J. Halti-

wanger "Gross Job Flows," in *Handbook of Labor Economics*, ed. O. Ashenfelter and D. Card, vol. 3B, 2711–2805 (Amsterdam: Elsevier / North-Holland, 1999); Haltiwanger, Jarmin, and Miranda, "Who Creates Jobs?"; R. Decker, J. Haltiwanger, R. Jarmin, and J. Miranda, "The Role of Entrepreneurship in US Job Creation and Economic Dynamism," *Journal of Economic Perspectives* 28, no. 3 (2014): 3–24; S. J. Davis and J. Haltiwanger, "Labor Market Fluidity and Economic Performance" (NBER Working Paper No. 20479, National Bureau of Economic Research, Cambridge, MA, September 2014).

14. U. Akcigit and W. R. Kerr, "Growth through Heterogeneous Innovations," *Journal of Political Economy* 126, no. 4 (2018): 1374–1443.

15. C. T. Hsieh and P. J. Klenow, "The Life Cycle of Plants in India and Mexico," *Quarterly Journal of Economics* 129, no. 3 (2014): 1035–1084.

16. P. Aghion, A. Bergeaud, T. Boppart, and S. Bunel, "Firm Dynamics and Growth Measurement in France," *Journal of the European Economic Association* 16, no. 4 (2018): 933–956.

17. A. Maddison, *The World Economy: A Millennial Perspective*, Development Centre Studies (Paris: OECD, 2001).

18. See R. Blundell, R. Griffith, and J. Van Reenen, "Dynamic Count Models of Technological Innovation," *Economic Journal* 105, no. 429 (1995): 333–344; R. Blundell, R. Griffith, and J. Van Reenen, "Market Share, Market Value and Innovation in a Panel of British Manufacturing Firms," *Review of Economic Studies* 66, no. 3 (1999): 529–554; and S. J. Nickell, "Competition and Corporate Performance," *Journal of Political Economy* 104, no. 4 (1996): 724–746.

19. A. Hansen, "Economic Progress and Declining Population Growth," presidential address, American Economic Association, December 28, 1938, *American Economic Review* 29, no. 1 (1939): 1–15.

20. L. Summers, presentation at the IMF Economic Forum: Policy Responses to Crises, 14th Jacques Polak Annual Research Conference, International Monetary Fund, Washington, DC, November 9, 2013.

21. R. Gordon, *The Rise and Fall of American Growth* (Princeton: Princeton University Press, 2016).

22. S. Baslandze, "The Role of the IT Revolution in Knowledge Diffusion, Innovation and Reallocation," 2016 Meeting Papers No. 1509, Society for Economic Dynamics, 2016.

23. A. B. Atkinson, T. Piketty, and E. Saez, "Top Incomes in the Long Run of History," *Journal of Economic Literature* 49, no. 1 (2011): 3–71; T. Piketty, *Capital in the Twenty-First Century* (Cambridge, MA: The Belknap Press of Harvard University Press, 2014).

24. P. Aghion, U. Akcigit, A. Bergeaud, R. Blundell, and D. Hémous, "Innovation and Top Income Inequality," *Review of Economic Studies* 86, no. 1 (2019): 1–45.

25. J. Williamson, "What Washington Means by Policy Reform," in *Latin American Adjustment: How Much Has Happened?* ed. J. Williamson, vol. 1, 90–120 (Washington, DC: Institution for International Economics, 1990).

26. R. Hausmann, D. Rodrik, and A. Velasco, "Growth Diagnostics," in *The Washington Consensus Reconsidered: Towards a New Global Governance,* ed. N. Serra and E. Stiglitz, 324–355 (Oxford: Oxford University Press, 2008).

27. Raghuram G. Rajan and Luigi Zingales, "The Great Reversals: The Politics of Financial Development in the 20th Century," *Journal of Financial Economics* 69, no. 1 (2003): 5–50.

28. The technological frontier is the most advanced state of technological development; in other words the most effective production technology available. Thanks to innovation, this frontier obviously moves forward over time.

29. D. Acemoglu, P. Aghion, and F. Zilibotti, "Distance to Frontier, Selection, and Economic Growth," *Journal of the European Economic Association* 4, no. 1 (2006): 37–74.

2. The Enigma of Takeoffs

1. Analysis in the following section is based on the two major works of Angus Maddison: A. Maddison, *The World Economy: A Millennial Perspective,* Development Centre Studies (Paris: OECD, 2001); and A. Maddison, *The World Economy: Historical Statistics,* Development Centre Studies (Paris: OECD, 2003). The Maddison Historical Statistics Project was initiated in 2010 at the Groningen Growth and Development Centre at the University of Groningen. Its aim is to perpetuate Maddison's work and continue the rigorous measurement of economic performance indicators for different regions and periods.

2. Paul Bairoch and Gary Goertz, "Factors of Urbanisation in the Nineteenth Century Developed Countries," *Urban Studies* 23, no. 4 (1986): 285–305.

3. The estimates differ slightly depending on the source we consider. In Bairoch and Goertz, "Factors of Urbanisation," the authors estimated that, in 1800, the industrialization level was 10.9 percent while the United Nations estimated it to be 7.6 percent. Note that the slight decrease we observe in the seventeenth century could be due to the Thirty Years' War.

4. J. V. Grauman, "Orders of Magnitude of the World's Urban Population in History," *Population Bulletin of the United Nations* 8 (1976): 16–33.

5. Jean-Claude Toutain, "Le produit intérieur brut de la France de 1789 à 1982," *Économies et Societé,* Cahiers de l'ISMEA, Série Histoire quantitative de l'économie française, 1987, 15.

6. M. Lévy-Leboyer and F. Bourguignon, *L'économie française au XIXe siècle: Analyse macro-économique* (Paris: Economica, 1985).

7. Cliometry is the study of economic history using econometric methods.

8. Roger Fouquet and Stephen Broadberry, "Seven Centuries of European Economic Growth and Decline," *Journal of Economic Perspectives* 29, no. 4 (2015): 227–244.

9. J. M. Keynes, "Economic Possibilities for Our Grandchildren," in *Essays in Persuasion* (New York: Norton, 1930; London: Palgrave Macmillan, 2010).

10. One can also mention the Netherlands: until 1570, the southern part of the country (now Belgium), constituted the center of economic activity and prosperity, but after 1590 the north of the country, which is today's Amsterdam, took the lead.

11. On the topic of intellectual property rights, see in particular Douglass C. North and Barry R. Weingast, "Constitutions and Commitment: The Evolution of Institutions Governing Public Choice in Seventeenth-Century England," *Journal of Economic History* 49, no. 4 (1989): 803–832.

12. Fouquet and Broadberry, "Seven Centuries of European Economic Growth and Decline."

13. T. R. Malthus, *An Essay on the Principle of Population* (London: J. Johnson, 1798; Harmondsworth: Penguin, 1970).

14. See, for example, K. M. Murphy, A. Shleifer, and R. W. Vishny, "Industrialization and the Big Push," *Journal of Political Economy* 97, no. 5 (1989): 1003–1026.

15. Michael Kremer, "Population Growth and Technological Change: One Million B.C. to 1990," *Quarterly Journal of Economics* 108, no. 3 (1993): 681–716. Oded Galor and David N. Weil, "Population, Technology, and Growth: From Malthusian Stagnation to the Demographic Transition and Beyond," *American Economic Review* 90, no. 4 (2000): 806–828.

16. This "market size" effect is inherent in models of innovation-driven growth, including the Schumpeterian model. We refer the reader to the following articles providing supportive evidence of this market size effect on sectoral data and firm data: Daron Acemoglu and Joshua Linn, "Market Size in Innovation: Theory and Evidence from the Pharmaceutical Industry," *Quarterly Journal of Economics* 119, no. 3 (2004): 1049–1090; and Philippe Aghion, Antonin Bergeaud, Matthieu Lequien, and Marc J. Melitz, "The Heterogeneous Impact of Market Size on Innovation: Evidence from French Firm-Level Exports" (NBER Working Paper No. 24600, National Bureau of Economic Research, Cambridge, MA, May 2018, rev. October 2019).

17. See Charles I. Jones and Paul M. Romer, "The New Kaldor Facts: Ideas, Institutions, Population, and Human Capital," *American Economic Journal: Macroeconomics* 2, no. 1 (2010): 224–245; and Chapter 10.

18. The idea is that technological progress leads to an increase in the return on education.

19. Richard R. Nelson and Edmund S. Phelps, "Investment in Humans, Technological Diffusion, and Economic Growth," *American Economic Review* 56, no. 1–2 (1966): 69–75.

20. Nelson and Phelps, "Investment in Humans."

21. Joel Mokyr and Hans-Joachim Voth, "Understanding Growth in Europe, 1700–1870: Theory and Evidence," in *The Cambridge Economic History of Modern Europe*, vol. 1: *1700–1870*, ed. Stephen Broadberry and Kevin H. O'Rourke (Cambridge: Cambridge University Press, 2009).

22. This section develops the analysis of Joel Mokyr, *The Gifts of Athena: Historical Origins of the Knowledge Economy* (Princeton: Princeton University Press, 2002). For an instructive analysis of this book, see Hal R. Varian, "Review of Mokyr's Gifts of Athena," *Journal of Economic Literature* 42, no. 3 (2004): 805–810.

23. Translated from David Encaoua, "Interactions science-technologie: quelles politiques publiques," *Revue Française d'Économie* 25, no. 4 (2011): 75–119.

24. Diego Puga and Daniel Trefler, "International Trade and Institutional Change: Medieval Venice's Response to Globalization," *Quarterly Journal of Economics* 129, no. 2 (2014): 753–821. R. R. John, *Spreading the News: The American Postal System from Franklin to Morse* (Cambridge, MA: Harvard University Press, 1995).

25. For example, Jean Le Rond d'Alembert for mathematics, Louis-Jean-Marie Daubenton for natural history, Théophile de Bordeu and Théodore Tronchin for medicine. Among the 72,000 themes that are developed in their *Encyclopédie*, we find information on various techniques such as glass making (forty-four pages) or the process for milling (twenty-five pages).

26. Puga and Trefler, "International Trade and Institutional Change."

27. D. C. North and B. R. Weingast, "Constitutions and Commitment: The Evolution of Institutions Governing Public Choice in Seventeenth-Century England," *Journal of Economic History* 49, no. 4 (1989): 803–832.

28. Georges Renard, *Guilds in the Middle Ages* (London: J. B. Bell and Sons, 1918).

29. Varian, "Review of Mokyr's Gifts of Athena."

30. As a starting point in the academic literature on patents, we refer the reader to the bibliographies of Pierre Azoulay, Bronwyn Hall, Adam Jaffe, Jacques Mairesse, Mark Schankerman, and Reinhilde Veugelers.

31. Raghuram Rajan and Luigi Zingales, *Saving Capitalism from the Capitalists* (New York: Crown Business, 2003).

32. We should mention that an indirect effect of Eli Whitney's invention was to escalate the use of slavery in the Southern states of the United States.

3. Should We Fear Technological Revolutions?

1. "One big wave," see Robert Gordon, "US Economic Growth since 1870: One Big Wave?" *American Economic Review* 89, no. 2 (1999): 123–128. Antonin Bergeaud, Gilbert Cette, and Rémy Lecat, "Productivity Trends in Advanced Countries between 1890 and 2012," *Review of Income and Wealth* 62, no. 3 (2016): 420–444.

2. Antonin Bergeaud, Gilbert Cette, and Rémy Lecat, *Le Bel Avenir de la croissance. Leçons du XXe siècle pour le futur* (Paris: Odile Jacob, 2018).

3. We will explore this question in Chapter 6.

4. See John M. Keynes, "Economic Possibilities for Our Grandchildren" (1930), in *Essays in Persuasion* (New York: W.W. Norton, 1963; repr. London: Palgrave Macmillan, 2010).

5. Robert M. Solow, "We'd Better Watch Out," *New York Times,* July 12, 1987.

6. See Timothy F. Bresnahan and Manuel Trajtenberg, "General Purpose Technologies 'Engines of Growth?'" *Journal of Econometrics* 65, no. 1 (1995): 83–108. We refer the reader to all of the authors who participated in the book by E. Helpman, ed., *General Purpose Technologies and Economic Growth* (Cambridge, MA: MIT Press, 1998).

7. Boyan Jovanovic and Peter L. Rousseau, "General Purpose Technologies," in *Handbook of Economic Growth,* ed. Philippe Aghion and Steven Durlauf, vol. 1, 1181–1224 (Amsterdam: Elsevier, 2005).

8. Elhanan Helpman and Manuel Trajtenberg, "Diffusion of General Purpose Technologies," in *General Purpose Technologies and Economic Growth,* ed. E. Helpman, 85–119 (Cambridge, MA: MIT Press, 1998).

9. This section is based on the main themes of Paul David, "The Dynamo and the Computer: An Historical Perspective on the Modern Productivity Paradox," *American Economic Review* 80, no. 2 (1990): 355–361.

10. Bergeaud, Cette, and Lecat, *Le Bel Avenir de la croissance.*

11. Salome Baslandze, "The Role of the IT Revolution in Knowledge Diffusion, Innovation and Reallocation," 2016 Meeting Papers No. 1509, Society for Economic Dynamics, 2016.

12. Eric Brynjolfsson and Shinkyu Yang, "Information Technology and Productivity: A Review of the Literature," in *Advances in Computers,* ed. Marvin Zelkowitz, vol. 43 (1996): 179–214.

13. See Joseph Zeira, "Workers, Machines, and Economic Growth," *Quarterly Journal of Economics* 113, no. 4 (1998): 1091–1117; Daron Acemoglu and Pascual Restrepo, "Robots and Jobs: Evidence from US Labor Markets," *Journal of Political Economy* 128, no. 6 (2020): 2188–2244; Philippe Aghion, Benjamin F. Jones, and Charles I. Jones, "Artificial Intelligence and Economic Growth" (NBER Working Paper No. 23928, National Bureau of Economic Research, Cambridge, MA, October 2017).

14. Aghion, Jones, and Jones, "Artificial Intelligence and Economic Growth."

15. Gravenor Henson, *The Civil, Political, and Mechanical History of the Framework-Knitters in Europe and America* (Nottingham: Richard Sutton, 1831), 45.

16. Not until the Reform Bill of 1832, however, did Parliament cease to be dominated by the large aristocratic landowners.

17. Keynes, "Economic Possibilities for Our Grandchildren."

18. Wassily Leontief, "Machines and Man," *Scientific American* 187, no. 3 (1952): 150–164.

19. For a more complete review of the literature, see Philippe Aghion, Céline Antonin, and Simon Bunel, "Artificial Intelligence, Growth and Employment: The Role of Policy," *Economics and Statistics,* 510-511-5 (2019): 149–164.

20. Data are also available for the service sector, but they are highly aggregated and more difficult to exploit.

21. Acemoglu and Restrepo, "Robots and Jobs."

22. Philippe Aghion, Celine Antonin, Simon Bunel, and Xavier Jaravel, "What Are the Labor and Product Market Effects of Automation? New Evidence from France," Working Papers, Observatoire Français des Conjonctures Economiques (OFCE), January 2020.

23. Definition from *Encyclopaedia Britannica* (2015), "Automation."

4. Is Competition a Good Thing?

1. See, for example, Richard Blundell, Rachel Griffith, and John Van Reenen, "Dynamic Count Data Models of Technological Innovation," *Economic Journal* 105 no. 429 (1995): 333–344; Richard Blundell, Rachel Griffith, and John Van Reenen, "Market Share, Market Value and Innovation in a Panel of British Manufacturing Firms," *Review of Economic Studies* 66, no. 3 (1999): 529–554; Steve Nickell, "Competition and Corporate Performance," *Journal of Political Economy* 104, no. 4 (1996): 724–746.

2. David Autor, David Dorn, Lawrence F. Katz, Christina Patterson, John Van Reenen, "The Fall of the Labor Share and the Rise of Superstar Firms," *Quarterly Journal of Economics* 135, no. 2 (2020): 645–709.

3. See William J. Baumol, *Microtheory: Applications and Origins* (Cambridge, MA: MIT Press, 1986), ch. 3, "Contestable Markets: An Uprising in the Theory of Industry Structure," 40–54.

4. For more details on the concept of contestable markets, see William J. Baumol, John C. Panzar, and Robert D. Willig, *Contestable Markets and the Theory of Industry Structure* (New York: Harcourt Brace Jovanovich, 1982).

5. Philippe Aghion and Peter Howitt, "A Model of Growth through Creative Destruction," *Econometrica* 60, no. 2 (1992): 323–351.

6. Blundell, Griffith, and Van Reenen, "Market Share, Market Value and Innovation"; Stephen Nickell and John Van Reenen, "The United Kingdom," in *Technological Innovation and Economic Performance,* ed. Benn Steil, David G. Victor, and Richard R. Nelson (Princeton: Princeton University Press, 2002).

7. See Philippe Aghion, Nick Bloom, Richard Blundell, Rachel Griffith, and Peter Howitt, "Competition and Innovation: An Inverted-U Relationship," *Quarterly*

Journal of Economics 120, no. 2 (2005): 701–728; Philippe Aghion, Rachel Griffith, and Peter Howitt, "Vertical Integration and Competition," *American Economic Review* 96, no. 2 (2006): 97–102; Philippe Aghion, Richard Blundell, Rachel Griffith, Peter Howitt, and Susanne Prantl, "The Effects of Entry on Incumbent Innovation and Productivity," *Review of Economics and Statistics* 91, no. 1 (2009): 20–32. See also Xavier Vives, "Innovation and Competitive Pressure," *Journal of Industrial Economics* 56, no. 3 (2008): 419–469.

8. We measure productivity either as the ratio of the aggregate firm's output to the number of employees or as the ratio of the aggregate output to aggregate input used in the production process.

9. Richard R. Nelson and Edmund S. Phelps, "Investment in Humans, Technological Diffusion and Economic Growth," *American Economics Review* 56, no. 1 (1966): 69–75.

10. Aghion, Blundell, Griffith, Howitt, and Prantl, "The Effects of Entry on Incumbent Innovation and Productivity."

11. Philippe Aghion, Antonin Bergeaud, Timothee Gigout, Matthieu Lequien, and Marc Melitz, "Spreading Knowledge across the World: Innovation Spillover through Trade Expansion," unpublished manuscript, March 2019, https://scholar.harvard.edu/files/aghion/files/spreading_knowledge_across_the_world.pdf.

12. Aghion, Bloom, Blundell, Griffith, and Howitt, "Competition and Innovation."

13. This is also an implication of the growth model in which innovation increases the variety of products. See, for example, Paul M. Romer, "Endogenous Technological Change," *Journal of Political Economy* 98, no. 5, pt. 2 (1990): 71–102.

14. See, for example, Michele Boldrin and David K. Levine, *Against Intellectual Monopoly* (Cambridge: Cambridge University Press, 2008); Michele Boldrin and David K. Levine, "Perfectly Competitive Innovation," *Journal of Monetary Economics* 55, no. 3 (2008): 435–453; Michele Boldrin and David K. Levine, "The Case against Patents," *Journal of Economic Perspectives* 27, no. 1 (2013): 3–22.

15. Philippe Aghion, Peter Howitt, and Susanne Prantl, "Patent Rights, Product Market Reforms, and Innovation," *Journal of Economic Growth* 20, no. 3 (2015): 223–262.

16. Thomas Philippon, *The Great Reversal: How America Gave Up on Free Markets* (Cambridge, MA: Harvard University Press, 2019).

17. Matilde Bombardini, "Firm Heterogeneity and Lobby Participation," *Journal of International Economics* 75, no. 2 (2008): 329–348; Matilde Bombardini and Francesco Trebbi, "Empirical Models of Lobbying," *Annual Review of Economics* 12, no. 1 (2020): 391–413; Marianne Bertrand, Matilde Bombardini, and Francesco Trebbi, "Is It Whom You Know or What You Know? An Empirical Assessment of the Lobbying Process," *American Economic Review* 104, no. 12 (2014): 3885–3920.

18. David Autor, David Dorn, Lawrence F. Katz, Christina Patterson, and John Van Reenen, "The Fall of the Labor Share and the Rise of Superstar Firms," *Quarterly Journal of Economics* 135, no. 2 (2020): 645-709.

19. Philippe Aghion, Antonin Bergeaud, Timo Boppart, Peter J. Klenow, and Huiyu Li, "A Theory of Falling Growth and Rising Rents" (NBER Working Paper No. 26448, National Bureau of Economic Research, Cambridge, MA, November 2019).

20. See, for instance, Friedrich List, *Das nationale System der politischen Ökonomie* (Stuttgart: J. G. Cotta, 1841).

21. Anne O. Krueger, *Political Economy of Policy Reform in Developing Countries* (Cambridge, MA: MIT Press, 1993); Anne O. Krueger, "Policy Lessons from Development Experience since the Second World War," in *Handbook of Development Economics*, ed. Jere Behrman and T. N. Srinivasan, vol. 3B, 2497-2550 (Amsterdam: Elsevier, 1995).

22. See, for example, Daron Acemoglu, Philippe Aghion, and Fabrizio Zilibotti, "Distance to Frontier, Selection, and Economic Growth," *Journal of the European Economic Association* 4, no. 1 (2006); Philippe Aghion and Peter Howitt, "Appropriate Growth Policy: A Unifying Framework" (Joseph Schumpeter Lecture), *Journal of the European Economic Association* 4, no. 2-3 (2006): 269-314.

23. Jean-Jacques Laffont and Jean Tirole, *A Theory of Incentives in Procurement and Regulation* (Cambridge, MA: MIT Press, 1993).

24. Philippe Aghion, Antoine Dechezleprêtre, David Hemous, Ralf Martin, and John Van Reenen, "Carbon Taxes, Path Dependency, and Directed Technical Change: Evidence from the Auto Industry," *Journal of Political Economy* 124, no. 1 (2016): 1-51.

25. Patrick Bolton and Joseph Farrell, "Decentralization, Duplication, and Delay," *Journal of Political Economy* 98, no. 4 (1990): 803-826; Rafael Rob, "Learning and Capacity Expansion under Demand Uncertainty," *Review of Economic Studies* 58, no. 4 (1991): 655-675.

26. See Pierre Azoulay, Erica Fuchs, Anna Goldstein, and Michael Kearney, "Funding Breakthrough Research: Promises and Challenges of the 'ARPA Model,'" *Innovation Policy and the Economy* 19 (2019): 69-96.

27. Nathan Nunn and Daniel Trefler, "The Structure of Tariffs and Long-Term Growth," *American Economic Journal: Macroeconomics* 2, no. 4 (2010): 158-194.

28. Philippe Aghion, Jing Cai, Mathias Dewatripont, Luosha Du, Ann Harrison, and Patrick Legros, "Industrial Policy and Competition," *American Economic Journal: Macroeconomics* 7, no. 4 (2015): 1-32.

29. Philippe Aghion, Antonin Bergeaud, Timo Boppart, and Simon Bunel, "Firm Dynamics and Growth Measurement in France," *Journal of the European Economic Association* 16, no. 4 (2018): 933-956.

30. See Philippe Aghion, Thibault Fally, and Stefano Scarpetta, "Credit Constraints as a Barrier to the Entry and Post-Entry Growth of Firms," *Economic Policy* 22, no. 52 (2007): 732–779; Philippe Aghion, John Van Reenen, and Luigi Zingales, "Innovation and Institutional Ownership," *American Economic Review* 103, no. 1 (2013): 277–304.

31. Philippe Aghion, Antonin Bergeaud, and John Van Reenen, "The Impact of Regulation on Innovation," unpublished manuscript, December 2019, https://www .college-de-france.fr/media/en-philippe-aghion/UPL9083408753564555677 _The_Impact_of_Regulation_on_Innovation.pdf.

32. Daron Acemoglu, Ufuk Akcigit, Harun Alp, Nicholas Bloom, and William Kerr, "Innovation, Reallocation, and Growth," *American Economic Review* 108, no. 11 (2018): 3450–3491.

33. Philippe Aghion, Antonin Bergeaud, Gilbert Cette, Remy Lecat, and Hélène Maghin, "The Inverted-U Relationship between Credit Access and Productivity Growth" (Coase Lecture), *Economica* 86 (2019): 1–31.

34. On the relationship between competition policy and industrial policy, and for a general framework on competition policy, we recommend Emmanuel Combe, *Economie et Politique de la Concurrence* (Paris: Dalloz, 2005). Another recent work on competition policy is Richard J. Gilbert, *Innovation Matters: Competition Policy for the High-Technology Economy* (Cambridge, MA: MIT Press, 2020).

5. Innovation, Inequality, and Taxation

1. A. B. Atkinson, *Inequality: What Can Be Done?* (Cambridge, MA: Harvard University Press, 2015); A. B. Atkinson, T. Piketty, and E. Saez, "Top Incomes in the Long Run of History," *Journal of Economic Literature* 49, no. 1 (2011): 3–71; Thomas Piketty, "Income Inequality in France, 1901–1998," *Journal of Political Economy* 111, no. 5 (2003): 1004–1042; Thomas Piketty, *Capital in the Twenty-First Century* (Cambridge, MA: The Belknap Press of Harvard University Press, 2014); Thomas Piketty, *Capital and Ideology* (Cambridge, MA: The Belknap Press of Harvard University Press, 2020); T. Piketty and E. Saez, "Income Inequality in the United States, 1913–1998," *Quarterly Journal of Economics* 118, no. 1 (2003): 1–41; E. Saez and G. Zucman, "Wealth Inequality in the United States since 1913: Evidence from Capitalized Income Tax Data," *Quarterly Journal of Economics* 131, no. 2 (2016): 519–578.

2. Piketty, *Capital in the Twenty-First Century.*

3. Miles Corak, "Income Inequality, Equality of Opportunity, and Intergenerational Mobility," *Journal of Economic Perspectives* 27, no. 3 (2013): 79–102.

4. Raj Chetty, Nathaniel Hendren, Patrick Kline, and Emmanuel Saez, "Where Is the Land of Opportunity? The Geography of Intergenerational Mobility in the United States," *Quarterly Journal of Economics* 129, no. 4 (2014): 1553–1623.

5. Abraham Lincoln, "Discoveries and Inventions," speech in Jacksonville, Illinois, February 11, 1859, quoted in Joel Mokyr, "Long-Term Economic Growth and the History of Technology," in *Handbook of Economic Growth,* ed. Philippe Aghion and Steven Durlauf, vol. 1B, 1113–1180 (Amsterdam: Elsevier, 2005). Also see B. Zorina Khan and Kenneth L. Sokoloff, "The Early Development of Intellectual Property Institutions in the United States," *Journal of Economic Perspectives* 15, no. 3 (2001): 233–246.

6. This prediction has been tested on American data and on Finnish data (see Chapter 10).

7. Philippe Aghion, Ufuk Akcigit, Antonin Bergeaud, Richard Blundell, and David Hémous, "Innovation and Top Income Inequality," *Review of Economic Studies* 86, no. 1 (2019): 1–45.

8. Charles Jones and Jihee Kim also use the paradigm of creative destruction to explain the dynamic of inequality at the top of the income distribution. In their article, growth results both from the cumulative experience acquired by incumbent firms and by the creative destruction generated by the entry of new firms. The former increases inequality while the latter reduces it. See Charles I. Jones and Jihee Kim, "A Schumpeterian Model of Top Income Inequality," *Journal of Political Economy* 126, no. 5 (2018): 1785–1826.

9. Philippe Aghion, Antonin Bergeaud, Richard Blundell, and Rachel Griffith, "The Innovation Premium to Soft Skills in Low-Skilled Occupations," unpublished manuscript, 2019.

10. Gallup annual survey of Honesty and Ethics in the Professions, 2017, https://news.gallup.com/poll/1654/honesty-ethics-professions.aspx.

11. Konstantinos Dellis and David Sondermann, "Lobbying in Europe: New Firm-Level Evidence," Working Paper 2071, European Central Bank, June 2017.

12. Ufuk Akcigit, Salomé Baslandze, and Francesca Lotti, "Connecting to Power: Political Connections, Innovation, and Firm Dynamics" (NBER Working Paper No. 25136, National Bureau of Economic Research, Cambridge, MA, October 2018).

13. Marianne Bertrand, Matilde Bombardini, and Francesco Trebbi, "Is It Whom You Know or What You Know? An Empirical Assessment of the Lobbying Process," *American Economic Review* 104, no. 12 (2014): 3885–3920.

14. Brian Kelleher Richter, Krislert Samphantharak, and Jeffrey F. Timmons, "Lobbying and Taxes," *American Journal of Political Science* 53, no. 4 (2009): 893–909.

15. The farther to the right a state is on the *x*-axis, the stronger the lobbying in that state. From year to year the same state moves on this axis because the intensity of lobbying in a given state varies from year to year.

16. For the theoretical underpinnings of this reform, which affected not only Sweden but also the three other Scandinavian nations (Norway, Finland, and Denmark),

see Céline Antonin and Vincent Touzé, "Loi des finances 2018 et fiscalité du capital. Fondements et impact sur les taux marginaux supérieurs," *Revue de l'OFCE* 161, no. 1 (2019): 77–112.

17. Philippe Aghion and Alexandra Roulet, *Repenser l'Etat. Pour une social-démocratie de l'innovation* (Paris: Seuil, in collaboration with La République des idées, 2011).

18. Thomas Blanchet, Lucas Chancel, and Amory Gethin, "Why Is Europe Less Unequal Than the United States?" unpublished manuscript, 2020, https://wid.world /wp-content/uploads/2020/10/WorldInequalityLab_WP2020_19_Europe-2.pdf.

19. This being said, recent critics have noted that Sweden went too far by eliminating property and inheritance taxes through subsequent reforms after the initial 1991 reform.

20. Ufuk Akcigit, Salomé Baslandze, and Stefanie Stantcheva, "Taxation and the International Mobility of Inventors," *American Economic Review* 106, no. 10 (2016): 2930–2981.

21. Ufuk Akcigit, John Grigsby, Tom Nicholas, and Stefanie Stantcheva, "Taxation and Innovation in the 20th Century" (NBER Working Paper No. 24982, National Bureau of Economic Research, Cambridge, MA, September 2018).

22. Philippe Aghion, Ufuk Akcigit, Julia Cagé, and William R. Kerr, "Taxation, Corruption, and Growth," *European Economic Review* 86 (2016): 24–51.

23. For each of these variables—growth, corruption, and tax revenues—the authors used the average over five subperiods and carried out regressions for forty-seven states and four sub-periods.

24. See Chapters 10, 11, and 14.

25. Philippe Aghion, Vlad Ciornohuz, Maxime Gravoueille, and Stefanie Stantcheva, "Reforms and Dynamics of Income: Evidence Using New Panel Data," unpublished manuscript, July 1, 2019, https://www.college-de-france.fr/media/philippe -aghion/UPL8158439681301526632_Tax_Reforms.pdf.

6. The Secular Stagnation Debate

1. Abhijit Banerjee and Esther Duflo, *Good Economics for Hard Times: Better Answers to Our Biggest Problems* (New York: Public Affairs, 2019).

2. Robert Gordon and Joel Mokyr, "Boom vs. Doom: Debating the Future of the US Economy Debate," presentation at the Chicago Council of Global Affairs, October 31, 2016. For a more complete development of each theme, see Robert Gordon, *The Rise and Fall of American Growth* (Princeton: Princeton University Press, 2016); and Joel Mokyr, "Secular Stagnation? Not in Your Life," in *Secular Stagnation: Facts, Causes and Cures,* ed. C. Teulings and R. Baldwin, 83–89 (London: CEPR Press, 2014).

3. Alvin Hansen, "Economic Progress and Declining Population Growth" (presidential address), *American Economic Review* 29, no. 1 (1939): 1–15.

4. Lawrence H. Summers, "Reflections on the New Secular Stagnation Hypothesis," in *Secular Stagnation: Facts, Causes and Cures,* ed. C. Teulings and R. Baldwin, 27–38 (London: CEPR Press, 2014).

5. The supersonic jet Concorde, introduced in 1969, made it possible to reduce travel time dramatically, but it only benefited a small number of passengers and was permanently withdrawn from service in 2003.

6. Salomé Baslandze, "The Role of the IT Revolution in Knowledge Diffusion, Innovation and Reallocation," 2016 Meeting Papers, No. 1509, Society for Economic Dynamics, 2016.

7. This phenomenon, known as the "middle-income trap," is discussed in greater detail in Chapter 7.

8. Ryan Banerjee and Boris Hofmann, "The Rise of Zombie Firms: Causes and Consequences," *BIS Quarterly Review* (September 2018): 67–78, https://www.bis.org/publ/qtrpdf/r_qt1809g.pdf.

9. Ricardo J. Caballero, Emmanuel Farhi, and Pierre-Olivier Gourinchas, "Rents, Technical Change, and Risk Premia Accounting for Secular Trends in Interest Rates, Returns on Capital, Earning Yields, and Factor Shares," *American Economic Review* 107, no. 5 (2017): 614–620.

10. Nicholas Bloom, Charles I. Jones, John Van Reenen, and Michael Webb, "Are Ideas Getting Harder to Find?" *American Economic Review* 110, no. 4 (2020): 1104–1144.

11. Charles I. Jones, "R&D-Based Models of Economic Growth," *Journal of Political Economy* 103, no. 4 (1995): 759–784.

12. Ufuk Akcigit and William R. Kerr, "Growth through Heterogeneous Innovations," *Journal of Political Economy* 126, no. 4 (2018): 1374–1443.

13. David Byrne, Stephen Oliner, and Daniel Sichel, "How Fast Are Semiconductor Prices Falling?" *Review of Income and Wealth* 64, no. 3 (2018): 679–702.

14. John Sutton, *Sunk Costs and Market Structure: Price Competition, Advertising, and the Evolution of Concentration* (Cambridge, MA: MIT Press, 1991).

15. Hal R. Varian, "Intelligent Technology," in special issue "Smart Technology Takes Flight," *Finance & Development* (IMF quarterly report) 53, no. 3 (2016): 6–9, https://www.imf.org/external/pubs/ft/fandd/2016/09/pdf/fd0916.pdf.

16. David M. Byrne, John G. Fernald, and Marshall B. Reinsdorf, "Does the United States Have a Productivity Slowdown or a Measurement Problem?" *Brookings Papers on Economic Activity* 1 (2016): 109–182.

17. Chad Syverson, "Challenges to Mismeasurement Explanations for the US Productivity Slowdown," *Journal of Economic Perspectives* 31, no. 2 (2017): 165–186.

18. Philippe Aghion, Antonin Bergeaud, Timo Boppart, Peter J. Klenow, and Huiyu Li, "Missing Growth from Creative Destruction," *American Economic Review* 109, no. 8 (2019): 2795–2822.

19. Although many countries, such as the United States, utilize this method, others, including France, use it sparingly.

20. Philippe Aghion, Antonin Bergeaud, Timo Boppart, and Simon Bunel, "Firm Dynamics and Growth Measurement in France," *Journal of the European Economic Association* 16, no. 4 (2018): 933–956.

21. For another view on this question, see the articles of Stephen Redding, in particular: Stephen J. Redding and David E. Weinstein, "Measuring Aggregate Price Indexes with Taste Shocks: Theory and Evidence for CES Preferences" (NBER Working Paper No. 22479, National Bureau of Economic Research, Cambridge, MA, 2016).

22. Thomas Philippon, *The Great Reversal: How America Gave Up on Free Markets* (Cambridge, MA: Harvard University Press, 2019).

23. Two other approaches, which also use the paradigm of creative destruction, deserve mention. The first, developed by Ernest Liu, Atif Mian, and Amir Sufi, highlights the idea that the continuous fall in interest rates over the past two decades increases the discounted value of being a leader. For a "leader" firm, this higher discounted value increases the present benefit of its technological leadership over other firms. It follows that the fall in interest rates will induce "leader" firms in each sector to innovate more in order to increase their leadership, which will discourage innovation by "nonleader" firms in that sector. As a result, concentration increases while innovation and aggregate growth potentially decrease. See Ernest Liu, Atif Mian, and Amir Sufi, "Low Interest Rates, Market Power, and Productivity Growth" (NBER Working Paper No. 25505, National Bureau of Economic Research, Cambridge, MA, June 2019).

    The second attempt, developed by Laurent Cavenaile, Murat Alp Celik, and Xu Tian, highlights the idea that increased concentration in production and innovation to the advantage of superstar firms is associated with less efficient aggregated R&D. See Laurent Cavenaile, Murat Alp Celik, and Xu Tian, "Are Markups Too High? Competition, Strategic Innovation, and Industry Dynamics," unpublished manuscript, rev. September 8, 2020, https://papers.ssrn.com/sol3/papers.cfm?abstract_id=3459775.

24. Ufuk Akcigit and Sina T. Ates, "Ten Facts on Declining Business Dynamism and Lessons from Endogenous Growth Theory" (NBER Working Paper No. 25755, National Bureau of Economic Research, Cambridge, MA, April 2019).

25. Philippe Aghion, Antonin Bergeaud, Timo Boppart, Peter J. Klenow, and Huiyu Li, "A Theory of Falling Growth and Rising Rents" (NBER Working Paper

No. 26448, National Bureau of Economic Research, Cambridge, MA, November 2019).

26. This fact was established both by David Rezza Bagaee and Emmanuel Farhi, "Productivity and Misallocation in General Equilibrium," *Quarterly Journal of Economics* 135, no. 1 (2019): 105–163; and by Jan De Loecker, Jan Eeckhout, and Gabriel Unger, "The Rise of Market Power and the Macroeconomic Implications," *Quarterly Journal of Economics* 135, no. 2 (2020): 561–644.

27. A recent article by Tania Babina, Anastassia Fedyk, Alex He, and James Hodson sheds light on the effect of artificial intelligence (AI), which is quite similar to the impact of the IT revolution that we describe in this chapter. The authors show that: (1) for a given sector, the factors that stimulate investment in AI also increase concentration in that sector; (2) this increase in concentration is not due to an increase in the firms' markups or the markup of any given product line; and (3) firms that are AI leaders increase the number of markets, products, or sectors within which they operate. Overall, this study confirms that the positive impact of AI on industrial concentration results essentially from the fact that superstar firms are the biggest investors in AI. Accordingly, these firms are the ones expanding the most the scope of their activities. In other words, the positive impact of AI on average concentration and markups is driven by a composition effect. See Tania Babina, Anastassia Fedyk, Alex He, and James Hodson, "Artificial Intelligence, Firm Growth, and Industry Concentration," unpublished manuscript, rev. September 22, 2020, https://papers.ssrn.com/sol3/papers.cfm?abstract_id=3651052.

28. Richard Gilbert, *Innovation Matters: Competition Policy for the High-Technology Economy* (Cambridge, MA: MIT Press, 2020).

7. Convergence, Divergence, and the Middle-Income Trap

1. Philippe Aghion, *Repenser la croissance économique* (Paris: Fayard, 2016).

2. Antonin Bergeaud, Gilbert Cette, and Remy Lecat, *Le Bel Avenir de la croissance— Leçons du XXème siècle pour le futur* (Paris: Editions Odile Jacob, 2018).

3. Lant Pritchett, "Divergence, Big Time," *Journal of Economic Perspectives* 11, no. 3 (1997): 3–17.

4. Xavier Sala-i-Martin, "The World Distribution of Income: Falling Poverty and . . . Convergence, Period," *Quarterly Journal of Economics* 121, no. 2 (2006): 351–397.

5. Chapter 5 explains in greater detail how this indicator is constructed.

6. Robert M. Solow, "A Contribution to the Theory of Economic Growth," *Quarterly Journal of Economics* 70, no. 1 (1956): 65–94.

7. Robert J. Barro and Xavier Sala-i-Martin, *Economic Growth* (New York: McGraw Hill, 1995).

8. Robert Lucas, "Why Doesn't Capital Flow from Rich to Poor Countries?" *American Economic Review* 80, no. 2 (1990): 92–96.

9. See Paul M. Romer, "Increasing Returns and Long-Run Growth," *Journal of Political Economy* 94, no. 5 (1986): 1002–1037. Paul Romer concentrates on the eleven OECD countries for which data, starting in 1870, are available.

10. David Coe and Elhanan Helpman, "International R&D Spillovers," *European Economic Review* 39, no. 5 (1995): 859–887.

11. Philippe Aghion, Antonin Bergeaud, Timothee Gigout, Matthieu Lequien, and Marc Melitz, "Spreading Knowledge Across the World: Innovation Spillover through Trade Expansion," unpublished manuscript, March 2019, https://scholar .harvard.edu/files/aghion/files/spreading_knowledge_across_the_world.pdf.

12. Daron Acemoglu, Philippe Aghion, and Fabrizio Zilibotti, "Distance to Frontier, Selection, and Economic Growth," *Journal of the European Economic Association* 4, no. 1 (2006): 37–74.

13. Jerome Vandenbussche, Philippe Aghion, and Costas Meghir, "Growth, Distance to Frontier and Composition of Human Capital," *Journal of Economic Growth* 11, no. 2 (2006): 97–127.

14. Philippe Aghion, Matthias Dewatripont, Caroline Hoxby, Andreu Mas-Colell, and André Sapir, "The Governance and Performance of Universities: Evidence from Europe and the US," *Economic Policy* 25, no. 61 (2010): 7–59.

15. Frontier firms are firms close to the technological frontier, that is, those whose productivity is close to that of the leader in their respective sectors.

16. Fabrizio Zilibotti, "Growing and Slowing Down Like China," *Journal of the European Economic Association* 15, no. 5 (2017): 943–988.

17. See Zilibotti, "Growing and Slowing Down Like China."

18. Boubacar Diallo and Wilfried Koch, "Bank Concentration and Schumpeterian Growth: Theory and International Evidence," *Review of Economics and Statistics* 100, no. 3 (2018): 489–501.

19. Chang T. Hsieh and Pete Klenow, "Misallocation and Manufacturing TFP in China and India," *Quarterly Journal of Economics* 124, no. 4 (2009): 1403–1448.

20. Chang T. Hsieh and Pete Klenow, "The Life Cycle of Plants in India and Mexico," *Quarterly Journal of Economics* 129, no. 3 (2014): 1035–1084.

21. Ufuk Akcigit, Harun Alp, and Michael Peters, "Lack of Selection and Limits to Delegation: Firm Dynamics in Developing Countries" (NBER Working Paper No. 21905, National Bureau of Economic Research, Cambridge, MA, January 2016).

22. This section is based on Philippe Aghion, Sergei Guriev, and Kangchul Jo, "Chaebols and Firm Dynamics in Korea," CEPR Discussion Paper No. DP13825, Center for Economic Policy Research, London, June 2019.

23. The analysis by Aghion, Guriev, and Jo, "Chaebols and Firm Dynamics in Korea," ends in 2003, as 1992–2003 is the period for which relevant data were available.

The fact that total factor productivity (TFP) growth slowed down after 2003 is consistent both with the slowdown in other advanced economies (see Chapter 6) and with the possibility that the *chaebols* were able to regain power more recently.

8. Can We Bypass Industrialization?

1. Simon Kuznets, "Modern Economic Growth: Findings and Reflections" (Nobel Lecture, December 11, 1971), *American Economic Review* 63, no. 3 (1973): 247–258.

2. Simon Alder, Timo Boppart, and Andreas Müller, "A Theory of Structural Change That Can Fit the Data," CEPR Discussion Paper No. 13469, Center for Economic Policy Research, London, January 2019.

3. Berthold Herrendorf, Richard Rogerson, and Akos Valentinyi, "Growth and Structural Transformation," in *Handbook of Economic Growth,* ed. Philippe Aghion and Steven Durlauf, vol. 2, 855–941 (Amsterdam: Elsevier, 2014).

4. Nicholas Kaldor, "Capital Accumulation and Economic Growth," in *The Theory of Capital,* ed. F. A. Lutz and D. C. Hague (New York: St. Martin's Press, 1961).

5. Nicholas Kaldor, "Alternative Theories of Distribution," *Review of Economic Studies* 23, no. 2 (1955): 83 -100.

6. Thomas Piketty, *Capital in the Twenty-First Century* (Cambridge, MA: The Belknap Press of Harvard University Press, 2014).

7. However, in Chapter 6 we pointed out the decrease in the share of labor income in the United States since the beginning of the 2000s. This suggests that the Kaldor facts have been less applicable in the United States over the last twenty years.

8. Timo Boppart, "Structural Change and the Kaldor Facts in a Growth Model with Relative Price Effects and Non-Gorman Preferences," *Econometrica* 82, no. 6 (2014): 2167–2196.

9. Boppart relied on two sources of American data, the Bureau of Economic Analysis and the Consumer Expenditure Survey.

10. This law was first formulated in William J. Baumol and William G. Bowen, "On the Performing Arts: The Anatomy of Their Economic Problems," *American Economic Review* 55, no. 1 / 2 (1965): 495–502. See also William J. Baumol, "Macroeconomics of Unbalanced Growth: The Anatomy of the Urban Crisis," *American Economic Review* 57, no. 3 (1967): 419–420.

11. Baumol and Bowen, "On the Performing Arts."

12. Ernst Engel, "Die Productions und Consumtionsverhältnisse des Königreichs Sachsen," *Zeitschrift des Statistischen Büreaus des Königlich-Sächsischen Ministeriums des Innern* 8 (1857): 1–54.

13. For the importance of the demand side in analyzing structural change, see Diego A. Comin, Danial Lashkari, and Martí Mestieri, "Structural Change with Long-Run Income and Price Effects" (NBER Working Paper No. 21595, National Bureau of Economic Research, Cambridge, MA, September 2015, rev. April 2020).

14. For the effect of market size on innovation see Daron Acemoglu and Joshua Linn, "Market Size in Innovation: Theory and Evidence from the Pharmaceutical Industry," *Quarterly Journal of Economics* 119, no. 3 (2004): 1049–1090; and Philippe Aghion, Antonin Bergeaud, Matthieu Lequien, and Marc J. Melitz, "The Heterogeneous Impact of Market Size on Innovation: Evidence from French Firm-Level Exports" (NBER Working Paper No. 24600, National Bureau of Economic Research, Cambridge, MA, May 2018, rev. October 2019).

    The idea that innovation and technical change could be directed was first modeled in Philippe Aghion and Peter Howitt, "Research and Development in the Growth Process," *Journal of Economic Growth* 1, no. 1 (1996): 49–93. The subsequent literature on directed technical change builds more directly on the work of Daron Acemoglu and his coauthors. In particular, see Daron Acemoglu, "Why Do New Technologies Complement Skills? Directed Technical Change and Wage Inequality," *Quarterly Journal of Economics* 113, no. 4 (1998): 1055–1089; Daron Acemoglu, "Directed Technical Change," *Review of Economic Studies* 69, no. 4 (2002): 781–809; Daron Acemoglu, "Equilibrium Bias of Technology," *Econometrica* 75, no. 5 (2007): 1371–1409. See also Daron Acemoglu and Pascual Restrepo, "The Race between Man and Machine: Implications of Technology for Growth, Factor Shares, and Employment," *American Economic Review* 108, no. 6 (2018): 1488–1542.

15. Philippe Aghion and Peter Howitt, *The Economics of Growth* (Cambridge, MA: MIT Press, 2008).

16. Acemoglu, "Why Do New Technologies Complement Skills?"

17. See, for example, David Popp, "Induced Innovation and Energy Prices," *American Economic Review* 92, no. 1 (2002): 160–180; Philippe Aghion, Antoine Dechezleprêtre, David Hémous, Ralf Martin, and John Van Reenen, "Carbon Taxes, Path Dependency, and Directed Technical Change: Evidence from the Auto Industry," *Journal of Political Economy* 124, no. 1 (2016): 1–51.

18. This section builds on the following two papers: Timo Boppart and Franziska J. Weiss, "Non-Homothetic Preferences and Industry Directed Technical Change," unpublished manuscript, June 2013; Acemoglu and Restrepo, "The Race between Man and Machine."

19. Philippe Aghion, Benjamin F. Jones, and Charles I. Jones, "Artificial Intelligence and Economic Growth," in *The Economics of Artificial Intelligence: An Agenda*, ed. Ajay Agrawal, Joshua Gans, and Avi Goldfarb (Chicago: University of Chicago Press, 2019).

20. Joseph Stiglitz, "From Resource Curse to Blessing," *Project Syndicate,* August 6, 2012.

21. In constant 2010 US dollars.

22. We are using here the terminology of Daron Acemoglu and James A. Robinson, *Why Nations Fail: The Origins of Power, Prosperity and Poverty* (New York: Crown, 2012), 529. These authors posit *inclusive* institutions, which encourage entrepreneurship and innovation, against *extractive* institutions, which discourage innovation and private enterprise with poor protection of property rights and an ineffective educational system.

23. Friedrich List, *Das nationale System der politischen Ökonomie* (Stuttgart: Cotta, 1841).

24. Note that List argued for temporary and not permanent protectionism. As soon as firms are sufficiently mature to face foreign competition, they should open to free trade. According to List, free trade is acceptable only in a universe of countries of comparable maturity.

25. Tianyu Fan, Michael Peters, and Fabrizio Zilibotti, "Service-Led or Service-Biased Growth? Equilibrium Development Accounting across Indian Districts," unpublished manuscript, August 2020.

26. Dani Rodrik, "Normalizing Industrial Policy," Working Paper no. 3, Commission on Growth and Development, 2008.

9. Green Innovation and Sustainable Growth

1. Donella H. Meadows, Denis L. Meadows, Jørgen Randers, and William W. Behrens, III, *The Limits to Growth* (New York: Universe Books, 1972).

2. Christian Gollier, *Le climat après la fin du mois* (Paris: Presses universitaires de France, 2019). Ppm is a measure of concentration used to determine levels of air pollution. It indicates the number of molecules of the pollutant, in this case carbon dioxide, per one million air molecules.

3. This is the same model as the Solow growth model that we discussed in Chapter 1, the only difference being that here final production also relies on natural resources.

4. Philippe Aghion, Antoine Dechezleprêtre, David Hémous, Ralf Martin, and John Van Reenen, "Carbon Taxes, Path Dependency, and Directed Technical Change: Evidence from the Auto Industry," *Journal of Political Economy* 124, no. 1 (2016): 1–51.

5. The question of whether electric vehicles should be considered "clean" is still under debate. Manufacturing an electric vehicle utilizes components whose production is not necessarily ecological, such as batteries (ADEME, April 2016, https://www.ademe.fr/sites/default/files/assets/documents/potential-electric -vehicles.pdf).

6. When the Yellow Vest movement started in France, during the fall of 2018, gas prices were already very high due to an increase in the price of imported oil, and not to an increase in the carbon tax, which is set each year on January 1. The intensity of the movement led the French government to lower the trajectory of these annual increases in the 2018 Budget Act.

7. We refer the reader to several seminal papers in environmental economics that build on the neoclassical paradigm: Martin L. Weitzman, "On Modeling and Interpreting the Economics of Catastrophic Climate Change," *Review of Economics and Statistics* 91, no. 1 (2009): 1–19; Mikhail Golosov, John Hassler, Per Krusell, and Aleh Tsyvinski, "Optimal Taxes on Fossil Fuel in General Equilibrium," *Econometrica* 82, no. 1 (2014): 41–88; John Hassler, Per Krusell, and A. A. Smith, "Environmental Macroeconomics," in *Handbook of Macroeconomics,* ed. John B. Taylor and Harald Uhlig, vol. 2, 1893–2008 (Amsterdam: Elsevier, 2016); Michael Greenstone and B. Kelsey Jack, "Envirodevonomics: A Research Agenda for an Emerging Field," *Journal of Economic Literature* 53, no. 1 (2015): 5–42.

8. William D. Nordhaus, "The 'DICE' Model: Background and Structure of a Dynamic Integrated Climate-Economy Model of the Economics of Global Warming," Cowles Foundation Discussion Paper 1009, Cowles Foundation for Research in Economics, Yale University, February 1992.

9. Nicholas Stern, *The Economics of Climate Change: The Stern Review* (Cambridge: Cambridge University Press, 2006).

10. William D. Nordhaus, "A Review of the Stern *Review on the Economics of Climate Change,*" *Journal of Economic Literature* 45, no. 3 (2007): 686–702.

11. Regarding this section, see Daron Acemoglu, Philippe Aghion, Leonardo Bursztyn, and David Hémous, "The Environment and Directed Technical Change," *American Economic Review* 102, no. 1 (2012): 131–166.

12. See note 5 above regarding the question of whether electric vehicles constitute a green technology.

13. We are distinguishing between developed and developing nations, but the argument also applies to groups of nations at different levels of technological development.

14. Milton Friedman, "The Social Responsibility of Business Is to Increase Its Profits," *New York Times Magazine,* September 13, 1970, 32–33, 122–124; Arthur C. Pigou, *The Economics of Welfare* (London: Macmillan, 1920).

15. Jean Tirole and Roland Bénabou, "Individual and Corporate Social Responsibility," *Economica* 77, no. 305 (2010): 1–19.

16. Philippe Aghion, Roland Bénabou, Ralf Martin, and Alexandra Roulet, "Environmental Preferences and Technological Choices: Is Market Competition Clean or Dirty?" (NBER Working Paper No. 26921, National Bureau of Economic Research, Cambridge, MA, April 2020).

17. "Americans' Preference for Environmental Protection vs. Economic Growth, 1984–2019," Gallup Poll, https://news.gallup.com/poll/248243/preference-environment-economy-largest-2000.aspx.

18. Shale gas is natural gas trapped in sedimentary rock. Unlike conventional natural gas stored in permeable rock that can be easily extracted, shale gas is found in rock of very low permeability and porosity. Its extraction is thus complex and requires techniques such as hydraulic fracturing (also known as fracking), in which water and chemicals are injected at high pressure in order to fracture the rock.

19. The environmental impact of shale gas is the subject of intense debate. As Robert Howarth and coauthors point out, fracking emits at least 30 percent more methane than conventional extraction of natural gas, and we know that methane contributes more to the greenhouse effect than does CO_2. In addition, fracking is controversial because of the associated risk of groundwater contamination. See Robert W. Howarth, Renee Santoro, and Anthony Ingraffea, "Methane and the Greenhouse-Gas Footprint of Natural Gas from Shale Formations," *Climatic Change* 106, no. 4 (2011): 679–690.

20. Daron Acemoglu, Philippe Aghion, Lint Barrage, and David Hémous, "Climate Change, Directed Innovation, and Energy Transition: The Long-Run Consequences of the Shale Gas Revolution," 2019 Meeting Papers, No. 1302, Society for Economic Dynamics. https://scholar.harvard.edu/aghion/publications/climate-change-directed-innovation-and-energy-transition-long-run-consequences.

10. Innovation: Behind the Scenes

1. It should be noted that, under a more comprehensive characterization of innovation, this definition may be considered too restrictive.

2. Alex Bell, Raj Chetty, Xavier Jaravel, Neviana Petkova, and John Van Reenen, "Who Becomes an Inventor in America? The Importance of Exposure to Innovation," *Quarterly Journal of Economics* 134, no. 2 (2019): 647–713.

3. U. Akcigit, J. Grigsby, and T. Nicholas, "The Rise of American Ingenuity: Innovation and Inventors of the Golden Age" (NBER Working Paper No. 23047, National Bureau of Economic Research, Cambridge, MA, January 2017).

4. Philippe Aghion, Ufuk Akcigit, Ari Hyytinen, and Otto Toivanen, "The Social Origins of Inventors" (NBER Working Paper No. 24110, National Bureau of Economic Research, Cambridge, MA, December 2017). Inventing was defined in this study as filing a patent application with the EPO.

5. Beyond the reading tests, when we look at the results in mathematics and science, Finland was tenth out of seventy-seven countries, and the United States and France ranked twenty-fifth and twenty-sixth, respectively.

6. Bell, Chetty, Jaravel, Petkova, and Van Reenen, "Who Becomes an Inventor in America?"

7. Aghion, Akcigit, Hyytinen, and Toivanen, "The Social Origins of Inventors."

8. We classified parental socioeconomic status in four categories: blue collar, junior white collar, senior white collar, and other.

9. A particularly illuminating book on this subject is Steven Pinker, *The Blank Slate: The Modern Denial of Human Nature* (New York: Viking, 2002).

10. Ufuk Akcigit, Jeremy G. Pearce, and Marta Prato, "Tapping into Talent: Coupling Education and Innovation Policies for Economic Growth" (NBER Working Paper No. 27862, National Bureau of Economic Research, Cambridge, MA, September 2020).

11. As in the Finnish study, the authors measure the initial abilities of individuals using IQ tests in their estimations, but this time using Danish data. We remind the reader that the American study by Bell et al., "Who Becomes an Inventor in America?" used third-grade math test scores as an alternative measure of ability.

12. Philippe Aghion, Ufuk Akcigit, Ari Hyytinen, and Otto Toivanen, "On the Returns to Invention within Firms: Evidence from Finland," *AEA Papers and Proceedings* 108 (2018): 208–212.

13. Shareholders holding at least 50 percent of the firm's capital are considered to be entrepreneurs.

14. Patrick Kline, Neviana Petkova, Heidi Williams, and Owen Zidar, "Who Profits from Patents? Rent-Sharing at Innovative Firms," *Quarterly Journal of Economics* 134 (2019): 1343–1404.

15. A patent's potential value is determined by the objective characteristics of the patent utilization.

16. In this section, unlike the preceding section, we do not differentiate between entrepreneurs and innovators.

17. Scott Stern looks at researchers who received competing offers from universities and firms and demonstrates the financial cost of choosing the university. See Scott Stern, "Do Scientists Pay to Be Scientists?" *Management Science* 50, no. 6 (2004): 835–853. See also Jeffrey L. Furman and Scott Stern, "Climbing atop the Shoulders of Giants: The Impact of Institutions on Cumulative Research," *American Economic Review* 101, no. 5 (2011): 1933–1963.

18. This linear representation of the research process is overly simplistic. In practice, new ideas in basic research frequently emerge from applied research at a stage close to being marketable.

19. Philippe Aghion, Mathias Dewatripont, and Jeremy C. Stein, "Academic Freedom, Private-Sector Focus, and the Process of Innovation," *RAND Journal of Economics* 39, no. 3 (2008): 617–635.

20. Our analysis of the role of the university focuses on research, without looking at teaching. For a sociological analysis of the complementarity of these two activities,

see Pierre-Michel Menger, "Academic Work: A Tale of Essential Tension between Research and Teaching," *Sociologisk Forsking* 53, no. 2 (2016): 175–192.

21. Michael A. Heller, "The Tragedy of the Anticommons: Property in the Transition from Marx to Markets," *Harvard Law Review* 111, no. 3 (1998): 621–688. Privatization has appeared to be a good way to avoid the overuse of public goods (the "commons"). Indeed, private owners are attentive to the preservation of a resource when their profits depend on it. Nonetheless, such privatization has led to an excessive fragmentation of property rights. Multiple and different private interests share ownership of the same resource, with each owner having the power to block the use of the commons by the others, as is the case with patents.

22. Fiona Murray, Philippe Aghion, Mathias Dewatripont, Julian Kolev, and Scott Stern, "Of Mice and Academics: Examining the Effect of Openness on Innovation," *American Economic Journal: Economic Policy* 8, no. 1 (2016): 212–252.

23. Biologists Mario R. Capecchi, Sir Martin J. Evans, and Oliver Smithies were awarded the 2007 Nobel Prize in Physiology or Medicine "for their discoveries of principles for introducing specific gene modifications in mice by the use of embryonic stem cells."

24. An oncogene is a gene whose expression can cause the proliferation of cancerous cells.

25. The novelty of the article was measured by the proportion of new keywords it contained.

26. Heidi L. Williams, "Intellectual Property Rights and Innovation: Evidence from the Human Genome," *Journal of Political Economy* 121, no. 1 (2013): 1–27.

27. In reality, the same gene can be part of multiple genotype-phenotype links, and a given genotype-phenotype link can involve more than one gene.

28. Ufuk Akcigit, Douglas Hanley, and Nicolas Serrano-Velarde, "Back to Basics: Basic Research Spillovers, Innovation Policy and Growth," *Review of Economic Studies* (2020), https://doi.org/10.1093/restud/rdaa061.

29. It is nevertheless possible to examine policies aimed at improving innovators' remuneration at Stage 0. This research topic is explored by Jerry Green and Suzanne Scotchmer. See Jerry Green and Suzanne Scotchmer, "On the Division of Profit in Sequential Innovation," *RAND Journal of Economics* 26, no. 1 (1995): 20–33. They argue that profits from a sequential innovation (where each stage in the process is performed in a different firm) should be more fairly apportioned between these stages. According to these authors, prolonging the duration of patents for Stage 0 innovations would enable the firm that bears the cost of the basic research to capture a greater share of profits, which would ultimately bring investment in basic research to a more desirable level. See also Suzanne Scotchmer, "Standing on the Shoulders of Giants: Cumulative Research and the Patent Law," *Journal of Economic Perspectives* 5, no. 1 (1991): 29–41; Suzanne Scotchmer, "Pro-

tecting Early Innovators: Should Second-Generation Products Be Patentable?" *RAND Journal of Economics* 27, no. 2 (1996): 322–331.

30. For initial answers, see Philippe Aghion, Mathias Dewatripont, Caroline Hoxby, Andreu Mas-Colell, and André Sapir, "Why Reform Europe's Universities?" Breugel Policy Brief 4 / 2007, Brussels, 2007.

11. Creative Destruction, Health, and Happiness

1. Anne Case and Angus Deaton, *Deaths of Despair and the Future of Capitalism* (Princeton: Princeton University Press, 2020).

2. The empirical results presented in this section and in section 3 come from: Philippe Aghion, Ufuk Akcigit, Angus Deaton, and Alexandra Roulet, "Creative Destruction and Subjective Wellbeing," *American Economic Review* 106, no. 12 (2016): 3869–3897.

3. For different perspectives on this question, see Philippe Aghion and Peter Howitt, "Growth and Unemployment," *Review of Economic Studies* 61, no. 3 (1994): 477–494; Dale T. Mortensen and Christopher A. Pissarides, "Job Creation and Job Destruction in the Theory of Unemployment," *Review of Economic Studies* 61, no. 3 (1994): 397–415; Andreas Hornstein, Per Krusell, and Giovanni L. Violante, "The Replacement Problem in Frictional Economies: A Near-Equivalence Result," *Journal of the European Economic Association* 3, no. 5 (2005): 1007–1057.

4. Aghion and Howitt, "Growth and Unemployment."

5. See Chapter 1 for bibliographic references; for example, Steven Davis and John Haltiwanger, "Labor Market Fluidity and Economic Performance" (NBER Working Paper No. 20479, National Bureau of Economic Research, Cambridge, MA, December 2014).

6. Aghion, Akcigit, Deaton, and Roulet, "Creative Destruction and Subjective Well-Being."

7. The job creation rate between date $t - 1$ and date t is the sum of all new jobs generated by the expansion of existing establishments or the creation of new establishments, divided by the average number of jobs in the same employment zone between dates t and $t - 1$. Similarly, the job destruction rate is the sum of job losses due to the contraction or closure of establishments, divided by the average number of jobs in the area between dates t and $t - 1$.

8. Philippe Aghion, Ufuk Akcigit, Ari Hyytinen, and Otto Toivanen, "On the Returns to Invention within Firms: Evidence from Finland," *AEA Papers and Proceedings* 108 (2018): 208–212.

9. Table 11.1 is directly inspired by Philippe Aghion, Peter Howitt, and Fabrice Murtin, "The Relationship between Health and Growth: When Lucas Meets Nelson-Phelps" (NBER Working Paper No. 15813, National Bureau of Economic Research, Cambridge, MA, March 2010), with updated data from 1961–2017.

10. A. Deaton, *The Great Escape: Health, Wealth, and the Origins of Inequality* (Princeton: Princeton University Press, 2013).

11. Anne Case and Angus Deaton, "Mortality and Morbidity in the 21st Century," *Brookings Papers on Economic Activity* 1 (2017): 397–476.

12. Daniel Sullivan and Till von Wachter, "Job Displacement and Mortality: An Analysis Using Administrative Data," *Quarterly Journal of Economics* 124, no. 3 (2009): 1265–1306.

13. Alexandra Roulet, "The Causal Effect of Job Loss on Health: The Danish Miracle," in "Essays in Labor Economics" (Ph.D. diss., Harvard University, 2017).

14. For management-level employees with less than twelve years' seniority, there is no severance pay. Severance pay is equal to one month of salary for twelve to seventeen years' seniority, and to a maximum of three months of salary for seniority exceeding seventeen years.

15. Andrew E. Clark and Claudia Senik-Leygonie, eds., *Happiness and Economic Growth: Lessons from Developing Countries* (Oxford: Oxford University Press, 2014). See also Cecile Daumas, "La croissance harmonise le bonheur de tous," interview with Claudia Senik, *Libération*, October 24, 2014.

16. See Richard A. Easterlin, "Does Economic Growth Improve the Human Lot? Some Empirical Evidence," in *Nations and Households in Economic Growth*, ed. Paul David and Melvin Reder, 89–125 (New York: Academic Press, 1974). Claudia Senik explains this paradox by noting that prosperity goes hand in hand with the standardization of happiness: the development of the welfare state generalizes access to tangible (education and health) and intangible (civil rights, political pluralism) public goods.

17. See Joseph Stiglitz, Amartya Sen, and Jean Fitoussi, "Report by the Commission on the Measurement of Economic Performance and Social Progress," CMEPSP, Paris, 2009.

18. Hadley Cantril, *Pattern of Human Concerns* (New Brunswick, NJ: Rutgers University Press, 1965).

19. Aghion, Akcigit, Deaton, and Roulet, "Creative Destruction and Subjective Well-Being."

20. Regarding flexicurity in France, see Olivier Blanchard and Jean Tirole, *Protection de l'emploi et procédures de licenciement* (Paris: La Documentation française, 2003).

21. See "Towards Common Principles of Flexicurity: More and Better Jobs through Flexibility and Security," Communication to the European Parliament, the Council, the European Economic and Social Committee and the Committee of the Regions, COM(2007) 359, Brussels, June 27, 2007, https://eur-lex.europa.eu /legal-content/EN/TXT/?uri=celex%3A52007DC0359.

22. See, for example, Ove K. Pedersen, "Flexicurity, mobication og europæisk beskæftigelsespolitik," in *Dansk flexicurity: Fleksibilitet og sikkerhed på arbejds-*

markedet, ed. Thomas Bredgaard and P. Kongshøj Madsen, 265–287 (Copenhagen: Hans Reitzels Forlag, 2015).

12. Financing Creative Destruction

1. A modern-day David Séchard could also have sold the patent to his invention on far more favorable terms than he got from the Cointet brothers. Ufuk Akcigit, Murat Alp Celik, and Jeremy Greenwood, "Buy, Keep, or Sell: Economic Growth and the Market for Ideas," *Econometrica* 84, no. 3 (2016): 943–984.

2. This phenomenon is known as the *Arrow replacement effect,* and it explains why important innovations usually come from new firms rather than from existing firms.

3. In their pioneering article on "architectural innovation," Rebecca Henderson and Kim Clark describe the example of a commercial jet that was not built by the dominant manufacturer of the 1950s, McDonnell Douglas, but rather by a new entrant, Boeing. See Rebecca M. Henderson and Kim B. Clark, "Architectural Innovation: The Reconfiguration of Existing Product Technologies and the Failure of Established Firms," *Administrative Science Quarterly* 35, no. 1 (1990): 9–30.

4. For a synthesis of finance and innovation-led growth, see Philippe Aghion, Peter Howitt, and Ross Levine, "Financial Development and Innovation-Led Growth," in *Handbook of Finance and Development,* ed. Thorson Beck and Ross Levine (Cheltenham, UK: Edward Elgar, 2018).

5. Philippe Aghion, Mathias Dewatripont, Caroline Hoxby, Andreu Mas-Colell, and André Sapir, "Why Reform Europe's Universities?" Policy Brief 34, Bruegel, Brussels, September 2007.

6. Philippe Aghion, Mathias Dewatripont, Caroline Hoxby, Andreu Mas-Colell, and André Sapir, "The Governance and Performance of Universities: Evidence from Europe and the US," *Economic Policy* 25, no. 61 (2010): 7–59.

7. Gustavo Manso, "Motivating Innovation," *Journal of Finance* 66 (2011): 1823–1860; Bengt Holmstrom and Paul Milgrom, "Multitask Principal-Agent Analyses: Incentive Contracts, Asset Ownership, and Job Design," *Journal of Law, Economics, and Organization* 7 (1991): 24–52.

8. The expression *principal-agent* refers to the relationship between an economic actor, the principal, whose actions depend on the action or the characteristics of another actor, the agent, about which the principal has imperfect information. For example, the principal could be a firm with imperfect information about how hard its employees work, or a bank that has imperfect information about its clients' profiles. Bengt Holmström and Paul Milgrom, in "Multitask Principal-Agent Analyses," discovered a new source of conflict of interests in the principal-agent relationship that can emerge when the agent is expected to accomplish several tasks in parallel.

9. In US bankruptcy law, placing a firm under Chapter 11 protection brings about the suspension of creditors' claims and legal actions for payment of debt. During the procedure, the firm continues to operate, which allows time for reorganization in agreement with the creditors.

10. Pierre Azoulay, Joshua S. Graff Zivin, and Gustavo Manso, "Incentives and Creativity: Evidence from the Academic Life Sciences," *RAND Journal of Economics* 42, no. 3 (2011): 527–554.

11. If the firm's profits are below the fixed amount due to the lender, the entire profits go to the lender.

12. Philippe Aghion and Patrick Bolton, "An Incomplete Contracts Approach to Financial Contracting," *Review of Economic Studies* 59, no. 3 (1992): 473–494.

13. Aghion and Bolton, "An Incomplete Contracts Approach to Financial Contracting"; Steven N. Kaplan and Per Strömberg, "Financial Contracting Theory Meets the Real World: An Empirical Analysis of Venture Capital Contracts," *Review of Economic Studies* 70, no. 2 (2003): 281–315.

14. A number of studies have highlighted the role of venture capital in financing innovation, beginning with Samuel S. Kortum and Josh Lerner, "Assessing the Contribution of Venture Capital to Innovation," *RAND Journal of Economics* 31, no. 4 (2000): 674–692. See also publications by Josh Lerner and Paul Gompers: Paul Gompers and Josh Lerner, *The Venture Capital Cycle* (Cambridge, MA: MIT Press, 2004); Paul Gompers and Josh Lerner, "The Venture Capital Revolution," *Journal of Economic Perspectives* 15, no. 2 (2001): 145–168.

15. Ufuk Akcigit, Emin Dinlersoz, Jeremy Greenwood, and Veronika Penciakova, "Synergizing Ventures" (NBER Working Paper No. 26196, National Bureau of Economic Research, Cambridge, MA, August 2019).

16. Innovation is measured by the total number of citations of the firm's patents within three years of its first patent.

17. Innovative activity is measured by the number of patents, taking into account their quality, which is measured by the number of citations of those patents.

18. Ghizlane Kettani, "Capital-risque, innovation et croissance" (Ph.D. diss., Université Paris-Dauphine, 2011).

19. Institutional investors are organizations that collect savings and invest their funds in the markets on their own behalf or on behalf of their clients. There are three types of institutional investors: pension funds, who manage retirement savings in countries where retirement is funded by capitalization (such as the United States and the United Kingdom); investment funds; and insurance companies.

20. Philippe Aghion, John Van Reenen, and Luigi Zingales, "Innovation and Institutional Ownership," *American Economic Review* 103, no. 1 (2013): 277–304.

21. We measured the intensity of innovation by the number of patents weighted by patent quality.

22. The "career concerns" theory was developed by Bengt Holmström in Bengt Holmström, "Managerial Incentive Problems: A Dynamic Perspective," *Review of Economic Studies* 66, no. 1 (1999): 169–182.

23. We assume implicitly that the market knows to what degree the project is innovative and that the manager's reputation improves more with the success of an innovative project than with the success of a more conventional project.

24. Aghion, Van Reenen, and Zingales, "Innovation and Institutional Ownership."

25. The degree of competition is measured as the opposite of monopoly rents.

26. World Bank data.

27. Figures from France Invest for France and from Prequin for the United States.

28. Unlike a tax allowance, a tax credit affects not the taxable income but the actual amount of tax owed. It is deducted directly from the amount of tax due and in some cases can even result in a refund if the amount of the tax credit exceeds the amount of tax due.

29. Antoine Dechezleprêtre, Elias Einiö, Ralf Martin, Kieu-Trang Nguyen, and John Van Reenen, "Do Tax Incentives for Research Increase Firm Innovation? An RD Design for R&D" (NBER Working Paper No. 22405, National Bureau of Economic Research, Cambridge, MA, July 2016).

30. Ufuk Akcigit and William R. Kerr, "Growth through Heterogeneous Innovations," *Journal of Political Economy* 126, no. 4 (2018): 1374–1443.

31. See the implied tax subsidy rates on R&D calculated by the OECD.

32. The size of the firm could be measured by its number of employees, its amount of assets, or its total sales.

13. How to Manage Globalization

1. For an excellent overview of the effects of the US trade war on prices and welfare, see M. Amiti, S. J. Redding, and D. Weinstein, "The Impact of the 2018 Trade War on U.S. Prices and Welfare," *Journal of Economic Perspectives* 33, no. 4 (2019): 187–210.

2. International Monetary Fund, *World Economic Outlook: The Great Lockdown*, April 2020.

3. N. Bloom, M. Draca, and J. Van Reenen, "Trade Induced Technical Change? The Impact of Chinese Imports on Innovation, IT and Productivity," *Review of Economic Studies* 83, no. 1 (2016): 87–117.

4. In 2018, the United States imported three times as much from China as it exported to China.

5. See A. B. Bernard, J. B. Jensen, and P. K. Schott, "Survival of the Best Fit: Exposure to Low-Wage Countries and the (Uneven) Growth of US Manufacturing Plants," *Journal of International Economics* 68, no. 1 (2006): 219–237; J. R. Pierce

and P. K. Schott, "The Surprisingly Swift Decline of US Manufacturing Employment," *American Economic Review* 106, no. 7 (2016): 1632–1662; D. Acemoglu, D. Autor, D. Dorn, G. H. Hanson, and B. Price, "Import Competition and the Great US Employment Sag of the 2000s," *Journal of Labor Economics* 34, no. S1 (2016): 141–198; D. H. Autor, D. Dorn, G. H. Hanson, and J. Song, "Trade Adjustment: Worker-Level Evidence," *Quarterly Journal of Economics* 129, no. 4 (2014): 1799–1860.

6. See D. H. Autor, D. Dorn, and G. H. Hanson, "The China Syndrome: Local Labor Market Effects of Import Competition in the United States," *American Economic Review* 103, no. 6 (2013): 2121–2168. The penetration rate of Chinese imports to the United States is the ratio of the value of Chinese imports to total sales on the US domestic market.

7. For the purposes of this analysis, the United States was divided into 722 regional labor markets.

8. The approach is quite similar to the one used to study the impact of Chinese imports on jobs and wages at the regional level. The only difference is that in this case the authors look at individual firms. See D. Autor, D. Dorn, G. H. Hanson, G. Pisano, and P. Shu, "Foreign Competition and Domestic Innovation: Evidence from US Patents," *American Economic Review: Insights* 2, no. 3 (2020): 357–374.

9. David Autor and his coauthors look only at large firms included in the Compustat database.

10. P. Aghion, A. Bergeaud, M. Lequien, M. Melitz, and T. Zuber, "Imports and Innovation: Evidence from French Firm-Level Data," unpublished manuscript, 2020.

11. More generally, Chinese import shocks were more often upstream shocks in Europe than in the United States.

12. Aghion, Bergeaud, Lequien, Melitz, and Zuber, "Imports and Innovation."

13. The fact that the effect of an upstream shock is positive, together with the fact that the Chinese import shock was more upstream in Europe than in the United States, might explain why Bloom, Draca, and Van Reenen, "Trade Induced Technical Change?" found an overall positive effect of the Chinese shock on innovation in their study of European data.

14. A. Lileeva and D. Trefler, "Improved Access to Foreign Markets Raises Plant-Level Productivity . . . for Some Plants," *Quarterly Journal of Economics* 125, no. 3 (2010): 1051–1099.

15. P. Aghion, A. Bergeaud, M. Lequien, and M. J. Melitz, "The Heterogeneous Impact of Market Size on Innovation: Evidence from French Firm-Level Exports" (NBER Working Paper No. 24600, National Bureau of Economic Research, Cambridge, MA, May 2018).

16. A. Flaaen, A. Hortaçsu, and F. Tintelnot, "The Production Relocation and Price Effects of U.S. Trade Policy: The Case of Washing Machines," *American Economic Review* 110, no. 7 (2020): 2103–2127.

17. U. Akcigit, S. T. Ates, and G. Impullitti, "Innovation and Trade Policy in a Globalized World" (NBER Working Paper No. 24543, National Bureau of Economic Research, Cambridge, MA, April 2018).

18. M. J. Melitz, "The Impact of Trade on Intra-Industry Reallocations and Aggregate Industry Productivity," *Econometrica* 71, no. 6 (2003): 1695–1725.

19. We took a detailed look at carbon taxes levied at borders in Chapter 9.

20. We particularly recommend reading the following papers on value chains: P. Antràs, "Conceptual Aspects of Global Value Chains," *World Bank Economic Review* 34, no. 3 (2020): 551–574; P. Antràs and D. Chor, "Organizing the Global Value Chain," *Econometrica* 81, no. 6 (2013): 2127–2204; and P. Antràs, D. Chor, T. Fally, and R. Hillberry, "Measuring the Upstreamness of Production and Trade Flows," *American Economic Review* 102, no. 3 (2012): 412–416.

21. An indispensable reference on the connection between immigration and innovation is the recent book by William Kerr, *The Gift of Global Talent: How Migration Shapes Business, Economy and Society* (Stanford: Stanford University Press, 2018).

22. Costas Arkolakis, Michael Peters, and Sun Kyoung Lee, "European Immigrants and the United States' Rise to the Technological Frontier," 2019 Meeting Paper No. 1420, Society for Economic Dynamics, 2019.

23. S. Bernstein, R. Diamond, T. McQuade, and B. Pousada, "The Contribution of High-Skilled Immigrants to Innovation in the United States," Working Paper no. 3748, Stanford Graduate School of Business, November 6, 2018.

24. This idea has already been used to good effect by P. Azoulay, J. S. Graff Zivin, and J. Wang, "Superstar Extinction," *Quarterly Journal of Economics* 125, no. 2 (2010): 549–589; and X. Jaravel, N. Petkova, and A. Bell, "Team-Specific Capital and Innovation," *American Economic Review* 108, no. 4–5 (2018): 1034–1073.

25. D. Bahar, P. Choudhury, and H. Rapoport, "Migrant Inventors and the Technological Advantage of Nations," *Research Policy* 49, no. 9 (2020). We also recommend that the reader review the bibliography associated with this article.

26. Similarly, George Borjas and Kirk Doran, "The Collapse of the Soviet Union and the Productivity of American Mathematicians," *Quarterly Journal of Economics* 127, no. 3 (2012): 1143–1203, shows that the immigration of Russian mathematicians after the fall of the USSR had a positive effect on the production of new knowledge in the United States.

27. A. Alesina, J. Harnoss, and H. Rapoport, "Birthplace Diversity and Economic Prosperity," *Journal of Economic Growth* 21, no. 2 (2016): 101–138. Note that the authors do not directly examine the impact of diversity on the number and quality of host-country patents.

28. Kerr, *The Gift of Global Talent.*

29. See P. E. Stephan and S. G. Levin, "Exceptional Contributions to US Science by the Foreign-Born and Foreign-Educated," *Population Research and Policy Review* 20, no. 1–2 (2001): 59–79.

30. See P. Aghion and A. Roulet, *Repenser l'État* (Paris: Seuil, in collaboration with La République des idées, 2011).

31. X. Jaravel and E. Sager, "What Are the Price Effects of Trade? Evidence from the U.S. and Implications for Quantitative Trade Models," Finance and Economics Discussion Series, no. 2019-068, Board of Governors of the Federal Reserve System, August 2019.

14. The Investor State and the Insurer State

1. Max Weber, "Politics as a Vocation" (1918–1919), in *The Vocation Lectures,* ed. David Owen and Tracy B. Strong, trans. Rodney Livingstone (Indianapolis: Hackett, 2004), 33.

2. Chapter 2 describes these evolutions in greater detail.

3. Montesquieu, *De l'esprit des lois* (Geneva: Barrillot & fils, 1748); Montesquieu, *The Spirit of the Laws,* ed. and trans. Anne M. Cohler, Basia Carolyn Miller, and Harold Samuel Stone (Cambridge: Cambridge University Press, 1989).

4. Timothy Besley and Torsten Persson, "Fragile States and Development Policy," *Journal of the European Economic Association* 9, no. 3 (2011): 371–398.

5. Timothy Besley, "State Capacity and Economic Development," Sir Arthur Lewis Distinguished Lecture, University of the West Indies, January 25, 2019.

6. Arthur Lewis, "The Slowing Down of the Engine of Growth," Nobel Prize Lecture, December 8, 1979.

7. J. A. Schumpeter, *Die Krise des Steuerstaats* (Austria: Leuschner and Lubensky, 1918). Translated as J. A. Schumpeter, "The Crisis of the Tax State," in Schumpeter, *The Economics and Sociology of Capitalism,* ed. Richard Swedberg, 99–140 (Princeton: Princeton University Press, 1991).

8. Tim Besley and Torsten Persson, "Taxation and Development," in *Handbook of Public Economics,* ed. A. J. Auerbach, R. Chetty, M. Feldstein, and E. Saez, vol. 5, 51–110 (Amsterdam: Elsevier, 2013). The nations in the sample were Argentina, Australia, Brazil, Canada, Chile, Colombia, Denmark, Finland, Ireland, Japan, Mexico, the Netherlands, New Zealand, Norway, Sweden, Switzerland, the United Kingdom, and the United States. Data are from Brian Mitchell, *International Historical Statistics,* 3 vols. (London: Palgrave Macmillan, 2007).

9. This section is based on Philippe Aghion, Xavier Jaravel, Torsten Persson, and Dorothée Rouzet, "Education and Military Rivalry," *Journal of the European Economic Association* 17, no. 2 (2019): 376–412.

10. Charles Tilly, *The Formation of National States in Western Europe* (Princeton: Princeton University Press, 1975); Besley and Persson, "Fragile States and Development Policy."

11. Napoleon I's victory over the Prussians at Iéna prompted the King of Prussia to invest massively in schools, universities, and infrastructure, for which he called upon the von Humboldt brothers.

12. Eugen Weber, *Peasants into Frenchmen: The Modernization of Rural France, 1870–1914* (Stanford: Stanford University Press, 1976).

13. Aghion, Jaravel, Persson, and Rouzet, "Education and Military Rivalry."

14. Lyndon B. Johnson, *The Vantage Point: Perspectives of the Presidency, 1963–1969* (New York: Holt, Rinehart and Winston, 1971).

15. Pierre Azoulay, Erica Fuchs, Anna P. Goldstein, and Michael Kearney, "Funding Breakthrough Research: Promises and Challenges of the 'ARPA Model,'" *Innovation Policy and the Economy* 19, no. 1 (2019): 69–96.

16. The top-down approach refers to a hierarchical process in which the state is the decision maker and imposes its decision on decentralized actors. Conversely, in a bottom-up approach, the state sets out the broad policy orientation, but allows local actors to determine how to implement it.

17. Several anti-socialist laws were adopted between 1878 and 1890.

18. Sir William Henry Beveridge, *Social Insurance and Allied Services* (New York: Macmillan, 1942).

19. National Council of the Resistance, "Programme du Conseil national de la Résistance," March 15, 1944.

20. The labor unions were well represented in the National Council of the Resistance, and the General Confederation of Labour (CGT) had 4 million members in 1945.

21. See Pierre Rosanvallon, *La Crise de l'Etat-providence* (Paris: Seuil, in collaboration with Points Politique, 1981).

22. The film *Adalen 31* deals with this tragic episode. See Bo Widerberg, dir., *Adalen 31*, Svensk Filmindustri, 1969.

23. Yuval Noah Harari, *21 Lessons for the 21st Century* (New York: Spiegel & Grau, 2018).

24. Monique Canto-Sperber, *La Fin des libertés: Ou comment refonder le libéralisme* (Paris: Robert Laffont, 2019).

25. Canto-Sperber, *La Fin des libertés.*

26. Milton Friedman, *Capitalism and Freedom* (Chicago: University of Chicago Press, 1962).

27. John M. Keynes and Hubert D. Henderson, *Can Lloyd George Do It? An Examination of the Liberal Pledge* (London: The Nation and Athenaeum, 1929), reprinted in John M. Keynes, "Can Lloyd George Do It?" in *Essays in Persuasion*, 86–125 (London: Palgrave Macmillan, 2010).

28. John M. Keynes, *The General Theory of Employment, Interest, and Money* (New York: Harcourt, Brace and World, 1936).

29. Willie O'Dea, "Why Our Response to Crisis Isn't Wrong," *Irish Independent*, January 4, 2009.

30. Philippe Aghion, George-Mario Angeletos, Abhijit Banerjee, and Kalina Manova, "Volatility and Growth: Credit Constraints and the Composition of Investment," *Journal of Monetary Economics* 57, no. 3 (2010): 246–265.

31. Quantitative easing is a fiscal policy whereby a central bank purchases massive quantities of debt from financial actors, in particular Treasury bonds and corporate bonds.

32. Philippe Aghion, David Hémous, and Enisse Kharroubi, "Cyclical Fiscal Policy, Credit Constraints, and Industry Growth," *Journal of Monetary Economics* 62 (2014): 41–58; Philippe Aghion, Emmanuel Farhi, and Enisse Kharroubi, "Monetary Policy, Product Market Competition and Growth," *Economica* 86, no. 343 (2019): 431–470.

33. Automatic stabilizers are adjustments in taxes and in government spending that occur in response to changing economic conditions, without requiring any legislative action. For example, during periods of expansion, income and payroll tax revenues rise due to increased consumption and employment, while spending on transfer programs such as unemployment benefits declines. Conversely, during a recession, lower taxes and increased spending on benefits help maintain economic activity.

34. Céline Antonin, "La fatalité grecque: un scénario prévisible?" *Lettre de l'OFCE* 323, September 21, 2010, 1–4, https://halshs.archives-ouvertes.fr/hal-01023902/.

35. Département analyse et prévision de l'OFCE, "Évaluation de l'impact économique de la pandémie de COVID-19 et des mesures de confinement sur l'économie mondiale en avril 2020," *OFCE Policy Brief*, no. 69, June 2020.

36. In the aftermath of the crisis, a consensus emerged that regulators should include a macroprudential dimension in their thinking. The Basel III Agreements not only strengthened the capital requirements, they also added a countercyclical buffer, ranging from 0 to 2.5 percent of assets. Basel III allows for increased capital requirements during periods of accelerated borrowing and for relaxing them during slowdowns.

15. Creative Destruction and the Golden Triangle

1. Jean-Jacques Laffont, "Étapes vers un État moderne: une analyse économique," in Report of the Conference of December 16, 1999, on State and Public Sector Management CAE, *Etat et gestion publique. Actes du Colloque du 16 décembre 1999*, 117–150, La Documentation française, 2000.

2. World economic history abounds in examples of collusion between incumbent firms and governments to block the entry of new firms into the market. Collusion occurs both at the national and the local levels. The Ruhr and Sarre regions in Germany provide an example of collusion at the local level. At the end of the twentieth century, incumbent firms in these regions utilized local governments to prevent the entry of new firms, which they claimed would spoil the local job market.

3. Diego Puga and Daniel Trefler, "International Trade and Institutional Change: Medieval Venice's Response to Globalization," *Quarterly Journal of Economics* 129, no. 2 (2014): 753-821.

4. In the rest of Europe, this contract was known as the *commenda*.

5. Daron Acemoglu and James Robinson, *Why Nations Fail: The Origins of Power, Prosperity, and Poverty* (New York: Crown, 2012).

6. Philippe Aghion and Alexandra Roulet, *Repenser l'État* (Paris: Seuil in collaboration with La République des idées, 2011).

7. The corruption perceptions index is published annually by the nongovernmental organization Transparency International. This index ranks countries based on how corrupt a country's public sector is perceived to be by experts and business executives. A score close to 0 corresponds to a high level of corruption, a score close to 100 to a low level of corruption. The Product Market Regulation index, computed by the OECD, is a synthetic indicator to measure the degree to which public policies promote or inhibit competition in the product market.

8. János Kornai, "Innovation and Dynamism: Interaction between Systems and Technical Progress," *Economics of Transition* 18, no. 4 (2010): 629-670.

9. The theory of incomplete contracts was recognized by the Royal Swedish Academy of Sciences, who awarded the Nobel Prize in Economic Sciences to Oliver Hart and Bengt Holmström in 2016. We recommend Hart's concise work: Oliver Hart, *Firms, Contracts, and Financial Structure* (Oxford: Clarendon Press, 1995). The first two articles that made use of the theory of incomplete contracts to analyze the nature and role of constitutions were: Philippe Aghion and Patrick Bolton, "Incomplete Social Contracts," *Journal of the European Economic Association* 1, no. 1 (2003): 38-67; and Philippe Aghion, Alberto Alesina, and Francesco Trebbi, "Endogenous Political Institutions," *Quarterly Journal of Economics* 119, no. 2 (2004): 565-611.

10. Montesquieu, *De l'esprit des lois* (Geneva: Barrillot & fils, 1748); Montesquieu, *The Spirit of the Laws*, ed. and trans. Anne M. Cohler, Basia Carolyn Miller, and Harold Samuel Stone (Cambridge: Cambridge University Press, 1989); Friedrich A. Hayek, *The Constitution of Liberty* (Abingdon, UK: Routledge, 1960); James M. Buchanan, *Fiscal Theory and Political Economy* (Chapel Hill: University of North Carolina Press, 1960); James M. Buchanan and Gordon Tullock, *The Calculus of Consent: Logical Foundations of Constitutional Democracy* (Ann Arbor: University of Michigan Press, 1962).

11. Alexis de Tocqueville, *Democracy in America*, ed. and trans. Harvey C. Mansfield and Delba Winthrop (1835; Chicago: University of Chicago Press, 2000).

12. Alexander Hamilton, James Madison, and John Jay, Federalist No. 70 (1788), in *The Federalist Papers*, ed. Clinton Rossiter (New York: New American Library, 1961).

13. Every nation has a constitution, even if no specific text bears this title. For example, the United Kingdom does not in a formal sense have an actual constitution; it nonetheless has, in material terms, written and unwritten rules that govern the functioning of political institutions. Great Britain also possesses a number of foundational texts, both ancient (Magna Carta of 1215, Bill of Rights of 1688) and modern (Parliament Acts of 1911, 1949).

14. Aghion and Bolton, "Incomplete Social Contracts."

15. See Aghion, Alesina, and Trebbi, "Endogenous Political Institutions"; and the precursor article on the political economy of vested interests: Per Krusel and Jose Victor Rios-Rull, "On the Size of U.S. Government: Political Economy in the Neoclassical Growth Model," *American Economic Review* 89, no. 5 (1999): 1156–1181.

16. Hayek, *The Constitution of Liberty.*

17. Rafael La Porta, Florencio López-de-Silanes, Christian Pop-Eleches, and Andrei Shleifer, "Judicial Checks and Balances," *Journal of Political Economy* 112, no. 2 (2004): 445–470.

18. La Porta et al., "Judicial Checks and Balances."

19. Daniel R. Pinello, "Linking Party to Judicial Ideology in American Courts: A Meta-Analysis," *Justice System Journal* 20, no. 3 (1999): 219–254.

20. Arnaud Philippe and Aurélie Ouss, "'No Hatred or Malice, Fear or Affection': Media and Sentencing," *Journal of Political Economy* 126, no. 5 (2018): 2134–2178.

21. Ioana Marinescu, "Are Judges Sensitive to Economic Conditions? Evidence from UK Employment Tribunals," *Industrial and Labour Relations Review* 64, no. 4 (2011): 673–698.

22. Daniel L. Chen, Tobias J. Moskowitz, and Kelly Shue, "Decision Making under the Gambler's Fallacy: Evidence from Asylum Judges, Loan Officers, and Baseball Umpires," *Quarterly Journal of Economics* 131, no. 3 (2016): 1181–1242.

23. Daniel L. Chen and Jess Eagel, "Can Machine Learning Help Predict the Outcome of Asylum Adjudications?" *Proceedings of the Sixteenth International Conference on Artificial Intelligence and Law* (2017): 237–240; Daniel L. Chen, "AI and Rule of Law: Machine Learning, Causal Inference, and Judicial Analytics," course at the Toulouse School of Economics, 2019.

24. Ozkan Eren and Naci Mocan, "Emotional Judges and Unlucky Juveniles," *American Economic Journal: Applied Economics* 10, no. 3 (2018): 171–205; Daniel L. Chen and Arnaud Philippe, "Clash of Norms: Judicial Leniency on Defendant Birthdays," unpublished manuscript, February 2020, https://papers.ssrn.com/sol3/papers.cfm?abstract_id=3203624.

25. Jon Kleinberg, Himabindu Lakkaraju, Jure Leskovec, Jens Ludwig, and Sendhil Mullainathan, "Human Decisions and Machine Predictions," *Quarterly Journal of Economics* 133, no. 1 (2018): 237–293.

26. Computers—or more precisely algorithms—can have biases. There is a large and growing literature on this. Algorithms based on machine learning incorporate

the biases of the human judges whose decisions form the basis of the machine's learning activity. See, for example, Cathy O'Neil, *Weapons of Math Destruction* (New York: Broadway Books, 2016).

27. Samuel Bowles and Wendy Carlin, "Shrinking Capitalism," *AEA Papers and Proceedings* 110 (2020): 372–377.

28. In their recent work on the "narrow corridor" between the state and civil society, Daron Acemoglu and James Robinson refer to the unrestricted state as the "despotic Leviathan." This view derives directly from Hobbes' *Leviathan* and describes the state as the entity capable of stopping the war of "all against all" and guaranteeing social peace by means of its sovereign power. See Daron Acemoglu and James A. Robinson, *The Narrow Corridor: States, Societies, and the Fate of Liberty* (London: Penguin, 2019).

29. On the necessary complementarity between the state and civil society, see also Monique Canto-Sperber, *La Fin des libertés. Ou comment refonder le libéralisme* (Paris: Robert Laffont, 2019).

30. Acemoglu and Robinson, *The Narrow Corridor*, refer to the "absent Leviathan" to describe a stateless society. They offer the Tiv society in Nigeria as an example where civil society negates the state. The Tiv have created a system in which norms and social sanctions prevent any individual from imposing his will on others.

31. Aghion and Bolton used an incomplete contracts approach to develop a theory of corporate and debt finance based on rights of control and the allocation of control rights between lenders and borrowers. See Philippe Aghion and Patrick Bolton, "An Incomplete Contracts Approach to Financial Contracting," *Review of Economic Studies* 59, no. 3 (1992): 473–494.

32. Samuel Bowles and Wendy Carlin, "The Coming Battle for the COVID-19 Narrative," *VOXeu*, April 10, 2020.

33. The state can encourage this mechanism by acting simultaneously on the degree of competition via its competition policy and on social values via its education and information policies.

34. Daron Acemoglu and James A. Robinson, "Why Did the West Extend the Franchise? Democracy, Inequality, and Growth in Historical Perspective," *Quarterly Journal of Economics* 115, no. 4 (2000): 1167–1199.

35. The idea of transferring control as a means of signaling commitment has been applied to organizational theory. See, for example, Philippe Aghion and Jean Tirole, "Formal and Real Authority in Organizations," *Journal of Political Economy* 105, no. 1 (1997): 1–29.

36. Toke S. Aidt and Peter S. Jensen, "Workers of the World, Unite! Franchise Extensions and the Threat of Revolution in Europe, 1820–1938," *European Economic Review* 72 (2014): 52–75.

37. The French Revolution of 1830 (the "Three Glorious Days"); the Revolutions of 1848 in France, Austria, Hungary, and Italy (the "Spring of Nations"); and the

October Revolution in Russia are among the major revolutions that occurred during this period.

38. Before that date, only prior referrals, that is, before the enactment of the law, were authorized by the Constitution.

39. The campaign rhetoric, which focused on going beyond the traditional political parties with the creation of a new party, "La République en Marche," undoubtedly played a decisive role in this victory. Macron's election also benefited from favorable circumstances, in particular primaries on both the left and the right that nominated candidates who were far from the center, as well as the legal proceedings embroiling François Fillon, winner of the right-wing primary.

40. The "Macron Laws" signed on September 22, 2017, capped damages for abusive dismissals and established the supremacy of labor negotiations within firms.

41. Laws adopted under this procedure are called *ordonnances*. To be sure, Parliament is not totally absent from the procedure because it votes twice: first to adopt the law authorizing the administration to pass *ordonnances* in a specific field; a second time to ratify those *ordonnances*. Nonetheless, Parliament's role is extremely limited, not only because it is difficult for legislators to modify an *ordonnance* that has already taken effect, but also because refusing to ratify it entails a vote of no confidence, provoking their own resignation and new legislative elections.

42. Frederic Joignot, "Coronavirus: La Dictature Chinoise Censure Les Médias, Le Public Ignore le Nombre de Personnes Contaminées. Faut-il Croire les Déclarations Officielles? Peut-on Combattre Efficacement une Épidémie Sans Liberté de la Presse?" *Journalisme pensif* (blog), *Le Monde*, February 29, 2020.

Conclusion

1. See János Kornai, "Innovation and Dynamism: Interaction between Systems and Technical Progress," *Economics of Transition* 18, no. 4 (2010): 629–670.

2. Henri Weber, *Rebelle jeunesse* (Paris: Robert Laffont, 2018).

3. Daron Acemoglu, James A. Robinson, and Thierry Verdier, "Asymmetric Growth and Institutions in an Interdependent World," *Journal of Political Economy* 125, no. 5 (2017): 1245–1305.

4. See Chapter 5.

5. P. Aghion, H. Maghin, and A. Sapir, "Covid and the Nature of Capitalism," VoxEU, 25 June 2020, https://voxeu.org/article/covid-and-nature-capitalism.

6. Prior to the reform, income on capital was taxed progressively with a maximum marginal rate of 72 percent and an average rate of 54 percent.

7. Some economists, including Per Molander, believe that Sweden went too far in its promarket reforms. For example, the reform of the education system, carried out in several stages, introduced competition between schools by granting gen-

erous subsidies to schools that attracted more students. This reform had the perverse effect of leading to grade inflation instead of improving the quality of instruction. In respect of taxation, in order to give an even stronger signal to investors, Prime Minister Goran Persson decided to eliminate the estate tax in 2002, and the Conservative Minister of Finance Per Nuder eliminated the property tax in 2006. See Per Molander, "Dags för omprövning" (2017), https://eso .expertgrupp.se/rapporter/politiken-forvaltningen/.

8. The political film *Adalen 31* portrays the bloody repression in 1931 of a workers' demonstration in the Adalen district of Sweden—specialized in sawmills—by Swedish military forces. See Bo Widerberg, dir., *Adalen 31*, Svensk Filmindustri, 1969. *Germinal,* one of the most prominent books of Emile Zola, also portrays a terrible episode of violence when a miners' strike is repressed by the French police and the army at the end of the nineteenth century. See Emile Zola, *Germinal,* trans. Roger Pearson (London: Penguin, 1885).

Acknowledgments

Ian Malcolm encouraged us to produce this book, and he helped us converge on its main arguments. Interacting with Ian over these past years has been a great privilege.

The book owes a lot to Jodie Cohen-Tanugi and her first-rate translation of the text from French into English. Jodie showed enormous patience with the authors and an unusual concern for perfection through all the stages until the manuscript was ready for print. Jodie acted as a virtual coauthor of this book.

Martin Hellwig and an anonymous referee provided extremely helpful comments that greatly improved the manuscript. Kate Brick did a wonderful job as copy editor. And we also thank Arthur Goldhammer, who read through a manuscript draft and made useful suggestions, as well as Louise Paul-Delvaux, who helped us finalize and complete the endnotes.

For intellectual interactions that directly influenced the content of this book, for their detailed comments on the manuscript, and for contributing material to the various chapters of the book, we thank Daron Acemoglu, Ufuk Akcigit, Nadia Antonin, Antonin Bergeaud, Benedicte Berner, Tim Besley, Olivier Blanchard, Nicholas Bloom, Richard Blundell, Patrick Bolton, Matilde Bombardini, Timo Boppart, Leonardo Bursztyn, Monique Canto-Sperber, Emmanuel Combe, Beatrice Couairon, Angus Deaton, Mathias Dewatripont, Timothée Gigout-Magiorani, Maxime Gravoueille, Jerry Green, Rachel Griffith, Oliver Hart, Martin Hellwig, David Hémous, Peter Howitt, Xavier Jaravel, Chad Jones, Enisse Kharroubi, Pete Klenow, Matthieu Lequien, Huiyu Li, Yinan Li, Eric Maskin, Marc Melitz, Pierre-Michel Menger, Joel Mokyr, Torsten Persson, Michael Peters, Edmund Phelps, Chris Pissarides, Anasuya Raj, Stephen Redding, Alexandra Roulet, Juliette Sagot, Michael Sohlman, Stefanie Stantcheva, Nicholas Stern, Jean Tirole, Otto Toivanen,

Francesco Trebbi, Daniel Trefler, John Van Reenen, Cyril Verluise, Fabrizio Zilibotti, and Thomas Zuber.

This book was written over a year that was dramatically affected by the COVID-19 pandemic and the resulting lockdowns. We are particularly grateful to our loved ones, who provided unfailing support and encouragement throughout.

Finally, we want to dedicate this book to Emmanuel Farhi, who passed away in July 2020. A beautiful mind and a genius economist, widely considered the best macroeconomist of his generation, Emmanuel was also an outstanding human being who never failed to find time to listen to us and to provide advice and support. We miss his great intelligence, his open-mindedness, his unbounded curiosity, and his uncommon generosity.

Index

Page numbers in italics refer to figures or tables.